MznLnx

Missing Links Exam Preps

Exam Prep for

MARKETING: Comprehensive Exam Preparation

Cram101, 1st Edition

The MznLnx Exam Prep is your link from the texbook and lecture to your exams.
The MznLnx Exam Preps are unauthorized and comprehensive reviews of your textbooks.

All material provided by MznLnx and Rico Publications (c) 2010
Textbook publishers and textbook authors do not particpate in or contribute to these reviews.

MznLnx

Rico Publications

Exam Prep for MARKETING: Comprehensive Exam Preparation
1st Edition
Cram101

Publisher: Raymond Houge
Assistant Editor: Michael Rouger
Text and Cover Designer: Lisa Buckner
Marketing Manager: Sara Swagger
Project Manager, Editorial Production: Jerry Emerson
Art Director: Vernon Lowerui

Product Manager: Dave Mason
Editorial Assitant: Rachel Guzmanji
Pedagogy: Debra Long
Cover Image: Jim Reed/Getty Images
Text and Cover Printer: City Printing, Inc.
Compositor: Media Mix, Inc.

(c) 2010 Rico Publications
ALL RIGHTS RESERVED. No part of this work covered by the copyright may be reproduced or used in any form or by an means--graphic, electronic, or mechanical, including photocopying, recording, taping, Web distribution, information storage, and retrieval systems, or in any other manner--without the written permission of the publisher.

Printed in the United States
ISBN:

For more information about our products, contact us at:
Dave.Mason@RicoPublications.com

For permission to use material from this text or product, submit a request online to:
Dave.Mason@RicoPublications.com

Contents

CHAPTER 1
Test Preparation Part 1 — 1
CHAPTER 2
Test Preparation Part 2 — 22
CHAPTER 3
Test Preparation Part 3 — 47
CHAPTER 4
Test Preparation Part 4 — 67
CHAPTER 5
Test Preparation Part 5 — 85
CHAPTER 6
Test Preparation Part 6 — 97
CHAPTER 7
Test Preparation Part 7 — 115
CHAPTER 8
Test Preparation Part 8 — 129
CHAPTER 9
Test Preparation Part 9 — 141
CHAPTER 10
Test Preparation Part 10 — 143
CHAPTER 11
Test Preparation Part 11 — 154
CHAPTER 12
Test Preparation Part 12 — 174
CHAPTER 13
Test Preparation Part 13 — 193
CHAPTER 14
Test Preparation Part 14 — 212
CHAPTER 15
Test Preparation Part 15 — 218
CHAPTER 16
Test Preparation Part 16 — 222
CHAPTER 17
Test Preparation Part 17 — 244
CHAPTER 18
Test Preparation Part 18 — 262
CHAPTER 19
Test Preparation Part 19 — 277
CHAPTER 20
Test Preparation Part 20 — 293

Contents (Cont.)

CHAPTER 21
  Test Preparation Part 21   311
ANSWER KEY   312

TO THE STUDENT

COMPREHENSIVE

The *MznLnx* Exam Prep series is designed to help you pass your exams. Editors at MznLnx review your textbooks and then prepare these practice exams to help you master the textbook material. Unlike study guides, workbooks, and practice tests provided by the texbook publisher and textbook authors, *MznLnx* gives you **all** of the material in each chapter in exam form, not just samples, so you can be sure to nail your exam.

MECHANICAL

The MznLnx Exam Prep series creates exams that will help you learn the subject matter as well as test you on your understanding. Each question is designed to help you master the concept. Just working through the exams, you gain an understanding of the subject--its a simple mechanical process that produces success.

INTEGRATED STUDY GUIDE AND REVIEW

MznLnx is not just a set of exams designed to test you, its also a comprehensive review of the subject content. Each exam question is also a review of the concept, making sure that you will get the answer correct without having to go to other sources of material. You learn as you go! Its the easiest way to pass an exam.

HUMOR

Studying can be tedious and dry. MznLnx's instructional design includes moderate humor within the exam questions on occassion, to break the tedium and revitalize the brain

Chapter 1. Test Preparation Part 1

1. The brand name of a product that is distributed nationally under a brand name owned by the producer or distributor, as opposed to local brands (products distributed only in some areas of the country), and private label brands (products that carry the brand of the retailer rather than the producer.)

    _____s must compete with local and private brands._____s are produced by ,widely distuted by, and carry the name of the manufacturer.

    - Local brands may appeal to those consumers who favor small, local producers over large national or global producers, and may be willing to pay a premium to 'buy local'

    - The private label producer can offer lower prices because they avoid the cost of marketing and advertising to create and protect the brand. In North America, large retailers such as Loblaws, Walgreen and Wal-Mart all offer private label products.

    a. Market intelligence
    c. Specialty catalogs
    b. National brand
    d. Line extension

2. A _____ is a collection of symbols, experiences and associations connected with a product, a service, a person or any other artifact or entity.

    _____s have become increasingly important components of culture and the economy, now being described as 'cultural accessories and personal philosophies'.

    Some people distinguish the psychological aspect of a _____ from the experiential aspect.

    a. Brand equity
    c. Brandable software
    b. Store brand
    d. Brand

3. _____ is defined by the American _____ Association as the activity, set of institutions, and processes for creating, communicating, delivering, and exchanging offerings that have value for customers, clients, partners, and society at large. The term developed from the original meaning which referred literally to going to market, as in shopping, or going to a market to sell goods or services.

    _____ practice tends to be seen as a creative industry, which includes advertising, distribution and selling.

    a. Product naming
    c. Customer acquisition management
    b. Marketing myopia
    d. Marketing

4. _____ is a global marketing research firm, with worldwide headquarters in New York City. Regional headquarters for North America are located in Schaumburg, IL. As of 2008, its the part of The Nielsen Company.
    a. InfoNU
    c. E-Detailing
    b. Alloy Entertainment
    d. ACNielsen

5. _____ is an Amazon.com affiliate product which website owners can use to create an online store on their site. The _____ interface is intended to be accessible to those without programming skills, using configuration pages to customise the content and design.

The store does not allow website owners to sell their own products directly.

    a. Ethan Allen
    c. Andre Kirk Agassi
    b. Ed Bradley
    d. AStore

6. _____ is a provider of business-related research services. It has its headquarters in Boston, Massachusetts and belongs to the Harte-Hanks group. Founded in 1988, Aberdeen's research is used by over 2.2 million readers in more than 40 countries; this includes 90% of the Fortune 1,000 and 93% of the Software 500.

    a. Aberdeen Group
    c. InfoUSA
    b. Adidas
    d. Outdoor Advertising Association of America

7. _____ is a strategic approach to business marketing in which an organisation considers and communicates with individual prospect or customer accounts as markets of one. The popularity of this approach is growing, with companies such as BearingPoint, HP, Progress Software and Xerox reported to be leading the way.

_____ has grown since the mid-1990s as a demonstration of the trend away from mass marketing towards more targeted approaches.

    a. InfoNU
    c. Alloy Entertainment
    b. Account-based marketing
    d. Outsourcing relationship management

8. _____ is a business practice that involves making the marketing activities of a company more accountable. Different names have been given to this process, such as: Marketing Performance Measurement, Marketing Performance Management, Marketing Accountability, Marketing ROI, 'ROMI, or _____.

Peter J. Rosenwald wrote a book about it in 2004.

    a. ACNielsen
    c. European Information Technology Observatory
    b. Accountable marketing
    d. Alloy Entertainment

9. _____ is a public relations professional certification provided by Universal Accreditation Board.

Accredited in Public Relations (APR) is a voluntary certification program for industry professionals, and is considered the mark of distinction for those who demonstrate commitment to the profession and to its ethical practice. Those who earn the APR demonstrate a broad knowledge, strategic perspective, and sound professional judgment of modern public relations.

    a. ACNielsen
    c. AMAX
    b. Accredited public relations professionals
    d. ADTECH

10. _____ is the practice of managing the flow of information between an organization and its publics. _____ - often referred to as _____ - gains an organization or individual exposure to their audiences using topics of public interest and news items that do not require direct payment. Because _____ places exposure in credible third-party outlets, it offers a third-party legitimacy that advertising does not have.

a. Power III
b. Symbolic analysis
c. Public Relations
d. Graphic communication

11. _____ is a specific category of age-targeted specialty shops and professional services strategically catering to the daily needs of active adults. Active adults, also known as baby boomers are characterized as people who are aged 55 years or older. The importance of active adults to the retail market are significant.
   a. ACNielsen
   b. AMAX
   c. ADTECH
   d. Active adult retail

12. _____ is a market research company for search engine advertisers. _____ monitors Google, Yahoo, MSN, Baidu, AOL, and Ask for paid search, natural rankings, and potential trademark infringement activity. The _____ service is a commercial platform whereby customers pay a monthly service fee to access data reports for the industry vertical.
   a. ADTECH
   b. Adbot
   c. Aberdeen Group
   d. Adgooroo

13. _____ is a recent term applied to a break away from the traditional model of television funding. Typically programmes have been funded by a broadcaster and they re-couped the money through selling advertising space around the content. This has worked fine for decades, but new technological advances have forced broadcasters and advertisers to re-think their relationship.
   a. EMarket trading platform
   b. Advertiser funded programming
   c. Outsourcing relationship management
   d. Incentive program

14. _____ is a form of communication that typically attempts to persuade potential customers to purchase or to consume more of a particular brand of product or service. 'While now central to the contemporary global economy and the reproduction of global production networks, it is only quite recently that _____ has been more than a marginal influence on patterns of sales and production. The formation of modern _____ was intimately bound up with the emergence of new forms of monopoly capitalism around the end of the 19th and beginning of the 20th century as one element in corporate strategies to create, organize and where possible control markets, especially for mass produced consumer goods.
   a. Advertising
   b. AMAX
   c. ACNielsen
   d. ADTECH

15. _____ is the process of choosing the most cost-effective media to achieve the necessary coverage, and number of exposures, among the target audience.

This is typically measured on two dimensions:

CovTo maximize overall awareness, the maximum number of the target audience should be reached by the advertising. There is a limit, however, for the last few per cent of the general population are always difficult (and accordingly very expensive) to reach; since they do not see the main media used by advertisers.

   a. All commodity volume
   b. Outsourcing relationship management
   c. Engagement marketing
   d. Advertising media selection

16. The notion of _____ emerged from the field of Human-Computer Interaction (HCI) (Norman, 1986) and more specifically from the developing area of affective computing (Picard, 1997.)

Affective computing aims to deliver affective interfaces (Reynolds, Picard, 2001) capable of eliciting certain emotional experiences from users (McCarthy, Wright, 2004.) Similarly, _____ attempts to define the subjective emotional relationships between consumers and products and to explore the affective properties that products intend to communicate through their physical attributes.

   a. AMAX
   c. ACNielsen
   b. Affective design
   d. ADTECH

17. _____ refers to any market where the customers who implement one product or service are likely to purchase a related, follow-on product.

The existence of an _____ is often a persuasive argument for manufacturers to stay in direct contact with end-users. Manufacturers will use postage-paid guarantee cards, for example, to keep track of the address of end-users.

   a. Online focus group
   c. After-market
   b. Individual branding
   d. Engagement

18. _____ represents the total annual sales volume of retailers that can be aggregated from individual store-level up to larger Geographical sets. This measure is typically presented millions dollars ($MM) in the United States, but may be represented in other currencies as appropriate.

The total dollar sales that go into _____ include the entire store inventory sales, rather than sales for a specific category of products - Hence the term '_____'.

   a. Incentive program
   c. Enterprise marketing management
   b. EMarket trading platform
   d. All commodity volume

19. _____ is the term used to describe marketing activity undertaken by more than one entity, jointly to promote and sell a concept, product or service which has benefit to all the stakeholders.

An example of _____ is a Destination Alliance where hotels, restaurants and attractions come together to jointly fund and market their destination. The Stakeholders understand that by marketing their destination jointly and pooling their resources that the marketing impact they can achieve will be stronger and benighted all stakeholders in that location.

   a. Alliance marketing
   c. EMarket trading platform
   b. All commodity volume
   d. InfoNU

20. _____ is a creative division of the Alloy Media + Marketing company--an American provider of targeted media programs. Alloy is a leading producer of novels created for teenage and young adult audiences. Additionally, the company produces or co-produces several television shows and films which are novel adaptations.

a. European Information Technology Observatory
b. Alloy Entertainment
c. Account-based marketing
d. Outsourcing relationship management

21.   The _____ is a professional association for marketers. As of 2008 it had approximately 40,000 members. There are collegiate chapters on 250 campuses.
   a. AMAX
   b. ADTECH
   c. ACNielsen
   d. American Marketing Association

22.   _____ is an international advertising research firm, headquartered in Albuquerque, New Mexico, which provides its clients with worldwide market research on their advertising concepts, and executions.

The company was founded in 1990 in Chicago, Illinois by Charles E. Young. _____, d.b.a. CY Research, uses highly visual or non-verbal approaches to measuring advertising in a variety of media, including television, print, direct response, packaging, internet and branded entertainment.

   a. Isobar
   b. Archos
   c. Asia Insight
   d. Ameritest

23.   _____ is a Digital agency, offering interactive web design, integrated digital marketing and technology services. The company is based in Bellevue, Washington.

Founded in 2001 by Jim Beebe, Curt Doolittle and Steven Salta, _____ has grown quickly .

   a. Eastman Chemical Company
   b. Advertising research
   c. ING Direct
   d. Ascentium

24.   _____ is an independent market research consultancy. They have a strong market presence around the Asia Pacific region including, Singapore, China, Japan and India. Their head office is in Singapore and a regional office is located in Shanghai, China.
   a. Ad pepper media
   b. Agency Republic
   c. Access Commerce
   d. Asia Insight

25.   In consumer marketing, an _____ means a large segment of its exposure audience wishes to own it, but for economical reasons cannot. An aspirational product implies certain positive characteristics to the user, but the supply appears limited due to limited production quantities.

An important characteristic of an aspirational product is that the part of its exposure audience that is at present economically unable to purchase it, thinks of itself as having a fair probability of at a certain point in the future being able to do so.

   a. ADTECH
   b. ACNielsen
   c. Electronic registration mark
   d. Aspirational brand

26. _____ is a marketing and service agency specialized in national and international student recruitment, release and branding of programs and academic institutions. The company was founded in October 2006 as spin-off from the University of Heidelberg. As one among very few spin-offs with a humanities background _____ is supported by the Research Department of the University.

   a. Oregon Tilth
   b. Arcis Communications
   c. ADTECH
   d. Athena Wissenschaftsmarketing

27. Media planning is a science and one that has seen growth and increased discipline over the last few years through the introduction of new technology. These technologies have morphed from audience segmentation to audience profiling, but the most recent wave of technology to affect media planning is based on _____, which can be defined as the opportunity to purchase an actual audience online rather than impressions.

_____ incorporates a number of different technologies including behavioral targeting and the more advanced Conversion optimization platforms.

   a. Ad rotation
   b. OpenX
   c. Enterprise Search Marketing
   d. Audience Screening

28. _____ is a UK producer of traditional British roast goods. The company produces foodstuffs such as yorkshire puddings, potato and vegetable dishes, main dishes, traditional puddings, cooking sauces, ready meals, and sweet dishes. _____'s is best known for producing yorkshire puddings however.

   a. ACNielsen
   b. ADTECH
   c. AMAX
   d. Aunt Bessie

29. The _____ is an academic journal publishing papers about management.

The journal was founded in 1976 by the Australian Graduate School of Management .

- Ray Ball (first editor)
- Chris Adam
- John Conybeare
- Vic Taylor
- Phillip Yetton
- John Roberts
- Robert Marks

Source:

In September 1995 the Australian Vice-Chancellor's Committee awarded a grant to a research team to study reader acceptance of an online version. The result was the creation of a freely available electronic archive of the AJM journal .

   a. Alliance marketing
   b. Australian Journal of Management
   c. Incentive program
   d. Advertiser funded programming

30. _____ are used to collect information and gain feedback via the telephone and the internet. _____ are used for customer research purposes by call centres for customer relationship management and performance management purposes. They are also used for political polling, market research and job satisfaction surveying.

   a. Individual branding   b. Engagement
   c. Intangibility   d. Automated surveys

31. _____ is a term commonly used to describe commerce transactions between businesses like the one between a manufacturer and a wholesaler or a wholesaler and a retailer i.e both the buyer and the seller are business entity.This is unlike business-to-consumers (B2C) which involve a business entity and end consumer, or business-to-government (B2G) which involve a business entity and government.

The volume of B2B transactions is much higher than the volume of B2C transactions. The primary reason for this is that in a typical supply chain there will be many B2B transactions involving subcomponent or raw materials, and only one B2C transaction, specifically sale of the finished product to the end customer.

   a. Disruptive technology   b. Social marketing
   c. Customer relationship management   d. Business-to-business

32. _____, in clothing retail, is a product season and is characterized by a display of items appropriate to a school wardrobe.

Many department stores, such as Target, Wal-Mart, and Kmart advertise _____ sales as a time when school supplies and children's and young adults' clothing goes on sale. Many states offer tax-free periods (usually about a week) at which time any school supplies and children's clothing purchased does not have sales tax added.

   a. Claritas Prizm   b. Fan loyalty
   c. Google Advertising Professional   d. Back to school

33. A _____ or few _____ is a rhetorical attempt to spin misdeeds within a group as isolated to a 'few bad apples'. The term has been applied to excuses for corporate fraud in the wake of the Enron scandal , for the Abu Ghraib torture and prison abuse case, the Chicago Police Department's response to off-duty officer Anthony Abatte's videotaped beating of a bartender and in a hypothetical sense involving projections about organizational accountability. The term became popular soon after the airing of a Canadian broadcast from the CBC's Fifth Estate television series called 'A Few Bad Apples'.

   a. 6-3-5 Brainwriting   b. Bad apples excuse
   c. Power III   d. 180SearchAssistant

34. The _____ was developed by Frank Bass and describes the process of how new products get adopted as an interaction between users and potential users. It has been described as one of the most famous empirical generalisations in marketing, along with the Dirichlet model of repeat buying and brand choice . The model is widely used in forecasting, especially product forecasting and technology forecasting.

   a. 6-3-5 Brainwriting   b. Bass diffusion model
   c. Power III   d. 180SearchAssistant

35. _____ is the process by which a new idea or new product is accepted by the market. The rate of _____ is the speed that the new idea spreads from one consumer to the next. Adoption is similar to _____ except that it deals with the psychological processes an individual goes through, rather than an aggregate market process.
   a. Market development
   b. Kano model
   c. Perceptual maps
   d. Diffusion

36. The _____ is a psychological finding: A person who has done someone a favor is more likely to do that person another favor than they would be if they had received a favor from that person. Similarly, one who harms another is more willing to harm them again than the victim is to retaliate.

For modern research on this phenomenon, see the foot-in-the-door technique.

   a. Borderless selling
   b. Ben Franklin effect
   c. AStore
   d. African Americans

37. _____ n. A short, sitcom-style video available over the Internet.

_____s or user generated adverts are the leading edge of marketing.

   a. Gimmick
   b. Perceptual mapping
   c. Kano model
   d. Bitcom

38. A _____ is a token asserting that someone qualifies under some criteria or has some status or right, without revealing 'who' that person is -- without including their name or address, for instance. It is used in maintaining medical privacy and increasingly for consumer privacy.

It can be quite difficult to ascertain that someone is not using another's credential -- identity theft -- therefore a great deal of effort goes into the application of cryptography to authentication.

   a. 6-3-5 Brainwriting
   b. Power III
   c. 180SearchAssistant
   d. Blind credential

39. In marketing, a _____ is often used as a tool for companies to compare their brand to another brand. For example, the Pepsi Challenge is a famous taste test that has been run by Pepsi since 1975 as a method to show their superiority to Coca-Cola. Taste tests are also a tool sometimes used by companies to develop their brand or new product.
   a. Mass marketing
   b. Business-to-business
   c. Primary research
   d. Blind taste test

40. _____ was developed by Richard Zultner for his clients in the software industry in the 1990s. The premise was that the House of Quality and other large matrices demanded too much time and resources when speed of development was a critical customer need. The _____ is an efficient subset of Comprehensive QFD as developed by Dr. Yoji Akao, that can be later upgraded with no wasted effort.
   a. Cyberdoc
   b. Market share
   c. Category management
   d. Blitz QFD

Chapter 1. Test Preparation Part 1 9

41. _____ is common parlance in the legal services sector and refers to the collection of clients that a lawyer (usually a partner) has assembled throughout his or her career. It is often used to refer to the valuation of such client following.

Since most law firms are organized as limited liability partnerships or professional corporations, each partner is usually responsible for cultivating his or her own clients in that partner's specific area of focus, e.g. litigation, tax or securities.

- a. Personalization
- b. Black PRies
- c. Private branding
- d. Book of business

42. _____ is a publishing activity in which a publishing company outsources the myriad tasks involved in putting together a book--writing, researching, editing, illustrating, and even printing--to an outside company called a _____ company. Once the _____ company has produced the book, they then sell it to the final publishing company.

In this arrangement, the _____ company acts as a liaison between a publishing company and the writers, researchers, editors, and printers that design and produce the book.

- a. Power III
- b. 6-3-5 Brainwriting
- c. Book-packaging
- d. 180SearchAssistant

43. _____ is an online marketplace that allows anyone with Internet access to submit ideas in response to creative briefs from top brands and be paid for them.

_____ was founded and launched in November 2007 by Pier Ludovico Bancale with a teaser website. Since its launch, creative briefs have been submitted from brands such as Auchan, Ferrero, Lego, Peugeot, among others.

- a. VoloMedia
- b. BootB
- c. Cirque du Soleil
- d. Mediox

44. _____ is the process of selling services to clients outside the country of origin of services through modern methods which eliminate the actions specifically designed to hinder international trade. International trade through '_____' is a new phenomenon born in the current 'Globalization' era.

_____ is defined as the process of performing sales transaction between two or more parties from different countries (an exporter and an importer) which is free from actions specifically designed to hinder international trade, such as tariff barriers, currency restrictions, and import quotas.

- a. African Americans
- b. Ben Franklin effect
- c. AStore
- d. Borderless selling

45. A _____ is a plan of action designed to achieve a particular goal.

_____ is different from tactics. In military terms, tactics is concerned with the conduct of an engagement while _____ is concerned with how different engagements are linked.

a. Power III
b. 6-3-5 Brainwriting
c. Strategy
d. 180SearchAssistant

46. _____ is a marketing practice that takes a specific approach to strategy, creativity and success tracking, where all three are driven by a thorough understanding of the business objective at hand. _____ insists that the organizational design of the marketing agency includes a team with broad skills, but that each staff member has creative and strategic leanings.

The strategy behind a _____ campaign is largely based on the business objective for a particular product, and is intended to be media-agnostic.

a. Lead scoring
b. Value chain
c. Brand infiltration
d. Customer Interaction Tracker

47. _____ refers to the implementation of brand modifications and life-cycle management of branded assets. The branded assets category includes managing digital brand execution.

Branding has emerged as a top management priority in the last decade due to the growing realization that brands are one of the most valuable assets that firms have.

a. Branded asset management
b. Risk management
c. Power III
d. 180SearchAssistant

48. _____ is a weekly American marketing trade publication. First published in 1986 as Adweek's Marketing Week, the publication changed its name in 1992 after facing a legal threat from the UK's Marketing Week magazine. _____ covers the world of marketing from big-budget ad campaigns to under-the-radar guerrilla efforts.

a. Magalog
b. Consumer Reports
c. Power III
d. Brandweek

49. _____, founded in 2006, is an independent branding and design agency, renowned for their creative and strategic excellence. They are based in Dubai Media City in the United Arab Emirates. As the creative agency behind the Burj Dubai brand, , Emaar's most prestigious luxury development, their work is highly visible throughout Dubai and the Middle East.

a. Fountain Fresh International
b. Brash Brands
c. Point of sale
d. Gerl

50. The break-even point for a product is the point where total revenue received equals the total costs associated with the sale of the product (TR=TC.) A break-even point is typically calculated in order for businesses to determine if it would be profitable to sell a proposed product, as opposed to attempting to modify an existing product instead so it can be made lucrative. _____ can also be used to analyse the potential profitability of an expenditure in a sales-based business.

In _____, margin of safety is how much output or sales level can fall before a business reaches its break-even point (BEP).

a. Contribution margin-based pricing
b. Pay Per Sale
c. Price skimming
d. Break even analysis

51. A _____ or pamphlet is a leaflet advertisement. _____s may advertise locations, events, hotels, products, services, etc. They are usually succinct in language and eye-catching in design.
   a. Marketspace
   b. Sweepstakes
   c. Customer relationship management
   d. Brochure

52. _____ is the practice of individuals including commercial businesses, governments and institutions, facilitating the sale of their products or services to other companies or organizations that in turn resell them, use them as components in products or services they offer _____ is also called business-to-_____ for short. (Note that while marketing to government entities shares some of the same dynamics of organizational marketing, B2G Marketing is meaningfully different.)
   a. Disruptive technology
   b. Mass marketing
   c. Law of disruption
   d. Business marketing

53. _____ is a term describing the different levels associated to an invividuals position or prominence in a business, market or group of associated business professionals. For example if a person in a company serves in a director level for a given department or division (of a company) he/she will look to work or relate to other people of equal level or 'stature' to have trust in and look to for sharing ideas and guidance.

Many folks inside of corporate situations are often left puzzled why they do not get the buy in, traction or respect from certain people within prospective clients or organizations.

   a. Time to market
   b. Price-weighted
   c. Chain stores
   d. Business stature

54. _____ describes activities of businesses serving end consumers with products and/or services.

An example of a B2C transaction would be a person buying a pair of shoes from a retailer. The transactions that led to the shoes being available for purchase, that is the purchase of the leather, laces, rubber, etc.

   a. Demand generation
   b. Societal marketing
   c. Corporate capabilities package
   d. Business-to-consumer

55. _____ electronic commerce uses an intrabusiness network which allows companies to provide products and/or services to their employees. Typically, companies use B2E networks to automate employee-related corporate processes.

Examples of B2E applications include:

- Online insurance policy management
- Corporate announcement dissemination
- Online supply requests
- Special employee offers
- Employee benefits reporting
- 401(k) Management

- e-business
- business-to-business
- business-to-consumer

a. Consumer-to-consumer
b. Spam Lit
c. Locator software
d. Business-to-employee

56. _____ is a derivative of B2B marketing and often referred to as a market definition of 'public sector marketing' which encompasses marketing products and services to government agencies through integrated marketing communications techniques such as strategic public relations, branding, marcom, advertising, and web-based communications.

B2G networks allow businesses to bid on government RFPs in a reverse auction fashion. Public sector organizations (PSO's) post tenders in the form of RFP's, RFI's, RFQ's etc.

a. Consumer privacy
b. Personalized marketing
c. Web banner
d. Business-to-government

57. '_____' is a common form of sales promotion. While rarely presented to customers in acronym form, this marketing technique is universally known in the marketing industry by the acronym _____ or just BOGO, and it is regarded as one of the most effective forms of special offers for goods.

Originally, 'buy one get one free' was a sudden end-of-season or stock clearance method used by shops who were left with a large quantity of stock that they were looking to sell quickly.

a. Blind taste test
b. Buy one, get one free
c. Pinstorm
d. Demand generation

58. _____ are the decision making processes undertaken by consumers in regard to a potential market transaction before, during, and after the purchase of a product or service.

More generally, decision making is the cognitive process of selecting a course of action from among multiple alternatives. Common examples include shopping, deciding what to eat.

a. Consumer confidence
b. Convenience
c. Demographic profile
d. Buyer decision processes

59. A _____, in marketing, procurement, and organizational studies, is a group of employees, family members, or members of any type of organization responsible for purchasing an item for the organization. In a business setting, major purchases typically require input from various parts of the organization, including finance, accounting, purchasing, information technology management, and senior management. Highly technical purchases, such as information systems or production equipment, also require the expertise of technical specialists.
   a. Buying center
   b. Marketing myopia
   c. Commercialization
   d. Packshot

60. In marketing and strategy, _____ refers to a reduction in the sales volume, sales revenue, or market share of one product as a result of the introduction of a new product by the same producer.

For example, if Coca Cola were to introduce a similar product (say, Diet Coke or Cherry Coke), this new product could take some of the sales away from the original Coke. _____ is a key consideration in product portfolio analysis.

   a. Business-to-consumer
   b. Co-marketing
   c. Marketing
   d. Cannibalization

61. In marketing, _____ refers to the total cost of holding inventory. This includes warehousing costs such as rent, utilities and salaries, financial costs such as opportunity cost, and inventory costs related to perishability, shrinkage and insurance.

When there are no transaction costs for shipment, _____s are minimized when no excess inventory is held at all, as in a Just In Time production system.

   a. Merchandise management system
   b. Vendor Managed Inventory
   c. Reverse auction
   d. Carrying cost

62. In economics, business, retail, and accounting, a _____ is the value of money that has been used up to produce something, and hence is not available for use anymore. In economics, a _____ is an alternative that is given up as a result of a decision. In business, the _____ may be one of acquisition, in which case the amount of money expended to acquire it is counted as _____.
   a. Transaction cost
   b. Variable cost
   c. Fixed costs
   d. Cost

63. _____ is a strategic business framework for dealing with economic turbulence defined and developed in 2008 by Philip Kotler of Northwestern University's Kellogg School of Management and John A. Caslione of GCS Business Capital LLC. Based on the concept that the world economy has entered into a new economic era of uncertainty, as put forth by Alan Greenspan in his book The Age of Turbulence, _____ provides methods to allow companies to live with increased risk and uncertainty in an age of heightened turbulence and its consequent chaos. This involves creating and implementing a set of new strategic behaviors defined by Philip Kotler and John A. Caslione as well as building an early warning system, a scenario construction system, and a quick response system to manage and market during recessions and other turbulent economic conditions.

a. Business strategy
b. Chaotics
c. Strategic group
d. Strategic business unit

64. _____ is a retailing concept in which the total range of products sold by a retailer is broken down into discrete groups of similar or related products; these groups are known as product categories. Examples of grocery categories may be: tinned fish, washing detergent, toothpastes, etc.Each category is then run like a 'mini business' (Business Unit) in its own right, with its own set of turnover and/or profitability targets and strategies. An important facet of _____ is the shift in relationship between retailer and supplier : instead of the traditional adversarial relationship, the relationship moves to one of collaboration, exchange of information and data and joint business building.The focus of all negotiations is centered around the effects of the turnover of the total category, not just the sales on the individual products therein.

a. Societal marketing
b. Market segment
c. Category management
d. Brochure

65. _____ occurs when manufacturers (brands) disintermediate their channel partners, such as distributors, retailers, dealers, and sales representatives, by selling their products direct to consumers through general marketing methods and/or over the internet through eCommerce.

Some manufacturers want their brands to capture the power of the internet but do not want to create conflict with their other distribution channels, as these partners are necessary and viable for any manufacturer to maintain and gain success. The Census Bureau of the U.S. Department of Commerce reported that online sales in 2005 grew 24.6 percent over 2004 to reach 86.3 billion dollars.

a. Store brand
b. Trade Symbols
c. Channel conflict
d. Retail design

66. In the United States, a _____ organization collects funds, sometimes called _____ dollars, from producers of a particular agricultural commodity and uses these funds to promote and do research on the commodity. The organizations must promote their commodity in a generic way, without reference to a particular producer. _____ programs attempt to improve the market position of the covered commodity by expanding markets, increasing demand, and developing new uses and markets.

a. JPMorgan Chase ' Co.
b. Compensation methods
c. Mapinfo
d. Checkoff

67. _____ offers pay for performance marketing services for retailers to deliver personalized display advertising and product recommendations. Retailers use _____ to present relevant products to consumers with the intention of increasing clickthrough and sales conversion.

_____ uses shopping data from retailers to generate personalized product recommendations for what consumers are likely to be in-market for next.

a. Partnership for a Drug-Free America
b. Multinational corporation
c. Superbrands
d. ChoiceStream

68. In the Northern Hemisphere, the _____ or (winter) holiday season (mainly in North American usage) is a late-year season that surrounds the Christmas holiday as well as other holidays during the November/December timeframe. It is sometimes synonymous with the winter season. It has been found to have a proportionate effect on health, compared to the rest of the year.
   a. Christmas creep
   b. Christmas season
   c. 180SearchAssistant
   d. Power III

69. _____ is a set of geo-demographic clusters for the United States, developed by Claritas Inc., which was then acquired by The Nielsen Company. It was a widely used customer segmentation system for marketing in the United States in the 1990s and continues to be used today.

The clusters were developed, in part, via the analysis of U.S. census data.

   a. Disruptive technology
   b. Claritas Prizm
   c. Gatefold
   d. Commercial operations management

70. _____ is a manga and cross-media tie-in to the 2008 film Cloverfield. It is published once a month on Kadokawa Shoten's website and consists of four chapters. It details the lives of two students seeking for shelter before what may seem to be the Chuai incident seen in the film's viral-marketing material, and their internal conflicts when the monster makes an appearance.
   a. 6-3-5 Brainwriting
   b. 180SearchAssistant
   c. Power III
   d. Cloverfield/Kishin

71. '_____' is a class of statistical techniques that can be applied to data that exhibit 'natural' groupings. _____ sorts through the raw data and groups them into clusters. A cluster is a group of relatively homogeneous cases or observations.
   a. 180SearchAssistant
   b. Cluster analysis
   c. Structure mining
   d. Power III

72. _____ is a marketing practice where two companies cooperate with separate distribution channels, sometimes including profit sharing. It is frequently confused with Co-promotion.

Cross-marketing describes the practice where two individual entities companies exchange marketing channels for mutual benefit.

   a. Confusion marketing
   b. SWOT analysis
   c. Vertical market
   d. Co-marketing

73. The _____ was a campaign of mutually-targeted television advertisements and marketing campaigns in the 1980s and 1990s between soft drink manufacturers The Coca-Cola Company and PepsiCo.

Pepsi and Coca-Cola had/have different brands of soda and other drinks competing with each other:

Coca-Cola and Pepsi focused particularly on rock stars; notable soft drink promoters included Michael Jackson and Ray Charles (for Pepsi) and Paula Abdul, Elton John (for Diet Coke.)

One example of a heated exchange that occurred during the _____ was Coca-Cola making a strategic retreat on July 11, 1985, by announcing its plans to bring back the original 'Classic' Coke after recently introducing New Coke.

a. 6-3-5 Brainwriting
b. Cola Wars
c. Power III
d. 180SearchAssistant

74. _____ combines all functional areas in the commercial process by integrating Branding, Innovation management, Product Management (PIM), Marketing Operations Management (MOM), Channel ' Sales Management and Customer Interaction Management. _____ is the alignment of people, process and technology to support commercial activities and improve both innovation and marketing effectiveness. _____ means that enterprises entering into a competitive process, whether 'in the market' or 'for the market', hold both the product innovation and marketing team accountable for their commercial and financial outcome.

a. Commercial operations management
b. Fan loyalty
c. Perceptual mapping
d. Lead scoring

75. _____ is term commonly used for commercializing a product. The success of a new product depends not only on the idea behind the product, but also on the marketing of the new product before, during and after the product launch. New Product Launching (NPL) is part of the New Product Development method.

a. Psychographic
b. Market share
c. Production orientation
d. Commercial planning

76. _____ in organizations and public policy is both the organizational process of creating and maintaining a plan; and the psychological process of thinking about the activities required to create a desired goal on some scale. As such, it is a fundamental property of intelligent behavior. This thought process is essential to the creation and refinement of a plan, or integration of it with other plans, that is, it combines forecasting of developments with the preparation of scenarios of how to react to them.

a. Power III
b. 6-3-5 Brainwriting
c. 180SearchAssistant
d. Planning

77. _____ identifies a business or similar entity, assists in wayfinding and attracts customers. In societies where literacy is not widespread, such signs are necessarily primarily based on images rather than words. Since the rise of mass literacy, such signs generally include the name of the business, often in the form of a logo, but also continue often to use images in addition to and in the place of words.

a. Kano model
b. Demand generation
c. Value chain
d. Commercial signage

78. _____ is the process or cycle of introducing a new product into the market. The actual launch of a new product is the final stage of new product development, and the one where the most money will have to be spent for advertising, sales promotion, and other marketing efforts. In the case of a new consumer packaged good, costs will be at least $ 10 million, but can reach up to $ 200 million.

a. Customer Interaction Tracker
b. Sweepstakes
c. Confusion marketing
d. Commercialization

Chapter 1. Test Preparation Part 1

79. A _____ is a sequential process used by firms to gather resources, transform them into goods or commodities and, finally, distribute them to consumers. In short, it is the connected path from which a good travels from producers to consumers. _____s can be unique depending on the product types or the types of markets.

a. Consumer-to-business
b. Commodity chain
c. Local purchasing
d. Niche market

80. _____ is a price setting technique used by marketers. Generally, it involves using the price of competitors' products in determining the price of your own products.

Variations of this strategy include:

- matching competitors price
- setting price at an amount above competitors' price (say $5 more)
- setting price at an amount below competitors' price (say $4 less)
- setting price at a percentage above competitors' price (say 3% more)
- setting price at a percentage below competitors' price (say 10% less)
- setting price within a range of the competitors' price (say no more than 5% more and no less than 8% less than competitors price)

This strategy is typically used by fringe firms, in an industry with one or two dominant companies (in fact, it is sometimes referred to as the 'follow the leader strategy'.)

Its main advantage is ease of use.

a. Penetration pricing
b. Premium pricing
c. Break even analysis
d. Competitor indexing

81. _____s can refer to a method of trading sometimes used by organizations when procuring large contracts for goods and/or services where the customer takes control of the selling process by issuing a Request for Proposal and requiring a proposal response from previously identified or interested suppliers. _____s involve long sales cycles with multiple decision makers. Multiple stakeholders and stakeholder groups contribute to every _____.

a. Complex sale
b. Motion Picture Association of America's film-rating system
c. Geo
d. Movin'

82. _____ is the process of using quantitative methods and qualitative methods to evaluate consumer response to a product idea prior to the introduction of a product to the market. It can also be used to generate communication designed to alter consumer attitudes toward existing products. These methods involve the evaluation by consumers of product concepts having certain rational benefits, such as 'a detergent that removes stains but is gentle on fabrics,' or non-rational benefits, such as 'a shampoo that lets you be yourself.' Such methods are commonly referred to as _____ and have been performed using field surveys, personal interviews and focus groups, in combination with various quantitative methods, to generate and evaluate product concepts.

a. Logit analysis
b. Market analysis
c. Cross tabulation
d. Concept testing

83. _____ is the practice of deliberately making confusing marketing material in order to hinder consumers' comparisons with other similar offers.

Financial products are sometimes said to employ the tactics of _____.

a. Product bundling
c. Product line
b. Customer franchise
d. Confusion marketing

84. _____ is a statistical technique used in market research to determine how people value different features that make up an individual product or service.

The objective of _____ is to determine what combination of a limited number of attributes is most influential on respondent choice or decision making. A controlled set of potential products or services is shown to respondents and by analyzing how they make preferences between these products, the implicit valuation of the individual elements making up the product or service can be determined.

a. Power III
c. Likert scale
b. Semantic differential
d. Conjoint analysis

85. _____ is a form of socio-economic organization that is posed in contrast with consumerist capitalism.

Under consumerist capitalism, it is assumed that market mechanisms are inherently guided by the solicitation of consumers' individualistic concerns (e.g., safety, accessibility, affordability of products) at the exclusion of other-regarding concerns.

This dogma however is substantially disproved by conservative efforts to prevent information about products reaching a consumer of those products, e.g. those on genetically modified organisms and work conditions.

a. Developed country
c. Consumocracy
b. Consumption Map
d. Cash and carry

86. _____ is a broad label that refers to any individuals or households that use goods and services generated within the economy. The concept of a _____ is used in different contexts, so that the usage and significance of the term may vary.

A _____ is a person who uses any product or service.

a. Consumer
c. Power III
b. 6-3-5 Brainwriting
d. 180SearchAssistant

87. _____ laws and regulations seek to protect any individual from loss of privacy due to failures or limitations of corporate customer privacy measures. They recognize that the damage done by privacy loss is typically not measurable, nor can it be undone, and that commercial organizations have little or no interest in taking unprofitable measures to drastically increase privacy of customers - indeed, their motivation is very often quite the opposite, to share data for commercial advantage, and to fail to officially recognize it as sensitive, so as to avoid legal liability for lapses of security that may occur.

_____ concerns date back to the first commercial couriers and bankers, who in every culture took strong measures to protect customer privacy, but also in every culture tended to be subject to very harsh punitive measures for failures to keep a customer's information private.

a. Locator software
b. Consumer privacy
c. Business-to-government
d. Personalized marketing

88. _____ is the ability of an individual or group to seclude themselves or information about themselves and thereby reveal themselves selectively. The boundaries and content of what is considered private differ among cultures and individuals, but share basic common themes. _____ is sometimes related to anonymity, the wish to remain unnoticed or unidentified in the public realm.

a. Power III
b. 180SearchAssistant
c. 6-3-5 Brainwriting
d. Privacy

89. _____ is an electronic commerce business model in which consumers (individuals) offer products and services to companies and the companies pay them. This business model is a complete reversal of traditional business model where companies offer goods and services to consumers (business-to-consumer = B2C.)

This kind of economic relationship is qualified as an inverted business model.

a. Consumer-to-business
b. Trade name
c. Niche market
d. Total benefits of ownership

90. _____ is a method to analyze the environment in which a business operates. Environmental scanning mainly focuses on the macro environment of a business. But _____ considers the entire environment of a business, its internal and external environment.

a. Commercial planning
b. Primary research
c. Confusion marketing
d. Context analysis

91. _____ maximizes the profit derived from an individual product, based on the difference between the product's price and variable costs (the product's contribution margin per unit), and on one's assumptions regarding the relationship between the product's price and the number of units that can be sold at that price. The product's contribution to total firm profit (i.e., to operating income) is maximized when a price is chosen that maximizes the following:

Contribution Margin Per Unit X Number of Units Sold

Contribution margin per unit is the difference between the price of a product and the sum of the variable costs of one unit of that product. Variable costs are all costs that will increase with greater unit sales of a product or decrease with fewer unit sales (i.e., leaving out fixed costs, which are costs that will not change with sales level over an assumed possible range of sales levels.)

a. Pay Per Sale
b. Contribution margin-based pricing
c. Price war
d. Cost-plus pricing

92. _____ is one of the four Ps of the marketing mix. The other three aspects are product, promotion, and place. It is also a key variable in microeconomic price allocation theory.

   a. Competitor indexing   b. Relationship based pricing
   c. Price   d. Pricing

93. A _____, also referred to as a 'corp capes,' is a collection of informational resources that describes and serves to market a company's products or services.

The standard _____ may include a letter from the CEO, mission statement and/or vision statement, fact sheet and/or brochure, staff bios, client list, case studies, client reference letters, press releases, and press coverage. The length of a _____ varies from company to company, but should be kept as concise as possible.

   a. Commercialization   b. Social marketing
   c. Category management   d. Corporate capabilities package

94. _____, are also called Company colours, which are one of the most instantly recognizable elements of a corporate visual identity and promote a strong non-verbal message on the company's behalf.

- Red for Coca-Cola
- Blue for Pepsi

- Corporate logo
- Corporate identity
- Corporate image

   a. Brand orientation   b. Visual merchandising
   c. Corporate colours   d. Brand equity

95. In marketing, a _____ is the 'persona' of a corporation which is designed to accord with and facilitate the attainment of business objectives. It is usually visibly manifested by way of branding and the use of trademarks.

_____ comes into being when there is a common ownership of an organisational philosophy that is manifest in a distinct corporate culture -- the corporate personality.

   a. Brand orientation   b. Brand ambassador
   c. Brand recognition   d. Corporate identity

96. A _____ refers to how a corporation is perceived. It is a generally accepted image of what a company 'stands for'. The creation of a _____ is an exercise in perception management.

   a. Demand generation   b. Corporate image
   c. Buying center   d. Lifetime value

97. _____ are cosmetic products that are claimed, primarily by those within the cosmetic industry, to have drug-like benefits. Examples of products typically labeled as _____ include anti-aging creams and moisturizers. The word is a portmanteau of the words 'cosmetic' and 'pharmaceutical'.
   a. 6-3-5 Brainwriting
   b. 180SearchAssistant
   c. Power III
   d. Cosmeceuticals

98. _____ is a pricing method used by companies. It is used primarily because it is easy to calculate and requires little information. There are several varieties, but the common thread in all of them is that one first calculates the cost of the product, then includes an additional amount to represent profit.
   a. Break even analysis
   b. Relationship based pricing
   c. Loss leader
   d. Cost-plus pricing

99. In economics, _____ is the ratio of the percent change in one variable to the percent change in another variable. It is a tool for measuring the responsiveness of a function to changes in parameters in a relative way. Commonly analyzed are _____ of substitution, price and wealth.
   a. Opinion leadership
   b. Elasticity
   c. ACNielsen
   d. Intellectual property

1. _____ , is the country of manufacture, production, or growth where an article or product comes from. There are differing rules of origin under various national laws and international treaties.

From a marketing perspective, '_____' gives a way to differentiate the product from the competitors.

  a. Mediation
  b. Joint venture
  c. Product liability
  d. Country of origin

2. In marketing a _____ is a ticket or document that can be exchanged for a financial discount or rebate when purchasing a product. Customarily, _____s are issued by manufacturers of consumer packaged goods or by retailers, to be used in retail stores as a part of sales promotions. They are often widely distributed through mail, magazines, newspapers, the Internet, and mobile devices such as cell phones.
  a. Merchandise
  b. Merchandising
  c. Marketing communication
  d. Coupon

3. _____ is the practice of marketing in order to generate additional revenue, known sometimes as add-on sales aimed at improving the overall customer experience.

Product selection in most retail environments is based on consumer usage patterns.

  a. Line extension
  b. Market intelligence
  c. Brand Development Index
  d. Cross merchandising

4. _____ refers to the methods, practices and operations conducted to promote and sustain certain categories of commercial activity. The term is understood to have different specific meanings depending on the context. Merchandise is a sale goods at a store

In marketing, one of the definitions of _____ is the practice in which the brand or image from one product or service is used to sell another.

  a. Marketing communication
  b. New Media Strategies
  c. Word of mouth
  d. Merchandising

5. A _____ displays the joint distribution of two or more variables. They are usually presented as a contingency table in a matrix format. Whereas a frequency distribution provides the distribution of one variable, a contingency table describes the distribution of two or more variables simultaneously.
  a. Logit analysis
  b. Marketing research
  c. Cross tabulation
  d. Marketing research process

6. _____ is a model for descriptive decisions under risk which has been introduced by Amos Tversky and Daniel Kahneman in 1992 (Tversky, Kahneman, 1992.) It is a further development and variant of prospect theory. The difference from the original version of prospect theory is that weighting is applied to the cumulative probability distribution function, as in rank-dependent expected utility theory, rather than to the probabilities of individual outcomes.
  a. Cumulative prospect theory
  b. 6-3-5 Brainwriting
  c. Power III
  d. 180SearchAssistant

Chapter 2. Test Preparation Part 2

7. _____ is a theory that describes decisions between alternatives that involve risk, i.e. alternatives with uncertain outcomes, where the probabilities are known. The model is descriptive: it tries to model real-life choices, rather than optimal decisions.

_____ was developed by Daniel Kahneman, professor at Princeton University's Department of Psychology, and Amos Tversky in 1979 as a psychologically realistic alternative to expected utility theory.

a. 6-3-5 Brainwriting
c. 180SearchAssistant
b. Power III
d. Prospect theory

8. _____ is a software and/or process of gathering information about customers interactions agains all levels throughout a business. A _____ does not only track customers who have actually bought a product or service, but also keeps track of future prospects and how they interact with sales organisations.

The difference between a CRM system and _____ is the approach and philosophy of what a customer actually is.

a. Customer Interaction Tracker
c. Value proposition
b. Customer insight
d. Sweepstakes

9. In statistics, an _____ is a term in a statistical model added when the effect of two or more variables is not simply additive. Such a term reflects that the effect of one variable depends on the values of one or more other variables.

Thus, for a response Y and two variables x_1 and x_2 an additive model would be:

$$Y = ax_1 + bx_2 + \text{error}$$

In contrast to this,

$$Y = ax_1 + bx_2 + c(x_1 \times x_2) + \text{error},$$

is an example of a model with an _____ between variables x_1 and x_2 ('error' refers to the random variable whose value by which y differs from the expected value of y.)

a. AMAX
c. ACNielsen
b. Interaction
d. ADTECH

10. _____ is the generic term for a class of software music sequencers which, in their purest form, allow the user to arrange sound samples stepwise on a timeline across several monophonic channels. A _____'s interface is primarily numeric; notes are entered via the alphanumeric keys of the computer keyboard, while parameters, effects and so forth are entered in hexadecimal. A complete song consists of several small multi-channel patterns chained together via a master list.

a. 6-3-5 Brainwriting
c. Power III

b. Tracker
d. 180SearchAssistant

11. _____ is a term used to describe the methodologies and systems to manage customer prospects and inquiries, generally generated by a variety of marketing techniques. It can be considered the connectivity between advertising and customer relationship management. This critical connectivity facilitates the acquisition of targeted customers, in the most effective fashion.

a. Mass marketing
c. Marketing

b. Value proposition
d. Customer acquisition management

12. _____ is a process by which data from customer behavior is used to help make key business decisions via market segmentation and predictive analytics. This information is used by businesses for direct marketing, site selection, and customer relationship management.

RetailGathering customer data and implementing it into some type of application that can enhance insight and the decision making process is a common application of _____ used by retailers.

a. Cyberdoc
c. Societal marketing

b. Disruptive technology
d. Customer analytics

13.

The net present value (NPV) of all of a company's customers in terms of customer loyalty and indirectly, the revenue that the company can obtain from them.

In deciding the value of a company, it is important to know of how much value its customer base is in terms of future revenues. The greater the _____ , the more future revenue in the lifetime of its clients; this means that a company with a higher _____ can get more money from its customers on average than another company that is identical in all other characteristics.

a. Total cost
c. Product proliferation

b. Marginal revenue
d. Customer equity

14. A _____ refers to the cumulative image of a product, held by the consumer, resulting from long exposure to the product or marketing of the product.

One of the most positive ways of consolidating the consumer as the most important focus of the organisation is to look on this relationship as a prime asset of the business; one that has been built up by a series of marketing investments over the years. As with any other asset, this investment can be expected to bring returns over subsequent years.

a. Commercialization
c. SWOT analysis

b. Customer relationship management
d. Customer franchise

15. _____ is the collection, deployment and translation of information that allows a business to acquire, develop and retain their customers.

Firslty, the collected data must be audited to fully understand the quality and opportunity within the database. Once this is done, there are a number of different types of analysis that can be applied.

    a. Societal marketing   b. Customer insight
    c. Customer analytics   d. Fifth screen

16. In marketing, customer _____, lifetime customer value (LCV), or _____ (LTV) and a new concept of 'customer life cycle management' is the present value of the future cash flows attributed to the customer relationship. Use of customer _____ as a marketing metric tends to place greater emphasis on customer service and long-term customer satisfaction, rather than on maximizing short-term sales.

Customer _____ has intuitive appeal as a marketing concept, because in theory it represents exactly how much each customer is worth in monetary terms, and therefore exactly how much a marketing department should be willing to spend to acquire each customer.

    a. Brand infiltration   b. Lifetime value
    c. Sweepstakes   d. Value chain

17. A personal and cultural _____ is a relative ethic _____, an assumption upon which implementation can be extrapolated. A _____ system is a set of consistent _____s and measures that is soo not true. A principle _____ is a foundation upon which other _____s and measures of integrity are based.
    a. Supreme Court of the United States   b. Perceptual maps
    c. Package-on-Package   d. Value

18. _____ consists of the processes a company uses to track and organize its contacts with its current and prospective customers. _____ software is used to support these processes; information about customers and customer interactions can be entered, stored and accessed by employees in different company departments. Typical _____ goals are to improve services provided to customers, and to use customer contact information for targeted marketing.
    a. Demand generation   b. Product bundling
    c. Customer relationship management   d. Commercialization

19. Customer _____ consists of the processes a company uses to track and organize its contacts with its current and prospective customers. CRelationship management software is used to support these processes; information about customers and customer interactions can be entered, stored and accessed by employees in different company departments. Typical CRelationship management goals are to improve services provided to customers, and to use customer contact information for targeted marketing.
    a. Product bundling   b. Green marketing
    c. Relationship management   d. Marketing

20. _____, a business term, is a measure of how products and services supplied by a company meet or surpass customer expectation. It is seen as a key performance indicator within business and is part of the four perspectives of a Balanced Scorecard.

In a competitive marketplace where businesses compete for customers, _____ is seen as a key differentiator and increasingly has become a key element of business strategy.

- a. Psychological pricing
- b. Customer base
- c. Supplier diversity
- d. Customer satisfaction

21. In the field of marketing, a _____ consists of the sum total of benefits which a vendor promises that a customer will receive in return for the customer's associated payment (or other value-transfer.)

Put simply, the value proposition is what the customer gets for his money.

Accordingly, a customer can evaluate a company's value-proposition on two broad dimensions with multiple subsets:

1. relative performance: what the customer gets from the vendor relative to a competitor's offering;
2. price: which consists of the payment the customer makes to acquire the product or service; plus the access cost

The vendor-company's marketing and sales efforts offer a _____; the vendor-company's delivery and customer-service processes then fulfill that value-proposition.

A value-proposition can assist in a firm's marketing strategy, and may guide a business to target a particular market segment.

- a. Customer value proposition
- b. Bitcom
- c. Psychographic
- d. Customer insight

22. In the field of marketing, a customer _____ consists of the sum total of benefits which a vendor promises that a customer will receive in return for the customer's associated payment (or other value-transfer.)

Put simply, the _____ is what the customer gets for his money.

Accordingly, a customer can evaluate a company's value-proposition on two broad dimensions with multiple subsets:

1. relative performance: what the customer gets from the vendor relative to a competitor's offering;
2. price: which consists of the payment the customer makes to acquire the product or service; plus the access cost

The vendor-company's marketing and sales efforts offer a customer _____; the vendor-company's delivery and customer-service processes then fulfill that value-proposition.

A value-proposition can assist in a firm's marketing strategy, and may guide a business to target a particular market segment.

a. Value proposition
b. Relationship management
c. DefCom Australia
d. Marketing performance measurement and management

23. _____ is a term coined by psychologist Gunther Eysenbach in 2001 to refer to the increasing number of websites that offer medical information and advice. This advice and information can be accessed as used as self-help self-medication without a consultation with a doctor.

This can be a problem as it discourages lay consultations which may be needed.

a. Business marketing
b. Prosumer
c. Cyberdoc
d. Customer analytics

24. The _____ is an independent index for brand marketers and agencies that determines a celebrity's ability to influence brand affinity and consumer purchase intent.

Developed by the talent division of Los Angeles-based Davie Brown Entertainment (DBE), an Omnicom Group Inc. agency and a member of The Marketing Arm network, the _____ provides marketers with a systematic approach for quantifying the use of celebrities in their advertising and marketing campaigns.

a. Per-inquiry advertising
b. Comparison-Shopping agent
c. Lobbying and Disclosure Act of 1995
d. Davie Brown Index

25. _____ is an American marketing research and consulting firm based in Arlington, Texas. It also operates the American Consumer Opinion online panel, which is made up of over seven million people. .

a. Power III
b. Chief executive officer
c. Financial analyst
d. Decision Analyst

26. In marketing, the _____ is the phenomenon whereby consumers will tend to have a specific change in preference between two options when also presented with a third option that is asymmetrically dominated. An option is asymmetrically dominated when it is inferior in all respects to one option; but, in comparison to the other option, it is inferior in some respects and superior in others. In other words, in terms of specific attributes determining preferability, it is completely dominated by (i.e., inferior to) one option and only partially dominated by the other.

a. Power III
b. 6-3-5 Brainwriting
c. Decoy effect
d. 180SearchAssistant

27. _____ is a loyalty card purchasing scheme for:

- regular and full-time Reserve members of the Australian Defence Force;
- certain 'Protector' organisations, such as firefighters, ambulance and emergency response personnel including the Wireless Institute of Australia's emergency response amateur radio personnel, etc;

and (fee may apply):

- Defence civilian staff;
- family members of the above (fee may apply); and
- certain other categories of people similar to these.

The Government of Australia established the scheme instead of establishing an organisation similar to the US' Base/Post exchange shops. The Defence Force Discount Buying Scheme commenced operations in April 1990. Known as the Defence Force Privilege Card scheme, it was developed by Defcom Pty.

    a. Cyberdoc   b. DefCom Australia
    c. Business-to-business   d. Kano model

28. In marketing and strategic management, marketing warfare strategies are a type of marketing strategy that uses military metaphor to craft a businesses strategy. See marketing warfare strategies for background and an overview. _____ are a type of marketing warfare strategy designed to protect a company's market share, profitability, product positioning, or mind share.

    a. Defensive marketing warfare strategies   b. Flanking marketing warfare strategies
    c. Power III   d. Mass customization

29. _____ is defined by the American _____ Association as the activity, set of institutions, and processes for creating, communicating, delivering, and exchanging offerings that have value for customers, clients, partners, and society at large. The term developed from the original meaning which referred literally to going to market, as in shopping, or going to a market to sell goods or services.

_____ practice tends to be seen as a creative industry, which includes advertising, distribution and selling.

    a. Customer acquisition management   b. Marketing myopia
    c. Product naming   d. Marketing

30. In economics, _____ is the desire to own something and the ability to pay for it. The term _____ signifies the ability or the willingness to buy a particular commodity at a given point of time .

    a. Market system   b. Market dominance
    c. Discretionary spending   d. Demand

31. _____ is the focus of targeted marketing programs to drive awareness and interest in a company's products and/or services. Commonly used in business to business, business to government, or longer sales cycle business to consumer sales cycles, _____ involves multiple areas of marketing and is really the marriage of marketing programs coupled with a structured sales process.

There are multiple components of a stepped _____ process that vary based on the size and complexity of a sale.

a. Marketing performance measurement and management	b. Bitcom
c. Blind taste test	d. Demand generation

32. A _____ is an example of something used in some kind of presentation or exhibit.

Sales and marketing people often need to show off an example of the product they are trying to sell, and demonstrate the use of the product. This has been accomplished in a variety of ways.

a. Targeted advertising	b. Market intelligence
c. Co-branding	d. Demonstrator model

33. A _____ is a term used to describe the form of a consortium of stakeholders coming together to undertake joint alliance marketing activities within a destination. An alliance can provide a way to increase marketing exposure that would otherwise be out of reach from individual stakeholders within a destination.

An example of a _____ is Destination Warsaw.

a. 6-3-5 Brainwriting	b. Destination alliance
c. Power III	d. 180SearchAssistant

34. _____ is the process by which a new idea or new product is accepted by the market. The rate of _____ is the speed that the new idea spreads from one consumer to the next. Adoption is similar to _____ except that it deals with the psychological processes an individual goes through, rather than an aggregate market process.

a. Kano model	b. Perceptual maps
c. Market development	d. Diffusion

35. _____ is a theory of how, why, and at what rate new ideas and technology spread through cultures. Everett Rogers introduced it in his 1962 book, _____s, writing that 'Diffusion is the process by which an innovation is communicated through certain channels over time among the members of a social system.' The adoption curve becomes an s-curve when cumulative adoption is used.

Rogers theorized that innovations would spread through a community in an S curve, as the early adopters select the innovation (which may be a technology) first, followed by the majority, until a technology or innovation has reached its saturation point in a community.

According to Rogers, diffusion research centers on the conditions which increase or decrease the likelihood that a new idea, product, or practice will be adopted by members of a given culture.

a. Power III	b. Diffusion of innovation
c. 6-3-5 Brainwriting	d. 180SearchAssistant

36. A _____ is a person who has grown up with digital technology such as computers, the Internet, mobile phones and MP3.

Marc Prensky claims to have coined the term _____, as it pertains to a new breed of student entering educational establishments. The term draws an analogy to a country's natives, for whom the local religion, language, and folkways are natural and indigenous, over against immigrants to a country who often are expected to adapt and assimilate to their newly adopted home.

  a. Reference group
  b. Digital native
  c. Minority
  d. Power III

37. In the fields of strategic management, marketing strategy, and operational strategy, _____ is the process of specifying an organization's vision, initiatives and processes in order to deploy their online assets (as of 2007, these include: web sites, mini-sites, mobile sites, digital audio and video content, rich Internet applications, community groups, banner ads, search engine marketing, affiliate programs, etc.) in a manner which maximizes the business benefits they provide to the organization.

There are numerous approaches to conducting _____, but at their core, all go through four steps:1.

  a. Goal setting
  b. Voice of the customer
  c. Business plan
  d. Digital strategy

38. A _____ is a plan of action designed to achieve a particular goal.

_____ is different from tactics. In military terms, tactics is concerned with the conduct of an engagement while _____ is concerned with how different engagements are linked.

  a. 6-3-5 Brainwriting
  b. Power III
  c. Strategy
  d. 180SearchAssistant

39. _____ includes any TV advertising that asks consumers to respond directly to the company --- usually either by calling an 800 number or by visiting a web site. This is a form of direct response marketing.

There are two types of _____, short form and long form.

  a. Barker channel
  b. Custom media
  c. History of Advertising Trust
  d. Direct response television

40. _____ are reductions to a basic price of goods or services. They can occur anywhere in the distribution channel, modifying either the manufacturer's list price (determined by the manufacturer and often printed on the package), the retail price (set by the retailer and often attached to the product with a sticker), or the list price (which is quoted to a potential buyer, usually in written form.) The market price (also called effective price) is the amount actually paid.
  a. Price points
  b. Discounts and allowances
  c. Price
  d. Price shading

41. A _____ or disruptive innovation is a technological innovation that improves a product or service in ways that the market does not expect, typically by being lower priced or designed for a different set of consumers.

Disruptive innovations can be broadly classified into low-end and new-market disruptive innovations. A new-market disruptive innovation is often aimed at non-consumption (i.e., consumers who would not have used the products already on the market), whereas a lower-end disruptive innovation is aimed at mainstream customers for whom price is more important than quality.

- a. Commercial operations management
- b. Law of disruption
- c. Google Advertising Professional
- d. Disruptive technology

42. _____ is a digital marketing term that means distributing a brand's presence through multiple communications channels to effectively reach target consumers. Brands have an arsenal of tactics today to reach and communicate with consumers, some of which include: video, audio, email, websites and microsites, paid media, search engine optimization and search engine marketing, blogging, social media, social influence programs, web content syndication and distribution, widgets, gadgets, word-of-mouth and viral marketing programs, mobile media, mobile text marketing, mobile applications, convergent media, etc.

The term was originally used by Sherry Turkle in her 1995 book, Life on the Screen: Identity in the Age of the Internet.

- a. Customer insight
- b. Marketing
- c. Product bundling
- d. Distributed presence

43. _____ is one of the four elements of marketing mix. An organization or set of organizations (go-betweens) involved in the process of making a product or service available for use or consumption by a consumer or business user.

The other three parts of the marketing mix are product, pricing, and promotion.

- a. Comparison-Shopping agent
- b. Japan Advertising Photographers' Association
- c. Better Living Through Chemistry
- d. Distribution

44. '_____' refers to the use of computer technology to enhance or bypass the pharmaceutical representative's traditional sales call to healthcare providers. (The traditional sales call is known as 'detailing.')

Either internet based or loaded onto a tablet PC, an e-detail is an interactive presentation which is backed up by robust CRM systems to allow for a tailored marketing approach for every single customer. Internet based _____ is seen by some as a method to overcome the challenge sales reps face to secure physician meeting, the e-detail effectively replacing the face-to-face contact.

- a. Interactive marketing
- b. Advertiser funded programming
- c. All commodity volume
- d. E-Detailing

45. _____s or 'eServices' is a highly general/generic term usually referring to the provision of services via the Internet (the prefix 'e' standing for 'electronic', as it does in many other uses.) It is true Web jargon, meaning just about anything done online. This page, for example, is an _____.

a. ACNielsen
b. ADTECH
c. AMAX
d. E-Service

46. A _____ is a relatively new executive level position at a corporation, company, organization typically reporting directly to the CEO or board of directors. The _____ is responsible for a brand's image, experience, and promise, and propagating it throughout all aspects of the company. The brand officer oversees marketing, advertising, design, public relations and customer service departments.
   a. Power III
   b. Chief executive officer
   c. Chief brand officer
   d. Financial analyst

47. _____ is a brand communications agency with offices in Hong Kong, Shanghai, Beijing and Macau employing approximately sixty staff and four senior partners. The company works on a project and a retainer basis for thirty leading local and international clients. Assignments range from brand definition and positioning to corporate identity, design and marketing communications.
   a. Ameritest
   b. Isobar
   c. Advertising Standards Canada
   d. Eight Partnership

48. A _____ is a type of business entity in which partners (owners) share with each other the profits or losses of the business undertaking in which all have invested. _____s are often favored over corporations for taxation purposes, as the _____ structure does not generally incur a tax on profits before it is distributed to the partners (i.e. there is no dividend tax levied.) However, depending on the _____ structure and the jurisdiction in which it operates, owners of a _____ may be exposed to greater personal liability than they would as shareholders of a corporation.
   a. Competition law
   b. Brand piracy
   c. Fair Debt Collection Practices Act
   d. Partnership

49. _____, commonly known as e-commerce or eCommerce, consists of the buying and selling of products or services over electronic systems such as the Internet and other computer networks. The amount of trade conducted electronically has grown extraordinarily with wide-spread Internet usage. A wide variety of commerce is conducted in this way, spurring and drawing on innovations in electronic funds transfer, supply chain management, Internet marketing, online transaction processing, electronic data interchange (EDI), inventory management systems, and automated data collection systems.
   a. ACNielsen
   b. ADTECH
   c. AMAX
   d. Electronic commerce

50. _____ refers to money or scrip which is exchanged only electronically. Typically, this involves use of computer networks, the internet and digital stored value systems. Electronic Funds Transfer and direct deposit are examples of _____.
   a. ADTECH
   b. AMAX
   c. ACNielsen
   d. Electronic money

51. _____ is anything that is generally accepted as payment for goods and services and repayment of debts. The main uses of _____ are as a medium of exchange, a unit of account, and a store of value. Some authors explicitly require _____ to be a standard of deferred payment.
   a. Law of supply
   b. Leading indicator
   c. Microeconomics
   d. Money

Chapter 2. Test Preparation Part 2

52. The _____ is a self-regulatory program created in 2004 by American business organizations to promote consumer confidence. _____ is a program of the Electronic Retailing Association in conjunction with the National Advertising Review Council (NARC) and administered by the Council of Better Business Bureaus. The mission of the program is to enhance consumer confidence in electronic retailing, by providing a forum to self-regulate direct response advertising.

   a. Interactive marketing   b. All commodity volume
   c. Electronic retailing self-regulation program   d. Engagement marketing

53. _____ consists of the sale of goods or merchandise from a fixed location, such as a department store or kiosk in small or individual lots for direct consumption by the purchaser. _____ may include subordinated services, such as delivery. Purchasers may be individuals or businesses.

   a. Warehouse store   b. Thrifting
   c. Charity shop   d. Retailing

54. _____ measures the extent to which a consumer has a meaningful brand experience when exposed to commercial advertising, sponsorship, television contact, or other experience.

In March 2006 the Advertising Research Foundation defined _____ as 'turning on a prospect to a brand idea enhanced by the surrounding context'. The ARF has also defined the function whereby _____ impacts a brand:

_____ is complex because a variety of exposure and relationship factors affect _____, making simplified rankings misleading.

   a. Engagement   b. Automated surveys
   c. Individual branding   d. Inseparability

55. _____, sometimes called 'participation marketing,' is a marketing strategy that invites and encourages consumers to participate in the evolution of a brand. Rather than looking at consumers as passive receivers of messages, engagement marketers believe that consumers should be actively involved in the production and co-creation of marketing programs.

Ultimately, _____ attempts to connect more strongly consumers with brands by 'engaging' them in a dialogue and two-way, cooperative interaction.

   a. Interactive marketing   b. Electronic retailing self-regulation program
   c. Australian Journal of Management   d. Engagement marketing

56. _____ defines a category of software used by marketing organizations to manage their end-to-end process from gathering and analyzing customer data across websites and other channels, to planning, budgeting and managing the creative production process, to executing targeted customer communications to measuring results and effectiveness. _____ is a superset of other marketing software categories such as Web Analytics, Campaign Management, Marketing Resource Management, Marketing Dashboards, Lead Management, Event-driven Marketing, Predictive Modeling and more. The goal of deploying and using _____ is to improve both the efficiency and effectiveness of marketing by increasing revenue generation, decreasing costs and waste, and reducing time to market.

a. Advertising media selection
b. Enterprise marketing management
c. Electronic retailing self-regulation program
d. ACNielsen

57. _____ is a business discipline which is focused on the practical application of marketing techniques and the management of a firm's marketing resources and activities. Marketing managers are often responsible for influencing the level, timing, and composition of customer demand accepted definition of the term. In part, this is because the role of a marketing manager can vary significantly based on a business' size, corporate culture, and industry context.

a. Door-to-door
b. Performance-based advertising
c. Marketing management
d. Business structure

58. _____ or _____ is a business method in relationship management beyond customer relationship management.

'_____ - Enterprise relationship management is basically a business strategy for value creation that is not based on cost containment, but rather on the leveraging of network-enabled processes and activities to transform the relationships between the organization and all its internal and external constituencies in order to maximize current and future opportunities.' [Galbreath, 2002]

The art of relationship management is not an entirely new one. In fact, it has taken on many forms, addressing specific organizational constituencies (customers, channel partners, specialized service providers, employees, suppliers, etc.)

a. ADTECH
b. AMAX
c. ACNielsen
d. Enterprise relationship management

59. _____ is to any mathematical method of comparing two or more generally unlike quantity/value scales.

A common example of the utility for an _____ standard comes in currency markets, where without established exchange rates there is great difficulty making comparisons. For example, dollars, euros, yen have different quantity amounts that would each equal the same implied value.

a. ACNielsen
b. AMAX
c. ADTECH
d. Equivalization

60. _____ is a broad label that refers to any individuals or households that use goods and services generated within the economy. The concept of a _____ is used in different contexts, so that the usage and significance of the term may vary.

A _____ is a person who uses any product or service.

a. Power III
b. 6-3-5 Brainwriting
c. Consumer
d. 180SearchAssistant

61. _____ is a UK magazine that also publishes a lot of its key information for free on its corresponding website [It is in its own words 'an alternative consumer organisation looking at the social and environmental records of the companies behind the brand names'.

Its stated reasons for existence are to promote universal human rights, environmental sustainability and animal welfare by informing consumers of which brands and products are ethical to buy.

The term _____ also describes someone who practices ethical consumerism.

a. Ethical Consumer
b. Entrepreneur magazine
c. American Booksellers Association
d. Adweek

62. The _____ gathers high quality and up-to-date information on European and global markets for information technology, telecommunications and consumer electronics. The _____ is managed by Bitkom Research GmbH, a wholly owned subsidiary of BITKOM, the German Association for Information Technology, Telecommunications and New Media. _____ is sponsored by CeBIT, KPMG, Simo, Systems and Telecom Italia.

a. Advertising media selection
b. Account-based marketing
c. E-Detailing
d. European Information Technology Observatory

63. The _____ represents those involved in sponsorship across Europe.

The _____ was formed in October 2003 by the merger of two bodies, the European Sponsorship Consultants Association and the Institute for Sports Sponsorship.

The European Sponsorship Consultants Association (ESCA) was founded in 1990.

a. ACNielsen
b. European Sponsorship Association
c. AMAX
d. ADTECH

64. _____ is a type of research conducted because a problem has not been clearly defined. _____ helps determine the best research design, data collection method and selection of subjects. Given its fundamental nature, _____ often concludes that a perceived problem does not actually exist.

a. Exploratory research
b. IDDEA
c. ACNielsen
d. Intent scale translation

65. _____ is a statistical method used to describe variability among observed variables in terms of fewer unobserved variables called factors. The observed variables are modeled as linear combinations of the factors, plus 'error' terms. The information gained about the interdependencies can be used later to reduce the set of variables in a dataset.

a. Power III
b. Semantic differential
c. Likert scale
d. Factor analysis

66. _____ is the loyalty felt and expressed by a fan towards the object of his/her fanaticism. Allegiances can be strong or weak. The loyalties of sports fans have been studied by psychologists, who have determined several factors that create such loyalties.

a. SWOT analysis
b. Product bundling
c. Law of disruption
d. Fan loyalty

67. _____ , are products that are sold quickly at relatively low cost. Though the absolute profit made on _____ products is relatively small, they generally sell in large quantities, so the cumulative profit on such products can be large. Examples of _____ generally include a wide range of frequently purchased consumer products such as toiletries, soap, cosmetics, teeth cleaning products, shaving products and detergents, as well as other non-durables such as glassware, light bulbs, batteries, paper products and plastic goods.

   a. Door-to-door
   b. Marketing management
   c. Performance-based advertising
   d. Fast moving consumer goods

68. _____ are final goods specifically intended for the mass market. For instance, _____ do not include investment assets, like precious antiques, even though these antiques are final goods.

Manufactured goods are goods that have been processed by way of machinery.

   a. Power III
   b. Consumer goods
   c. Durable good
   d. Free good

69. _____/primary market research has traditionally been thought different from methods of research conducted in a laboratory or academic setting. It was developed originally from anthropology and is sometimes know as participant research, or as ethnography in anthropology

   a. Questionnaire
   b. Mystery shopping
   c. Field research
   d. Market research

70. The _____ is the most recent in a historic line of communication screens. It is commonly called Digital Signage or Digital Out Of Home.

The _____ represents the combination of the World Wide Web and mobile 2G and 3G technologies or data delivered via physical uploads at screens placed in various environments.

   a. Fan loyalty
   b. Fifth screen
   c. Commercial operations management
   d. Marketing plan

71. _____ is a challenger branding agency based in Pittsburgh, Pennsylvania, that provides clients with strategic marketing and advertising services. The agency received international media coverage when it launched a controversial marketing campaign featuring a whip-bearing dominatrix to promote _____'s Brand Spanking process.

_____ was founded in 1986 by Andrea Fitting, Ph.D. The agency's notable clients include the Mason School of Business at The College of William ' Mary and Butler Health System.

   a. Brand ambassador
   b. Retail design
   c. Brand culture
   d. Fitting Group

72. In marketing and strategic management, marketing warfare strategies are a type of marketing strategy that uses military metaphor to craft a businesses strategy. See marketing warfare strategies for background and an overview. _____ are a type of marketing warfare strategy designed to minimize confrontational losses.

a. Vertical integration
b. Mass customization
c. Power III
d. Flanking marketing warfare strategies

73. _____ brings together the producer and the consumer. It is the chain of activities that brings food from 'farm gate to plate.' The marketing of even a single food product can be a complicated process involving many producers and companies. For example, fifty-six companies are involved in making one can of chicken noodle soup.
   a. Co-marketing
   b. Cyberdoc
   c. Law of disruption
   d. Food marketing

74. _____ is a defunct company that operated soft drink and water dispensers at retail locations. Based in Salt Lake City, Utah, Fountain Fresh developed and marketed in-store, self-serve soft drink and pure drinking water beverage centers in the mid-1990s.

The original value proposition was for consumers to enjoy low-priced beverages by washing and refilling reusable soft-drink bottles in the Fountain Fresh dispenser.

   a. CoolBrands
   b. Point of sale
   c. Fountain Fresh International
   d. Partnership for a Drug-Free America

75. '_____' is a generally accepted term used in a number of advertising and technology industries, to refer to a small portable video screen such as those found in mobile (cellular) phones or other portable electronic devices such as a video iPod player. Sometimes referred to as the 'Third Screen.'

While the term is gaining acceptance into popular usage, it is not as well known as 'Cell 'PDA' and 'mobile' which are other terms used in the English-speaking world to refer to these very popular electronic devices.

Today, people use mobile devices in ways that open new possibilities for Documentary Practice.

   a. Business marketing
   b. Fourth screen
   c. Prosumer
   d. Corporate capabilities package

76. A _____ is a fee that a person pays to operate a franchise branch of a larger company and enjoy the profits therefrom.

By joining a franchise an investor or franchisee is able to run a business under the umbrella of the franchise.

The franchisee must pay a _____, which may become costly.

   a. Franchise fee
   b. Franchising
   c. 180SearchAssistant
   d. Power III

77. A _____ is the price one pays as remuneration for services, especially the honorarium paid to a doctor, lawyer, consultant, or other member of a learned profession. _____s usually allow for overhead, wages, costs, and markup.

Traditionally, professionals in Great Britain received a _____ in contradistinction to a payment, salary, or wage, and would often use guineas rather than pounds as units of account.

a. Price shading
b. Price war
c. Transfer pricing
d. Fee

78. _____ refers to the methods of practicing and using another person's philosophy of business. The franchisor grants the independent operator the right to distribute its products, techniques, and trademarks for a percentage of gross monthly sales and a royalty fee. Various tangibles and intangibles such as national or international advertising, training, and other support services are commonly made available by the franchisor.

a. Power III
b. Franchising
c. Franchise fee
d. 180SearchAssistant

79. _____ is an annual promotional effort by the North American comic book industry to help bring new readers into independent comic book stores. Brainstormed by retailer Joe Field of Flying Colors Comics in Concord CA in his 'Big Picture' column in the August 2001 issue of Comics ' Games Retailer magazine, it was started in 2002 and is coordinated by the industry's single large distributor, Diamond Comic Distributors. The next event will be on May 2, 2009.

a. Power III
b. 180SearchAssistant
c. 6-3-5 Brainwriting
d. Free Comic Book Day

80. _____, which requires a Rockwick Capital Proof of Funds, can be used to create any market by customizing built-in account, order, user management systems along with infrastructure to create an online market for selling/buying/exchanging their products. Markets can be auction-based, over-the-counter or hybrid. _____ is currently specialized for stock brokerages, that can be customized for any other business.

a. Outsourcing relationship management
b. Enterprise marketing management
c. EMarket trading platform
d. Advertising media selection

81. In market research, _____ is 'fund-raising under the guise of research'. This behavior occurs when a product marketer falsely purports to be a market researcher conducting a statistical survey, when in reality the 'researcher' is attempting to solicit a donation.

Generally considered unethical, this tactic is strictly prohibited by trade groups, such as CASRO and the Marketing Research Association, for their member research companies.

a. 180SearchAssistant
b. Power III
c. Frugging
d. 6-3-5 Brainwriting

82. The _____ is an alternative technique used in brand marketing and product management to help a company decide what product(s) to add to its product portfolio, and which market opportunities are worthy of continued investment. Also known as the 'Directional Policy Matrix,' the GE multi-factor model was first developed by General Electric in the 1970s.

Conceptually, the _____ is similar to the Boston Box as it is plotted on a two-dimensional grid.

a. Parity Product
b. Reinforcement
c. Perceptual maps
d. GE matrix

83. _____ is the promotion of gambling by casinos, lotteries, bookmakers or other organisations that provide the opportunity to make bets. It is usually conducted through a variety of media or through sponsorship deals, particularly with sporting events or people.

Chapter 2. Test Preparation Part 2   39

Although not as highly regulated as tobacco advertising and alcohol advertising, in many countries there are strict laws about the way in which such services can be marketed.

a. Here Comes the King
c. BidClix
b. Gambling advertising
d. Puffery

84. _____ is a form of communication that typically attempts to persuade potential customers to purchase or to consume more of a particular brand of product or service. 'While now central to the contemporary global economy and the reproduction of global production networks, it is only quite recently that _____ has been more than a marginal influence on patterns of sales and production. The formation of modern _____ was intimately bound up with the emergence of new forms of monopoly capitalism around the end of the 19th and beginning of the 20th century as one element in corporate strategies to create, organize and where possible control markets, especially for mass produced consumer goods.

a. Advertising
c. ADTECH
b. ACNielsen
d. AMAX

85. A _____ is a type of fold used for advertising around a magazine or section, and for packaging of media such as vinyl records.

A _____ cover or _____ LP is a form of packaging for LP records which became popular in the mid-1960s. A _____ cover, when folded, is the same size as a standard LP cover (i.e., a 12 inch, or 30 centimetre, square.)

a. Fifth screen
c. Law of disruption
b. Fan loyalty
d. Gatefold

86. _____ of consumer products (often supermarket goods) are distinguished by the absence of a brand name. They are identifed more by product characterstics.

They may be manufactured by less [prominent companies], or manufactured on the same production line as a 'named' brand. _____ are usually priced below those products sold by supermarkets under their own brand (frequently referred to as 'store brands' or 'own brands'.)

a. Micro ads
c. M80
b. Gross Margin Return on Inventory Investment
d. Generic brands

87. A _____ is a collection of symbols, experiences and associations connected with a product, a service, a person or any other artifact or entity.

_____s have become increasingly important components of culture and the economy, now being described as 'cultural accessories and personal philosophies'.

Some people distinguish the psychological aspect of a _____ from the experiential aspect.

a. Store brand
b. Brandable software
c. Brand equity
d. Brand

88. A _____ is a trademark or brand name that has become the colloquial or generic description for a general class of product or service, rather than the specific meaning intended by the trademark's holder. Using a _____ to refer to the general form of what that trademark represents is a form of metonymy.
   a. Trade Symbols
   b. Retail design
   c. Lovemarks
   d. Genericized trademark

89. A _____ or trade mark, identified by the symbols ™ (not yet registered) and ® (registered) business organization or other legal entity to identify that the products and/or services to consumers with which the _____ appears originate from a unique source of origin, and to distinguish its products or services from those of other entities. A _____ is a type of intellectual property, and typically a name, word, phrase, logo, symbol, design, image, or a combination of these elements. There is also a range of non-conventional _____s comprising marks which do not fall into these standard categories.
   a. Risk management
   b. Trademark
   c. 180SearchAssistant
   d. Power III

90. In marketing, _____ is a discipline within marketing analysis which uses geolocation in the process of planning and implementation of marketing activities. It can be used in any aspect of the marketing mix - the Product, Price, Promotion, or Place Market segments can also correlate with location, and this can be useful in targeted marketing.
   a. Quantitative
   b. Parity Product
   c. Containerization
   d. Geo

91. _____, in marketing, is the practice of modifying a basic list price based on the geographical location of the buyer. It is intended to reflect the costs of shipping to different locations.

There are several types of geographic pricing:

- FOB origin (Free on Board origin) - The shipping cost from the factory or warehouse is paid by the purchaser. Ownership of the goods is transferred to the buyer as soon as it leaves the point of origin. It can be either the buyer or seller that arranges for the transportation.
- Uniform delivery pricing - (also called postage stamp pricing) - The same price is charged to all.
- Zone pricing - Prices increase as shipping distances increase. This is sometimes done by drawing concentric circles on a map with the plant or warehouse at the center and each circle defining the boundary of a price zone. Instead of using circles, irregularly shaped price boundaries can be drawn that reflect geography, population density, transportation infrastructure, and shipping cost. (The term 'zone pricing' can also refer to the practice of setting prices that reflect local competitive conditions, i.e., the market forces of supply and demand, rather than actual cost of transportation.)

Zone pricing, as practiced in the gasoline industry in the United States, is the pricing of gasoline based on a complex and secret weighting of factors, such as the number of competing stations, number of vehicles, average traffic flow, population density, and geographic characteristics. This can result in two branded gas stations only a few miles apart selling gasoline at a price differential of as much as $0.50 per gallon.

a. Green market
c. Competitive

b. Geographical pricing
d. Countervailing duties

92. _____ is one of the four Ps of the marketing mix. The other three aspects are product, promotion, and place. It is also a key variable in microeconomic price allocation theory.
   a. Competitor indexing
   c. Relationship based pricing

   b. Price
   d. Pricing

93. _____ is a flexible e-commerce solution for Plone, a content management system written in the Python programming language. In essence, _____ is an add-on framework to Plone which allows processing credit cards for online payments. It provides solutions for the most common e-commerce use cases out of the box.
   a. 6-3-5 Brainwriting
   c. Power III

   b. GetPaid
   d. 180SearchAssistant

94. In marketing language, a _____ is a unique or quirky special feature that makes something 'stand out' from its contemporaries. However, the special feature is typically thought to be of little relevance or use. Thus, a _____ is a special feature for the sake of having a special feature.
   a. Customer Interaction Tracker
   c. Prosumer

   b. Marketing plan
   d. Gimmick

95. _____, Inc. is a technology services company which provides a search engine of engineering and industrial products, indexing over 180 million parts divided into 2,300,000 product families, from over 24,000 manufacturer and distributor catalogs. _____ is a domain-specific (or 'vertical search') tool, in that its focused domain allows for optimized results.
   a. Fountain Fresh International
   c. Mapinfo

   b. Green Earth Market
   d. GlobalSpec

96. In Marketing Management, _____ strategy encompasses the channels that a company uses to connect with its customers/business and the organizational processes it develops (such as high tech product development) to guide customer interactions from initial contact through fulfilment.

A firm _____ is the delivery mechanism for their unique value proposition. That value proposition is based on the choices the business has made to focus on and invest in markets and solutions that they believe will respond positively to the increased attention.

   a. Gold Key Matching Service
   c. Net Promoter[R] score

   b. Go-to-market
   d. Better Living Through Chemistry

97. A _____ is a sample produced by a manufacturer that is perfect in almost all ways so that when sent to the media it can be tested and receive a high standard review. The term _____ can also be used to describe a product that is a very rare find and is perfect in almost all ways and has been found just by chance. Contract Manufacturers and Original Design Manufacturers use the term _____ to describe the final sample that is sent to the customer or OEM for approval before mass production.
   a. 6-3-5 Brainwriting
   c. Golden sample

   b. Power III
   d. 180SearchAssistant

98. Google launched the _____s program in November, 2004, in response to the growing need for consultants to help the increasing number of new Google AdWords clients with their AdWords campaigns.

In terms of work performed by _____s, they typically handle the following tasks:

1. Top to bottom review of client website, business model, and industry.
2. Analysis to determine client's core keywords.
3. Creation of ad copy to promote client's website on Google AdWords.
4. Determination of appropriate daily budget, ad scheduling, network targeting, and match type(s.)
5. Determination of appropriate maximum cost-per-click and landing pages for specific keywords.
6. Appropriate follow-up and campaign monitoring.

Although Google AdWords is primarily a self service program, clients bring on _____s for many reasons:

1. So that the clients can focus on their business itself, not the search campaigns.
2. It is less expensive to hire a _____ than to hire an in-house employee.
3. Clients are displeased with their existing campaigns' results.
4. Clients simply want to have a specialist handling this important part of their marketing mix.

Typically, _____s fees may or may not include: a set-up fee, a monthly management fee, an hourly fee, and/or a percentage of total ad spend. To locate a _____, Google recommends that you do a Google Maps search for _____s.

_____s range from self-employed individuals specializing in search engine marketing to full service ad agencies that cover all types of media (both online ' offline.)

a. Blitz QFD
b. Distributed presence
c. Corporate capabilities package
d. Google Advertising Professional

99. The _____ is the distribution of refurbished, used, repaired, recycled, discontinued or new products that are in working condition. They are sold through brokers and resellers, not through the original manufacturer. These goods are suitable for resale to customers as a lower cost alternative to buying new goods from standard distribution channels such as retail stores.

a. Customs union
b. Free trade zone
c. Grey market
d. Green market

100. _____ has offices in Australia, Bangladesh, China, Hong Kong, India, Indonesia, Japan, Korea, Malaysia, New Zealand, Pakistan, Philippines, Singapore, Sri Lanka, Taiwan, Thailand and Vietnam.

Eye on Asia is Grey Group's annual proprietary study that looks at the hopes and dreams of the Asia Pacific region, and determines the powerful underlying trends that will shape branding and communications today and in the future. One of the most comprehensive, in-depth surveys ever done on the Asian consumer, Eye on Asia is a thought leadership initiative that aims to get closer to the peoples of Asia.

a. 180SearchAssistant
b. 6-3-5 Brainwriting
c. Grey Group Asia Pacific
d. Power III

101. A _____ or gray market is the trade of a commodity through distribution channels which, while legal, are unofficial, unauthorized, or unintended by the original manufacturer. In contrast, a black market is the trade of goods and services that are illegal in themselves and/or distributed through illegal channels, such as the selling of stolen goods or illegal items such as heroin or unregistered handguns.

The two main types of _____ are imported manufactured goods that would be normally unavailable or more expensive in a certain country and unissued securities that are not yet traded in official markets.

a. Green market
b. Zone pricing
c. Countervailing duties
d. Grey market

102. _____ is a marketing practice that takes a specific approach to strategy, creativity and success tracking, where all three are driven by a thorough understanding of the business objective at hand. _____ insists that the organizational design of the marketing agency includes a team with broad skills, but that each staff member has creative and strategic leanings.

The strategy behind a _____ campaign is largely based on the business objective for a particular product, and is intended to be media-agnostic.

a. Lead scoring
b. Value chain
c. Customer Interaction Tracker
d. Brand infiltration

103. The _____ is an independent marketing agency specializing in all areas of the marketing and promotions in the entertainment industry, including but not limited to Commercial/non-Commercial Radio Promotion, Publicity, Street/Lifestyle Marketing, Online Marketing, Viral Video Dissemination. Founded in 1999 by Ted Chung, _____ has grown to be one of the west coast largest independent integrated marketing companies, and recently went international opening offices in New York and Mumbai, India. They have coordinated campaigns for the likes of Snoop Dogg, Warner Bros.

a. Comprehensive,
b. Clutter
c. Customization
d. Cashmere Agency

104. _____ is the practice of promoting products and services using digital distribution channels to reach consumers in a timely, relevant, personal and cost-effective manner.

Whilst _____ does include many of the techniques and practices contained within the category of Internet Marketing, it extends beyond this by including other channels with which to reach people that do not require the use of The Internet. As a result of this non-reliance on the Internet, the field of _____ includes a whole host of elements such as mobile phones, sms/mms, display / banner ads and digital outdoor.

a. Diversity marketing
b. Global marketing
c. Digital marketing
d. Relationship marketing

105. _____ is the marketing efforts using today modern technologies (mobile phones, laptops, etc..). This includes using a medium which involves text messaging over a mobile device. A very high percentage of Americans today carry around with them a mobile phone.

   a. Viral marketing   b. Direct Text Marketing
   c. Power III   d. 180SearchAssistant

106. _____, also referred to as i-marketing, web marketing, online marketing is the marketing of products or services over the Internet.

The Internet has brought many unique benefits to marketing, one of which being lower costs for the distribution of information and media to a global audience. The interactive nature of _____, both in terms of providing instant response and eliciting responses, is a unique quality of the medium.

   a. ACNielsen   b. ADTECH
   c. AMAX   d. Internet marketing

107. _____ is a relatively new concept utilized by businesses in developing an online community, which allows satisfied customers to congregate and extol the virtues of a particular brand. In most cases, the online community includes mechanisms such as blogs, podcasts, message boards, and product reviews, all of which contribute to a transparent forum to post praises, criticisms, questions, and suggestions.

One of the primary arguments to promote _____ is the premise that traditional advertising is losing its influence on consumers.

   a. Viral marketing   b. Power III
   c. 180SearchAssistant   d. New Media Marketing

108. A _____ is a term used in marketing to describe a group of people who 'hit the streets' promoting an event or a product. '_____s' are a powerful promotional tool that has been adopted industry wide as a standard line item in marketing budgets by entertainment companies, record labels, the tech industry, corporate brand marketers, new media companies and direct marketers worldwide. _____ members that are highly trained are now called Brand Ambassadors

The now ubiquitous '_____' model was originally developed by urban record labels such as Loud Records, Jive, Bad Boy and Priority Records.

   a. AStore   b. Albert Einstein
   c. African Americans   d. Street team

109. _____ is an Amazon.com affiliate product which website owners can use to create an online store on their site. The _____ interface is intended to be accessible to those without programming skills, using configuration pages to customise the content and design.

The store does not allow website owners to sell their own products directly.

a. Ed Bradley
c. Andre Kirk Agassi
b. Ethan Allen
d. AStore

110. _____ is an advertisement Software as a Service (SaaS) application run by Google.

GAd Manager can be used as an Ad Server but it also provides a variety of useful features for managing the sales process of online ads using a publishers dedicated sales team.

Should a publisher not sell out all their available ad inventory they can choose to run either other Ad Networks or AdSense Ads as Remnant Inventory in GAd Manager.

a. Ad Manager
c. ACNielsen
b. AMAX
d. ADTECH

111. _____ product trial and usage, and attitudes about the brand versus their competition.

Depending on the speed of the purchase cycle in the category, tracking can be done continuously or it can be 'pulsed,' with interviews conducted in widely spaced waves

a. Advertising agency
c. Industrial musical
b. Ad Tracking
d. Ambient media

112. _____s are rapidly growing and accepted online advertising technology platforms for buying, selling and trading online ad impressions and is a field beyond ad networks cited by the Interactive Advertising Bureau (IAB)) advertising trade publications Advertising Age, iMediaConnectionClickZ, and others that provide ways to purchase advertising on many advertising networks or thousands of websites or the pages of websites at the same time to effectively reach the largest or most targeted audience very efficiently in an increasingly fragmented online media world.

They give buyers (online advertisers and ad agency media planners and buyers) places to advertise where audiences are engaged with content today and at the same time give sellers (publisher websites online advertising sellers) a place to compete for advertiser revenue they otherwise would have a difficult time acquiring on their own and a place for these same publisher online advertising sellers to be able to sell various parts of their website(s) ad impression inventory.

_____s offer ways for advertisers to reach more audience efficiently as well as an effective method for managing campaigns to see which ads on which networks perform better or to contextually see how advertising is best performing.

a. Automated Bid Managers
c. Advertising network
b. Ad rotation
d. Ad exchange

113. _____ describes the technology and service that places advertisements on web sites. _____ technology companies provide software to web sites and advertisers to serve ads, count them, choose the ads that will make the website or advertiser most money, and monitor progress of different advertising campaigns.

An ad server is a computer server, specifically a web server, that stores advertisements used in online marketing and delivers them to website visitors.

- a. Online reputation management
- b. Organic search
- c. Online identity management
- d. Ad serving

114. _____ is the advertising industry standard unique identifier for all commercial assets. It replaced the ISCI system in 2003. It is used to track advertising from the point of concept, through creation and on to distribution, and the media.
- a. AMAX
- b. Ad-ID
- c. ADTECH
- d. ACNielsen

115. _____ is a magazine, delivering news, analysis and data on marketing and media. The magazine was started as a broadsheet newspaper in Chicago in 1930. Today, its content appears in a print weekly distributed around the world and on many electronic platforms, including: AdAge.com, daily e-mail newsletters called Ad Age Daily, Ad Age's Mediaworks and Ad Age Digital; weekly newsletters such as Madison ' Vine (about branded entertainment) and Ad Age China; podcasts called Why It Matters and various videos.
- a. Adweek
- b. Ethical Consumer
- c. Outsert
- d. Advertising Age

116. _____ is the advertising industry's non-profit self-regulating body created in 1957 to ensure the integrity and viability of advertising in Canada through industry self-regulation. The organization includes over 160 advertisers, advertising agencies, media organizations, and suppliers to the advertising sector.
- a. Eastman Kodak Company
- b. Advertising Standards Canada
- c. IMS Health
- d. Oodle

Chapter 3. Test Preparation Part 3

1. _____ is a form of communication that typically attempts to persuade potential customers to purchase or to consume more of a particular brand of product or service. 'While now central to the contemporary global economy and the reproduction of global production networks, it is only quite recently that _____ has been more than a marginal influence on patterns of sales and production. The formation of modern _____ was intimately bound up with the emergence of new forms of monopoly capitalism around the end of the 19th and beginning of the 20th century as one element in corporate strategies to create, organize and where possible control markets, especially for mass produced consumer goods.
   a. ADTECH
   b. ACNielsen
   c. AMAX
   d. Advertising

2. An _____ or ad agency is a service business dedicated to creating, planning and handling advertising (and sometimes other forms of promotion) for its clients. An ad agency is independent from the client and provides an outside point of view to the effort of selling the client's products or services. An agency can also handle overall marketing and branding strategies and sales promotions for its clients.
   a. Openad
   b. Onsert
   c. Advertising research
   d. Advertising agency

3. A _____ is a relatively new executive level position at a corporation, company, organization typically reporting directly to the CEO or board of directors. The _____ is responsible for a brand's image, experience, and promise, and propagating it throughout all aspects of the company. The brand officer oversees marketing, advertising, design, public relations and customer service departments.
   a. Chief brand officer
   b. Financial analyst
   c. Power III
   d. Chief executive officer

4. _____ or morris columns are cylindrical outdoor sidewalk structures with a characteristic style that are used for advertising and other purposes. They are common in the city of Berlin, Germany, where 1855, the first 100 columns where installed. _____ were invented by the German printer Ernst Litfaß in 1854.
   a. ADTECH
   b. AMAX
   c. ACNielsen
   d. Advertising columns

5. Advertising is a management function. While advertising is the event, _____ is the whole process - a function of marketing starting from market research continuing through advertising leading to actual sales or achievement of objective. It goes further in regard to evaluation of the whole cost-benefits that were involved in the whole exercise.
   a. ADTECH
   b. ACNielsen
   c. Advertising management
   d. AMAX

6. _____ is the process of choosing the most cost-effective media to achieve the necessary coverage, and number of exposures, among the target audience.

This is typically measured on two dimensions:

CovTo maximize overall awareness, the maximum number of the target audience should be reached by the advertising. There is a limit, however, for the last few per cent of the general population are always difficult (and accordingly very expensive) to reach; since they do not see the main media used by advertisers.

   a. Engagement marketing
   b. All commodity volume
   c. Outsourcing relationship management
   d. Advertising media selection

7. _____ refers to the laws and rules defining the ways in which products can be advertised in a particular region. Rules can define a wide number of different aspects, such as placement, timing, and content. In the United States, false advertising and health-related ads are regulated the most.
   a. ACNielsen
   b. AMAX
   c. ADTECH
   d. Advertising regulation

8. _____ refers to 'controlling human or societal behaviour by rules or restrictions.' _____ can take many forms: legal restrictions promulgated by a government authority, self-_____, social _____, co-_____ and market _____. One can consider _____ as actions of conduct imposing sanctions (such as a fine.) This action of administrative law, or implementing regulatory law, may be contrasted with statutory or case law.
   a. Non-conventional trademark
   b. Regulation
   c. CAN-SPAM
   d. Rule of four

9. _____ is a specialized form of marketing research conducted to improve the efficiency of advertising. According to MarketConscious.com, 'It may focus on a specific ad or campaign, or may be directed at a more general understanding of how advertising works or how consumers use the information in advertising. It can entail a variety of research approaches, including psychological, sociological, economic, and other perspectives.'

1879 - N.W. Ayer conducts custom research in an attempt to win the advertising business of Nichols-Shepard Co., a manufacturer of agricultural machinery.

   a. Advertising research
   b. Electrolux
   c. INVISTA
   d. American Medical Association

10. _____ are short, often memorable phrases used in advertising campaigns. They are claimed to be the most effective means of drawing attention to one or more aspects of a product. A strapline is a British term used as a secondary sentence attached to a brand name.
    a. Inprint
    b. Autosurf
    c. Interactive Urinal Communicator
    d. Advertising slogans

11. _____ is the act of marketing or advertising products or services to young people. In 2000, children under 13 years old impacted the spending of over $600 billion in the United States alone. This has created a large incentive to advertise to children which has led to the development to a multimillion dollar industry.
    a. Advertising research
    b. Industrial musical
    c. In-game advertising
    d. Advertising to children

12. _____ is an interactive communications agency. Based in Battersea, London with a staff of around 100, they were Marketing Magazine's Digital Agency of the Year in 2008 , 2005, 2004 and 2002, and Campaign Magazine's Digital Agency of the Year for 2006. _____ opened their first international office in New York in June of 2008, and soon won the Boots Retail International USA account.
    a. Agency Republic
    b. Advertising Standards Canada
    c. ADTECH
    d. Aberdeen Group

13. _____ is the promotion of alcoholic beverages by alcohol producers through a variety of media. Along with tobacco advertising, it is one of the most highly-regulated forms of marketing.

Scientific research around the world conducted by governments, health agencies and universities has, over decades, been able to demonstrate a causal relationship between alcohol beverage advertising and alcohol consumption.

   a. ADTECH   b. AMAX
   c. ACNielsen   d. Alcohol advertising

14. _____ started to appear in British media jargon around 1999, but now seems to be firmly established as a standard term within the advertising industry. It is the name given to a new breed of out-of-home products and services determined by some as Non-Traditional or Alternative Media. _____ advertising can be used in conjunction with mainstream traditional media, or used equally effectively as a stand-alone activity.

   a. Openad   b. Autosurf
   c. Advertising agency   d. Ambient media

15. In the past two decades, _____ has become appreciated for the 'artistic' and free-thinking messages of its advertisements, which reflect a business plan of marketing their products to creative individuals. Their most significant ad campaigns include the '1984' Super Bowl commercial, which introduced their company as revolutionary, independent, and subversive, as well as the 1990s Think Different campaign, which featured major artists, and the 'iPod people' of the 2000s, featuring several colorful, dancing silhouetted people.

   a. ACNielsen   b. ADTECH
   c. AMAX   d. Apple Inc.

16. _____ constitutes demand for something that, in the absence of exposure to the vehicle of creating demand, would not exist. It has controversial applications in microeconomics (pump and dump strategy) and advertising. Synonyms for '_____' include 'fake demand' and 'false need'.

   a. ACNielsen   b. Artificial demand
   c. ADTECH   d. AMAX

17. In economics, _____ is the desire to own something and the ability to pay for it. The term _____ signifies the ability or the willingness to buy a particular commodity at a given point of time .

   a. Market dominance   b. Market system
   c. Discretionary spending   d. Demand

18. Throughout the twentieth century, _____, located in Manhattan, New York, was the preeminent designer and creator of Times Square's iconic signs and displays. These included the 'smoking' Camel sign, which wafted giant smoke rings over the Square; the Bond Clothing Stores display, a block-long extravaganza with a perpetual waterfall; and the high-neon north-Square 'spectaculars' created for Canadian Club and Admiral Television. For almost a century, _____ was also responsible for the annual midnight ball-lowering that signaled the new year's arrival.

   a. Arbitron   b. Ethics Resource Center
   c. United States Steel Corporation   d. Artkraft Strauss

19. _____, born Angelo Siciliano (October 30, 1894, Acri, Italy - December 23, 1972, Long Beach, New York) was the developer of a bodybuilding method and its associated exercise program, most well-known for a landmark advertising campaign featuring his name and likeness, which has been described as one of the most lasting and memorable ad campaigns of all time.

According to Atlas, he trained himself to develop his body from that of a 'scrawny weakling', eventually becoming the most popular muscleman of his day. He took the name '_____' after a friend told him he resembled the statue of Atlas on top of a hotel in Coney Island, and legally changed his name in 1922.

    a. Nouveau riche   b. Paschal Eze
    c. Rick Boyce   d. Charles Atlas

20. _____s are traffic exchanges that automatically rotate advertised websites in one's web browser. Therefore, they are capable of bringing a large amount of traffic to the advertised websites. Members earn credits for each site that they view, which can then be spent to advertise members' sites by adding them to the _____ rotation.

    a. Openad   b. Onsert
    c. Advertising slogans   d. Autosurf

21. _____ is a 13 letter acronym used in Metlink advertising in Melbourne, Australia. It stands for 'Buying A Ticket Before You Get On Board Saves Time Or Problems Later'.

The acronym was the centre of a Metlink advertising campaign which ran from January 2006, to remind people they can save time (saving time meaning they don't have to worry about buying tickets on the vehicle or at the railway station) or problems later (problems later meaning getting caught without a ticket and being issued with a fine) by visiting a retail outlet which sells metcards (usually a Milk Bar or Newsagent.)

    a. 6-3-5 Brainwriting   b. Power III
    c. 180SearchAssistant   d. BATBYGOBSTOPL

22. _____ is a global distribution network built for the advertising industry.

The idea was created in 1998 when a group of people in the technology department of London facilities house The Mill had to find a way to please director Ridley Scott who was creating the movie Gladiator in LA, whilst the visual effects were being created by The Mill in London. Rather than couriering videotapes of work-in-progress from London to LA for Ridley Scott's approval, the team applied the idea of uploading material to the internet as a means of speeding-up the approval process.

    a. 6-3-5 Brainwriting   b. BEAM.TV
    c. Power III   d. 180SearchAssistant

23. _____ were a brand of cigarettes produced in the United States beginning in 1973. This product was notable during the 1970s and 1980s for heavy advertising, which became one of the more obvious examples of how companies at the time reacted to changing laws and cultural views on public health and the smoking culture.

_____ were released in the United States shortly after the Public Health Cigarette Smoking Act was enacted by President Richard Nixon on 1 April 1970.

a. Bumvertising
c. Custom media
b. Backwoods Smokes
d. Fast food advertising

24. A _____ is a TV channel that is used almost entirely for promotion and advertising, usually marketing various features of the service carrying the channel. The name is analogous to a dog barking to attract attention.

There are several of these channels on digital cable systems and especially on direct broadcast satellite systems like DirecTV.

a. Helicopter banner
c. Barker channel
b. Local advertising
d. Media planner

25. The _____ is the largest illuminated advertisement in the world. The advertisement is for Bayer, the multinational pharmaceutical company based in Leverkusen. The advertisement, installed in 1958, shows the emblem of the company Bayer.

a. High School National Ad Network
c. Law of primacy in persuasion
b. Bayer Cross Leverkusen
d. Heinz pickle pin

26. _____ is a comic strip character, featured on small comics included inside individually wrapped pieces of Bazooka bubble gum.

He wears an eyepatch, lending him a distinctive appearance. He is one of the more recognizable American advertising characters of the 20th century--and one of the few identifiable ones associated with a candy.

a. Bazooka Joe
c. 6-3-5 Brainwriting
b. Power III
d. 180SearchAssistant

27. _____, more commonly known as Beattie, was a character from a series of television advertisements by British Telecom, famously played by Maureen Lipman. She was created, originally named Dora, by Richard Phillips, a Jewish advertising copywriter, based on his mother.

Beattie was a stereotypical Jewish mother and her adventures largely involved her nagging her family over the telephone, thus promoting communication.

a. GoSasa
c. Local advertising
b. Jingle
d. Beatrice Bellman

28. In environmental modeling and especially in hydrology, a _____ model means a model that is acceptably consistent with observed natural processes, i.e. that simulates well, for example, observed river discharge. It is a key concept of the so-called Generalized Likelihood Uncertainty Estimation (GLUE) methodology to quantify how uncertain environmental predictions are.

a. 6-3-5 Brainwriting
c. Behavioral

b. 180SearchAssistant
d. Power III

29. _____ is a form of online targeted advertising by which online advertising is delivered to consumers based on previous Internet actions that did not in the past result in a conversion

Various Internet Marketing companies have added retargeting to their list of methods of purchasing advertising.

Some companies, such as FetchBack, specialize in Retargeting. Retargeting helps companies advertise to the 98% of people who visit a website but leave without converting.

a. Mobile phone content advertising
c. Brring

b. Here Comes the King
d. Behavioral retargeting

30. The _____ Advertising Marketplace was an online advertising network with over 5,200 registered publishers and 10,400 registered advertisers. _____ served approximately 1.1 billion ads per month, reaching an estimated 25 million individual consumers in the US and international markets.

_____ was a corporate partner of NetAid, a New York based anti-poverty organization.

a. BidClix
c. Copy testing

b. Driven media
d. Norm of reciprocity

31. Although arguably neologism '_____' is gradually gaining ground as a common term for the provision of any small digital media to suitable media provisioning enabled devices over Bluetooth via the OBEX protocol. Where by 'small digital media' does not exclusively mean advertisements but could include photos, podcast style audio content, video, mobile ticketing, text messages, games (especially those written in Java ME) or even other applications.

A bluecast is generally provisioned by a Bluetooth Kiosk a physical server provisioning the digital media over Bluetooth to interested devices.

a. 180SearchAssistant
c. 6-3-5 Brainwriting

b. Bluecasting
d. Power III

32. A _____ is a collection of symbols, experiences and associations connected with a product, a service, a person or any other artifact or entity.

_____s have become increasingly important components of culture and the economy, now being described as 'cultural accessories and personal philosophies'.

Some people distinguish the psychological aspect of a _____ from the experiential aspect.

a. Brandable software
c. Store brand

b. Brand equity
d. Brand

Chapter 3. Test Preparation Part 3

33. _____ or measures the relative sales strength of a brand within a specific market (e.g. Pepsi brand in 10 - 50 year old's.) It is a measure of the relative sales strength of a given brand in a specific market area.

_____ or is the index of brand sales to category sales.

a. Perishability
b. Hoover free flights promotion
c. Brand parity
d. Brand Development Index

34. _____ is a term loosely used to describe the process of forming an attachment (emotional and rational) between a person and a brand. It comprises one aspect of brand management. What makes the topic complex is that _____ is partly created by institutions and organizations, but is equally created by the perceptions, attitudes, beliefs and behaviors of those with whom these institutions and organizations are communicating or engaging with.

a. Power III
b. Symbolic analysis
c. Brand engagement
d. Graphic communication

35. _____ measures the extent to which a consumer has a meaningful brand experience when exposed to commercial advertising, sponsorship, television contact, or other experience.

In March 2006 the Advertising Research Foundation defined _____ as 'turning on a prospect to a brand idea enhanced by the surrounding context'. The ARF has also defined the function whereby _____ impacts a brand:

_____ is complex because a variety of exposure and relationship factors affect _____, making simplified rankings misleading.

a. Engagement
b. Individual branding
c. Automated surveys
d. Inseparability

36. _____ is a marketing practice that takes a specific approach to strategy, creativity and success tracking, where all three are driven by a thorough understanding of the business objective at hand. _____ insists that the organizational design of the marketing agency includes a team with broad skills, but that each staff member has creative and strategic leanings.

The strategy behind a _____ campaign is largely based on the business objective for a particular product, and is intended to be media-agnostic.

a. Customer Interaction Tracker
b. Brand infiltration
c. Lead scoring
d. Value chain

37. _____ are an award-winning Tradigital advertising agency. They are currently located in Ireland at 30 -32 Rear Warehouse, Sir John Rogersons Quay, Dublin 2. They were founded in 2005 by Darren McGrath (Managing Director) and Brendan O'Flaherty (Creative Director) .

a. Brando
b. Consumption Map
c. LIFO
d. Self branding

38. _____ is a free service allowing users to create phone numbers with embedded preroll advertising. _____ allows users to create custom 'ringback tones', or sounds played before the phone is answered. _____ also pays users to refer users to their service.

  a. Geo targeting
  b. Content marketing
  c. Brring
  d. Fast food advertising

39. _____ is a form of informal employment in which a homeless person is paid to display advertising.

The _____ website publicizing this form of advertising was launched in August 2005 by Benjamin Rogovy, a 22-year-old entrepreneur who hired homeless men in the U.S. city of Seattle, Washington, to carry signs with the URL of his poker player match-up site.

In high traffic areas, such as intersections many beggars hold up a sign describing their plight but most people that pass by do not contribute to the beggar.

  a. Bumvertising
  b. Forehead advertising
  c. Link flooding
  d. Pixel advertising

40. _____ refers to either a German art movement of the early 1960s, or the characteristic style of advertising in the 1980s.

The phrase's earliest appearance was as the title of the 1963 art exhibition in Düsseldorf, Demonstration for _____, featuring the work of Gerhard Richter, Sigmar Polke, Wolf Vostell and Konrad Lueg. Lueg went on to represent his friend's work as the gallerist Konrad Fischer (in the exhibition he had used his mother's maiden name.)

  a. 180SearchAssistant
  b. 6-3-5 Brainwriting
  c. Power III
  d. Capitalist realism

41. _____ was the second mascot for Hostess brand baked goods along with Twinkie the Kid. He is very rarely seen on the cupcake containers anymore. He promoted Hostess Cupcakes.

  a. Power III
  b. 6-3-5 Brainwriting
  c. 180SearchAssistant
  d. Captain Cupcake

42. _____ is the main cinema advertising company of the Republic of Ireland and Northern Ireland. The company is owned by ITV plc

The company was founded in 1938 as Rank Screen Advertising, part of the Rank Organisation. It was set up to sell advertising time for Rank's cinema chain, Odeon.

  a. BidClix
  b. Carlton Screen Advertising
  c. Mobile phone content advertising
  d. Here Comes the King

43. _____ or measures the sales strength of a particular category of product, within a specific market (e.g. Soft drinks in 10 - 50 year old's.)

Chapter 3. Test Preparation Part 3

To calculate the _____:

A% / X% * 100

Simply divide product 'A''s total sales in the specific market, then divide it by the population in that specific market. Finally you multiply the result by one hundred to get an index number.

   a. Package-on-Package   b. Category Development Index
   c. Bringin' Home the Oil   d. Push

44. _____ is the name of the advertising campaign used to advertise the Olympic Games. Developed by Saatchi ' Saatchi, it has been used for both the winter and summer Olympics since the games in 2000. It features famous people explaining the significance of the Olympics to them.
   a. Norm of reciprocity   b. Direct response television
   c. Fast food advertising   d. Celebrate Humanity

45. _____ offers pay for performance marketing services for retailers to deliver personalized display advertising and product recommendations. Retailers use _____ to present relevant products to consumers with the intention of increasing clickthrough and sales conversion.

_____ uses shopping data from retailers to generate personalized product recommendations for what consumers are likely to be in-market for next.

   a. Partnership for a Drug-Free America   b. Superbrands
   c. ChoiceStream   d. Multinational corporation

46. A _____ is a magazine that publishes small ads and announcements for free or at relatively low cost. Typically these include items for sale and wanted, and services offered; they may also include personal ads. Some _____s specialise in particular areas, for example the sale of cars.
   a. Non-commercial advertising   b. History of Advertising Trust
   c. Classified magazine   d. Forehead advertising

47. The _____ was a large photographic display located on the east balcony inside New York City's Grand Central Terminal from 1950 to 1990. Used as advertisements by the Eastman Kodak Company, the photographs were backlit transparencies 18 feet tall by 60 feet wide. They were described as 'The World's Largest Photographs.'
   a. 6-3-5 Brainwriting   b. 180SearchAssistant
   c. Power III   d. Colorama

48. _____ is speech done on behalf of a company or individual for the intent of making a profit. It is economic in nature and usually has the intent of convincing the audience to partake in a particular action, often purchasing a specific product.

The idea of '_____' was first introduced by the Supreme Court when it upheld Valentine v. Chrestensen (1942).

a. 6-3-5 Brainwriting
b. 180SearchAssistant
c. Commercial speech
d. Power III

49. _____ is a mixed discipline between design and information-development which is concerned with how media intermission such as printed, crafted, electronic media or presentations communicate with people. A _____ approach is not only concerned with developing the message aside from the aesthetics in media, but also with creating new media channels to ensure the message reaches the target audience.

_____ seeks to attract, inspire, create desires and motivate the people to respond to messages, with a view to making a favorable impact to the bottom line of the commissioning body, which can be either to build a brand, move sales, or for humanitarian purposes.

a. 180SearchAssistant
b. 6-3-5 Brainwriting
c. Communication design
d. Power III

50. _____ as used in the Advertising industry, is a means to deploy an advertisement for one's products or services adjacent to editorial content relating to the competitor or the competitors' products.

A common practice is to purchase advertisements in magazines and newspapers where editors and reporters write about the products or company. The goal is to reinforce the marketing message and earn even greater levels of awareness and recall of the Brand.

a. Conquesting
b. Remainder advertising
c. History of Advertising Trust
d. Here Comes the King

51. _____ is an umbrella term encompassing all marketing formats that involve the creation or sharing of content for the purpose of engaging current and potential consumer bases. In contrast to traditional marketing methods that aim to increase sales or awareness through interruption techniques, _____ subscribes to the notion that delivering high-quality, relevant and valuable information to prospects and customers drives profitable consumer action.

The idea of sharing content as a means of persuading decision-making has driven content marketers to make their once-proprietary informational assets available to selected audiences.

a. Fast food advertising
b. Media planner
c. Norm of reciprocity
d. Content marketing

52. _____ is defined by the American _____ Association as the activity, set of institutions, and processes for creating, communicating, delivering, and exchanging offerings that have value for customers, clients, partners, and society at large. The term developed from the original meaning which referred literally to going to market, as in shopping, or going to a market to sell goods or services.

_____ practice tends to be seen as a creative industry, which includes advertising, distribution and selling.

a. Product naming
b. Customer acquisition management
c. Marketing myopia
d. Marketing

Chapter 3. Test Preparation Part 3

53. _____ is a specialized field of marketing research, it is the study of television commercials prior to airing them. It is defined as research to determine an ad's effectiveness based on consumers' responses to the ad and covers all media including print, TV, radio, Internet etcAlthough also known as _____, pre-testing is considered the more accurate, modern name (Young, p.4) for the prediction of how effectively an ad will perform, based on the analysis of feedback gathered from the target audience. Each test will either qualify the ad as strong enough to meet company action standards for airing or identify opportunities to improve the performance of the ad through editing.
   a. Johnson Box
   b. Heinz pickle pin
   c. Copy testing
   d. Custom media

54. _____ is the promotion of cosmetics and beauty products by the cosmetics industry through a variety of media. The advertising campaigns are usually aimed at women wishing to improve their appearance, commonly to increase physical attractiveness and reduce the signs of ageing.

Many campaigns have come under fire through their alleged use of pseudoscience and their promotion of unrealistic goals.

   a. Cosmetic advertising
   b. Power III
   c. 6-3-5 Brainwriting
   d. 180SearchAssistant

55. _____ or amphimacer feet are a unit of prosody that contain three syllables, metrically long, short, long. In Greek poetry, the amphimacer was usually a form of paeon or aeolic verse. However, any line mixing iambs and trochees could employ a _____ foot as a transition.
   a. Cretic
   b. 6-3-5 Brainwriting
   c. 180SearchAssistant
   d. Power III

56. _____ is a marketing term referring broadly to the development, production and delivery of media (print, digital, audio, video, events) designed to strengthen the relationship between the sponsor of the medium and the medium's audience. It is also called branded media, customer media, member media, content marketing, and custom publishing in the US; contract publishing and customer publishing in the UK. In-flight magazines, sponsored by airlines, were one of the first _____ and remain typical of the genre.
   a. Gambling advertising
   b. Custom media
   c. Forehead advertising
   d. Geo targeting

57. _____ is one of the first and now-defunct online casinos, which gained it notoriety for one of the largest organised international sponsorship (and gambling) frauds, through its ad serving program. Formed in 1997 and located in Nassau, Bahamas, the company was represented by the Canadian firm Internet Entertainment Enterprises, Inc. (based in Montreal, Canada) which also handled the casino's marketing and banner advertising program.
   a. 180SearchAssistant
   b. Power III
   c. CyberThrill
   d. 6-3-5 Brainwriting

58. _____ includes any TV advertising that asks consumers to respond directly to the company --- usually either by calling an 800 number or by visiting a web site. This is a form of direct response marketing.

There are two types of _____, short form and long form.

a. Direct response television
b. Barker channel
c. History of Advertising Trust
d. Custom media

59. _____ usually refers to the marketing of pharmaceutical products but can apply in other areas as well. This form of advertising is directed toward patients, rather than healthcare professionals. Forms of DTC advertising include TV, print, and other mass media.
a. Local advertising
b. History of Advertising Trust
c. Recruitment tool
d. Direct-to-consumer advertising

60. _____ is the practice of covering or wrapping any vehicle in vibrant, custom designed state of the art vinyl sheets, turning any vehicle into a mobile billboard. The purpose of this is to provide impressionable advertising, creating tremendous value for anyone wanting to take their message right to their audience in places that traditional media outlets cannot reach. This extremely innovative, unique and cost-effective advertising/marketing medium is a relatively unexplored and previously untapped resource.
a. History of Advertising Trust
b. Public service advertising
c. Jingle
d. Driven media

61. The _____ Awards are advertising awards given yearly by the New York American Marketing Association. _____ appears to be an acronym since it is usually written in capital letters, but it is a pseudo-acronym, since the letters don't stand for individual words. They are from the word effectiveness, a desirable trait in an advertisement.
a. ACNielsen
b. ADTECH
c. AMAX
d. EFFIE

62. An _____ shows the major editorial features planned for forthcoming issues of a newspaper, magazine, and similar. It is used by the advertising sales function of the publication to attract advertisers. For example, if Newsweek plans to print an editorial feature on hybrid cars, then manufacturers of those cars might want to place advertisements in that issue.
a. Editorial calendar
b. ACNielsen
c. AMAX
d. ADTECH

63. In economics, business, retail, and accounting, a _____ is the value of money that has been used up to produce something, and hence is not available for use anymore. In economics, a _____ is an alternative that is given up as a result of a decision. In business, the _____ may be one of acquisition, in which case the amount of money expended to acquire it is counted as _____.
a. Cost
b. Transaction cost
c. Fixed costs
d. Variable cost

64. _____ is a commonly used measurement in advertising. Radio, television, newspaper, magazine, Out-of-home advertising and online advertising can be purchased on the basis of what it costs to show the ad to one thousand viewers. It is used in marketing as a benchmark to calculate the relative cost of an advertising campaign or an ad message in a given medium.
a. Cost per time
b. Cost per mille
c. Link exchange
d. Frequency capping

Chapter 3. Test Preparation Part 3

65. _____ is a brand communications agency with offices in Hong Kong, Shanghai, Beijing and Macau employing approximately sixty staff and four senior partners. The company works on a project and a retainer basis for thirty leading local and international clients. Assignments range from brand definition and positioning to corporate identity, design and marketing communications.

   a. Advertising Standards Canada
   b. Ameritest
   c. Isobar
   d. Eight Partnership

66. A _____ is a type of business entity in which partners (owners) share with each other the profits or losses of the business undertaking in which all have invested. _____s are often favored over corporations for taxation purposes, as the _____ structure does not generally incur a tax on profits before it is distributed to the partners (i.e. there is no dividend tax levied.) However, depending on the _____ structure and the jurisdiction in which it operates, owners of a _____ may be exposed to greater personal liability than they would as shareholders of a corporation.

   a. Partnership
   b. Fair Debt Collection Practices Act
   c. Brand piracy
   d. Competition law

67. The _____ is a self-regulatory program created in 2004 by American business organizations to promote consumer confidence. _____ is a program of the Electronic Retailing Association in conjunction with the National Advertising Review Council (NARC) and administered by the Council of Better Business Bureaus. The mission of the program is to enhance consumer confidence in electronic retailing, by providing a forum to self-regulate direct response advertising.

   a. Interactive marketing
   b. Engagement marketing
   c. All commodity volume
   d. Electronic retailing self-regulation program

68. _____ consists of the sale of goods or merchandise from a fixed location, such as a department store or kiosk in small or individual lots for direct consumption by the purchaser. _____ may include subordinated services, such as delivery. Purchasers may be individuals or businesses.

   a. Warehouse store
   b. Charity shop
   c. Retailing
   d. Thrifting

69. _____ or deceptive advertising is the use of false or misleading statements in advertising. As advertising has the potential to persuade people into commercial transactions that they might otherwise avoid, many governments around the world use regulations to control false, deceptive or misleading advertising. Truth in labeling refers to essentially the same concept, that customers have the right to know what they are buying, and that all necessary information should be on the label.

   a. Power III
   b. False advertising
   c. Fine print
   d. Misleading advertising

70. _____ is the term given to food that can be prepared and served very quickly. While any meal with low preparation time can be considered to be _____, typically the term refers to food sold in a restaurant or store with low quality preparation and served to the customer in a packaged form for take-out/take-away. The term '_____' was recognized in a dictionary by Merriam-Webster in 1951.

   a. 180SearchAssistant
   b. 6-3-5 Brainwriting
   c. Fast food
   d. Power III

71. _____ is the promotion of fast food products and ventures through a variety of media. _____ campaigns are not as highly regulated as some other products, such as those imposed on alcohol advertising, but there are often public calls for their promotion to be minimized.

Advertising campaigns for fast food restaurants have changed in their intent over time.

   a. Copy testing
   c. Media agency
   b. Jingle
   d. Fast food advertising

72. The _____ is the most recent in a historic line of communication screens. It is commonly called Digital Signage or Digital Out Of Home.

The _____ represents the combination of the World Wide Web and mobile 2G and 3G technologies or data delivered via physical uploads at screens placed in various environments.

   a. Fifth screen
   c. Fan loyalty
   b. Commercial operations management
   d. Marketing plan

73. _____ is an advertising term for a timing pattern in which commercials are scheduled to run during intervals that are separated by periods in which no advertising messages appear for the advertised item. Any period of time during which the messages are appearing is called a flight, and a period of message inactivity is usually called a hiatus.

The advantage of the _____ technique is that it allows an advertiser who does not have funds for running spots continuously to conserve money and maximize the impact of the commercials by airing them at key strategic times.

   a. Consumocracy
   c. Flighting
   b. Concession
   d. Strict liability

74. _____ is an advertising concept that uses people's foreheads as advertising spaces.

The concept was created by Justin Kapust through his organization, called Headvertise (Kapust-Allen Enterprises, now defunct) in late 2002.

Soon after its launch, and the media frenzy that came along with it, Ebay started hosting auctions for _____ and other tattoo advertising.

   a. Forehead advertising
   c. Local advertising
   b. Heinz pickle pin
   d. The Centaur Company

75. _____ is a popular form of advertising in parts of Asia, Eastern Europe and Latin America. The phenomenon is most pronounced when English-speaking celebrities do print advertisements or commercials for a non-English speaking market.

American and British dramatic actors have traditionally been reluctant to appear in widespread advertising campaigns, on the assumption that it cheapens their respectability and can be perceived as selling out by their fanbase or the critical public at large.

   a. BidClix
   b. Remainder advertising
   c. Custom media
   d. Foreign celebrity advertising

76. '_____' is a generally accepted term used in a number of advertising and technology industries, to refer to a small portable video screen such as those found in mobile (cellular) phones or other portable electronic devices such as a video iPod player. Sometimes referred to as the 'Third Screen.'

While the term is gaining acceptance into popular usage, it is not as well known as 'Cell 'PDA' and 'mobile' which are other terms used in the English-speaking world to refer to these very popular electronic devices.

Today, people use mobile devices in ways that open new possibilities for Documentary Practice.

   a. Prosumer
   b. Corporate capabilities package
   c. Fourth screen
   d. Business marketing

77. _____ Díaz Mestre first rose to fame as a catwalk and photographic model in the 1960s and 70s. She later became a successful businesswoman when she started running a modelling school and agency.

_____ was born in Albi (France) and at nine months old moved to Barcelona, which she has come to adopt as her birthplace.

   a. AStore
   b. African Americans
   c. Albert Einstein
   d. Francina

78. _____ is a term in advertising that means restricting (capping) the amount of times (frequency) a specific visitor to a website is shown a particular advertisement. This restriction is applied to all websites that serve ads from the same advertising network.

_____ is a feature within ad serving that allows to limit the maximum number of impressions/views a visitor can see a specific ad within a period of time.

   a. Cost per mille
   b. Link exchange
   c. Cost per time
   d. Frequency capping

79. _____ was what Gleem toothpaste, in the 1950s, advertised as its unique decay and mouth-odor fighting ingredient. Whether or not _____ was a real ingredient or what it was is unknown.

   a. GL-70
   b. Heavy-up
   c. Comparative advertising
   d. Rack card

Chapter 3. Test Preparation Part 3

80. _____ is the promotion of gambling by casinos, lotteries, bookmakers or other organisations that provide the opportunity to make bets. It is usually conducted through a variety of media or through sponsorship deals, particularly with sporting events or people.

Although not as highly regulated as tobacco advertising and alcohol advertising, in many countries there are strict laws about the way in which such services can be marketed.

   a. Gambling advertising
   b. Puffery
   c. Here Comes the King
   d. BidClix

81. In marketing, _____ is a discipline within marketing analysis which uses geolocation in the process of planning and implementation of marketing activities. It can be used in any aspect of the marketing mix - the Product, Price, Promotion, or Place Market segments can also correlate with location, and this can be useful in targeted marketing.
   a. Parity Product
   b. Quantitative
   c. Containerization
   d. Geo

82. _____ in geomarketing and internet marketing is the method of determining the geolocation (the physical location) of a website visitor and delivering different content to that visitor based on his or her location, such as country, region/state, city, metro code/zip code, organization, Internet Protocol (IP) address, ISP or other criteria.

In _____ with geolocation software, the geolocation is based on geographical and other personal information that is provided by the visitor or others.

A typical example for different content by choice in _____ is the FedEx website at FedEx

   a. Geo targeting
   b. Recruitment tool
   c. Driven media
   d. Puffery

83. _____, Inc. is a search engine aggregator for online classifieds within the United States. The San Diego based company is owned by founders Juan Santiago and Steve Schindler and was officially launched in early 2007 having been live since its soft launch in fall 2006.
   a. Remainder advertising
   b. Direct-to-consumer advertising
   c. Recruitment tool
   d. GoSasa

84. _____ has offices in Australia, Bangladesh, China, Hong Kong, India, Indonesia, Japan, Korea, Malaysia, New Zealand, Pakistan, Philippines, Singapore, Sri Lanka, Taiwan, Thailand and Vietnam.

Eye on Asia is Grey Group's annual proprietary study that looks at the hopes and dreams of the Asia Pacific region, and determines the powerful underlying trends that will shape branding and communications today and in the future. One of the most comprehensive, in-depth surveys ever done on the Asian consumer, Eye on Asia is a thought leadership initiative that aims to get closer to the peoples of Asia.

   a. Grey Group Asia Pacific
   b. Power III
   c. 180SearchAssistant
   d. 6-3-5 Brainwriting

Chapter 3. Test Preparation Part 3

85. The _____ is an advertising item from the H. J. Heinz Company, being a small green pin made in the shape of a pickle. Being continuously offered for more than a century, and with more than 100 million pins produced over the years, it is both one of the longest-running and most successful promotions in history.

Because its retro feel and long tradition are part of the appeal of the pickle pin, the design has changed relatively little in over a century of production.

   a. Direct-to-consumer advertising
   b. Foreign celebrity advertising
   c. Logojet
   d. Heinz pickle pin

86. A _____ is a form of aerial advertising, developed over 10+ years ago.

_____s are made from highly durable light weight polyester. These are manufactured from designs taken from vector graphics; however, standard jpeg images may also be used.

   a. Norm of reciprocity
   b. Pay per ship
   c. BidClix
   d. Helicopter banner

87. _____ is a well-known advertising jingle written for Budweiser, the flagship brand of the Anheuser-Busch brewery, and whose slogan is, 'The King of Beers'. First played in 1967, it is often played as a theme song for the Budweiser Clydesdale horses pulling the Budweiser beer wagon (such as winter-themed TV commercials around Christmas time.) It was written, words and music, by Steve Karmen.
   a. Remainder advertising
   b. Here Comes the King
   c. Classified magazine
   d. Link flooding

88. The _____ is a project by the American Society of Newspaper Editors' High School Journalism Initiative to steer national print advertising into high school newspapers. It is one of six projects in the initiative, which aims to improve scholastic journalism.

The non-profit advertising network, launched in 2006, includes hundreds of high schools.

   a. Non-commercial advertising
   b. High School National Ad Network
   c. Conquesting
   d. Law of primacy in persuasion

89. The _____ was established in 1976 to preserve and protect the heritage of UK advertising history and to offer it for research and study. It was registered as a UK charity (no. 276194) in 1978 and operates on a not-for-profit basis.
   a. Logojet
   b. History of Advertising Trust
   c. Brring
   d. Media agency

90. _____ is a music production company specializing in radio jingles and library production music based in Seattle, Washington, composed of Michael Berlin (Co-Owner, CEO, Sales/Marketing), Steven Scalfati (Co-owner, Creative Director, Composer/Producer) Kip Beelman (Engineer/Producer), Patrick Napper (Composer/Producer), Dudley Taft (Composer/Producer) and is represented in the UK and Ireland by Mark Hall, in Australia by Big Bang ' Fuzz, and in Europe by Music ' Images.

Formed in the summer of 2002 by Reelworld alumni Michael Berlin and Steven Scalfati, the pair started with a bang by landing a custom commission for a new Fox FM package that has since gone on to be the most syndicated _____ package ever. The immediate success of this package generated a buzz in the UK radio world that lead to a rapid-fire succession of commissions for The Century Network, WKTU and Heart 106.2 in London as well as a slew of orders for syndication.

    a. Adbot
    c. Emerging technologies
    b. IQ Beats
    d. Arcis Communications

91. An _____ (ISCI) code conforms to a standard used to identify commercials (aka 'spots') aired on commercial television worldwide, for TV stations, ad agencies, video post-production houses, radio stations and other related entities to identify commercials for airing.

It was first developed in 1970 by and for American local affiliate TV stations, the TV networks that serve the affiliates, and ad agencies, to distribute commercial television advertisements more efficiently. The _____ coding system has been maintained and operated by the American Association of Advertising Agencies (AAAA) and the Association of National Advertisers (ANA) since 1992.

    a. ADTECH
    c. ACNielsen
    b. AMAX
    d. ISCI

92. An _____ is a musical performed internally for the employees or shareholders of a business, to create a feeling of being part of a team, to entertain, and/or to educate and motivate the management and salespeople to improve sales and profit. It can be used to increase staff awareness of public relations, advertising, marketing or corporate image.

Other terms for _____s include the corporate musical or industrial show, but the latter can also refer to trade shows, which are publicity events organized by businesses in a specific industry to promote their products to potential buyers.

    a. Autosurf
    c. Industrial musical
    b. Openad
    d. Advertising agency

93. _____ is an open and extensible web-based mobile mass communication environment for mobile marketers. It provides support for a tasks such as mobile permission marketing, WAP Push, and automatic creation of mobile applications in Java ME.

_____ attempts to uniformly capture all aspects of mobile marketing, rather than just specialized areas.

    a. EMarket trading platform
    c. InfoNU
    b. Australian Journal of Management
    d. Engagement marketing

94. _____ are long-format television commercials, typically five minutes or longer.. _____ are also known as paid programming (or teleshopping in Europe.) Originally, they were a phenomenon that started in the United States where they were typically shown overnight (usually 2:00 a.m. to 6:00 a.m.)

a. AMAX
b. Infomercials
c. ADTECH
d. ACNielsen

95. _____ is an award winning design and branding agency based in Vinton, Virginia. The firm serves a broad range of clients, with a specialty in the tourism, hospitality and foodservice industries. Located in the Roanoke Valley, _____'s clients have included start-up companies and Fortune 500 corporations all across the United States.

a. Advertising agency
b. Ambient media
c. Interactive Urinal Communicator
d. Inprint

96. The _____ is an advertising device invented by bioengineer Dr. Richard Deutsch for the Islip, New York company Wizmark. The 3.5 inch screen is placed in a urinal to promote products or services. Deutsch commented, 'Now when nature calls, there is going to be something entertaining to look at and listen to.'

Features of the advertising include:

- Flashing lights that are activated by physical presence, or actual urination
- A lenticular image that changes depending on viewpoint
- A 16-second pre-recorded audio message
- A temperature-sensitive image

Deutsch commented to Marketing Magazine that 'Beginning with early attempts at writing one's name in the snow, there has always been an element of recreation associated with urination for men.'

Such advertising vehicles are not entirely new: some plain screens have carried advertising for a few years now and poster style ads in washrooms are quite common. The use of interactive urinal screens is being advocated by guerrilla marketers.

a. Interactive Urinal Communicator
b. Advertising research
c. In-game advertising
d. Inprint

97. _____ are a type of advertisement that is used in political campaigns.

It has been a political tool dating back to the invention of TV and radio. In modern history, issue advocacy advertisements have become more distasteful.

a. Autosurf
b. Osborne bull
c. Advertising research
d. Issue advocacy ads

98. _____ is the pursuit of influencing outcomes -- including public-policy and resource allocation decisions within political, economic, and social systems and institutions -- that directly affect people's current lives. (Cohen, 2001)

Therefore, _____ can be seen as a deliberate process of speaking out on issues of concern in order to exert some influence on behalf of ideas or persons. Based on this definition, Cohen (2001) states that 'ideologues of all persuasions advocate' to bring a change in people's lives.

a. Advocacy
c. AMAX
b. ACNielsen
d. ADTECH

Chapter 4. Test Preparation Part 4

1. A _____ is a memorable slogan, set to an engaging melody, mainly broadcast on radio and sometimes on television commercials.

The _____ had no definitive debut: its infiltration of the radio was more of an evolutionary process than a sudden innovation. Product advertisements with a musical tilt can be traced back to 1923, around the same time commercial radio came to the public.

 a. Custom media
 b. Non-commercial advertising
 c. Link flooding
 d. Jingle

2. A _____ is a box commonly found at the top of direct mail letters, containing the key message of the letter. The purpose of it is to draw the reader's attention to this key message first, and hopefully grab their attention, enticing them to read the rest of the letter.

A _____ is very effective, but it lends a 'salesy' air to a letter, and so is considered inappropriate for letters that are intended to be formal or personal.

 a. Classified magazine
 b. N2 Effect
 c. Logojet
 d. Johnson Box

3. The _____ is a symbol of the Green Giant food company of the United States, appearing as a smiling green-skinned giant wearing a tunic, wreath and boots made of leaves. In 1973, _____ teamed up with 'Little Green Sprout', the diminutive young green giant. Created by Leo Burnett, the Giant first appeared in advertisements in 1928; the name originally came from a variety of unusually large pea called the 'Green Giant' that the company canned and sold.
 a. 180SearchAssistant
 b. Power III
 c. Morris the Cat
 d. Jolly Green Giant

4. In advertising and public communications, the _____ as postulated by Frederick Hansen Lund in 1925 holds that the side of an issue presented first will have greater effectiveness than the side presented subsequently. Lund gave college students document in support of one side of a controversial issue and then presented a second taking the opposite position. He found the document read first had greater influence, regardless of which position it expressed.
 a. Bayer Cross Leverkusen
 b. Conquesting
 c. Driven media
 d. Law of primacy in persuasion

5. _____ is a form of social influence. It is the process of guiding people toward the adoption of an idea, attitude, or action by rational and symbolic (though not always logical) means. It is strategy of problem-solving relying on 'appeals' rather than coercion.
 a. 6-3-5 Brainwriting
 b. 180SearchAssistant
 c. Power III
 d. Persuasion

6. _____ is advertising by lawyers (attorneys-at-law) and law firms.

Legal marketing is a broader term referring to advertising and other practices, such as client relations and public relations.

There is no standard definition of what constitutes _____, or marketing.

a. Customs
c. Trademark infringement
b. Regulatory
d. Legal advertising

7. _____ is a form of communication that typically attempts to persuade potential customers to purchase or to consume more of a particular brand of product or service. 'While now central to the contemporary global economy and the reproduction of global production networks, it is only quite recently that _____ has been more than a marginal influence on patterns of sales and production. The formation of modern _____ was intimately bound up with the emergence of new forms of monopoly capitalism around the end of the 19th and beginning of the 20th century as one element in corporate strategies to create, organize and where possible control markets, especially for mass produced consumer goods.
   a. ACNielsen
   c. Advertising
   b. ADTECH
   d. AMAX

8. _____ or link injection is the act of inserting links to promote a service, wiki, internet forum, blog or company. Often this technique is used to increase search engine rankings. _____/injection also occurs frequently in blogs with spam comments.
   a. Custom media
   c. BidClix
   b. Link flooding
   d. Celebrate Humanity

9. _____ refers to optimizing delivering ads according to the position of the recipient (client, user.) It is used in Geo (marketing.) Local search (Internet) often fuels uses optimization for targeting the advertising.
   a. Puffery
   c. Bumvertising
   b. Jingle
   d. Local advertising

10. A _____ is an airliner with an advertising paint scheme. _____s used for advertising companies remain uncommon due to the time and cost of repainting an entire airliner.

When accommodating advertisements, the aircraft's normal livery often disappears completely from the fuselage, leaving only the airline's logo painted, for example, on the engine's cowling.

   a. Custom media
   c. Norm of reciprocity
   b. Johnson Box
   d. Logojet

11. The _____ was a device and regimen sold by the Mark Eden company of San Francisco, California, that promised to enlarge a woman's breasts. Jack Feather, a California based figure salon entrepreneur, was the promoter of the device. The product was widely marketed in women's magazines during the 1960s and 1970s, making claims such as, 'For thousands, Mark Eden has transformed flat bustlines into firm, shapely fullness.'

The product consisted of a regimen of exercises using a clamshell-like device with a spring to provide resistance.

   a. 180SearchAssistant
   c. 6-3-5 Brainwriting
   b. Power III
   d. Mark Eden bust developer

12. The _____ is (or, in many areas, was) part of a tobacco advertising campaign for Marlboro cigarettes. In the United States, where the campaign originated, it was used from 1954 to 1999. The _____ was first conceived by Leo Burnett in 1954.

Chapter 4. Test Preparation Part 4

a. 6-3-5 Brainwriting
c. 180SearchAssistant
b. Power III
d. Marlboro Man

13. A _____ is a company which help companies to communicate with current and potential consumers and/or the general public.

Media agencies work with their clients to understand the business issues, their markets and their consumers. The _____ then identifies the consumer insights, which can help to devise a channel-neutral communication strategy which really connects with those consumers; using channels ranging from public relations (PR), events and sponsorship to advertising, interactive advertising, word of mouth and direct mail; to build a genuinely integrated campaign.

a. Public service advertising
c. Media agency
b. Heinz pickle pin
d. Copy testing

14. A _____ is a relatively new executive level position at a corporation, company, organization typically reporting directly to the CEO or board of directors. The _____ is responsible for a brand's image, experience, and promise, and propagating it throughout all aspects of the company. The brand officer oversees marketing, advertising, design, public relations and customer service departments.

a. Power III
c. Financial analyst
b. Chief brand officer
d. Chief executive officer

15. A _____, broadcast market, media region, designated market area (DMA), Television Market Area (FCC term) or simply market is a region where the population can receive the same (or similar) television and radio station offerings, and may also include other types of media including newspapers and Internet content. They can coincide with metropolitan areas, though rural regions with few significant population centers can also be designated as markets. Conversely, very large metropolitan areas can sometimes be subdivided into multiple segments.

a. 180SearchAssistant
c. 6-3-5 Brainwriting
b. Media market
d. Power III

16. _____ is a job title in an advertising agency or media planning and buying agency, responsible for selecting media for advertisement placement on behalf of their clients. The main aim of a _____ is to assist their client in achieving business objectives through their advertising budgets by recommending the best possible use of various media platforms available to advertisers. Their roles may include analyzing target audiences, keeping abreast of media developments, reading market trends and understanding motivations of consumers (often including psychology and neuroscience.)

a. Johnson Box
c. Helicopter banner
b. Mobile phone content advertising
d. Media planner

17. A _____ is a person who controls, either through personal ownership or a dominant position in a public company, a significant part of the mass media. _____s are commonly called 'media moguls', 'tycoons', 'barons', or 'bosses'.

The figure of the _____ first became prominent in the 19th century with the development of mass circulation newspapers.

a. Power III
b. 180SearchAssistant
c. Media proprietor
d. 6-3-5 Brainwriting

18. _____ is a company specializing in the design of high tech multimedia equipment for the food service industry. The company has a patent pending in the United States for both a product and a method of content delivery that, together, are capable of revolutionizing the fast food industry. _____ Smart Tray, an advanced multimedia-enabled food service tray, is a wide-reach advertising medium that the company has created for the food service industry.
   a. GlobalSpec
   b. BSI Group
   c. Mediox
   d. Fountain Fresh International

19. _____ is defined by the American _____ Association as the activity, set of institutions, and processes for creating, communicating, delivering, and exchanging offerings that have value for customers, clients, partners, and society at large. The term developed from the original meaning which referred literally to going to market, as in shopping, or going to a market to sell goods or services.

_____ practice tends to be seen as a creative industry, which includes advertising, distribution and selling.

   a. Customer acquisition management
   b. Marketing myopia
   c. Product naming
   d. Marketing

20. _____ is the promotion of ring tones, games and other mobile phone services. Such services are usually subscription-based and use the short message service (SMS) system to join up to them. Another method is broadcasting messages to the mobile phone's idle-screen, enabling the mobile operators or advertisers to reach millions in real-time.
   a. Pixel advertising
   b. Foreign celebrity advertising
   c. Mobile phone content advertising
   d. BidClix

21. _____ is a radio jingle production company which is based in the USA.

The company was founded by Chris Cline and Tony Valdez.

Chris Cline's interest in radio jingles began when he was eight years of age while listening to WLS in Chicago.

   a. Non-commercial advertising
   b. Media planner
   c. Beatrice Bellman
   d. N2 Effect

22. _____ is the largest outdoor advertising company in Eastern Europe, a subsidiary of News Corporation. NewsCorp entered the OOH advertising market in 1999 and _____ has since become the leading emerging market OOH advertising company in the world. _____ has more than 4,500 employees and operates approximately 60,000 advertising displays in more than 300 cities spread across 13 time zones.
   a. Local advertising
   b. Recruitment tool
   c. Puffery
   d. News Outdoor Group

23. _____ is sponsored by or for a charitable institution or civic group or religious or political organization. Many noncommercial advertisements seek money and placed in the hope of raising funds. Others hope to change consumer behavior.

a. Media planner
b. Here Comes the King
c. Pay per ship
d. Non-commercial advertising

24. The _____ is the social expectation that people will respond to each other in kind -- returning benefits for benefits, and responding with either indifference or hostility to harms. The social _____ often takes different forms in different areas of social life, or in different societies. All of them, however, are distinct from related ideas such as gratitude, the Golden Rule, or mutual goodwill.
   a. Driven media
   b. Classified magazine
   c. Gambling advertising
   d. Norm of reciprocity

25. In the entertainment industry, a one-sheet or _____ is a single document that summarizes a product for publicity and sales.

A _____ is a specific size (typically 27' x 41' in size before 1985; 27' x 40' in size after 1985) of film poster advertising. Multiple one-sheets are used to assemble larger advertisements, which are referred to by their sheet count, including 24-sheet billboards, and 30-sheet billboards.

   a. AMAX
   b. One sheet
   c. ACNielsen
   d. ADTECH

26. In advertising, an _____ is a separate advertisement put in a magazine, newspaper, or other publication. _____s are affixed to a page, and may be a sample of a product, a compact disk, magnet, a small booklet or even a targeted advertisement.
   a. Issue advocacy ads
   b. Onsert
   c. Advertising research
   d. Interactive Urinal Communicator

27. _____, Inc. is a privately held local classifieds metasearch company based out of San Mateo, California. It was founded in 2004 by ex-Excite executives Craig Donato, Scott Kister and Faith Sedlin.
   a. Association of National Advertisers
   b. Oodle
   c. United States Steel Corporation
   d. Interpublic Group

28. _____.net is an online marketplace for buying and selling creative ideas for use in advertising, marketing and design. The core of its services is giving idea buyers (marketers, advertisers) direct access to a variety of unpublished ideas offered to them by over 11,500 freelance 'creatives' from 125 countries worldwide.

The whole process of buying ideas takes place on-line, directly between advertisers/marketers and creatives, disintermediating agencies in the process.

   a. Onsert
   b. Interactive Urinal Communicator
   c. Advertising slogans
   d. Openad

29. The _____ is a 14 meters high black silhouetted image of a bull in semi-profile, and is regarded as the unofficial national symbol of Spain. The bull was created in 1956 by Manolo Prieto. Nowadays the conservation of the bulls is handled by the family of Felix Tejada.

a. Osborne bull
b. In-game advertising
c. Ambient media
d. Advertising slogans

30. An _____ is a four page card wrapped around and attached to the outside of a magazine or other publication. Its purpose is to advertise a product (such as a subscription and/or free gift) and also to act as a flag for the publication to distinguish it from other titles on newsstand shelves. The _____ was first used on Running Magazine in the UK in 1981.
   a. American Booksellers Association
   b. Outsert
   c. Adweek
   d. Ethical Consumer

31. _____ is new forms of advertising which are designed specifically to still appear despite a user skipping through the commercials when using a device such as a Tivo or other PVR.

This was used first by cable network FX when advertising 'Brotherhood'.

   a. Bumvertising
   b. PVR-resistant advertising
   c. Puffery
   d. The Centaur Company

32. A _____ is a still or moving image of a product, usually including its packaging and labeling, used to portray the product's reputation in advertising or other media. It is an important stimulus to sales, with the goal of triggering in-store, on-shelf product recognition. The term _____ also refers to product placement in a movie or television show.
   a. Product bundling
   b. Relationship management
   c. Market share
   d. Packshot

33. A _____ is a fictional advertisement for a non-existent product, either done within another advertisement for an actual product or as a comedic device, such as in a comedy skit or sketch.

A _____ should not be confused with a fictional brand name used in a program to avoid giving free advertising to an actual product which is sometimes done as opposed to comparing the product to an actual competitor it is illegal to make disparaging comments about a competitor's product in an advertisement, even if the statements are proven to be true.)

A _____ can be one in which the advertisement appears to actually be a real ad for the false product, but then the advertisement is somehow exposed to be a parody and if it is an actual advertisement the actual brand becomes clear.

   a. Parody advertisement
   b. Albert Einstein
   c. African Americans
   d. AStore

34. A _____ is a type of business entity in which partners (owners) share with each other the profits or losses of the business undertaking in which all have invested. _____s are often favored over corporations for taxation purposes, as the _____ structure does not generally incur a tax on profits before it is distributed to the partners (i.e. there is no dividend tax levied.) However, depending on the _____ structure and the jurisdiction in which it operates, owners of a _____ may be exposed to greater personal liability than they would as shareholders of a corporation.

a. Competition law
b. Fair Debt Collection Practices Act
c. Brand piracy
d. Partnership

35. _____ is a non-profit organization founded by Richard T O'Reilly in 1986 as a project of the American Association of Advertising Agencies. Its publicly stated goal, to reduce the demand for narcotics amongst young people by using the various advertising outlets of the mass media to change their attitudes towards illegal drugs, is based on an idea by Philip Joanou, (chairman of Dailey and Associates in Los Angeles), that marketing techniques can be used to help 'unsell' narcotics. The presumption being that if advertising can influence individuals to purchase products, then it may also be possible to influence the choice of whether or not to experiment with or use narcotics.
a. Checkoff
b. Hechsher
c. Partnership for a Drug-Free America
d. Point of sale

36. A _____ is a set of exclusive rights granted by a State to an inventor or his assignee for a limited period of time in exchange for a disclosure of an invention.

The procedure for granting _____s, the requirements placed on the _____ee and the extent of the exclusive rights vary widely between countries according to national laws and international agreements. Typically, however, a _____ application must include one or more claims defining the invention which must be new, inventive, and useful or industrially applicable.

a. Foreign Corrupt Practices Act
b. Reasonable person standard
c. Product liability
d. Patent

37. _____ is the somewhat misleading term given to various medical compounds sold under a variety of names and labels, though they were, for the most part, actually medicines with trademarks, not patented medicines. In ancient times, such medicine was called nostrum remedium, 'our remedy' in Latin, hence the name 'nostrum,' that is also used for such medicines; it is a medicine whose efficacy is questionable and whose ingredients are usually kept secret. The name _____ has become particularly associated with the sale of drug compounds in the nineteenth century under cover of colourful names and even more colourful claims.
a. 6-3-5 Brainwriting
b. Power III
c. 180SearchAssistant
d. Patent medicine

38. _____ is a term used in Internet marketing to define a popular pricing model whereby a marketing agency will receive a bounty from an advertiser for each new lead or new customer obtained for the advertiser through the agency's online marketing efforts. The agency creates advertising campaigns and promotions to convert the maximum number of new leads or customers and gets paid for its work only when a new lead or a new customer is passed on to the advertiser.

PPP advertising became popular with the advent of the world wide web that allows real time measurement of an advertising campaign's ROI (return on investment.)

a. 6-3-5 Brainwriting
b. Pay for performance advertising
c. Power III
d. 180SearchAssistant

39. _____ is an advertising model and direct marketing method whereby advertisers only pay for each individual ad sent via trackable courier service or express mail. The ad itself is an advertising insert printed by the shipper along with the shipping label, and subsequently included in a letter or package as contextual advertising. Advertisers bid on keywords or target market that they believe best fit the product or service being advertised.
   a. Book of business
   b. Just-In-Case
   c. Lobbying and Disclosure Act of 1995
   d. Pay per ship

40. _____ is a concept similar to pay-per-click (PPC) advertising which is the dominant form of online advertising. In _____, however, the advertiser receives a phone call, a majority of current pay per call provider use web forms to generate phone calls. On web based only platforms, merchants define their relevant keyterms, choose their desired categories and decide upon the geographic area where they'd like their ad to appear (local, regional or national) From there, they create their ad, containing their company name, address, a short description and a trackable toll-free telephone number which redirects to the advertiser's actual phone number.
   a. Gambling advertising
   b. Driven media
   c. The Centaur Company
   d. Pay-per-call

41. _____ is a website which helps content creators such as bloggers find advertisers willing to sponsor specific content. The advertisers create opportunities ('opps') that describe the content they are looking for (e.g. feedback, reviews, buzz, creative, video.) The bloggers (sometimes referred to as 'Posties') then choose opportunities in their area of interest.
   a. VoloMedia
   b. Forrester Research
   c. M80
   d. PayPerPost

42. A _____ is a kind of free community periodical available in North America (typically weekly or monthly publications) that advertises items for sale. Frequently _____s are actually called The _____ (or Penny Saver, Penny-saver, _____.) Many _____s offer local news and entertainment, as well as generic advice information, various syndicated or locally-written columns on various topics of interest, limited comics and primetime TV listings grids in some papers.
   a. Power III
   b. 180SearchAssistant
   c. Pennysaver
   d. 6-3-5 Brainwriting

43. With _____, the advertiser pays only for measurable results.

With other forms of advertising they pay regardless of results. _____ is becoming more common with the spread of electronic media, notably the Internet, where it is possible to directly measure user actions that result from the advertisement.

   a. Door-to-door
   b. Performance-based advertising
   c. Fast moving consumer goods
   d. Business structure

44. _____ is a pay-for-performance digital marketing firm. _____ is based out of offices in Bombay - also known as Mumbai - and Delhi in India, along with offices in Singapore, Malaysia, Europe and the United States. They service clients in North America, Europe, Australia and Asia from these offices.
   a. Pinstorm
   b. Prosumer
   c. Customer insight
   d. DefCom Australia

45. A _____ is a marketing device used by an investment bank. It consists of a careful arrangement and analysis of the investment considerations of a potential or current client, and/or a reference for comparison for an employee in an investment or commercial bank. Its purpose is to secure a deal for the investment bank with the potential client.
  a. 6-3-5 Brainwriting
  b. Pitch Book
  c. Power III
  d. 180SearchAssistant

46. _____ is a form of display advertising on the web, in which the cost of each advertisement is calculated dependent on the number of pixels it occupies.

_____ gained popularity in the last quarter of 2005 when British student Alex Tew created a website named The Million Dollar Homepage, and solicited advertisers to buy ad space measured in pixels on the homepage. The price was set at $1 USD per pixel, and there were 1 million pixels of space available.

  a. Pay per ship
  b. Driven media
  c. Copy testing
  d. Pixel advertising

47. _____ is a full-service advertising and marketing agency specializing in higher education. PlattForm employs more than 350 professionals and is headquartered in Lenexa, Kansas.
  a. Brando
  b. Hospitality point of sales systems
  c. M80
  d. PlattForm, Inc.

48. _____ is the use of commercial advertising techniques for non-commercial purposes Typical topics for _____ include public health/public safety issues, emergency preparedness instructions, natural resources conservation information, and other topics of broad interest.

_____ campaigns are widespread around the world.

  a. Helicopter banner
  b. Logojet
  c. Geo targeting
  d. Public service advertising

49. _____ is an advertisement in which a particular product specifically mentions a competitor by name for the express purpose of showing why the competitor is inferior to the product naming it.

This should not be confused with parody advertisements, where a fictional product is being advertised for the purpose of poking fun at the particular advertisement, nor should it be confused with the use of a coined brand name for the purpose of comparing the product without actually naming an actual competitor. ('Wikipedia tastes better and is less filling than the Encyclopedia Galactica.')

In the 1980s, during what has been referred to as the cola wars, soft-drink manufacturer Pepsi ran a series of advertisements where people, caught on hidden camera, in a blind taste test, chose Pepsi over rival Coca-Cola.

  a. Cost per conversion
  b. Comparative advertising
  c. GL-70
  d. Heavy-up

50. _____ as a legal term refers to promotional statements and claims that express subjective rather than objective views, such that no reasonable person would take literally. _____ is especially featured in testimonials.

In a legal context, the term originated in the English Court of Appeal case Carlill v Carbolic Smoke Ball Company, which centred on whether a monetary reimbursement should be paid when an influenza preventative device failed to work.

   a. Heinz pickle pin
   b. Conquesting
   c. Custom media
   d. Puffery

51. A _____ is a document used for commercial advertising, frequently in convenience stores, hotels, landmarks, restaurants, rest areas and other locations that enjoy significant foot traffic. _____s are typically 4 by 9 inches in size and sport high-impact graphic design.

   a. Rack card
   b. GL-70
   c. Hard sell
   d. Cost per conversion

52. A _____ is a document containing prices and descriptions for the various ad placement options available from a media outlet.

Like the rack rate at a hotel, this is generally the maximum price that one may pay. Most advertising buyers will pay significantly less than this, receiving discounts due to volume, a desire to sell unused space, or other factors.

   a. Rate card
   b. Hard sell
   c. GL-70
   d. Comparative advertising

53. _____ includes all communications used by an organization to attract talent to work within it.

Recruitment advertisements may be the first experience of a company for many people, and the impression they make goes a long way to determining interest in the post being advertised. Recruitment advertisements should have a uniform layout and contain the following elements:

- the job title heading and location
- an explanatory paragraph describing the company, including the Employer Brand
- a description of the position
- entry qualifications
- the remuneration package
- further details and from where application forms may be sought

In the United Kingdom many recruitment advertisements fail to provide all the information listed above and this is frustrating for potential applicants.

Compared to using recruitment consultancies, many organisations find it more cost effective to advertise vacancies themselves or via a _____ agency who obtain their remuneration via commission from the releavnt media, thus no fees are incurred.

a. Power III
b. 180SearchAssistant
c. Recruitment advertising
d. 6-3-5 Brainwriting

54. A _____ is an advertising method that aids in creating interest in and getting people for a typically political organization. The term can not properly be applied to commercial advertising. Historically _____s have often taken the form of posters or films, though in modern times _____s have taken the form of advergame video games.
   a. BidClix
   b. Carlton Screen Advertising
   c. Recruitment tool
   d. Content marketing

55. A _____ is a collection of symbols, experiences and associations connected with a product, a service, a person or any other artifact or entity.

_____s have become increasingly important components of culture and the economy, now being described as 'cultural accessories and personal philosophies'.

Some people distinguish the psychological aspect of a _____ from the experiential aspect.

   a. Store brand
   b. Brandable software
   c. Brand
   d. Brand equity

56. _____ is the structure of brands within an organizational entity. It is the way in which the brands within a company's portfolio are related to, and differentiated from, one another. The architecture should define the different leagues of branding within the organization; how the corporate brand and sub-brands relate to and support each other; and how the sub-brands reflect or reinforce the core purpose of the corporate brand to which they belong.
   a. Status brand
   b. Channel conflict
   c. Corporate colours
   d. Brand architecture

57. _____ is a term loosely used to describe the process of forming an attachment (emotional and rational) between a person and a brand. It comprises one aspect of brand management. What makes the topic complex is that _____ is partly created by institutions and organizations, but is equally created by the perceptions, attitudes, beliefs and behaviors of those with whom these institutions and organizations are communicating or engaging with.
   a. Power III
   b. Graphic communication
   c. Brand engagement
   d. Symbolic analysis

58. _____ measures the extent to which a consumer has a meaningful brand experience when exposed to commercial advertising, sponsorship, television contact, or other experience.

In March 2006 the Advertising Research Foundation defined _____ as 'turning on a prospect to a brand idea enhanced by the surrounding context'. The ARF has also defined the function whereby _____ impacts a brand:

_____ is complex because a variety of exposure and relationship factors affect _____, making simplified rankings misleading.

a. Inseparability
c. Engagement
b. Individual branding
d. Automated surveys

59. _____ refers to the physical application of brand identity across visual identity carriers. This can include signage, uniforms, liveries and branded merchandise. _____ encompasses facets of architecture, product design, industrial design, quantity surveying, engineering, procurement, project management and retail design.
   a. Brand implementation
   b. Web 2.0
   c. Visual merchandising
   d. Corporate identity

60. _____ is the realization of an application idea, model, design, specification, standard, algorithm an _____ is a realization of a technical specification or algorithm as a program, software component, or other computer system. Many _____s may exist for a given specification or standard.
   a. Implementation
   b. ACNielsen
   c. AMAX
   d. ADTECH

61. The brand name of a product that is distributed nationally under a brand name owned by the producer or distributor, as opposed to local brands (products distributed only in some areas of the country), and private label brands (products that carry the brand of the retailer rather than the producer.)

_____s must compete with local and private brands. _____s are produced by ,widely distuted by, and carry the name of the manufacturer.

- Local brands may appeal to those consumers who favor small, local producers over large national or global producers, and may be willing to pay a premium to 'buy local'

- The private label producer can offer lower prices because they avoid the cost of marketing and advertising to create and protect the brand. In North America, large retailers such as Loblaws, Walgreen and Wal-Mart all offer private label products.

   a. Specialty catalogs
   b. Market intelligence
   c. National brand
   d. Line extension

62. _____ is a Public Relations and Branding agency based in Kuala Lumpur, Malaysia

_____ was formed by former journalists, psychologists, public relations and branding professionals from several regional and international network firms in Malaysia and Singapore. The collective experience of this group includes decades of experience in journalism, public relations, branding, issues and crisis communications, marketing communications and design services.

With a young team - and a network of freelance and agency partners around the South East Asian region - _____ is establishing itself as an integrated communications solutions provider in the areas of Public Relations, Branding and Marketing Communications.

A team of account directors, brand managers, designers and other specialist talents work with the firm's clients to help identify, discuss and address public relations and branding concerns or goals in Malaysia and the Asia Pacific region.

a. Underwriters Laboratories
b. Adbot
c. United States Steel Corporation
d. Arcis Communications

63. In consumer marketing, an _____ means a large segment of its exposure audience wishes to own it, but for economical reasons cannot. An aspirational product implies certain positive characteristics to the user, but the supply appears limited due to limited production quantities.

An important characteristic of an aspirational product is that the part of its exposure audience that is at present economically unable to purchase it, thinks of itself as having a fair probability of at a certain point in the future being able to do so.

a. Aspirational brand
b. ADTECH
c. Electronic registration mark
d. ACNielsen

64. _____ is an international branding agency with offices on four continents. Founded in London in 1993 as Morning Star Media, it changed to its present name in 2003. It employs brand directors, managers and consultants to work with brand owners and custodians to deliver branding solutions.

a. 180SearchAssistant
b. Power III
c. 6-3-5 Brainwriting
d. Brand Mercatus

65. _____ is a branding strategy used in a business alliance. _____ are divided into three types: A typical Yum! Brands co-branded restaurant that offer products from two or more of the company's brands (in this case, Taco Bell and KFC)

Cobrands are the usage of two or more brands on one certain product. For example, Dell computers carries three brands on their packages and cases: Dell, Microsoft Windows, and Intel.

a. Brand alliances
b. Rack card
c. Comparative advertising
d. Rate card

66. A _____ a well-connected person or a celebrity who is used to promote and advertise a product or service. Pictorial view of _____

A diplomat; a representative of an organization, institution or corporation that best portrays the product or service. _____s are the face and fingers of the brand, everything they touch, the brand is touching.

a. Brand ambassador
b. Brand aversion
c. Brand implementation
d. Brand architecture

67. _____ is an antonym of brand loyalty. It is when a consumer experiences distrust or a disliking of products from a particular brand based on past experiences with that brand and its products, similar to taste aversion.

_____ usually happens after recent bad press, a mass product recall, or other poor product launches.

- a. Brand image
- b. Brand aversion
- c. Lovemarks
- d. Brand strength analysis

68. _____ is a marketing concept that refers to a consumer knowing of a brand's existence; at aggregate (brand) level it refers to the proportion of consumers who know of the brand.

_____ can be measured by showing a consumer the brand and asking whether or not they knew of it beforehand. However, in common market research practice a variety of recognition and recall measures of _____ are employed all of which test the brand name's association to a product category cue, this came about because most market research in the 20th Century was conducted by post or telephone, actually showing the brand to consumers usually required more expensive face-to-face interviews (until web-based interviews became possible.)

- a. Brand awareness
- b. Brand orientation
- c. Fitting Group
- d. Brand equity

69. _____ refers to the goof ups associated with the branding of a product, especially a new product in a new market. There could be many reasons for such slips. For example, the lack of understanding of the language, culture, consumer attitude etc.
- a. Channel conflict
- b. Visual merchandising
- c. Retail design
- d. Brand blunder

70. A _____ is a community formed on the basis of attachment to a product or marque. Recent developments in marketing and in research in consumer behavior result in stressing the connection between brand, individual identity and culture. Among the concepts developed to explain the behavior of consumers, the concept of a _____ focuses on the connections between consumers.
- a. Customer Integrated System
- b. Foviance
- c. Customer intimacy
- d. Brand community

71. _____ is a company culture in which employees 'live' to brand values, to solve problems and make decisions internally, and deliver a branded customer experience externally. It is the desired outcome of an internal branding, internal brand alignment or employee engagement effort that elevates beyond communications and training.
- a. Brand culture
- b. Web 2.0
- c. Channel conflict
- d. Visual merchandising

Chapter 4. Test Preparation Part 4   81

72. _____ is difficult to define. For example, in 1952, Alfred Kroeber and Clyde Kluckhohn compiled a list of 164 definitions of '_____' in _____: A Critical Review of Concepts and Definitions. However, the word '_____' is most commonly used in three basic senses:

- excellence of taste in the fine arts and humanities
- an integrated pattern of human knowledge, belief, and behavior that depends upon the capacity for symbolic thought and social learning
- the set of shared attitudes, values, goals, and practices that characterizes an institution, organization or group.

When the concept first emerged in eighteenth- and nineteenth-century Europe, it connoted a process of cultivation or improvement, as in agriculture or horticulture. In the nineteenth century, it came to refer first to the betterment or refinement of the individual, especially through education, and then to the fulfillment of national aspirations or ideals.

a. AStore
b. African Americans
c. Albert Einstein
d. Culture

73. _____ refers to the marketing effects or outcomes that accrue to a product with its brand name compared with those that would accrue if the same product did not have the brand name . And, at the root of these marketing effects is consumers' knowledge. In other words, consumers' knowledge about a brand makes manufacturers/advertisers respond differently or adopt appropriately adapt measures for the marketing of the brand .

a. Brand aversion
b. Product extension
c. Brand image
d. Brand equity

74. _____ or brand stretching is a marketing strategy in which a firm marketing a product with a well-developed image uses the same brand name in a different product category. Organizations use this strategy to increase and leverage brand equity (definition: the net worth and long-term sustainability just from the renowned name.) An example of a _____ is Jello-gelatin creating Jello pudding pops.

a. Brand awareness
b. Brand orientation
c. Web 2.0
d. Brand extension

75. _____ is the process of creating and managing contracts between the owner of a brand and a company or individual who wants to use the brand in association with a product, for an agreed period of time, within an agreed territory. Licensing is used by brand owners to extend a trademark or character onto products of a completely different nature.

_____ a is well-established business, both in the area of patents and trademarks.

a. Brand loyalty
b. Brand strength analysis
c. Brand culture
d. Brand licensing

76. The verb _____ or grant _____ means to give permission. The noun _____ refers to that permission as well as to the document memorializing that permission. _____ may be granted by a party to another party as an element of an agreement between those parties.

a. Power III
b. 6-3-5 Brainwriting
c. License
d. 180SearchAssistant

77. _____, in marketing, consists of a consumer's commitment to repurchase the brand and can be demonstrated by repeated buying of a product or service or other positive behaviors such as word of mouth advocacy. True _____ implies that the consumer is willing, at least on occasion, to put aside their own desires in the interest of the brand. _____ has been proclaimed by some to be the ultimate goal of marketing.
- a. Brand awareness
- b. Brand implementation
- c. Trade Symbols
- d. Brand loyalty

78. _____ is a deliberate approach to working with brands, both internally and externally. The most important driving force behind this increased interest in strong brands is the accelerating pace of globalization. This has resulted in an ever-tougher competitive situation on many markets.
- a. Brand extension
- b. Web 2.0
- c. Brand orientation
- d. Distinctiveness

79. _____ is the act of naming a product in a manner which can result in confusion with other better known brands. It can occur with either partial integration of the name of the better known brand, or simply by changing the spelling of the product's name. The effect is similar to that of phishing, whereby the trust of the customer is gained through association with the brand name version of the product.
- a. Rule of four
- b. Trademark dilution
- c. Colour trademark
- d. Brand piracy

80. _____ describes efforts to determine the strength a brand has compared with its competitors.

Software brand strength is hard to measure accurately. Techniques from competitor analysis can be used to compare companies over time.

- a. Brand recognition
- b. Trade Symbols
- c. Distinctiveness
- d. Brand strength analysis

81. _____ is a relatively new form of advertising medium that blurs conventional distinctions between what constitutes advertising and what constitutes entertainment. _____ is essentially a fusion of the two into one product intended to be distributed as entertainment content, albeit with a highly branded quality. _____, unlike conventional forms of entertainment content, is generally funded entirely by a brand or corporation rather than, for example, a Movie studio or a group of producers.
- a. 6-3-5 Brainwriting
- b. 180SearchAssistant
- c. Power III
- d. Branded content

82. _____ is the combination of an audio-visual program and a brand. It can be initiated either by the brand or by the broadcaster.
- a. Channel conflict
- b. Branded entertainment
- c. Brand loyalty
- d. Brand image

83. _____ is the application of marketing techniques to a specific product, product line, or brand. It seeks to increase the product's perceived value to the customer and thereby increase brand franchise and brand equity. Marketers see a brand as an implied promise that the level of quality people have come to expect from a brand will continue with future purchases of the same product.

Chapter 4. Test Preparation Part 4

a. Brand management
c. Trademark distinctiveness
b. Store brand
d. Naming rights

84. _____ is a type of branding in which a celebrity uses his or her status in society to promote a product, service or charity. _____ can take several different forms, from a celebrity simply appearing in advertisements for a product, service or charity, to a celebrity attending PR events, creating his or her own line of products or services, and/or using his or her name as a brand. The most popular forms of celebrity brand lines are for clothing and perfume.

a. Master-McNeil
c. Celebrity branding
b. Gee, Your Hair Smells Terrific
d. Fu Yan Jie

85. _____ occurs when manufacturers (brands) disintermediate their channel partners, such as distributors, retailers, dealers, and sales representatives, by selling their products direct to consumers through general marketing methods and/or over the internet through eCommerce.

Some manufacturers want their brands to capture the power of the internet but do not want to create conflict with their other distribution channels, as these partners are necessary and viable for any manufacturer to maintain and gain success. The Census Bureau of the U.S. Department of Commerce reported that online sales in 2005 grew 24.6 percent over 2004 to reach 86.3 billion dollars.

a. Channel conflict
c. Retail design
b. Trade Symbols
d. Store brand

86. _____ is an annual initiative to identify the UK's coolest brands. The list has been compiled by Superbrands annually since 2001; the results are published every September. The survey seeks the opinion of independent experts and thousands of consumers.

a. Checkoff
c. National Asset Recovery Services
b. CoolBrands
d. Mapinfo

87. _____, are also called Company colours, which are one of the most instantly recognizable elements of a corporate visual identity and promote a strong non-verbal message on the company's behalf.

- Red for Coca-Cola
- Blue for Pepsi

- Corporate logo
- Corporate identity
- Corporate image

a. Brand equity
c. Visual merchandising
b. Corporate colours
d. Brand orientation

88. In marketing, a _____ is the 'persona' of a corporation which is designed to accord with and facilitate the attainment of business objectives. It is usually visibly manifested by way of branding and the use of trademarks.

_____ comes into being when there is a common ownership of an organisational philosophy that is manifest in a distinct corporate culture -- the corporate personality.

a. Brand orientation
c. Brand recognition
b. Corporate identity
d. Brand ambassador

89. An _____ is a proposed category of trademark that would restrict the use of trademarked words and phrases in online advertising.

The State of Utah proposed this in response to trademark owners' claims that online advertisers have abused trademarked terms. Some online advertisers, particularly search engines, allow trademarked keywords to generate advertisements for a trademark holder's competitors.

a. Umbrella brand
c. Electronic registration mark
b. ACNielsen
d. ADTECH

90. _____ is a former Gambian daily newspaper and monthly business magazine editor in chief. In 2001, Eze resigned from his position as editor in chief of The Gambia's largest selling independent daily newspaper, The Daily Observer, in response to being told not to publish interviews or stories about United Democratic Party politician Lamin Waa Juwara. Ten other member of the editorial staff resigned along with Eze.

a. Peter Ferdinand Drucker
c. Paschal Eze
b. Rick Boyce
d. Nouveau riche

Chapter 5. Test Preparation Part 5

1. A _____ is a non-existing brand used in artistic or entertainment productions -- paintings, books, comics, movies, TV serials, etc. The _____ may be designed to imitate a real corporate brand, satirize a real corporate brand, or differentiate itself from real corporate brands.

Works of fiction often mention or show specific brands to give more realism to the plot or scenery.

a. Fictional brand
c. 180SearchAssistant
b. Power III
d. 6-3-5 Brainwriting

2. A _____ is a collection of symbols, experiences and associations connected with a product, a service, a person or any other artifact or entity.

_____s have become increasingly important components of culture and the economy, now being described as 'cultural accessories and personal philosophies'.

Some people distinguish the psychological aspect of a _____ from the experiential aspect.

a. Store brand
c. Brand equity
b. Brandable software
d. Brand

3. _____ is a challenger branding agency based in Pittsburgh, Pennsylvania, that provides clients with strategic marketing and advertising services. The agency received international media coverage when it launched a controversial marketing campaign featuring a whip-bearing dominatrix to promote _____'s Brand Spanking process.

_____ was founded in 1986 by Andrea Fitting, Ph.D. The agency's notable clients include the Mason School of Business at The College of William ' Mary and Butler Health System.

a. Retail design
c. Brand culture
b. Fitting Group
d. Brand ambassador

4. A _____ is a trademark or brand name that has become the colloquial or generic description for a general class of product or service, rather than the specific meaning intended by the trademark's holder. Using a _____ to refer to the general form of what that trademark represents is a form of metonymy.

a. Lovemarks
c. Retail design
b. Trade Symbols
d. Genericized trademark

5. A _____ or trade mark, identified by the symbols â„¢ (not yet registered) and Â® (registered) business organization or other legal entity to identify that the products and/or services to consumers with which the _____ appears originate from a unique source of origin, and to distinguish its products or services from those of other entities. A _____ is a type of intellectual property, and typically a name, word, phrase, logo, symbol, design, image, or a combination of these elements. There is also a range of non-conventional _____s comprising marks which do not fall into these standard categories.

a. 180SearchAssistant
c. Power III
b. Risk management
d. Trademark

6. _____ is an award winning design and branding agency based in Vinton, Virginia. The firm serves a broad range of clients, with a specialty in the tourism, hospitality and foodservice industries. Located in the Roanoke Valley, _____'s clients have included start-up companies and Fortune 500 corporations all across the United States.

a. Inprint
b. Advertising agency
c. Ambient media
d. Interactive Urinal Communicator

7. Custom _____ are floor mats used by businesses to send a message or advertise a brand name on the first place people look when they enter a building. They provide a greeting and make a first impression on customers and clients, promoting brand recognition. Creative logo placement is one of the ways companies can use custom made mats to enhance their business operation.

a. 6-3-5 Brainwriting
b. Logo mats
c. 180SearchAssistant
d. Power III

8. _____ is a marketing technique that is intended to replace the idea of brands. _____ were invented by Kevin Roberts, Chief Executive Officer Worldwide of the advertising agency Saatchi ' Saatchi, and are promoted by him and his company. Roberts claims, 'Brands are running out of juice.' He considers that love is what is needed to rescue brands.

a. Corporate identity
b. Brand licensing
c. Brand architecture
d. Lovemarks

9. In economics, a _____ is a good for which demand increases more than proportionally as income rises, in contrast to a 'necessity good', for which demand increases less than proportionally as income rises.

_____s are said to have high income elasticity of demand: as people become wealthier, they will buy more and more of the _____. This also means, however, that should there be a decline in income its demand will drop.

a. Power III
b. Durable good
c. Free good
d. Luxury good

10. _____s function as professionals who deal with trade, dealing in commodities that they do not produce themselves, in order to produce profit.

_____s can be of two types:

1. A wholesale _____ operates in the chain between producer and retail _____. Some wholesale _____s only organize the movement of goods rather than move the goods themselves.
2. A retail _____ or retailer, sells commodities to consumers (including businesses.) A shop owner is a retail _____.

A _____ class characterizes many pre-modern societies. Its status can range from high (even achieving titles like that of _____ prince or nabob) to low, such as in Chinese culture, due to the soiling capabilities of profiting from 'mere' trade, rather than from the labor of others reflected in agricultural produce, craftsmanship, and tribute.

In the United States, '_____' is defined (under the Uniform Commercial Code) as any person while engaged in a business or profession or a seller who deals regularly in the type of goods sold.

a. RFM	b. Merchant
c. Retail loss prevention	d. Trade credit

11. _____ are the right to name a piece of property, either tangible property or an event, usually granted in exchange for financial considerations. Institutions like schools, places of worship and hospitals have a tradition of granting donors the right to name facilities in exchange for contributions. Securing the _____ for stadiums, theaters, and other public gathering places is seen by companies as a form of advertising, and _____ deals worth millions of dollars have been consummated.

a. Distinctiveness	b. Trademark distinctiveness
c. Brand blunder	d. Naming rights

12. _____ MCSD is a brand strategist, writer, columnist, editor, publisher, designer, creative director, public speaker, corporate celebrity, radio and television personality from Malaysia. He is best known as the creative director of New Nation, a British tabloid; the editor-in-chief of Food ' Beverage magazine; publisher of Malaysian Superbrands; and for his work in branding.

He is a host and judge of the corporate reality television series The Firm, where he plays himself, acting as a corporate leader and mentor.

a. 180SearchAssistant	b. 6-3-5 Brainwriting
c. Peter Pek	d. Power III

13. _____ is when a large distribution channel member (usually a retailer), buys from a manufacturer in bulk and puts its own name on the product. This strategy is only practical when the retailer does very high levels of volume. The advantages to the retailer are:

- more freedom and flexibility in pricing
- more control over product attributes and quality
- higher margins (or lower selling price)
- eliminates much of the manufacturer's promotional costs

The advantages to the manufacturer are:

- reduced promotional costs
- stability of sales volume (at least while the contract is operative)

- Kumar, Nirmalya; Steenkamp, Jan-Benedict E.M., Private Label Strategy - How to Meet the Store Brand Challenge. Harvard Business Press 2007

- private label
- brand management
- brand
- product management
- marketing

a. Customization
c. Rural market
b. Promotion
d. Private branding

14. _____ is the discipline of deciding what a product will be called, and is very similar in concept and approach to the process of deciding on a name for a company or organization. _____ is considered a critical part of the branding process, which includes all of the marketing activities that affect the brand image, such as positioning and the design of logo, packaging and the product itself. _____ involves the application of creative and linguistic strategy and results in a brand name that becomes a product's shorthand.

a. Psychographic
c. Customer insight
b. Product naming
d. DefCom Australia

15. _____ is a creative and commercial discipline that combines and utilizes many different design concepts together in the conceptualizing and construction of retail space. _____ is primarily a specialized practice of architecture and interior design, however it also incorporates elements of interior decoration, graphic design, ergonomics, and advertising.

_____ is a very specialized discipline due to the heavy demands placed on retail space.

a. Retail design
c. Channel conflict
b. Distinctiveness
d. Web 2.0

16. Throughout the long history of consumer research, there has been much interest regarding how consumers choose which brand to buy and why they continue to purchase these brands. _____ describes the process in which consumers match their own self-concept with the images of a certain brand.

People engaged in consumption do not merely buy certain products to satisfy basic needs.

a. Self branding

b. Lifestyle city

c. Maturity of Organizations and Business Excellence - The Four-Phase Model

d. Lifestyles of Health and Sustainability

17. _____ is typically software created by one company for the purpose of allowing other companies to obtain resell rights or giveaway rights to the software, change the brand associated with it, and sell it as if it were their own. It may also be referred to as private label software or Rebranded Software.

_____ is usually presented as an alternative to more expensive software development.

a. Brand management
b. Brandable software
c. Brand awareness
d. Status brand

18. _____s are brands that, through association, inherently increase their owner's popularity in a certain community. Unlike luxury brands, _____s are usually available at different price points and thus are available to shoppers of various demographics.

Trendsetters determine the societal and cultural status ultimately associated with a given _____.

a. Corporate identity
b. Brand management
c. Brand equity
d. Status brand

19. _____s (house brands in the United States, own brands in the UK, and home brands in Australia) are brands which are specific to a retail store or store chain. The retailer can manufacture goods under its own label, re-brand private label goods, or outsource manufacture of _____ items to multiple third parties - often the same manufacturers that produce brand label goods. _____ goods are generally cheaper than national brand goods because the retailer can optimize the production to suit consumer demand and reduce advertising costs.

a. Brand strength analysis
b. Brand ambassador
c. Brand loyalty
d. Store brand

20. The _____ organization is an independent arbiter on branding. It pays tribute to brands that it considers exceptional through its programs. The organization also publishes a series of brand-focused books and publications.

a. CoolBrands
b. Green Earth Market
c. China Compulsory Certificate
d. Superbrands

21. In each country that Superbrands operates in, it elects a _____, which usually comprises industry experts and practitioners, which selects the top brands under various categories and awards them the status of 'Superbrands'.

Brands are invited to participate in the Superbrands project based on the following criteria: market dominance, longevity, goodwill, customer loyalty and market acceptancy.

a. Kahala-Cold Stone
b. MySpace
c. Superbrands Council
d. MyToons

22. The Trade Mark Extensible Markup Language (_____) is an XML open standard for the trademark business and for the exchange of trademark information between the Industrial Property Offices and its partners or users.

Chapter 5. Test Preparation Part 5

The initial objective was the definition of XML Standard for trademark information exchange. During the specifications and after the creation of WIPO Standard ST.66, other objectives have been added as following:

- Define XML Standards for Trade Mark Offices and Trade Mark Business
- Propose Useful Outcomes as Base for the Creation of WIPO Standards
- Define Trademark Web Service Standards
- Provide Examples of Implementations and Tools
- Share Experiences, Practices and Knowledge
- Promote Collaboration and Harmonization of Trade Mark Information and Knowledge Representations
- Prepare the Emerging Semantic Web for the Trade Mark Domain in the Intellectual Property Context (hTrademark Microformat, TM-RDF, TM-OWL)

_____ was defined by a working group created by the Office for Harmonization in the Internal Market in June 2003. 8 draft versions for comment have been published (versions 0.1 to 0.7 and 1.0 Draft) before the version 1.0 Final published on 26 May, 2006 on its website: http://www._____.org.

a. Power III
c. 6-3-5 Brainwriting
b. 180SearchAssistant
d. TM-XML

23. _____

There are four type of _____

1. Trade mark - Unique Symbol, word, picture, name or combination of these, e.g. Apple Symbol of Apple Computer.
2. Service mark - Which identifies one service from another, e.g. Golden Arches of McDonalds.
3. Certification mark - Which is used or intended to be used, in commerce with the owner's permission by someone other than its owner, to certify regional or other geographic origin or other characteristics of someone's goods or services.
4. Collective mark - Which used by the members of a cooperative, an association including a mark which indicates membership an association

All of these symbols are recognized by the Lanham Act.

Registrations issued on or after November 16, 1989 have a ten-year term, renewable every ten years. The previous validity period was twenty years. For a trademark registration to remain valid, an Affidavit of Use must be filed: (1) between the fifth and sixth year following registration, and (2) within the year before the end of every ten-year period after the date of registration.

a. Fitting Group
c. Brand loyalty
b. Brand recognition
d. Trade Symbols

Chapter 5. Test Preparation Part 5

24. _____ is an important concept in the law governing trademarks and service marks. A trademark may be eligible for registration, or registrable, if amongst other things it performs the essential trademark function, and has distinctive character. Registrability can be understood as a continuum, with 'inherently distinctive' marks at one end, 'generic' and 'descriptive' marks with no distinctive character at the other end, and 'suggestive' and 'arbitrary' marks lying between these two points.
   a. Lovemarks
   b. Brand ambassador
   c. Web 2.0
   d. Trademark distinctiveness

25. Trademark _____ is an important concept in the law governing trademarks and service marks. A trademark may be eligible for registration, or registrable, if amongst other things it performs the essential trademark function, and has distinctive character. Registrability can be understood as a continuum, with 'inherently distinctive' marks at one end, 'generic' and 'descriptive' marks with no distinctive character at the other end, and 'suggestive' and 'arbitrary' marks lying between these two points.
   a. Corporate colours
   b. Distinctiveness
   c. Brand implementation
   d. Brand ambassador

26. An _____ is a brand that covers diverse kinds of products which are more or less related.

It applies also to any company that is identified only by its brand and history. Such a company now only acts as designer and distributor.

   a. Electronic registration mark
   b. ACNielsen
   c. ADTECH
   d. Umbrella brand

27. The _____ is Virginia Commonwealth University's Monroe Park campus located in downtown Richmond, Virginia. The Brandcenter program is composed of five tracks in advertising; Art Direction, Copywriting, Communication Strategy, Creative Brand Management, and Creative Technology.

Founded in 1996 as the VCU Adcenter, _____ was the first graduate program in marketing communications to combine business-oriented brand management and strategic tracks with a creative program for art directors, writers, and technologists in an agency setting.

   a. Power III
   b. VCU Brandcenter
   c. 6-3-5 Brainwriting
   d. 180SearchAssistant

28. _____, until recently called simply merchandising, is the activity of promoting the sale of goods, especially by their presentation in retail outlets.. This includes combining product, environment, and space into a stimulating and engaging display to encourage the sale of a product or service. It has become an important element in retailing that is a team effort involving senior management, architects, merchandising managers, buyers, the _____ director, designers, and staff.
   a. Trade Symbols
   b. Status brand
   c. Brand licensing
   d. Visual merchandising

29. _____ refers to the methods, practices and operations conducted to promote and sustain certain categories of commercial activity. The term is understood to have different specific meanings depending on the context. Merchandise is a sale goods at a store

In marketing, one of the definitions of _____ is the practice in which the brand or image from one product or service is used to sell another.

a. Marketing communication
b. Merchandising
c. New Media Strategies
d. Word of mouth

30. Windows Hardware Quality Labs testing or _____ is a testing process which involves running a series of tests on third-party (i.e. non-Microsoft) hardware or software, and then submitting the log files from these tests to Microsoft for review. The procedure may also include Microsoft running their own tests on a wide range of equipment, like different hardware and different Microsoft Windows editions.

New since June 2007 is the requirement of a Fidelity Test equipment (Audio Precision SYS-2722-A-M) for System Submissions.

a. Power III
b. 180SearchAssistant
c. 6-3-5 Brainwriting
d. WHQL Testing

31. The term '_____' refers to a perceived second generation of web development and design, that aims to facilitate communication, secure information sharing, interoperability, and collaboration on the World Wide Web. _____ concepts have led to the development and evolution of web-based communities, hosted services, and applications; such as social-networking sites, video-sharing sites, wikis, blogs, and folksonomies.

The term was first used by Dale Dougherty and Craig Cline and shortly after became notable after the O'Reilly Media _____ conference in 2004.

a. Corporate colours
b. Brand image
c. Web 2.0
d. Product extension

32. _____ is the structure of brands within an organizational entity. It is the way in which the brands within a company's portfolio are related to, and differentiated from, one another. The architecture should define the different leagues of branding within the organization; how the corporate brand and sub-brands relate to and support each other; and how the sub-brands reflect or reinforce the core purpose of the corporate brand to which they belong.

a. Channel conflict
b. Corporate colours
c. Status brand
d. Brand architecture

33. _____ refers to the physical application of brand identity across visual identity carriers. This can include signage, uniforms, liveries and branded merchandise. _____ encompasses facets of architecture, product design, industrial design, quantity surveying, engineering, procurement, project management and retail design.

a. Visual merchandising
b. Web 2.0
c. Brand implementation
d. Corporate identity

34. _____ is the realization of an application idea, model, design, specification, standard, algorithm an _____ is a realization of a technical specification or algorithm as a program, software component, or other computer system. Many _____s may exist for a given specification or standard.

a. AMAX
b. ACNielsen
c. Implementation
d. ADTECH

35. The brand name of a product that is distributed nationally under a brand name owned by the producer or distributor, as opposed to local brands (products distributed only in some areas of the country), and private label brands (products that carry the brand of the retailer rather than the producer.)

_____s must compete with local and private brands._____s are produced by ,widely distuted by, and carry the name of the manufacturer.

- Local brands may appeal to those consumers who favor small, local producers over large national or global producers, and may be willing to pay a premium to 'buy local'
- The private label producer can offer lower prices because they avoid the cost of marketing and advertising to create and protect the brand. In North America, large retailers such as Loblaws, Walgreen and Wal-Mart all offer private label products.

a. Specialty catalogs
b. Line extension
c. Market intelligence
d. National brand

36. _____ is a French consumer electronics company that was established in 1988 by Henri Crohas. _____ manufactures portable media players and portable storage devices. The name is an anagram of Crohas' last name, and it is also Greek for 'master'.
a. Athena Wissenschaftsmarketing
b. Adgooroo
c. Asia Insight
d. Archos

37. _____ is a company active on the promotional products market with its headquarters in Hamburg and markets in 14 European states. According to the company, the annual turnover amounts to approx. EUR 80 million.
a. Fountain Fresh International
b. Multinational corporation
c. VideoJug
d. Berendsohn AG

38. _____ is the application of marketing techniques to a specific product, product line, or brand. It seeks to increase the product's perceived value to the customer and thereby increase brand franchise and brand equity. Marketers see a brand as an implied promise that the level of quality people have come to expect from a brand will continue with future purchases of the same product.
a. Trademark distinctiveness
b. Store brand
c. Naming rights
d. Brand management

39. _____ is a type of branding in which a celebrity uses his or her status in society to promote a product, service or charity. _____ can take several different forms, from a celebrity simply appearing in advertisements for a product, service or charity, to a celebrity attending PR events, creating his or her own line of products or services, and/or using his or her name as a brand. The most popular forms of celebrity brand lines are for clothing and perfume.
a. Fu Yan Jie
b. Master-McNeil
c. Celebrity branding
d. Gee, Your Hair Smells Terrific

40. The _____ is an independent index for brand marketers and agencies that determines a celebrity's ability to influence brand affinity and consumer purchase intent.

Developed by the talent division of Los Angeles-based Davie Brown Entertainment (DBE), an Omnicom Group Inc. agency and a member of The Marketing Arm network, the _____ provides marketers with a systematic approach for quantifying the use of celebrities in their advertising and marketing campaigns.

   a. Comparison-Shopping agent   b. Lobbying and Disclosure Act of 1995
   c. Per-inquiry advertising   d. Davie Brown Index

41. _____ was a trade name assigned to a product line of automotive lacquer developed by the DuPont Company in the 1920s. Under the _____ brand, DuPont introduced the first quick drying multi-color line of lacquers especially for the automotive industry. It is now used by Nexa Autocolor -- formerly ICI Autocolor and now a division of Pittsburgh-based PPG Industries -- as a tradename for automotive enamels in Asia.
   a. 180SearchAssistant   b. Duco
   c. 6-3-5 Brainwriting   d. Power III

42. _____ was originally a brand of tyre produced by the _____ Pneumatic Tyre Company at the end of the 19th century, taking its name from John _____. The brand is now used for many other products either derived from rubber or with a looser connection to rubber.

Ownership of the brand has become fragmented over the years.

   a. Retail floor planning   b. Product line extension
   c. Market specialization   d. Dunlop

43. The _____ is the official currency of 16 out of 27 member states of the European Union (EU.) The states, known collectively as the Eurozone are: Austria, Belgium, Cyprus, Finland, France, Germany, Greece, Ireland, Italy, Luxembourg, Malta, the Netherlands, Portugal, Slovakia, Slovenia, and Spain. The currency is also used in a further five European countries, with and without formal agreements and is consequently used daily by some 327 million Europeans.
   a. ADTECH   b. ACNielsen
   c. Eurozone   d. Euro

44. _____ is a discount brand of everyday commodities developed and marketed by AMS Sourcing B.V.. It was introduced to the market in 1996 and _____ branded products have been sold by some of the AMS members in different countries in Europe ever since. Countries in which _____ is active

_____ products mostly include commodities with long shelf life.

   a. ADTECH   b. Euro Shopper
   c. ACNielsen   d. AMAX

45. _____ is a product brand belonging to Nickelodeon and Viacom aimed at children, and described as 'a lifestyle brand specifically created for tween girls'. The products include dolls, clothes, music CDs, digital cameras and a virtual community. Currently, the site is getting a 'makeover' and has been getting a 'makeover' for more than two years now.

Chapter 5. Test Preparation Part 5   95

a. ACNielsen
b. ADTECH
c. EverGirl
d. AMAX

46. _____ is a personal bodily cleanser product for females, which is popular in China.

_____ is a women's hygiene solution made from herbal medicine. It is available in single bottled packs or boxed bundles.

a. Marque
b. Thomson Directories
c. Fu Yan Jie
d. Master-McNeil

47. _____ was a popular shampoo from the 1970s by the Andrew Jergens Company.

The shampoo became popular, especially with teenage girls and young women, because of its strong, but pleasant floral scent, that softened after rinsing, and remained with the user's hair for hours.

While out of production in the United States, the formula was sold to Vibelle Manufacturing Corporation of Malabon City, Philippines and is currently sold in the Philippines, where it is still popular.

a. Marque
b. Master-McNeil
c. Fu Yan Jie
d. Gee, Your Hair Smells Terrific

48. A _____ is a compact multi-function tool from a range made by Gerber Legendary Blades, part of the Fiskars Corporation.

There are many similarities with Leatherman tools, as well as some interesting differences. Some of the Gerber tools are accessed by opening the handles, but unique to Gerber is a system in which the pliers slide straight out from the end.

a. 180SearchAssistant
b. Power III
c. Gerber multitool
d. 6-3-5 Brainwriting

49. _____ is a German manufacturer of wood crafts. The artist Egon _____ is known by Celebrities and Politicians as a specialist for unique and extraordinary designs.

_____ Manufactur was established in 1992 as a private company in Landshut in Bavaria, Germany.

a. Hechsher
b. Partnership for a Drug-Free America
c. Superbrands Council
d. Gerl

50. _____ is a branded product line from IBM under its Information Management Software brand, announced in February 2008, which includes software products from its WebSphere and Information Server product lines. Upon its announcement, included in the Infosphere product line were the _____ Master Data Management Server and _____ Warehouse. _____ falls under IBM's Information On Demand initiative.

a. IBM InfoSphere
c. AMAX
b. ACNielsen
d. ADTECH

51. _____ refers to a brand of software products, although the term also popularly refers to one specific product: _____ Application Server (WAS.) WebSphere is designed to set up, operate and integrate electronic business applications across multiple computing platforms, using Java-based Web technologies. It includes both the run-time components and the tools to develop applications, that will run on WAS.
   a. IBM WebSphere
   c. AMAX
   b. ADTECH
   d. ACNielsen

52. A _____ is a brand name, especially in the automobile industry. For example, Chevrolet and Pontiac are _____s of their maker, General Motors . A company may have many _____s: GM has used more than a dozen in the North American market alone.
   a. Marque
   c. Thomson Directories
   b. Fu Yan Jie
   d. Gee, Your Hair Smells Terrific

53. _____ is a Korean fictional character who resembles a fat rabbit, created by Kim Jae In He is also known as Yupki Tokki He debuted in a series of Flash animations on the internet.
   a. 180SearchAssistant
   c. Mashimaro
   b. 6-3-5 Brainwriting
   d. Power III

54. _____, Inc. is a naming firm that focuses on naming products, companies, and brands. The Berkeley, California firm was founded in 1988 by SB Master and is one of the four original naming firms in the world.
   a. Master-McNeil
   c. Gee, Your Hair Smells Terrific
   b. Fu Yan Jie
   d. Marque

55. _____ Electronic Technology is a Chinese electronics manufacturer. _____ is the developer of the M6 Mini Player, the M3 Music Card, released in March 2007, and the upcoming M8 miniOne mobile phone. Later they plan to release another MP3 player based on the M8 miniOne, named the M7.
   a. National Asset Recovery Services
   c. Brash Brands
   b. Dunkin' Donuts
   d. Meizu

56. _____ is a certified organic product range from Organic and Natural Enterprises Pty Ltd (ONE Group), an organic cosmetic and beauty company from Australia. The founder of the _____ range, Narelle Chenery first began to use organic ingredients in 1997, realising that products making claims of being 'natural' still contained synthetic toxins in them. Narelle says that up to 99% of 'natural' ingredients are synthetically processed after they are derived from a natural source.
   a. Power III
   c. 6-3-5 Brainwriting
   b. 180SearchAssistant
   d. Miessence

Chapter 6. Test Preparation Part 6

1. The _____ organization is an independent arbiter on branding. It pays tribute to brands that it considers exceptional through its programs. The organization also publishes a series of brand-focused books and publications.
   a. China Compulsory Certificate
   b. Green Earth Market
   c. CoolBrands
   d. Superbrands

2. In each country that Superbrands operates in, it elects a _____, which usually comprises industry experts and practitioners, which selects the top brands under various categories and awards them the status of 'Superbrands'.

Brands are invited to participate in the Superbrands project based on the following criteria: market dominance, longevity, goodwill, customer loyalty and market acceptancy.

   a. Kahala-Cold Stone
   b. MySpace
   c. Superbrands Council
   d. MyToons

3. _____ is a publisher of local directories based in Farnborough, Hampshire, England including the Thomson Local. They are a subsidiary of Seat Pagine Gialle, and a competitor to the Yellow Pages. They are responsible for innovative features such as local guides and colour directory advertising.
   a. Fu Yan Jie
   b. Marque
   c. Gee, Your Hair Smells Terrific
   d. Thomson Directories

4. _____ is a local business telephone directory published in the United Kingdom by Thomson Directories Ltd. It is the principal rival (and for the 1980s and some of the 1990s the sole rival) to the Yellow Pages (published by Thomson as the Thomson Yellow Pages until it was sold off to the privatised BT.)

_____ is a focused local area directory which has continually innovated with features such as colour and knock-out white advertisements.

   a. 180SearchAssistant
   b. Thomson Local
   c. Power III
   d. 6-3-5 Brainwriting

5. The _____ was a campaign of mutually-targeted television advertisements and marketing campaigns in the 1980s and 1990s between soft drink manufacturers The Coca-Cola Company and PepsiCo.

Pepsi and Coca-Cola had/have different brands of soda and other drinks competing with each other:

Coca-Cola and Pepsi focused particularly on rock stars; notable soft drink promoters included Michael Jackson and Ray Charles (for Pepsi) and Paula Abdul, Elton John (for Diet Coke.)

One example of a heated exchange that occurred during the _____ was Coca-Cola making a strategic retreat on July 11, 1985, by announcing its plans to bring back the original 'Classic' Coke after recently introducing New Coke.

   a. Cola Wars
   b. 180SearchAssistant
   c. 6-3-5 Brainwriting
   d. Power III

6. The _____ were conflicts in the East End of Glasgow in Scotland in the 1980s between rival ice cream van operators, over lucrative territory and suggested use of ice cream vans as a cover for selling drugs. The conflicts involved daily violence and intimidation, and led to the deaths by arson of several members of the family of one ice cream van driver and a consequent court case that lasted for 20 years. The conflicts generated widespread public outrage, and earned the Strathclyde Police the nickname the 'serious chimes squad' (a pun on Serious Crime Squad) for its perceived failure to address them.
   a. Power III
   b. 180SearchAssistant
   c. 6-3-5 Brainwriting
   d. Glasgow Ice Cream Wars

7. _____ in economics and business is the result of an exchange and from that trade we assign a numerical monetary value to a good, service or asset. If I trade 4 apples for an orange, the _____ of an orange is 4 - apples. Inversely, the _____ of an apple is 1/4 oranges.
   a. Price
   b. Discounts and allowances
   c. Contribution margin-based pricing
   d. Pricing

8. _____ is a term used in business to indicate a state of intense competitive rivalry accompanied by a multi-lateral series of price reduction. One competitor will lower its price, then others will lower their prices to match. If one of them reduces their price again, a new round of reductions starts.
   a. Resale price maintenance
   b. Pricing objectives
   c. Competitor indexing
   d. Price war

9. _____ refers to a self-organizing tactical relationship between opposing organizations (which can be countries, terrorist organizations, businesses, religious institutions, etc. and mixes of any of these, i.e. terrorist org. vs. country) in which both opposing sides benefit (gain/concentrate power or wealth) by attacking each other.
   a. Power III
   b. 6-3-5 Brainwriting
   c. Promoting adversaries
   d. 180SearchAssistant

10. The _____ were a series of conflicts between two competing railroads in the Old West of the late 1870s.

In 1878, the Atchison, Topeka and Santa Fe Railway and the smaller Denver and Rio Grande were competing to put the first line through Raton Pass. Both railroads had extended lines into Trinidad, Colorado and the pass was the only access to continue on to New Mexico.

   a. Power III
   b. 180SearchAssistant
   c. Railroad Wars
   d. 6-3-5 Brainwriting

11. _____, Pricing models and business models used for the different types of internet marketing, including affiliate marketing, contextual advertising, search engine marketing (including vertical comparison shopping search engines and local search engines) and display advertising.

The following models are also referred to as performance based pricing/compensation model, because they only pay if a visitor performs an action that is desired by the advertisers or completes a purchase. Advertisers and publishers share the risk of a visitor that does not convert.

a. Compensation methods
b. Phorm
c. Hennes ' Mauritz
d. Sustainable Forestry Initiative

12. In economics, business, retail, and accounting, a _____ is the value of money that has been used up to produce something, and hence is not available for use anymore. In economics, a _____ is an alternative that is given up as a result of a decision. In business, the _____ may be one of acquisition, in which case the amount of money expended to acquire it is counted as _____.
   a. Cost
   b. Fixed costs
   c. Variable cost
   d. Transaction cost

13. _____ is an online advertising pricing model, where the advertiser pays for each specified action (a purchase, a form submission, and so on) linked to the advertisement.

Direct response advertisers consider _____ the optimal way to buy online advertising, as an advertiser only pays for the ad when the desired action has occurred. An action can be a product being purchased, a form being filled, etc.

   a. Cost per Lead
   b. Cost per action
   c. Value Per Action
   d. Display advertising

14. _____ is the amount of money an advertiser pays search engines and other Internet publishers for a single click on its advertisement that brings one visitor to its website.

- Ad serving
- Click-through rate (CTR)
- Compensation methods
- Cost per action (CPA)
- Cost per impression (CPI)
- Cost per mille (CPM), Also Cost per thousand
- Google AdSense
- Interactive advertising
- Internet marketing
- Online advertising
- Pay Per Click (PPC)
- Search engine marketing (SEM)
- Search engine optimization (SEO)

   a. Comparative advertising
   b. Flighting
   c. Cost per conversion
   d. Cost per click

15. _____, often abbreviated to _____, is a phrase often used in online advertising and marketing related to web traffic. It is used for measuring the worth and cost of a specific e-marketing campaign. This technique is applied with web banners, text links, e-mail spam, and opt-in e-mail advertising, although opt-in e-mail advertising is more commonly charged on a cost per action (CPA) basis.

a. Frequency capping
b. Cost per impression
c. Cost per time
d. Cost per mille

16. _____ is a commonly used measurement in advertising. Radio, television, newspaper, magazine, Out-of-home advertising and online advertising can be purchased on the basis of what it costs to show the ad to one thousand viewers . It is used in marketing as a benchmark to calculate the relative cost of an advertising campaign or an ad message in a given medium.

a. Frequency capping
b. Cost per mille
c. Link exchange
d. Cost per time

17. _____ is an online advertisement pricing system where the publisher or website owner is paid on the basis of the number of sales that are directly generated by an advertisement. It is a variant of the CPA (Cost Per Action) model where the advertiser pays the publisher/website only and in proportion to the number of actions committed by the readers or visitors to the website.

In many cases it's not practical to track all the sales generated by an advertisement, however it is more easily tracked for full online transactions, such as for selling songs directly on the internet.

a. Price war
b. Break even analysis
c. Price points
d. Pay Per Sale

18. _____ is a term used in Internet marketing to define a popular pricing model whereby a marketing agency will receive a bounty from an advertiser for each new lead or new customer obtained for the advertiser through the agency's online marketing efforts. The agency creates advertising campaigns and promotions to convert the maximum number of new leads or customers and gets paid for its work only when a new lead or a new customer is passed on to the advertiser.

PPP advertising became popular with the advent of the world wide web that allows real time measurement of an advertising campaign's ROI (return on investment.)

a. Power III
b. Pay for performance advertising
c. 180SearchAssistant
d. 6-3-5 Brainwriting

19. _____ is a form of communication that typically attempts to persuade potential customers to purchase or to consume more of a particular brand of product or service. 'While now central to the contemporary global economy and the reproduction of global production networks, it is only quite recently that _____ has been more than a marginal influence on patterns of sales and production. The formation of modern _____ was intimately bound up with the emergence of new forms of monopoly capitalism around the end of the 19th and beginning of the 20th century as one element in corporate strategies to create, organize and where possible control markets, especially for mass produced consumer goods.

a. ADTECH
b. ACNielsen
c. AMAX
d. Advertising

20. _____ is an Internet advertising model used on search engines, advertising networks, and content sites, such as blogs, in which advertisers pay their host only when their ad is clicked. With search engines, advertisers typically bid on keyword phrases relevant to their target market. Content sites commonly charge a fixed price per click rather than use a bidding system.

a. Navigation Catalyst Systems
b. Hit inflation attack
c. Videoplaza
d. Pay per click

21. _____ is a broad label that refers to any individuals or households that use goods and services generated within the economy. The concept of a _____ is used in different contexts, so that the usage and significance of the term may vary.

A _____ is a person who uses any product or service.

a. 180SearchAssistant
b. Power III
c. Consumer
d. 6-3-5 Brainwriting

22. _____ is the study of when, why, how, where and what people do or do not buy products. It blends elements from psychology, sociology, social psychology, anthropology and economics. It attempts to understand the buyer decision making process, both individually and in groups. It studies characteristics of individual consumers such as demographics and behavioural variables in an attempt to understand people's wants. It also tries to assess influences on the consumer from groups such as family, friends, reference groups, and society in general.
a. Multidimensional scaling
b. Communal marketing
c. Consumer confidence
d. Consumer behavior

23. _____ is the term John Maynard Keynes used to describe emotion or affect which influences human behavior and can be measured in terms of consumer confidence. Trust is also included or produced by _____. Several articles and at least one book with a focus on _____ have been published in 2009 as a part of a so-called Keynesian resurgence.
a. ADTECH
b. ACNielsen
c. Animal spirits
d. AMAX

24. _____ refers to the socio-political movement against consumerism, the equation of personal happiness with consumption and the purchase of material possessions. Consumerism is a term used to describe the effects of the market economy on the individual. Concern over the treatment of consumers has spawned substantial activism, and the incorporation of consumer education into school curricula.
a. ACNielsen
b. AMAX
c. ADTECH
d. Anti-consumerism

25. _____ is a social psychology theory developed by Fritz Heider, Harold Kelley, Edward E. Jones, and Lee Ross.

The theory is concerned with the ways in which people explain (or attribute) the behavior of others or themselves (self-attribution) with something else. It explores how individuals 'attribute' causes to events and how this cognitive perception affects their usefulness in an organization.

a. ACNielsen
b. AMAX
c. ADTECH
d. Attribution theory

26. _____ are the decision making processes undertaken by consumers in regard to a potential market transaction before, during, and after the purchase of a product or service.

More generally, decision making is the cognitive process of selecting a course of action from among multiple alternatives. Common examples include shopping, deciding what to eat.

a. Consumer confidence
b. Convenience
c. Demographic profile
d. Buyer decision processes

27. The _____ is a non-profit organization based in Takoma Park, Maryland, on the border of Washington, DC. A primary focus of New American Dream is promoting sustainable consumption. New American Dream's stated mission is to 'help Americans consume responsibly to protect the environment, enhance quality of life, and promote social justice.' The organization works with individuals, institutions, communities, and businesses to conserve natural resources, counter the commercialization of the culture, and change the way goods are produced and consumed.
a. Partnership for a Drug-Free America
b. National Asset Recovery Services
c. Hennes ' Mauritz
d. Center for a New American Dream

28. _____ is the name given to the trend that sees individuals socializing less and retreating into their home more. Individuals tend to stay away from society and lack in social confidence leading to '_____'. The term was coined in the 1990s by Faith Popcorn a trend forecaster and marketing consultant.
a. Diderot effect
b. Shopping Neutral
c. Gruppi di Acquisto Solidale
d. Cocooning

29. _____ refers to a marketing practice that incorporates public involvement in the development of an advertising/marketing campaign. A 'communal advertising' campaign invites consumers to share their ideas or express their articulation of what the brand means to them through their own personal stories, with the use of print media, film or audio. The resulting 'consumer generated content' is then incorporated into the campaign.
a. Cocooning
b. Conspicuous consumption
c. Communal marketing
d. Shopping Neutral

30. _____ is defined by the American _____ Association as the activity, set of institutions, and processes for creating, communicating, delivering, and exchanging offerings that have value for customers, clients, partners, and society at large. The term developed from the original meaning which referred literally to going to market, as in shopping, or going to a market to sell goods or services.

_____ practice tends to be seen as a creative industry, which includes advertising, distribution and selling.

a. Customer acquisition management
b. Marketing myopia
c. Product naming
d. Marketing

31. A _____ is an expert that utilizes and perfects means of gaining influence. Though the means of gaining influence are common, their aims vary from political, economic, to personal. Thus the label of _____ applies to diverse groups of people, including propagandists, marketers, pollsters, salesmen and political advocates.
a. Shopping Neutral
b. Convenience
c. MaxDiff
d. Compliance professional

32. _____ is a statistical technique used in market research to determine how people value different features that make up an individual product or service.

Chapter 6. Test Preparation Part 6   103

The objective of _____ is to determine what combination of a limited number of attributes is most influential on respondent choice or decision making. A controlled set of potential products or services is shown to respondents and by analyzing how they make preferences between these products, the implicit valuation of the individual elements making up the product or service can be determined.

a. Conjoint analysis
b. Likert scale
c. Semantic differential
d. Power III

33. _____ is a term used to describe the lavish spending on goods and services acquired mainly for the purpose of displaying income or wealth. In the mind of a conspicuous consumer, such display serves as a means of attaining or maintaining social status. A very similar but more colloquial term is 'keeping up with the Joneses'.

a. Consumption smoothing
b. Marketing buzz
c. Cocooning
d. Conspicuous consumption

34. _____ describes a theoretical economic and cultural condition in which consumer demand is manipulated, in a deliberate and coordinated way, on a very large scale, through mass-marketing techniques, to the advantage of sellers.

The phrase is controversial. It suggests manipulation of consumer demand so potent that it has a coercive effect, amounts to a departure from free-market capitalism, and has an adverse effect on society in general.

a. Power III
b. 6-3-5 Brainwriting
c. 180SearchAssistant
d. Consumer capitalism

35. _____ is the degree of optimism that consumers feel about the overall state of the economy and their personal financial situation. How confident people feel about stability of their incomes determines their spending activity and therefore serves as one of the key indicators for the overall shape of the economy. In essence, if _____ is higher, consumers are making more purchases, boosting the economic expansion.

a. Rule Developing Experimentation
b. Communal marketing
c. Consumer confidence
d. Diderot effect

36. _____ is derived from the more general psychological concept of ethnocentrism.

Basically, ethnocentric individuals tend to view their group as superior to others. As such, they view other groups from the perspective of their own, and reject those which are different while accepting those which are similar (Netemeyer et al., 1991; Shimp ' Sharma, 1987.)

a. Power III
b. 6-3-5 Brainwriting
c. 180SearchAssistant
d. Consumer ethnocentrism

37. _____ is the tendency to believe that one's own race or ethnic group is the most important and that some or all aspects of its culture are superior to those of other groups. Since within this ideology, individuals will judge other groups in relation to their own particular ethnic group or culture, especially with concern to language, behavior, customs, and religion. These ethnic distinctions and sub-divisions serve to define each ethnicity's unique cultural identity.

a. Albert Einstein
b. AStore
c. Ethnocentrism
d. African Americans

38. The term _____ refers to the period from the late sixteenth century to the nineteenth century in which there was a marked increase in consumption of various goods and products by individuals from different economic and social backgrounds. The _____ allowed a diverse group of individuals to purchase similar items, that previously may have only been available to those of middle to upper classes. This revolution allowed individuals who were not necessarily wealthy to indulge, and consume products that were necessity as well as those that were not.
   a. Power III
   b. 6-3-5 Brainwriting
   c. Consumer revolution
   d. 180SearchAssistant

39. _____ is the equation of personal happiness with consumption and the purchase of material possessions.

The term is often associated with criticisms of consumption starting with Thorstein Veblen.

Veblen's subject of examination, the newly emergent middle class arising at the turn of the twentieth century, comes to full fruition by the end of the twentieth century through the process of globalization.

In economics, _____ refers to economic policies placing emphasis on consumption.

   a. Consumerism
   b. 6-3-5 Brainwriting
   c. Power III
   d. 180SearchAssistant

40. _____s are designed to help managers understand the customer's viewpoint while going through the company's business process. In analyzing the process, managers are able to question the value of certain steps while working to create an ideal experience for the customer. In determining value, it can be defined as something that the customer is willing to pay for in working to solve his/her problem.
   a. Statistical surveys
   b. Ghost marks
   c. Book of business
   d. Consumption Map

41. _____ is an economic concept which refers to balancing out spending and saving to attain and maintain the highest possible living standard over the course of one's life. This idea is notable because of its difference in approach to common knowledge about preparing for retirement, in which individuals are encouraged to save a particular % of their income throughout their life. Some believe that this approach is flawed and typically leads to one of two outcomes: over-saving or over-spending.
   a. Compliance professional
   b. Consumption smoothing
   c. Consumer confidence
   d. Rule Developing Experimentation

42. In statistics and image processing, to smooth a data set is to create an approximating function that attempts to capture important patterns in the data, while leaving out noise or other fine-scale structures/rapid phenomena. Many different algorithms are used in _____. One of the most common algorithms is the 'moving average', often used to try to capture important trends in repeated statistical surveys.
   a. Power III
   b. 180SearchAssistant
   c. 6-3-5 Brainwriting
   d. Smoothing

Chapter 6. Test Preparation Part 6

43. _____ is anything that is intended to save time, energy or frustration. A _____ store at a petrol station, for example, sells items that have nothing to do with gasoline/petrol, but it saves the consumer from having to go to a grocery store. '_____' is a very relative term and its meaning tends to change over time.

   a. Demographic profile
   b. Convenience
   c. MaxDiff
   d. Marketing buzz

44. _____ is a model for descriptive decisions under risk which has been introduced by Amos Tversky and Daniel Kahneman in 1992 (Tversky, Kahneman, 1992.) It is a further development and variant of prospect theory. The difference from the original version of prospect theory is that weighting is applied to the cumulative probability distribution function, as in rank-dependent expected utility theory, rather than to the probabilities of individual outcomes.

   a. 6-3-5 Brainwriting
   b. Power III
   c. 180SearchAssistant
   d. Cumulative prospect theory

45. _____ is a theory that describes decisions between alternatives that involve risk, i.e. alternatives with uncertain outcomes, where the probabilities are known. The model is descriptive: it tries to model real-life choices, rather than optimal decisions.

   _____ was developed by Daniel Kahneman, professor at Princeton University's Department of Psychology, and Amos Tversky in 1979 as a psychologically realistic alternative to expected utility theory.

   a. 180SearchAssistant
   b. Power III
   c. 6-3-5 Brainwriting
   d. Prospect theory

46. _____ is a process by which data from customer behavior is used to help make key business decisions via market segmentation and predictive analytics. This information is used by businesses for direct marketing, site selection, and customer relationship management.

   RetailGathering customer data and implementing it into some type of application that can enhance insight and the decision making process is a common application of _____ used by retailers.

   a. Societal marketing
   b. Customer analytics
   c. Disruptive technology
   d. Cyberdoc

47. _____ measures the extent to which a consumer has a meaningful brand experience when exposed to commercial advertising, sponsorship, television contact, or other experience.

   In March 2006 the Advertising Research Foundation defined _____ as 'turning on a prospect to a brand idea enhanced by the surrounding context'. The ARF has also defined the function whereby _____ impacts a brand:

   _____ is complex because a variety of exposure and relationship factors affect _____, making simplified rankings misleading.

   a. Individual branding
   b. Automated surveys
   c. Inseparability
   d. Engagement

48. _____ is the activity that the selling organization undertakes to reduce customer account defections. The success of this activity is when the customer account places an additional order before a 12-month period has expired. Note that ideally these orders will need to contribute similar financial amounts to the previous 12 months.
   a. Customer centricity
   b. Customer base
   c. First-mover advantage
   d. Customer retention

49. _____, a business term, is a measure of how products and services supplied by a company meet or surpass customer expectation. It is seen as a key performance indicator within business and is part of the four perspectives of a Balanced Scorecard.

In a competitive marketplace where businesses compete for customers, _____ is seen as a key differentiator and increasingly has become a key element of business strategy.

   a. Customer base
   b. Customer satisfaction
   c. Supplier diversity
   d. Psychological pricing

50. In marketing, the _____ is the phenomenon whereby consumers will tend to have a specific change in preference between two options when also presented with a third option that is asymmetrically dominated. An option is asymmetrically dominated when it is inferior in all respects to one option; but, in comparison to the other option, it is inferior in some respects and superior in others. In other words, in terms of specific attributes determining preferability, it is completely dominated by (i.e., inferior to) one option and only partially dominated by the other.
   a. Power III
   b. 180SearchAssistant
   c. 6-3-5 Brainwriting
   d. Decoy effect

51. _____ or _____ data refers to selected population characteristics as used in government, marketing or opinion research, or the _____ profiles used in such research. Note the distinction from the term 'demography' Commonly-used _____ include race, age, income, disabilities, mobility (in terms of travel time to work or number of vehicles available), educational attainment, home ownership, employment status, and even location.
   a. African Americans
   b. Demographic
   c. AStore
   d. Albert Einstein

52. A demographic or _____ is a term used in marketing and broadcasting, to describe a demographic grouping or a market segment. This typically involves age bands (as teenagers do not wish to purchase denture fixant), social class bands (as the rich may want different products than middle and lower classes and may be willing to pay more) and gender (partially because different physical attributes require different hygiene and clothing products, and partially because of the male/female mindsets.)

A _____ can be used to determine when and where advertising should be placed so as to achieve maximum results.

   a. Shopping Neutral
   b. Cocooning
   c. Demographic profile
   d. Diderot effect

53. _____ was a psychologist and marketing expert who is widely considered to be the 'father of motivational research.'

He received his doctorate from the University of Vienna in 1934 and emigrated with his wife Hedy (née Langfelder) to the United States in 1937. In 1946 he founded the Institute of Motivational Research in Croton-on-Hudson, New York (later moved to his home in Peekskill), and in the succeeding years founded similar institutes in Switzerland and Germany.

Dichter pioneered the application of Freudian psychoanalytic concepts and techniques to business--in particular to the study of consumer behavior in the marketplace.

a. Elmer Davis
b. AStore
c. Andre Kirk Agassi
d. Ernest Dichter

54. The _____ is a social phenomenon related to consumer goods that form culturally defined groups that are considered cohesive. The term was coined by anthropologist and scholar of consumption patterns Grant McCracken in 1988, and is named after the French philosopher Denis Diderot (1713-84) who first described the effect in an essay.

The _____ is the result of the interaction between objects within 'product complements', or 'Diderot unities', and consumers.

a. Cocooning
b. Compliance professional
c. Consumer behavior
d. Diderot effect

55. _____ is an approach in science and technology studies and media studies that describes the processes by which innovations, especially new technology is 'tamed' or appropriated by its users. First, technologies are integrated into everyday life and adapted to daily practices. Secondly, the user and its environment change and adapt accordingly.
a. 180SearchAssistant
b. Power III
c. 6-3-5 Brainwriting
d. Domestication theory

56. _____ is a statistical phenomenon in marketing where, with few exceptions, brand loyalty is lower among buyers of low market share brands than buyers of high market share brands. The market leader in an industry enjoys a high level of sales due to customer loyalty, with a higher probability of repeat purchase. This phenomenon occurs because consumers believe the high sales product to be of high quality.
a. 6-3-5 Brainwriting
b. Double jeopardy
c. 180SearchAssistant
d. Power III

57. _____ includes the application or study of geodemographic classifications for business, social research and public policy but has a shorter history in academic research seeking to understand the processes by which settlements (notably, cities) evolve and neighborhoods are formed. It links the sciences of demography, the study of human population dynamics, geography, the study of the locational and spatial variation of both physical and human phenomena on Earth, and also sociology. In short, _____ is the science of profiling people based on where they live.
a. Geodemography
b. 6-3-5 Brainwriting
c. Power III
d. 180SearchAssistant

58. Launched in 2006, _____ is an American online retailer of environmentally friendly goods, offering products that are made locally (North America), of natural, organic and/or produced in a fair trade, sustainable practices of ecological economics and ethical consumerism are growing and the big box stores are taking environmental initiatives.

a. Green Earth Market
b. Gerl
c. HD share
d. China Compulsory Certificate

59. _____, a buying group is set up from a number of consumers that cooperate in order to buy food and other commonly used goods directly from the producers or from big retailers at a discounted rate.

When a buying group doesn't search for the ultimate discounted rate, but instead puts people and environment before profit the group become a Solidal buyers group.

a. Gruppi di Acquisto Solidale
b. Conspicuous consumption
c. Communal marketing
d. Multidimensional scaling

60. _____ is a general term for the accumulation of food or other items. The term is used to describe both animal and human behavior.

_____ of food is a natural behaviour in certain species of animals.

a. Hoarding
b. Marginal revenue
c. Household production function
d. Product proliferation

61. Consumers often choose not directly from the commodities that they purchase but from commodities they transform into goods through a _____. It is these goods that they value. The idea was originally proposed by Gary Becker and Kelvin Lancaster in the mid 1960s.

a. Total cost
b. Hoarding
c. Product proliferation
d. Household production function

62. An _____ is an unplanned or otherwise spontaneous purchase. One who tends to make such purchases is referred to as an impulse purchaser or impulse buyer.

Marketers and retailers tend to exploit these impulses which are tied to the basic want for instant gratification.

a. Impulse purchase
b. ADTECH
c. ACNielsen
d. AMAX

63. _____ is a mathematical technique used by marketers to convert stated purchase intentions into purchase probabilities, that is, into an estimate of actual buying behaviour. It takes survey data on consumers purchase intentions and converts it into actual purchase probabilities.

A survey might ask a question using a five-point scale such as :

Which is most true about product X?

___ I definitely would use product X
___ I probably would use product X
___ I might use product X
___ I probably would not use product X
___ I definitely would not use product X

A marketing researcher will first assign numerical values to these intention categories.

a. Intent scale translation
b. IDDEA
c. ACNielsen
d. Exploratory research

64. An _____ is a term used in behavioral economics to describe those types of behaviors that impose costs on a person in the long-run that are not taken into account when making decisions in the present. Classical Economics discourages government from creating legislation that targets internalities, because it is assumed that the consumer takes these personal costs into account when paying for the good that causes the _____. For example, cigarettes should be taxed because of the negative consumption externalities that they impose, such as second-hand smoke, not because the smoker harms him or herself by smoking.

a. Income distribution
b. ACNielsen
c. Inflation rate
d. Internality

65. _____ is the study of the relative value people assign to two or more payoffs at different points in time. This relationship is usually simplified to today and some future date. _____ was introduced by John Rae in 1834 in the 'Sociological Theory of Capital'.

a. AMAX
b. Intertemporal choice
c. ACNielsen
d. ADTECH

66. _____ was originally coined by Austrian psychologist Alfred Adler in 1929. The current broader sense of the word dates from 1961.

In sociology, a _____ is the way a person lives.

a. 180SearchAssistant
b. 6-3-5 Brainwriting
c. Power III
d. Lifestyle

67. A _____ is a city which is widely recognized as an attractive place to live. People are attracted to the lifestyle, conditions, and other advantages of such a city. Usually such cities are either cultural capitals or growing cities with a reputation for career opportunities.

a. LIFO
b. Lifestyle city
c. Customization
d. Supreme Court of the United States

68. _____ and the related Fisher's linear discriminant are methods used in statistics and machine learning to find the linear combination of features which best separate two or more classes of objects or events. The resulting combination may be used as a linear classifier, or, more commonly, for dimensionality reduction before later classification.

_____ is closely related to ANOVA (analysis of variance) and regression analysis, which also attempt to express one dependent variable as a linear combination of other features or measurements.

a. Geodemographic segmentation
c. Multiple discriminant analysis
b. Discriminant analysis
d. Linear discriminant analysis

69. In algebra, the _____ of a polynomial with real or complex coefficients is a certain expression in the coefficients of the polynomial which is equal to zero if and only if the polynomial has a multiple root (i.e. a root with multiplicity greater than one) in the complex numbers. For example, the _____ of the quadratic polynomial

$$ax^2 + bx + c \text{ is } b^2 - 4ac.$$

The _____ of the cubic polynomial

$$ax^3 + bx^2 + cx + d \text{ is } b^2c^2 - 4ac^3 - 4b^3d - 27a^2d^2 + 18abcd.$$

a. Consumption Map
c. Discriminant
b. Flighting
d. Lifestyle center

70. Linear _____ and the related Fisher's linear discriminant are methods used in statistics and machine learning to find the linear combination of features which best separate two or more classes of objects or events. The resulting combination may be used as a linear classifier, or, more commonly, for dimensionality reduction before later classification.

LDiscriminant analysis is closely related to ANOVA (analysis of variance) and regression analysis, which also attempt to express one dependent variable as a linear combination of other features or measurements.

a. Geodemographic segmentation
c. Discriminant analysis
b. Multiple discriminant analysis
d. Linear discriminant analysis

71. _____ is a preference to buy locally produced goods and services over those produced more distantly. It is very often abbreviated as a positive goal 'buy local' to parallel the phrase think globally, act locally common in green politics.

On the national level, the equivalent of _____ is import substitution, the deliberate industrial policy or agricultural policy of replacing goods or services produced on the far side of a national border with those produced on the near side, i.e. in the same country or trade bloc.

a. Total benefits of ownership
c. Commodity chain
b. Trade name
d. Local purchasing

72. _____ refers to a business or organization attempting to acquire goods or services to accomplish the goals of the enterprise. Though there are several organizations that attempt to set standards in the _____ process, processes can vary greatly between organizations. Typically the word '_____' is not used interchangeably with the word 'procurement', since procurement typically includes Expediting, Supplier Quality, and Traffic and Logistics (T'L) in addition to _____.

a. Supply chain
b. Purchasing
c. Supply network
d. Drop shipping

73. In prospect theory, _____ refers to people's tendency to strongly prefer avoiding losses to acquiring gains. Some studies suggest that losses are twice as powerful, psychologically, as gains. _____ was first convincingly demonstrated by Amos Tversky and Daniel Kahneman.
a. 6-3-5 Brainwriting
b. 180SearchAssistant
c. Power III
d. Loss aversion

74. _____ or simply buzz is a term used in word-of-mouth marketing. The interaction of consumers and users of a product or service serve to amplify the original marketing message.

Some describe buzz as a form of hype among consumers, a vague but positive association, excitement, or anticipation about a product or service.

a. Consumption smoothing
b. Multidimensional scaling
c. Consumer confidence
d. Marketing buzz

75. _____ is a statistical method invented by Jordan Louviere in 1987 while on the faculty at the University of Alberta. The first working papers and publications occurred in the early 1990s. With _____, survey respondents are shown a set of the possible items and are asked to indicate the best and worst items (or most and least important, or most and least appealing , etc.).
a. Gruppi di Acquisto Solidale
b. Situational theory of publics
c. Consumer confidence
d. MaxDiff

76. _____ is an online virtual fashion community/game. It is owned and developed by Blouzar Ltd., London. It was originally an English expansion of a French game called Ma Bimbo.
a. Power III
b. 180SearchAssistant
c. Miss Bimbo
d. 6-3-5 Brainwriting

77. _____ is defined as the study of human behavior in a mobile world and the study of mobile device/phone lifestyles. The word is probably a combination of 'mobile' and 'sociology'.

This is the direct by-product of how mobile phones and mobility in modern life lifestyles are affecting and changing human interaction, behavior, and consumption in the 21st century.

a. Power III
b. Reference group
c. Minority
d. Mociology

78. _____ is a set of related statistical techniques often used in information visualization for exploring similarities or dissimilarities in data. MDS is a special case of ordination. An MDS algorithm starts with a matrix of item-item similarities, then assigns a location to each item in N-dimensional space, where N is specified a priori.
a. Situational theory of publics
b. Cocooning
c. Convenience
d. Multidimensional scaling

79. The _____ is a management tool that can be used to gauge the loyalty of a firm's customer relationships. It serves as an alternative to traditional customer satisfaction research.

Net Promoter is a customer loyalty metric co-founded by (and a registered trademark of) Frederick F. Reichheld, Bain ' Company and Satmetrix.

a. Category Development Index
b. Lifestyle city
c. Black Friday
d. Net Promoter^R score

80. _____ is a graphics technique used by asset marketers that attempts to visually display the perceptions of customers or potential customers. Typically the position of a product, product line, brand, or company is displayed relative to their competition.

Perceptual maps can have any number of dimensions but the most common is two dimensions.

a. Kano model
b. Customer franchise
c. Perceptual mapping
d. Market environment

81. _____ is a blanket concept including fair trade and moral purchasing. It could be seen as more general, or as more specific.

It takes the word Consumerism which is nowerdays portrayed as a bad thing, a sort of hysteric drive to consume, where consumption is no longer motivated by physiological (hunger, thirst, avoidance of incomfort) motives but more by psychological, cultural and social influences many of them overly fuelled by advertising.

a. Political consumerism
b. Product stewardship
c. Power III
d. SA8000

82. _____ is a common phenomenon after people have invested a lot of time, money, or effort in something to convince themselves that it must have been worth it. Many decisions are made emotionally, and so are often rationalized retrospectively in an attempt to justify the choice.

This rationalization is based on the principle of commitment and the psychological desire to stay consistent to that commitment.

a. 180SearchAssistant
b. Von Restorff effect
c. Power III
d. Post-purchase rationalization

83. _____ is a stage of human development through childhood that occurs in a child's years before adolescence. Sigmund Freud termed this the latency period, which he saw as a period of unparalleled repression of sexual desires and erogenous impulses. During the latency period, children direct this repressed libidal energy into asexual pursuits such as school, athletics, and same-sex friendships.

a. Test market
b. 180SearchAssistant
c. Power III
d. Preadolescence

Chapter 6. Test Preparation Part 6   113

84. _____ is a statistical technique used by marketers to determine consumers' preferred core benefits. It usually supplements product positioning techniques like multi dimensional scaling or factor analysis and is used to create ideal vectors on perceptual maps.

Starting with raw data from surveys, researchers apply positioning techniques to determine important dimensions and plot the position of competing products on these dimensions. Next they regress the survey data against the dimensions.

a. Preference regression
c. Marketing research process
b. Cross tabulation
d. Focus group

85. _____ is a mathematical technique used by marketers to convert stated preferences into purchase probabilities, that is, into an estimate of actual buying behaviour. It takes survey data on consumers' preferences and converts it into actual purchase probabilities.

A survey might ask a question using a ranking scale such as :

Please rate the following products from 1 (most preferred) to 5 (least preferred.)

    ___ product A
    ___ product B
    ___ product C
    ___ product D
    ___ product E

A marketing researcher will re-specify the numerical values during codification.

a. Preference-rank translation
c. Logit analysis
b. Market analysis
d. Marketing research

86. _____ is a creative and commercial discipline that combines and utilizes many different design concepts together in the conceptualizing and construction of retail space. _____ is primarily a specialized practice of architecture and interior design, however it also incorporates elements of interior decoration, graphic design, ergonomics, and advertising.

_____ is a very specialized discipline due to the heavy demands placed on retail space.

a. Distinctiveness
c. Channel conflict
b. Retail design
d. Web 2.0

87. _____ is the examining of goods or services from retailers with the intent to purchase at that time. _____ is an activity of selection and/or purchase. In some contexts it is considered a leisure activity as well as an economic one.

a. Shopping
c. Khodebshchik
b. Discount store
d. Hawkers

88. _____ is the term given to the shopping trend whereby consumers offset almost all of their spending by making money from selling goods online. The trend was identified amongst users of eBay.co.uk based on analysis of over 100 million online transactions during 2007-2008.

Researchers at eBay documented the _____ trend in the 2008 eBaynomics[1] report, which identified the activity of a growing number of users who bought and sold on the site within a 10% value range.

- a. Situational theory of publics
- b. Rule Developing Experimentation
- c. Shopping Neutral
- d. Marketing buzz

89. The _____ defines that publics can be identified and classified in the context to which they are aware of the problem and the extent to which they do something about the problem.

The _____, developed by Professor James E. Grunig in University of Maryland, College Park, defines that publics can be identified and classified in the context to which they are aware of the problem and the extent to which they do something about the problem. This theory explains when people communicate and when communications aimed at people are most likely to be effective.

- a. Rule Developing Experimentation
- b. Diderot effect
- c. Consumer confidence
- d. Situational theory of publics

90. The _____ is an environmental strategy gaining ground in health campaigns. While conducting research in the mid 1980s, two researchers, H.W. Perkins and A.D. Berkowitz, discovered that students at a small U.S. college held exaggerated beliefs about the normal frequency and consumption habits of other students with regard to alcohol. These inflated perceptions were later found in universities of all types, with varying populations and locations.

- a. Trade secret
- b. Madrid system
- c. Social Norms Approach
- d. Comparative negligence

Chapter 7. Test Preparation Part 7

1. _____ is defined by the American _____ Association as the activity, set of institutions, and processes for creating, communicating, delivering, and exchanging offerings that have value for customers, clients, partners, and society at large. The term developed from the original meaning which referred literally to going to market, as in shopping, or going to a market to sell goods or services.

_____ practice tends to be seen as a creative industry, which includes advertising, distribution and selling.

  a. Marketing myopia
  b. Product naming
  c. Customer acquisition management
  d. Marketing

2. _____ was founded in 1986 by its founder, Nye Lavalle and his family, the Pews. Established first in Boca Raton, Florida, to serve advertising agencies and public relations firms, _____ by 1988 became a more client-centric organization moving to Detroit, New York and Dallas to advise clients directly, while maintaining its connections with leading advertising and PR firms on Madison Avenue.

Unlike other sports marketing agencies, _____ was created as a sports and sponsorship research consultancy using the application of scientific marketing research principles in the emerging sports, sponsorship and sports marketing industries.

  a. AStore
  b. Sampling
  c. Richard Buckminster 'Bucky' Fuller
  d. Sports Marketing Group

3. _____ is a United States term for the feeling of surprise experienced by consumers upon finding unexpectedly high prices on the price tags (stickers) of products they are considering purchasing. The term is commonly thought to have originated with high automobile sticker prices in the U.S. in the late 1970s or early 1980s, as inflation and increasing government regulation of automotive safety and environmental issues greatly increased car prices.
  a. 180SearchAssistant
  b. Power III
  c. 6-3-5 Brainwriting
  d. Sticker shock

4. A _____ is a collection of symbols, experiences and associations connected with a product, a service, a person or any other artifact or entity.

_____s have become increasingly important components of culture and the economy, now being described as 'cultural accessories and personal philosophies'.

Some people distinguish the psychological aspect of a _____ from the experiential aspect.

  a. Store brand
  b. Brand
  c. Brand equity
  d. Brandable software

5. A _____ is a community formed on the basis of attachment to a product or marque. Recent developments in marketing and in research in consumer behavior result in stressing the connection between brand, individual identity and culture. Among the concepts developed to explain the behavior of consumers, the concept of a _____ focuses on the connections between consumers.
  a. Customer intimacy
  b. Customer Integrated System
  c. Foviance
  d. Brand community

6. Customer Operations Performance Center Incorporated is a privately held international customer service support company based in Austin, Texas. _____ redesigns business processes for customer contact center and business process outsourcing services, offering training, consulting and certification services.

   a. COPC Inc.
   b. Customer service
   c. Facing
   d. Customer lifecycle management

7. _____ is the sum of all experiences a customer has with a supplier of goods or services, over the duration of their relationship with that supplier. It can also be used to mean an individual experience over one transaction; the distinction is usually clear in context.

Analysts and commentators who write about _____ and CRM have increasingly recognized the importance of managing the customer's experience.

   a. Customer Integrated System
   b. COPC Inc.
   c. Customer Experience
   d. Customer service

8. _____ uses software to identify and analyze customer behavior patterns within and across multiple access points.

_____ solutions use sophisticated data modeling techniques to analyze customer experiences with a company. Customers contact companies for a variety of reasons (service, sales, feedback) and use a variety of methods to interact (websites, phone, kiosks, mobile devices, etc.).

   a. Customer service
   b. Customer experience
   c. Customer Experience Analytics
   d. Customer lifecycle management

9. A _____ is an extension or hybrid of the Transaction Processing System (TPS) that places technology in the hands of the customer and allows them to process their own transactions. _____ represents a way of doing business at substantial savings; customers save time and organizations can lower their human resource costs.

In 1992, Bergen Brunswig, a distributor of diversified drug and health care products, unintentionally created a _____.

   a. Customer experience
   b. Customer Integrated System
   c. Music on hold
   d. Customer lifecycle management

10. _____ are integrated business and operational support systems (BSS/OSS) that particularly address service providers' mandate of focusing on the customer experience.

In the past, service providers (wireline, wireless, broadband cable, satellite) and other companies competed through product differentiation and price points. Today, with products more and more commoditized and price differences negligible, the remaining differentiator is how well a company can deliver a customer experience that is personalized, rewarding, and meets customer needs.

a. 6-3-5 Brainwriting
c. Power III
b. Customer experience systems
d. 180SearchAssistant

11. _____ is the collection, deployment and translation of information that allows a business to acquire, develop and retain their customers.

Firslty, the collected data must be audited to fully understand the quality and opportunity within the database. Once this is done, there are a number of different types of analysis that can be applied.

a. Fifth screen
c. Societal marketing
b. Customer analytics
d. Customer insight

12. _____ is the process of gathering and analysing information regarding customers; their details and their activities, in order to build deeper and more effective customer relationships and improve strategic decision making.

Consumer Intelligence is also the name of a leading company within the UK Research industry that is referenced in large number of Advertising campaigns by companies such as Asda, Budget Compare The Market, Churchill, Direct Line, MoneySupermarket, Norwich Union and many others.

_____ is a key component of effective Customer Relationship Management, and when effectively implemented it is a rich source of insight into the behaviour and experience of a company's customer base.

a. Pop-up ads
c. Power III
b. Project Portfolio Management
d. Customer intelligence

13. _____ is based on the ability of the supplier to become accepted and known as the regular partner. _____ creates a virtuous circle: the better the supplier knows the customer company with its objectives and difficulties, the better able he is to provide an optimal solution. The more adapted the supplier's product or service is, the happier the customer will be, and the stronger the 'intimacy' between the two parties.

a. COPC Inc.
c. Customer experience
b. Customer intimacy
d. Customer lifecycle management

14. _____, or _____ is the measurement of multiple customer related metrics, which, when analyzed for a period of time, indicate performance of a business. The overall scope of the _____ implementation process encompasses all domains or departments of an organization, which generally brings all sources of static and dynamic data, marketing processes, and value added services to a unified decision supporting platform through iterative phases of customer acquisition, retention, cross and up-selling, and lapsed customer win-back.

Some detailed _____ models further breakdown these phases into acquisition, introduction to products, profiling of customers, growth of customer base, cultivation of loyalty among customers, and termination of customer relationship.

a. Customer service
c. Customer Integrated System
b. Customer lifecycle management
d. Customer experience

Chapter 7. Test Preparation Part 7

15. _____ consists of the processes a company uses to track and organize its contacts with its current and prospective customers. _____ software is used to support these processes; information about customers and customer interactions can be entered, stored and accessed by employees in different company departments. Typical _____ goals are to improve services provided to customers, and to use customer contact information for targeted marketing.
- a. Product bundling
- b. Commercialization
- c. Demand generation
- d. Customer relationship management

16. Customer _____ consists of the processes a company uses to track and organize its contacts with its current and prospective customers. CRelationship management software is used to support these processes; information about customers and customer interactions can be entered, stored and accessed by employees in different company departments. Typical CRelationship management goals are to improve services provided to customers, and to use customer contact information for targeted marketing.
- a. Relationship management
- b. Green marketing
- c. Marketing
- d. Product bundling

17. _____ is the provision of service to customers before, during and after a purchase.

According to Turban et al., '_____ is a series of activities designed to enhance the level of customer satisfaction - that is, the feeling that a product or service has met the customer expectation.'

Its importance varies by product, industry and customer.

- a. Facing
- b. COPC Inc.
- c. Customer experience
- d. Customer service

18. _____ is an advertisement in which a particular product specifically mentions a competitor by name for the express purpose of showing why the competitor is inferior to the product naming it.

This should not be confused with parody advertisements, where a fictional product is being advertised for the purpose of poking fun at the particular advertisement, nor should it be confused with the use of a coined brand name for the purpose of comparing the product without actually naming an actual competitor. ('Wikipedia tastes better and is less filling than the Encyclopedia Galactica.')

In the 1980s, during what has been referred to as the cola wars, soft-drink manufacturer Pepsi ran a series of advertisements where people, caught on hidden camera, in a blind taste test, chose Pepsi over rival Coca-Cola.

- a. Heavy-up
- b. Comparative advertising
- c. GL-70
- d. Cost per conversion

19. _____ or _____ is a business method in relationship management beyond customer relationship management.

'_____ - Enterprise relationship management is basically a business strategy for value creation that is not based on cost containment, but rather on the leveraging of network-enabled processes and activities to transform the relationships between the organization and all its internal and external constituencies in order to maximize current and future opportunities.' [Galbreath, 2002]

The art of relationship management is not an entirely new one. In fact, it has taken on many forms, addressing specific organizational constituencies (customers, channel partners, specialized service providers, employees, suppliers, etc.)

a. ACNielsen
b. ADTECH
c. AMAX
d. Enterprise relationship management

20. _____,, is a common tool in the retail industry to create the look of a perfectly stocked store by pulling all of the products on a display or shelf to the front, as well as downstacking all the canned and stacked items. It is also done to keep the store appearing neat and organized.

The workers who face commonly have jobs doing other things in the store such as customer service, stocking shelves, daytime cleaning, bagging and carryouts, etc.

a. Foviance
b. Customer Experience Analytics
c. Customer Integrated System
d. Facing

21. _____ is a customer experience consultancy based in London, UK. The company provides user experience, usability, analytics, accessibility and research consulting services to clients worldwide. _____ was originally founded as The Usability Company in 2001, by Catriona Campbell, a noted figure in the UK internet industry.

a. Customer Integrated System
b. Facing
c. Customer experience
d. Foviance

22. In economics and sociology, an _____ is any factor (financial or non-financial) that enables or motivates a particular course of action, or counts as a reason for preferring one choice to the alternatives. It is an expectation that encourages people to behave in a certain way. Since human beings are purposeful creatures, the study of _____ structures is central to the study of all economic activity (both in terms of individual decision-making and in terms of co-operation and competition within a larger institutional structure.)

a. Incentive
b. AMAX
c. ACNielsen
d. ADTECH

23. An _____ is a formal scheme used to promote or encourage specific actions or behavior by a specific group of people during a defined period of time. _____s are particularly used in business management to motivate employees, and in sales in order to attract and retain customers.

If programs are to be effective, all the factors that affect behavior must be recognized, including: motivation, skills, recognition, an understanding of the goals, and the ability to measure progress.

a. Incentive program
b. Advertiser funded programming
c. All commodity volume
d. Electronic retailing self-regulation program

24. _____

Algorithmic based profiling of leads in order to filter based on a set of predefined criteria.

The practice is becoming increasingly popular in a world of web based server centric CRM software.

An example of this would be generating a score for each client visiting a web site, or reading an email, to determine who is interested in a specific page or offer on a website, or email.

a. Macromarketing
b. Customer acquisition management
c. SWOT analysis
d. Lead scoring

25. On an intranet or B2E Enterprise Web portals, personalization is often based on user attributes such as department, functional area, or role. The term _____ in this context refers to the ability of users to modify the page layout or specify what content should be displayed.

There are two categories of personalizations:

1. Rule-based
2. Content-based

Web personalization models include rules-based filtering, based on 'if this, then that' rules processing, and collaborative filtering, which serves relevant material to customers by combining their own personal preferences with the preferences of like-minded others. Collaborative filtering works well for books, music, video, etc.

a. Cashmere Agency
b. Customization
c. Movin'
d. Self branding

26. _____ refers to the business practice of playing pre-recorded music to fill the silence that would be heard by telephone callers that have been placed on hold. It is especially common in situations involving customer service.

Most _____ systems are integrated into a businesses telephone system via an audio jack on the telephone equipment labeled '_____'.

a. Foviance
b. Facing
c. Music on hold
d. Customer lifecycle management

27. _____ is a company that specializes in call center solutions. Headquartered in Saint Louis, Missouri, _____, Inc. is a Business Process Outsourcing (BPO) Company that ranks among the top consumer collection agencies in the United States.

Chapter 7. Test Preparation Part 7

a. Superbrands Council
c. Phorm

b. Hechsher
d. National Asset Recovery Services

28. _____ is subcontracting a process, such as product design or manufacturing, to a third-party company. The decision to outsource is often made in the interest of lowering cost or making better use of time and energy costs, redirecting or conserving energy directed at the competencies of a particular business, or to make more efficient use of land, labor, capital, (information) technology and resources. _____ became part of the business lexicon during the 1980s.
   a. Outsourcing
   c. Intangible assets

b. In-house
d. ACNielsen

29. _____ is the business discipline widely adopted by companies and public institutions to manage one or more external service providers as part of an outsourcing strategy. _____ is a broadly used term that encompasses elements of organizational structure, management strategy and information technology infrastructure.

Outsourcing gained prominence as a business strategy in the early/mid 1980's and was originally driven by the desire to reduce costs in labor-intensive business processes.

   a. European Information Technology Observatory
   c. All commodity volume

b. Outsourcing relationship management
d. Account-based marketing

30. _____ is a service provided by many retailers of various products, primarily electronics, that provides the end-user with a resource for information regarding the product, and help if the product should malfunction. _____ can be found in most manuals for products in the form of a phone number, website address, or physical location.

The Internet has allowed for a new form of _____ to develop.

   a. Product support
   c. Psychological pricing

b. Price-weighted
d. Product life cycle

31. _____ refers to planned and systematic production processes that provide confidence in a product's suitability for its intended purpose. Refer to the definition by Merriam-Webster for further information. It is a set of activities intended to ensure that products (goods and/or services) satisfy customer requirements in a systematic, reliable fashion.
   a. Power III
   c. 6-3-5 Brainwriting

b. 180SearchAssistant
d. Quality Assurance

32. _____ is a service provided by SWIFT to manage the business relationships between financial institutions.

_____ operates by managing which message types are permitted to be exchanged between users of a SWIFT service:

- the receiver specifies which message types are permitted, and sends this permission data to the sender,
- the sender checks the message type against the permission data before sending a message to the receiver.

_____ uses a SWIFTNet InterAct Store and Forward service to exchange the permission data between financial institutions.

_____ is initially scheduled for roll-out on the SWIFT FIN service as part of the SWIFTNet Phase 2 project in 2008 .

a. Personalization
c. Lobbying and Disclosure Act of 1995
b. Parity Product
d. Relationship Management Application

33. _____ is a protocol designed and supported by SWIFT. The protocol is used to exchange financial messages between organizations connected to services on the SWIFTNet network .

_____ is a client-server protocol.

a. 180SearchAssistant
c. Power III
b. SWIFTNet InterAct Realtime
d. 6-3-5 Brainwriting

34. _____ is a protocol designed and supported by SWIFT. The protocol is used to exchange financial messages between organizations connected to services on to the SWIFTNet network . The FIN messaging Service , via which currently most SWIFT messages are still exchanged, is an InterAct Store and Forward Service.

a. Customer intimacy
c. Customer service
b. SWIFTNet InterAct Store and Forward
d. Customer Integrated System

35. A _____ is a systematic approach to selling a product or service. A growing body of published literature approaches the _____ from the point of view of an engineering discipline

Reasons for having a well thought-out _____ include seller and buyer risk management, standardized customer interaction in sales, and scalable revenue generation.

a. Request for proposal
c. Lead generation
b. Sales management
d. Sales process

36. _____ has been described as 'the systematic application of scientific and mathematical principles to achieve the practical goals of a particular sales process'. Selden pointed out that in this context, sales referred to the output of a process involving a variety of functions across an organization, and not that of a 'sales department' alone. Primary areas of application span functions including sales, marketing, and customer service.

a. 6-3-5 Brainwriting
c. Power III
b. Sales process engineering
d. 180SearchAssistant

Chapter 7. Test Preparation Part 7   123

37. _____ is a term used to describe automatic methods of analyzing speech to extract useful information about the speech content or the speakers. Although it often includes elements of automatic speech recognition, where the identities of spoken words or phrases are determined, it may also include analysis of one or more of the following:

- the topic(s) being discussed
- the identities of the speaker(s)
- the genders of the speakers
- the emotional character of the speech
- the amount and locations of speech versus non-speech (e.g. background noise or silence)

One use of _____ applications is to spot spoken keywords or phrases, either as real-time alerts on live audio or as a post-processing step on recorded speech. This technique is also known as audio mining. Other uses include categorization of speech, for example in the contact center environment, to identify calls from unsatisfied customers.

a. 180SearchAssistant
b. 6-3-5 Brainwriting
c. Power III
d. Speech analytics

38. _____ is a range of services providing assistance with technology products such as mobile phones, televisions, computers, or other electronic or mechanical goods. In general, _____ services attempt to help the user solve specific problems with a product--rather than providing training, customization, or other support services.

Most companies offer _____ for the products they sell, either freely available or for a fee.

a. 6-3-5 Brainwriting
b. 180SearchAssistant
c. Power III
d. Technical support

39. _____ is a customer experience business that helps large commercial clients monitor and improve their user experiences. The company was founded in 1988 with a focus on usability testing and has since grown to provide 20 user experience testing, research, consulting and software services. Offerings include: attitudinal analytics, usability testing, online user experience research, persona development, information architecture and taxonomy consulting and ethnography.

a. AMAX
b. ACNielsen
c. Usability Sciences
d. ADTECH

40. _____ is an international provider of E-Commerce and Configurator software with global annual revenue of â,¬11.07 million as of 2007. It develops, manufactures, licenses, and supports a Software Suite called Cameleon Commerce Suite. The company is headquartered in Toulouse, France and Chicago, Illinois, USA and has branches in cities such as Paris, France and Lyon, France.

a. Arbitron
b. IQ Beats
c. United States Patent and Trademark Office
d. Access Commerce

41. _____ is a method that involves compiling information from different accounts, which may include bank accounts, credit card accounts, investment accounts, and other consumer or business accounts, into a single place. This may include a database or may be provided through 'screen scraping' where a user provides the requisite account-access information for an automated system to gather and compile the information into a single page. Usually this database resides in a web-based application or in client-side software.

a. ACNielsen   b. ADTECH
c. AMAX   d. Account aggregation

42. An _____ is a computerized system which provides a non-profit organization basic database features to run its operations, such as member services, dues, event management, communications, product databases and fundraising.

Typically, an _____ will be linked to an association's public-facing website so that members and customers may interact with the association. These interactions may include purchasing memberships, products, events, and more.

a. Association Management System   b. ADTECH
c. AMAX   d. ACNielsen

43. _____, Inc. supplies product configurator, quoting, and proposal software to companies that sell complex products. The company's software aims to streamline the inquiry-to-order process for companies with large sales teams or distributor/VAR networks.
a. Mapinfo   b. ChoiceStream
c. Chief marketing officer   d. BigMachines

44. _____: A distribution term that refers to the status of items on a purchase order in the event that some or all of the inventory required to fulfill the order is insufficient to satisfy demand. This differs from a forward order where stock is available but delivery is postponed for another reason.

_____ Cost: A cost incurred by a business when it is unable to fill an order and must complete it later.

a. Discontinuation   b. Chief privacy officer
c. Backorder   d. Shop fitting

45. _____ is a term used in the retail industry. Retailers contract with their suppliers to supply a quantity of product in a specified time period to a specific location at an agreed price. The retailer 'calls off' the production of the product to match the expected or actual sales curves, depending on the stage in the life-cycle of the product.
a. Balance of contract   b. Nielsen VideoScan
c. Gear Acquisition Syndrome   d. Pallet Rack Mover

46. _____ was cofounded in 1994 by Billy Prim and Andrew Filipowski, both North Carolina businessmen, with the goal of building a national brand of propane tank exchange that would capitalize on the growth in gas grill sales and year-round grilling. At the time, propane tank exchange was viewed as a commodity and a large number of consumers got their tanks filled by various vendors.

A national distribution network was constructed and retailer partnerships were established.

a. Wholesale list   b. Teleflorist
c. Blue Rhino   d. Factory direct

47. The _____ is an observed phenomenon in forecast-driven distribution channels. The concept has its roots in J Forrester's Industrial Dynamics (1961) and thus it is also known as the Forrester Effect. Since the oscillating demand magnification upstream a supply chain reminds someone of a cracking whip it became famous as the _____.
   a. Wholesale list
   b. Free box
   c. Bullwhip effect
   d. Nielsen VideoScan

48. _____ wholesale represents a type of operation within the wholesale sector. Its main features are summarized best by the following definitions:

   - _____ is a form of trade in which goods are sold from a wholesale warehouse operated either on a self-service basis, or on the basis of samples (with the customer selecting from specimen articles using a manual or computerized ordering system but not serving himself) or a combination of the two. Customers (retailers, professional users, caterers, institutional buyers, etc.) settle the invoice on the spot and in cash, and carry the goods away themselves.

   - Though wholesalers buy primarily from manufacturers and sell mostly to retailers, industrial users and other wholesalers, they also perform many value added functions. The wholesaler, an intermediary, is used based on principles of specialisation and division of labour as well as contractual efficiency. (OECD -Organisation for Economic Cooperation and Development.)

   a. Self branding
   b. Davie Brown Index
   c. Containerization
   d. Cash and carry

49. Wholesaling, historically called jobbing, is the sale of goods or merchandise to retailers, to industrial, commercial, institutional or to other wholesalers and related subordinated services.

According to the United Nations Statistics Division, '_____' is the resale (sale without transformation) of new and used goods to retailers, to industrial, commercial, institutional or professional users or involves acting as an agent or broker in buying merchandise for such persons or companies. Wholesalers frequently physically assemble, sort and grade goods in large lots, break bulk, repack and redistribute in smaller lots.

   a. Wholesale
   b. Supply network
   c. Purchasing
   d. Supply chain network

50. A _____ is a business operated under a contract or license associated with a degree of exclusivity in business within a certain geographical area. For example, sports arenas or public parks may have _____ stands. Many department stores contain numerous _____s operated by other retailers.
   a. Promotion
   b. Strict liability
   c. Gross Margin Return on Inventory Investment
   d. Concession

51. In a _____, end-user demand drives all activities among trading partners.

_____ distinguishes between actions that provide customers with real value, and actions which just add costs. It facilitates and possibly maximizes collaboration with suppliers.

a. Reverse auction
b. Materials management
c. Customer driven supply chain
d. Vendor Managed Inventory

52. A _____ or logistics network is the system of organizations, people, technology, activities, information and resources involved in moving a product or service from supplier to customer. _____ activities transform natural resources, raw materials and components into a finished product that is delivered to the end customer. In sophisticated _____ systems, used products may re-enter the _____ at any point where residual value is recyclable.
   a. Supply chain network
   b. Supply chain
   c. Purchasing
   d. Demand chain management

53. A _____ is an inventory management procedure where a small subset of inventory is counted on any given day. _____s contrast with traditional physical inventory in that physical inventory stops operation at a facility and all items are counted, audited, and recounted at one time. _____s are less disruptive to daily operations, provide an ongoing measure of inventory accuracy and procedure execution, and can be tailored to focus on items with higher value or higher movement.
   a. Free box
   b. Cycle count
   c. Pallet rack
   d. Blue Rhino

54. In economics, _____ is the desire to own something and the ability to pay for it. The term _____ signifies the ability or the willingness to buy a particular commodity at a given point of time .

   a. Market dominance
   b. Discretionary spending
   c. Market system
   d. Demand

55. _____ is the management of upstream and downstream relationships between suppliers and customers to deliver the best value to the customer at the least cost to the demand chain as a whole. The term _____ is used to denote the concept commonly referred to as supply chain management, however with special regard to the customer pull . In that sense, _____ software tools bridge the gap between the customer relationship management and the supply chain management .
   a. Purchasing
   b. Wholesale
   c. Demand chain management
   d. Supply chain

56. _____, Inc. (often called Diamond Comics, _____, or casually Diamond) is the largest comic book distributor serving North America. They transport comic books from both big and small comic book publishers, or suppliers, to the retailers.
   a. New Media Strategies
   b. VoloMedia
   c. Point of sale
   d. Diamond Comic Distributors

57. _____ is one of the four elements of marketing mix. An organization or set of organizations (go-betweens) involved in the process of making a product or service available for use or consumption by a consumer or business user.

The other three parts of the marketing mix are product, pricing, and promotion.

a. Comparison-Shopping agent
b. Better Living Through Chemistry
c. Japan Advertising Photographers' Association
d. Distribution

58. The _____ is the dominant distribution and retail network for North American comic books. It consists of one dominant distributor and the majority of comics specialty stores, as well as other retailers of comic books and related merchandise. The name is no longer a fully accurate description of the model by which it operates, but derives from its original implementation: retailers bypassing existing distributors to make 'direct' purchases from publishers.
   a. 6-3-5 Brainwriting
   b. Direct market
   c. 180SearchAssistant
   d. Power III

59. _____ are reductions to a basic price of goods or services. They can occur anywhere in the distribution channel, modifying either the manufacturer's list price (determined by the manufacturer and often printed on the package), the retail price (set by the retailer and often attached to the product with a sticker), or the list price (which is quoted to a potential buyer, usually in written form.) The market price (also called effective price) is the amount actually paid.
   a. Price points
   b. Price shading
   c. Discounts and allowances
   d. Price

60. A _____ for a set of products is a warehouse or other specialized building, often with refrigeration or air conditioning, which is stocked with products (goods) to be re-distributed to retailers, wholesalers or directly to consumers. A _____ is a principle part, the 'order processing' element, of the entire 'order fulfillment' process. _____s are usually thought of as being 'demand driven'.
   a. 180SearchAssistant
   b. 6-3-5 Brainwriting
   c. Distribution center
   d. Power III

61. _____ is a supply chain management technique in which the retailer does not keep goods in stock, but instead transfers customer orders and shipment details to either the manufacturer or a wholesaler, who then ships the goods directly to the customer. As in all retail businesses, the retailers make their profit on the difference between the wholesale and retail price.

Some _____ retailers may keep 'show' items on display in stores, so that customers can inspect an item similar to those that they can purchase.

   a. Supply chain
   b. Supply chain network
   c. Supply network
   d. Drop shipping

62. _____ is a term used to explain when a manufacturer sells directly to the end-user of a product. Most products bought and sold by consumers are purchased through intermediaries and in many cases can include two tiers made up of distributors and resellers.

Each selling tier adds cost to the product.

   a. Symbol group
   b. Supply chain optimization
   c. Factory direct
   d. Teleflorist

63. _____ is anytime that you leave the origin of a product or things of that nature intentionally vauge to try and profit from it.

a. False designation of origin
c. Blue Rhino
b. Gear Acquisition Syndrome
d. Supply chain optimization

Chapter 8. Test Preparation Part 8

1. _____ is one of the four elements of marketing mix. An organization or set of organizations (go-betweens) involved in the process of making a product or service available for use or consumption by a consumer or business user.

The other three parts of the marketing mix are product, pricing, and promotion.

   a. Distribution
   b. Japan Advertising Photographers' Association
   c. Better Living Through Chemistry
   d. Comparison-Shopping agent

2. A _____ is a fee that a person pays to operate a franchise branch of a larger company and enjoy the profits therefrom.

By joining a franchise an investor or franchisee is able to run a business under the umbrella of the franchise.

The franchisee must pay a _____, which may become costly.

   a. Franchising
   b. Franchise fee
   c. Power III
   d. 180SearchAssistant

3. A _____ is the price one pays as remuneration for services, especially the honorarium paid to a doctor, lawyer, consultant, or other member of a learned profession. _____s usually allow for overhead, wages, costs, and markup.

Traditionally, professionals in Great Britain received a _____ in contradistinction to a payment, salary, or wage, and would often use guineas rather than pounds as units of account.

   a. Fee
   b. Transfer pricing
   c. Price war
   d. Price shading

4. _____ refers to the methods of practicing and using another person's philosophy of business. The franchisor grants the independent operator the right to distribute its products, techniques, and trademarks for a percentage of gross monthly sales and a royalty fee. Various tangibles and intangibles such as national or international advertising, training, and other support services are commonly made available by the franchisor.

   a. Franchising
   b. Power III
   c. Franchise fee
   d. 180SearchAssistant

5. A _____ is a box used to allow for people to rid themselves of excess items without the inconvenience of a garage sale. When someone has items they wish to be rid of, but which might be useful to another person, they are set out and given to whomever wants them. If, after a period, no one has claimed the items, the contents of the box may be dumped.

   a. Nielsen VideoScan
   b. Supply chain optimization
   c. Reverse vending machine
   d. Free box

6. A _____ is a payment card for petrol (gasoline), diesel and other fuels at filling stations. Account balances are cleared in full when due and payment terms vary depending on the supplier and can be anything from weekly to monthly. One of the main reasons _____s are popular is the elimination of the requirement for cash at filling stations and the perceived increase in security.

   a. Fuel card
   b. 6-3-5 Brainwriting
   c. Power III
   d. 180SearchAssistant

7. A _____ is a company specializing in product fulfillment services, on behalf of the product owner.

Fulfillment, also known as order fulfillment or product fulfillment, is the process where by a person or company fulfills their obligations to send a person an item or product that the person has ordered, purchased, or requested from the organization.

Fulfillment typically will refer to the services provided by a company that offers to store, receive the orders, package, and then ship the ordered item to the end consumer.

a. Vendor Managed Inventory
b. Materials management
c. Fulfillment house
d. Reverse auction

8. _____ is the company with the most widespread sales network in Serbia and own distribution to support the company's basic activity - wholesale and retail sale of consumer goods, newspapers, non-alcoholic beverages and confectionery.

In addition to being the leader in its segment in Serbia, _____ has established itself as one of the leading companies in this activity in south-eastern Europe.

In 2006, _____ opened the first of its Minut2 retail outlets, a true novelty in this part of the Balkans.

a. Physical inventory
b. Supply chain optimization
c. Futura plus
d. Symbol group

9. _____ is a term used to describe an urge to acquire and accumulate lots of gear. This term commonly associated with:

- Guitarists (tend to acquire guitars, guitar amplifiers, pedals, effects processors, etc.)
- Keyboard / synth players (keyboards, synthesizers, samplers, effects units, etc.)
- Drummers (various drums, percussion, drumsticks, etc.)
- Photographers (cameras, its parts and accessories -- bodies, video cameras, lens, mounts, filters, flashes, lighting rigs, etc.)
- Audiophiles (high-end preamps, amplifiers, converters, CD players, speakers, etc.)
- Clarinetists (clarinets, reeds, barrels, bells, mouthpieces, ligatures, reed cases, etc.)
- Saxophonists (saxophones, reeds, mouthpieces, etcA.S. in Guitar Player as 'Guitar Acquisition Syndrome'. The term started to be frequently used by guitarists and spread out to other people of creative professions who were familiar with similar tendencies. As it no longer concerned guitars only, _____ became a backronym for '_____'.

a. Gear Acquisition Syndrome
b. Thomas Register
c. Blue Rhino
d. Symbol group

10. The _____ is the distribution of refurbished, used, repaired, recycled, discontinued or new products that are in working condition. They are sold through brokers and resellers, not through the original manufacturer. These goods are suitable for resale to customers as a lower cost alternative to buying new goods from standard distribution channels such as retail stores.

a. Customs union
c. Grey market
b. Free trade zone
d. Green market

11. A _____ or gray market is the trade of a commodity through distribution channels which, while legal, are unofficial, unauthorized, or unintended by the original manufacturer. In contrast, a black market is the trade of goods and services that are illegal in themselves and/or distributed through illegal channels, such as the selling of stolen goods or illegal items such as heroin or unregistered handguns.

The two main types of _____ are imported manufactured goods that would be normally unavailable or more expensive in a certain country and unissued securities that are not yet traded in official markets.

a. Green market
c. Grey market
b. Countervailing duties
d. Zone pricing

12. _____ is a blanket term used for pre-recorded media that is either sold or hired for home entertainment. The term originates from the VHS/Betamax era but has carried over into the current DVD/Blu-ray Disc age. The first company to duplicate and distribute _____ was Magnetic Video, established in 1968.
a. Power III
c. 180SearchAssistant
b. Home video
d. 6-3-5 Brainwriting

13. In commerce, a _____ is a superstore which combines a supermarket and a department store. The result is a very large retail facility which carries an enormous range of products under one roof, including full lines of groceries and general merchandise. In theory, _____s allow customers to satisfy all their routine weekly shopping needs in one trip.
a. 180SearchAssistant
c. Hypermarket
b. Power III
d. 6-3-5 Brainwriting

14. Radio-frequency identification (_____) is the use of an object (typically referred to as an _____ tag) applied to or incorporated into a product, animal, or person for the purpose of identification and tracking using radio waves. Some tags can be read from several meters away and beyond the line of sight of the reader.

Most _____ tags contain at least two parts.

a. 180SearchAssistant
c. RFID
b. Power III
d. 6-3-5 Brainwriting

15. _____ is a book distributor, founded in 1971 to exclusively market titles from independent client publishers to the book trade. _____ combines its client publishers' books into a single list, offering small and mid-size publishers the advantages of a marketing and sales force comparable to that of a major publishing house. _____'s distribution services include warehousing, bill collecting, customer service, and trade sales management, all of which allow publishers to concentrate on the acquisition, editorial, design, and promotional sides of the business.
a. Independent Publishers Group
c. ADTECH
b. ACNielsen
d. AMAX

16. _____ is a list for goods and materials held available in stock by a business. It is also used for a list of the contents of a household and for a list for testamentary purposes of the possessions of someone who has died. In accounting _____ is considered an asset.

a. Ending Inventory
c. Inventory
b. ADTECH
d. ACNielsen

17. _____ is a point-of-sale technology used by retailers that accept FSA debit cards, which are issued for use with medical flexible spending accounts (FSAs), health reimbursement accounts (HRAs), and some health savings accounts (HSAs) in the United States.

By the end of 2007, all grocery stores, discount stores, and online pharmacies that accept FSA debit cards must have an _____; by the end of 2008, most chain pharmacies must have an _____ as well.

The predecessor to the current _____ was developed by the online retailer drugstore.com for its 'FSA store' in 2005; it was first introduced to brick-and-mortar retailing by Walgreens in 2006.

a. ADTECH
c. AMAX
b. Inventory Information Approval System
d. ACNielsen

18. A _____ is a type of wholesale merchant business that buys goods and bulk products from importers, other wholesalers and then sells to retailers. _____s can deal in any commodity destined for the retail market. Typical categories are food, lumber, hardware, fuel, and textiles.

a. Chief privacy officer
c. Jobbing house
b. Refusal to deal
d. Tacit collusion

19. _____ describes an unwanted loss of something which escapes from its proper location. In everyday usage, _____ is the gradual escape of matter through a leak-hole. In different fields, the term may have specialized meanings.

a. 6-3-5 Brainwriting
c. Power III
b. 180SearchAssistant
d. Leakage

20. Merchandising refers to the methods, practices and operations conducted to promote and sustain certain categories of commercial activity. The term is understood to have different specific meanings depending on the context. _____ is a sale goods at a store

In marketing, one of the definitions of merchandising is the practice in which the brand or image from one product or service is used to sell another.

a. Merchandise
c. Sales promotion
b. New Media Strategies
d. Merchandising

21. When opened in 1930, the _____ or the Mart, located in Chicago, Illinois, was the largest building in the world with 4,000,000 square feet (372,000 m^2) of floor space. Previously owned by the Marshall Field family, the Mart centralized Chicago's wholesale goods business by consolidating vendors and trade under a single roof. Massive in its construction, and serving as a monument to early 20th century merchandising and architecture, the art deco landmark anchors the daytime skyline at the junction of the Chicago River branches.

a. John F. Kennedy International Airport
c. BSI Group
b. Merchandise Mart
d. Population Reference Bureau

Chapter 8. Test Preparation Part 8

22. A _____ is an automated information system to keep track of the inventory in a warehouse or store. Usually the merchandise can be grouped into product lines. Thus, the _____ shows the exact number of products a business has in stock at any particular time.
   a. Materials management
   b. Reverse auction
   c. Fulfillment house
   d. Merchandise management system

23. _____s function as professionals who deal with trade, dealing in commodities that they do not produce themselves, in order to produce profit.

   _____s can be of two types:

   1. A wholesale _____ operates in the chain between producer and retail _____. Some wholesale _____s only organize the movement of goods rather than move the goods themselves.
   2. A retail _____ or retailer, sells commodities to consumers (including businesses.) A shop owner is a retail _____.

   A _____ class characterizes many pre-modern societies. Its status can range from high (even achieving titles like that of _____ prince or nabob) to low, such as in Chinese culture, due to the soiling capabilities of profiting from 'mere' trade, rather than from the labor of others reflected in agricultural produce, craftsmanship, and tribute.

   In the United States, '_____' is defined (under the Uniform Commercial Code) as any person while engaged in a business or profession or a seller who deals regularly in the type of goods sold.

   a. Retail loss prevention
   b. RFM
   c. Trade credit
   d. Merchant

24. _____ or Mystery Consumer is a tool used by market research companies to measure quality of retail service or gather specific information about products and services. Mystery shoppers posing as normal customers perform specific tasks-- such as purchasing a product, asking questions, registering complaints or behaving in a certain way - and then provide detailed reports or feedback about their experiences.

   _____ began in the 1940s as a way to measure employee integrity.

   a. Questionnaire
   b. Market research
   c. Mystery shoppers
   d. Mystery shopping

25. _____ is the examining of goods or services from retailers with the intent to purchase at that time. _____ is an activity of selection and/or purchase. In some contexts it is considered a leisure activity as well as an economic one.
   a. Shopping
   b. Khodebshchik
   c. Hawkers
   d. Discount store

26. _____ is an information system created by Mike Fine and Mike Shalett that tracks sales of music and music video products throughout the United States and Canada. Data is collected weekly and made available every Wednesday to subscribers, which include executives from all facets of record companies, publishing firms, music retailers, independent promoters, film and TV, and artist management. SoundScan is the sales source for the Billboard music charts.

a. Teleflorist
b. Factory direct
c. Nielsen VideoScan
d. Nielsen SoundScan

27. _____ is the partnership formed between the VideoScan and ACNielsen companies, each of which is owned by The Nielsen Company. _____ provides detailed point-of-sale data regarding sales of VHS videotape cassettes, DVDs, HD DVDs and Blu-ray Discs. The data is collected from VHS and DVD distribution outlets, such as retail stores, in the United States and Canada and then made available to clients in customized report form through the VideoScan website.
a. Nielsen VideoScan
b. Stock management
c. Gear Acquisition Syndrome
d. Reverse vending machine

28. The _____ was launched to standardize the application interface between the EPOS application and any cashless payments solution installed on the EFT/PoS terminal. The specification for this interface focused mainly on international and cross-industry aspects. Today, the interface is already a de facto European standard, which is spreading from Germany to retailing and mineral oil projects throughout Europe.
a. ACNielsen
b. Open Payment Initiative
c. ADTECH
d. AMAX

29. _____ is in the most general sense the complete process from point of sales inquiry to delivery of a product to the customer. Sometimes _____ is used to describe the more narrow act of distribution or the logistics function, however, in the broader sense it refers to the way firms respond to customer orders.

The first research towards defining _____ strategies was published by Mather and his discussion of the P:D ratio, whereby P is defined as the production lead-time, i.e. how long it takes to manufacture a product, and D is the demand lead-time, i.e. how long customers are willing to wait for the order to be completed.

a. Order fulfillment
b. AMAX
c. ACNielsen
d. ADTECH

30. _____, also referred to as 'pallet racking,' is a material handling storage aid system designed to store materials on pallets (or 'skids'.) Although there are many varieties of _____, all types allow for the storage of palletized materials in horizontal rows with multiple levels. All types of _____ create some level of increase storage density with the least dense being the least expensive and cost increasing with storage denisity.
a. Nielsen VideoScan
b. Bullwhip effect
c. Gear Acquisition Syndrome
d. Pallet Rack

31. A _____ is a device that makes it possible to move pallet rack without demo or the re-assembly of the storage system. They are designed to move the entire rack assembly as one unit rather than individual pieces, saving valuable labor costs.

_____s are typically separated into different classes depending on the weight capacity of the mover.

a. Factory direct
b. Reverse vending machine
c. Stock management
d. Pallet Rack Mover

32. _____ is a common expression for goods that an inventory accounting system considers to be on-hand at a storage location, but are not actually available. This could be due to the items being moved without recording the change in the inventory accounting system, breakage, theft, data entry errors or deliberate fraud. The resulting discrepancy between the online inventory balance and physical availability can delay automated reordering and lead to out-of-stock incidents.
- a. Phantom inventory
- b. Reorder point
- c. Finished good
- d. Cost of goods sold

33. _____ is a process where a business physically counts its entire inventory. A _____ may be mandated by financial accounting rules or the tax regulations to place an accurate value on the inventory, or the business may need to count inventory so component parts or raw materials can be restocked. Businesses may use several different tactics to minimize the disruption caused by _____.
- a. Reverse vending machine
- b. Teleflorist
- c. Blue Rhino
- d. Physical inventory

34. _____ is a part of a complete supply chain management focused on the needs of small retailers. It entails processing small to large quantities of product, often truck or train loads and disassembling them, picking the relevant product for each destination and re-packaging with shipping label affixed and invoice included. Usual service includes obtaining a fair rate of shipping from common as well as expediting truck carriers.
- a. Power III
- b. Pick and pack
- c. Promotional mix
- d. Product manager

35. A _____ is a device that accepts used (empty) beverage containers and returns money to the user (the reverse of the typical vending cycle.) The machines are popular in places that have mandatory recycling laws or container deposit legislation. In some places, bottlers paid funds into a centralized pool to be dispersed to people who recycled the containers. Any excess funds were to be used for general environmental cleanup. In other places, such as Norway, the state mandated that a vendor pay for recycled bottles, but left the system in the hands of private industry.
- a. Nielsen VideoScan
- b. Reverse vending machine
- c. Physical inventory
- d. Stock management

36. _____ is the difference between actual sales and budget sales. It is used to measure the performance of a sales function, and/or analyze business results to better understand market conditions.

There are two reasons actual sales can vary from planned sales: either the volume sold varied from plan (sales volume variance), or sales were at a different price from what was planned (sales price variance.)

- a. Sample sales
- b. Power III
- c. Sales variance
- d. 180SearchAssistant

37. In probability theory and statistics, the _____ of a random variable, probability distribution, or sample is a measure of statistical dispersion, averaging the squared distance of its possible values from the expected value (mean.) Whereas the mean is a way to describe the location of a distribution, the _____ is a way to capture its scale or degree of being spread out. The unit of _____ is the square of the unit of the original variable.
- a. Sample size
- b. Variance
- c. Correlation
- d. Standard deviation

38. _____ is an advertisement in which a particular product specifically mentions a competitor by name for the express purpose of showing why the competitor is inferior to the product naming it.

This should not be confused with parody advertisements, where a fictional product is being advertised for the purpose of poking fun at the particular advertisement, nor should it be confused with the use of a coined brand name for the purpose of comparing the product without actually naming an actual competitor. ('Wikipedia tastes better and is less filling than the Encyclopedia Galactica.')

In the 1980s, during what has been referred to as the cola wars, soft-drink manufacturer Pepsi ran a series of advertisements where people, caught on hidden camera, in a blind taste test, chose Pepsi over rival Coca-Cola.

a. Comparative advertising
b. Cost per conversion
c. GL-70
d. Heavy-up

39. _____ measures the performance of a system. Certain goals are defined and the _____ gives the percentage to which they should be achieved.

Examples

- Percentage of calls answered in a call center.
- Percentage of customers waiting less than a given fixed time.
- Percentage of customers that do not experience a stock out.

_____ is used in supply chain management and in inventory management to measure the performance of inventory systems.

Under stochastic conditions it is unavoidable that in some periods the inventory on hand is not sufficient to deliver the complete demand and, as a consequence, that part of the demand is filled only after an inventory-related waiting time.

a. False designation of origin
b. Symbol group
c. Nielsen SoundScan
d. Service level

40. In financial accounting the term inventory _____ is the loss of products between point of manufacture or purchase from supplier and point of sale. The total shrink percentage of the retail industry in the United States was 1.7% of sales in 2001 according to the University of Florida's, National Retail Security Survey.

48.5% of _____ in that time period was due to employee theft and 31.7% due to shoplifting.

a. Better Living Through Chemistry
b. M80
c. Davie Brown Index
d. Shrinkage

41. _____ is the function of understanding the stock mix of a company and the different demands on that stock. The demands are influenced by both external and internal factors and are balanced by the creation of Purchase order requests to keep supplies at a reasonable or prescribed level.

_____ in the retail supply chain follows the following sequence:

1. Request for new stock from stores to head office
2. Head office issues purchase orders to the vendor
3. Vendor ships the goods
4. Warehouse receives the goods
5. Warehouse stocks and distributes to the stores
6. Stores receive the goods
7. Goods are sold to customers at the stores

The management of the inventory in the supply chain involves managing the physical quantities as well as the costing of the goods as it flows through the supply chain.

In managing the cost prices of the goods throughout the supply chain, several costing methods are employed:

1. Retail method
2. Weighted Average Price method
3. FIFO (First In First Out) method
4. LIFO (Last In First Out) method
5. LPP (Last Purchase Price) method
6. BNM (Bottle neck method)

This is able to going with closer lead time of procurement on this method we save the company money very much, for this method we have to make a proper plan of their requirements, we plan for sub divisional equipments and less important products of concern but it must be plan the date of availability and near by vendor,to save money

The calculation can be done for different periods. If the calculation is done on a monthly basis, then it is referred to the periodic method.

a. Futura plus
c. Stock management

b. Pallet rack
d. Wholesale list

42. Obsolete stock or _____ calculations are done by companies to determine how much of their stock on hand is unlikely to be used in the future.

The financial value of _____ that is calculated can be entered into a general ledger system to create a '_____ provision' which can reduce the tax liability of a company. For this reason, a systematic and auditable approach to designing a _____ report should be used.

a. Stock obsolescence
c. Stock mix

b. Phantom inventory
d. Perpetual inventory

Chapter 8. Test Preparation Part 8

43. A _____ or logistics network is the system of organizations, people, technology, activities, information and resources involved in moving a product or service from supplier to customer. _____ activities transform natural resources, raw materials and components into a finished product that is delivered to the end customer. In sophisticated _____ systems, used products may re-enter the _____ at any point where residual value is recyclable.
   a. Supply chain network
   b. Purchasing
   c. Demand chain management
   d. Supply chain

44. Due to the rapid advancement of technology such as pervasive or ubiquitous wireless and internet networks, connective product marking technologies like RFID and emerging standards for the use of these defining specific locations using Global Location Number(s), the basic supply chain is rapidly evolving into what is known as a _____.

One of the first references to this term and concept was in the book 'The _____ @Internet Speed: Preparing Your Company for the E-Commerce Revolution' by Fred A.; Rosenbaum, Barbara A. Kuglin (Hardcover - 2000.)

The book 'Supply Chain Architecture' by William T. Walker (2004) was the first to integrate APICS concepts with inter-enterprise business processes.

   a. Slip sheet
   b. Demand chain management
   c. Megalister
   d. Supply chain network

45. _____ is the application of processes and tools to ensure the optimal operation of a manufacturing and distribution supply chain. This includes the optimal placement of inventory within the supply chain, minimizing operating costs (including manufacturing costs, transportation costs, and distribution costs.) This often involves the application of mathematical modelling techniques using computer software.
   a. Blue Rhino
   b. Supply chain optimization
   c. Futura plus
   d. Reverse vending machine

46. A _____ is a pattern of temporal and spatial processes carried out at facility nodes and over distribution links, which adds value for customers through the manufacturing and delivery of products. It comprises the general state of business affairs in which all kinds of material (work-in-process material as well as finished products) are transformed and moved between various value-add points to maximize the value added for customers.

A supply chain is a special instance of a _____ in which raw materials, intermediate materials and finished goods are procured exclusively as products through a chain of processes that supply one another.

   a. Wholesale
   b. Drop shipping
   c. Slip sheet
   d. Supply network

47. _____ is a mainly British term for a form of franchise in the retail sector. They do not own or operate stores, but act as suppliers to independent grocers and small supermarkets and produce stores which then trade under a common banner. Unlike other forms of franchise, they have expanded primarily by selling their services to existing stores, rather than by actively developing new outlets.
   a. Stock management
   b. Nielsen VideoScan
   c. Supply chain optimization
   d. Symbol group

Chapter 8. Test Preparation Part 8

48. _____ is the trading name for British Teleflower Service Limited, the largest flower relay service network in the UK and Ireland, with about 2000 florist members. _____ was established in 1947 in Hampshire, England, and has remained privately owned. _____ is part of Teleflor International and provides local flower delivery in 140 countries.
   a. False designation of origin
   b. Supply chain optimization
   c. Gear Acquisition Syndrome
   d. Teleflorist

49. The _____ of American Manufacturers is a multi-volume directory of industrial product information covering 650,000 distributors, manufacturers and service companies within 67,000-plus industrial categories. It was first published in 1898 by Harvey Mark Thomas as Hardware and Kindred Trades. The company stopped publishing its print products in 2006 due to declining circulation as Internet searches eroded the products' usability.
   a. Thomas Register
   b. Free box
   c. Stock management
   d. Futura plus

50. _____ is an abbreviation for '_____', a legal document used in the franchising process in the United States.

Franchisors must give a _____ to franchisees at least 10 business days before any contract is signed and before any money changes hands. It contains extensive information about a franchisor, which is intended to give potential franchisees enough information to make educated decisions about their investments.

   a. UFOC
   b. ACNielsen
   c. AMAX
   d. ADTECH

51. A _____ is a commercial building for storage of goods. _____s are used by manufacturers, importers, exporters, wholesalers, transport businesses, customs, etc. They are usually large plain buildings in industrial areas of cities and towns.
   a. Power III
   b. 6-3-5 Brainwriting
   c. 180SearchAssistant
   d. Warehouse

52. Wholesaling, historically called jobbing, is the sale of goods or merchandise to retailers, to industrial, commercial, institutional or to other wholesalers and related subordinated services.

According to the United Nations Statistics Division, '_____' is the resale (sale without transformation) of new and used goods to retailers, to industrial, commercial, institutional or professional users or involves acting as an agent or broker in buying merchandise for such persons or companies. Wholesalers frequently physically assemble, sort and grade goods in large lots, break bulk, repack and redistribute in smaller lots.

   a. Wholesale
   b. Purchasing
   c. Supply network
   d. Supply chain network

53. A _____ is a piece of compilational media (collection of information) providing details for various wholesale companies. One can use a _____ to save hours of researching about wholesaling companies as the producer of a _____ will already have done it. For example a _____ may contain details of companies which sell computers at wholesaler prices to customers.
   a. Wholesale list
   b. Teleflorist
   c. Pallet rack
   d. Pallet Rack Mover

54. _____ generally refers to a list of all planned expenses and revenues. It is a plan for saving and spending. A _____ is an important concept in microeconomics, which uses a _____ line to illustrate the trade-offs between two or more goods.

   a. Power III
   c. Budget
   b. 180SearchAssistant
   d. 6-3-5 Brainwriting

55. _____ is an international chain of convenience stores, originally founded in 1951, in El Paso, Texas. It is currently owned and operated by Alimentation Couche-Tard.

_____ is the largest company-owned convenience store chain in the U.S, and second in overall number of U.S. stores to 7-Eleven.

   a. Diamond Comic Distributors
   c. PayPerPost
   b. Circle K
   d. Checkoff

Chapter 9. Test Preparation Part 9

1. _____, a specialized category of professional assistance for investors, entrepreneurs, and enterprises, is a field which has arisen from the increased popularity and profitability of franchising.

Potential franchise owners employ franchise consultants to help choose the correct franchise company ('franchiser') in which to invest. Conversely, franchisers employ the franchise consultant to act as an agent between themselves and interested franchisees.

a. Franchising
b. Franchise consulting
c. Power III
d. 180SearchAssistant

2. A _____ is a fee that a person pays to operate a franchise branch of a larger company and enjoy the profits therefrom.

By joining a franchise an investor or franchisee is able to run a business under the umbrella of the franchise.

The franchisee must pay a _____, which may become costly.

a. Power III
b. Franchising
c. 180SearchAssistant
d. Franchise fee

3. A _____ is the price one pays as remuneration for services, especially the honorarium paid to a doctor, lawyer, consultant, or other member of a learned profession. _____s usually allow for overhead, wages, costs, and markup.

Traditionally, professionals in Great Britain received a _____ in contradistinction to a payment, salary, or wage, and would often use guineas rather than pounds as units of account.

a. Price war
b. Price shading
c. Transfer pricing
d. Fee

4. _____ is an advertisement in which a particular product specifically mentions a competitor by name for the express purpose of showing why the competitor is inferior to the product naming it.

This should not be confused with parody advertisements, where a fictional product is being advertised for the purpose of poking fun at the particular advertisement, nor should it be confused with the use of a coined brand name for the purpose of comparing the product without actually naming an actual competitor. ('Wikipedia tastes better and is less filling than the Encyclopedia Galactica.')

In the 1980s, during what has been referred to as the cola wars, soft-drink manufacturer Pepsi ran a series of advertisements where people, caught on hidden camera, in a blind taste test, chose Pepsi over rival Coca-Cola.

a. Heavy-up
b. GL-70
c. Cost per conversion
d. Comparative advertising

5. _____ is the management of the flow of goods, information and other resources, including energy and people, between the point of origin and the point of consumption in order to meet the requirements of consumers (frequently, and originally, military organizations.) _____ involves the integration of information, transportation, inventory, warehousing, material-handling, and packaging. _____ is a channel of the supply chain which adds the value of time and place utility.
   a. 180SearchAssistant
   b. 6-3-5 Brainwriting
   c. Logistics
   d. Power III

6. _____ is anything that is intended to save time, energy or frustration. A _____ store at a petrol station, for example, sells items that have nothing to do with gasoline/petrol, but it saves the consumer from having to go to a grocery store. '_____' is a very relative term and its meaning tends to change over time.
   a. Marketing buzz
   b. Demographic profile
   c. MaxDiff
   d. Convenience

Chapter 10. Test Preparation Part 10

1. _____ is a mainly British term for a form of franchise in the retail sector. They do not own or operate stores, but act as suppliers to independent grocers and small supermarkets and produce stores which then trade under a common banner. Unlike other forms of franchise, they have expanded primarily by selling their services to existing stores, rather than by actively developing new outlets.

   a. Supply chain optimization
   b. Symbol group
   c. Stock management
   d. Nielsen VideoScan

2. _____ is an abbreviation for '_____', a legal document used in the franchising process in the United States.

Franchisors must give a _____ to franchisees at least 10 business days before any contract is signed and before any money changes hands. It contains extensive information about a franchisor, which is intended to give potential franchisees enough information to make educated decisions about their investments.

   a. ACNielsen
   b. UFOC
   c. AMAX
   d. ADTECH

3. _____ is the practice of using video games to advertise a product, organization or viewpoint. The term 'advergames' was coined in January 2000 by Anthony Giallourakis, and later mentioned by Wired's 'Jargon Watch' column in 2001. It has been applied to various free online games commissioned by major companies.

   a. AMAX
   b. Advergaming
   c. ACNielsen
   d. ADTECH

4. _____ is a form of communication that typically attempts to persuade potential customers to purchase or to consume more of a particular brand of product or service. 'While now central to the contemporary global economy and the reproduction of global production networks, it is only quite recently that _____ has been more than a marginal influence on patterns of sales and production. The formation of modern _____ was intimately bound up with the emergence of new forms of monopoly capitalism around the end of the 19th and beginning of the 20th century as one element in corporate strategies to create, organize and where possible control markets, especially for mass produced consumer goods.

   a. ADTECH
   b. ACNielsen
   c. AMAX
   d. Advertising

5. An _____ is usually a term reserved for the advertising hoardings seen at football (soccer) matches, although there are other more general forms such as billboards and posters.

_____s first appeared around football stadiums in the 1980s after the influence of on-shirt advertising, and are now commonplace in professional football grounds.

They are a source of humour when a player shoots for goal and misses the target but hits the _____s instead, sometimes knocking them over.

   a. ACNielsen
   b. ADTECH
   c. AMAX
   d. Advertising board

6. An _____ is a postcard used for advertising purposes (as opposed to tourism and greeting postcards.) Because the postcard begins as a blank sheet of paper, the options for what may be advertised are endless. Postcards are used in advertising as an alternative to or complementary addition to other print advertising such as catalogs, letters, and flyers.

a. ACNielsen
b. AMAX
c. Advertising postcard
d. ADTECH

7. The _____ aims to place 'peaceful and upbeat' messages about atheism on transport media in the UK, in response to evangelical Christian advertising. It was created by comedy writer Ariane Sherine and launched on 21 October 2008, with official support from the British Humanist Association and Richard Dawkins. The campaign's original goal was to raise Â£5,500 to run 30 buses across London for four weeks early in 2009 with the slogan: 'There's probably no God.
a. AMAX
b. ADTECH
c. ACNielsen
d. Atheist Bus Campaign

8. _____ is a form of advertising which is particularly common in newspapers, online and other periodicals, e.g. free ads papers or Pennysavers. _____ differs from standard advertising or business models in that it allows private individuals (not simply companies or corporate entities) to solicit sales for products and services.

_____ is usually textually based and can consist of as little as the type of item being sold and a telephone number to call for more information.

a. Classified advertising
b. Radio commercial
c. Television advertisement
d. Ghost sign

9. The _____ is a magazine sent free to members of the warehouse club Costco and includes articles which regularly tie into the corporation along with business, health and social articles. .
a. Ghost sign
b. Transit media
c. Television advertisement
d. Costco Connection

10. A _____ is a window in a shop displaying items for sale. Usually, the term points to the larger windows in the front facade of the shop.

_____s at boutiques usually have dressed-up mannequins in them.

a. Display window
b. Power III
c. 6-3-5 Brainwriting
d. 180SearchAssistant

11. A _____ is a single page leaflet advertising a nightclub, event, service, or other activity. _____s are typically used by individuals or businesses to promote their products or services. They are a form of mass marketing or small scale, community communication.
a. Quantitative
b. Flyer
c. Just-In-Case
d. Consumption Map

12. A _____ is an unbound booklet (that is, without a hard cover or binding.) It may consist of a single sheet of paper that is printed on both sides and folded in half, in thirds or it may consist of a few pages that are folded in half and stapled at the crease to make a simple book. In order to count as a _____, UNESCO requires a publication (other than a periodical) to have 'at least 5 but not more than 48 pages exclusive of the cover pages'; a longer item is a book.
a. Pamphlet
b. 6-3-5 Brainwriting
c. Power III
d. 180SearchAssistant

Chapter 10. Test Preparation Part 10

13. A _____ is a term for old hand painted advertising or signage that has been preserved on a building for an extended period of time, whether by actively keeping it or choosing not to destroy it.

They are found across the world with America, France and Canada having many surviving examples. _____s are also called fading ads.

- a. Transit media
- b. Television advertisement
- c. Radio commercial
- d. Ghost sign

14. _____ uses online or offline interactive media to communicate with consumers and to promote products, brands, services, and public service announcements, corporate or political groups.

In the inaugural issue of the Journal of _____ , editors Li and Leckenby (2000) defined _____ as the 'paid and unpaid presentation and promotion of products, services and ideas by an identified sponsor through mediated means involving mutual action between consumers and producers.' This is most commonly performed through the Internet as a medium.

It is these mutual actions or interactions that enhance what _____ is trying to achieve.

- a. Internet currency
- b. Interactive advertising
- c. Enterprise Search Marketing
- d. Audience Screening

15. A _____ is the marketing practice of advertising on the side of a truck or trailer that is typically mobile. _____s are a form of Out-Of-Home (OOH) Advertising. Radio, static billboards, and mall/airport advertising fall into the same category.

- a. Power III
- b. 6-3-5 Brainwriting
- c. 180SearchAssistant
- d. Mobile billboard

16. A _____ is a large outdoor advertising structure (a billing board), typically found in high traffic areas such as alongside busy roads. _____s present large advertisements to passing pedestrians and drivers. Typically showing large, ostensibly witty slogans, and distinctive visuals, _____s are highly visible in the top designated market areas.

- a. Power III
- b. 180SearchAssistant
- c. 6-3-5 Brainwriting
- d. Billboard

17. _____ is the use of advertising in outer space or related to space flight. While there have only been a few examples of successful marketing campaigns, there have been several proposals to advertise in space, some even planning to launch giant billboards visible from the Earth. Obtrusive _____ is the term used for such ventures.

- a. Space advertising
- b. 180SearchAssistant
- c. 6-3-5 Brainwriting
- d. Power III

18. A '_____' or television commercial (often just commercial (US) or advert or ad (UK) or ad-film (India)) is a span of television programming produced and paid for by an organisation that conveys a message. Advertisement revenue provides a significant portion of the funding for most privately owned television networks. The vast majority of _____s today consist of brief advertising spots, ranging in length from a few seconds to several minutes (as well as program-length infomercials.)

a. Television advertisement
b. Ghost sign
c. Radio commercial
d. Transit media

19. _____ is a form of out-of-home advertising that uses vehicular platforms to establish a mobile brand presence.

Typically, _____ campaigns are employed in denser urban environments to maximize brand exposure to both pedestrian and on-road traffic. The medium has traditionally been limited to featured advertisements on buses and trams, but in recent years has extended to various sub-categories, such as dedicated car, van or truck advertising.

a. Television advertisement
b. Transit media
c. Costco Connection
d. Ghost sign

20. In the past two decades, _____ has become appreciated for the 'artistic' and free-thinking messages of its advertisements, which reflect a business plan of marketing their products to creative individuals. Their most significant ad campaigns include the '1984' Super Bowl commercial, which introduced their company as revolutionary, independent, and subversive, as well as the 1990s Think Different campaign, which featured major artists, and the 'iPod people' of the 2000s, featuring several colorful, dancing silhouetted people.
a. ADTECH
b. ACNielsen
c. AMAX
d. Apple Inc.

21. '_____' is a recruiting slogan that is used by the United States Army. It replaced the slogan 'Army of One' in 2006.

The composer of the song used in the _____ television commercials is Mark Isham .

a. ACNielsen
b. Army Strong
c. ADTECH
d. AMAX

22. '_____' is a former recruiting slogan that was used by the United States Army. It replaced 'Be All You Can Be', the Army's slogan for twenty years. It was replaced in 2006 by the slogan 'Army Strong'.
a. ADTECH
b. ACNielsen
c. Army of One
d. AMAX

23. _____ was the recruiting slogan of the United States Army for over twenty years. It was followed by the slogan, 'Army of One', which was followed by 'Army Strong.'

This popular slogan was created by E. N. J. Carter while at the advertising firm N. W. Ayer ' Son.

a. 180SearchAssistant
b. 6-3-5 Brainwriting
c. Power III
d. Be All You Can Be

24. The phrase '_____' is a variant of a DuPont advertising slogan, 'Better Things for Better Living...Through Chemistry.' DuPont adopted it in 1935 and was their slogan until 1982 when the 'Through Chemistry' part was dropped. Since 1999, their slogan has been 'The miracles of science'.

This phrase became popular as culture shifted from mod to hippie in the later half of the 1960s.

a. Black PRies
b. Pay per ship
c. Surcharge
d. Better Living Through Chemistry

25. '_____' was an advertising campaign for Nike cross-training shoes that ran in 1989 and 1990 and featured professional baseball and American football player Bo Jackson.

Jackson was the first athlete in the modern era to play professional baseball and football in the same year. He was the perfect spokesman for a shoe geared toward an athlete actively engaged in more than one sport at a time or with little time between activities to switch to sport-specific footwear.

a. Slip-Slop-Slap
b. Buy Kiwi Made
c. Who Makes Movies?
d. Bo Knows

26. _____ is a Government campaign aimed at promoting consumer and retailer awareness of Kiwi made products and encouraging domestic manufacturers to label their goods New Zealand made. It uses the slogan 'Buy Kiwi and We've Got it Made'. It is complementary to the Buy New Zealand Made Campaign Ltd which was formed in 1988 and which licenses use of the kiwi in a triangle logo.

a. Go to work on an egg
b. Life. Be in it.
c. Slip-Slop-Slap
d. Buy Kiwi Made

27. '_____' was the slogan of a series of British public information films sponsored by the Royal Society for the Prevention of Accidents, commencing in January 1971 and starring Jimmy Savile. The slogan was introduced during the previous campaign, fronted by Shaw Taylor and featuring the slogan 'Your Seatbelt Is Their Security'. However, it was the onomatopoeia used by Taylor to describe the act of closing the door and fastening a seatbelt that proved the most memorable aspect of that campaign, and so it was upgraded to act as the slogan when the films moved into colour.

a. Clunk Click Every Trip
b. 180SearchAssistant
c. Power III
d. 6-3-5 Brainwriting

28. 'It _____' is a popular phrase in the United Kingdom, which originated in a series of television advertisements by the woodstain and wood-dye manufacturer Ronseal, initiated in 1994 and still being broadcast as of 2008. The slogan was created by Liz Whiston and Dave Shelton at the London advertising agency HHCL. The idea of the phrase was to emphasise that the company's products would act and last for the amount of time exactly as described on the tin can.

a. 180SearchAssistant
b. 6-3-5 Brainwriting
c. Power III
d. Does exactly what it says on the tin

29. In May 1987, Wendy's International followed up the 'Where's the Beef?' campaign with the US television commercial '_____'. The tag line was to be a catchy phrase that would capture the attention of consumers and help make Wendy's major player on the fast-food scene once again. This television commercial was a flop and sent Wendy's hunting for a new advertising agency.

a. You Got the Right One, Baby
b. Life. Be in it.
c. Go to work on an egg
d. Give a little nibble

30. '_____' was an advertising slogan used by the United Kingdom's Egg Marketing Board during the 1950s as part of more than £12 million it spent on advertising, including a series of television adverts starring the comedian Tony Hancock and actress Patricia Hayes. The proposition was that having an egg for breakfast was the best way to start the working day.

The slogan is often said to have been created by Fay Weldon, who has since said that she was just the manager of the person who created the phrase.

   a. Give a little nibble
   b. For Your Consideration
   c. Got Milk?
   d. Go to work on an egg

31. '_____' is an advertising slogan used by Diageo in television, cinema, and print advertising campaigns promoting Guinness-brand draught stout in the United Kingdom. The slogan formed the cornerstone of advertising agency Abbott Mead Vickers BBDO's successful pitch to secure the Guinness account in 1996. Their proposal was to turn around the negative consumer opinion of the length of time required to correctly pour a pint of Guinness from the tap, usually quoted as 119.5 seconds, as well as to encourage bartenders to take the time to do so.

   a. Pearson's chi-square
   b. Clustering
   c. Market specialization
   d. Good things come to those who wait

32. _____? is an American advertising campaign encouraging the consumption of cow's milk, which was created by the advertising agency Goodby Silverstein ' Partners for the California Milk Processor Board in 1993 and later licensed for use by milk processors and dairy farmers. It has been running since October 1993. The campaign has been credited with greatly increasing milk sales nationwide after a 20-year slump.

   a. You Got the Right One, Baby
   b. Got Milk?
   c. Slip-Slop-Slap
   d. Who Makes Movies?

33. _____ was the slogan of Molson Canadian Beer from 1994 until 1998 (via ad agency Maclaren Lintas and then MacLaren McCann), and between 2000 and 2005 (Bensimon Byrne.) It was also the subject of an extremely popular ad campaign centered on Canadian nationalism, the most famous examples of which are 'The Rant' and 'The Anthem'. The ads aired in both English Canada and the United States.

   a. ACNielsen
   b. ADTECH
   c. I Am Canadian
   d. AMAX

34. _____ is an advertising campaign launched by Discovery Channel in 2008 in promotion of their new tagline: 'The World is Just... Awesome'. The song used in the ad is a re-writing of a traditional camping song known as I Love the Mountains or I Love the Flowers, depending on the lyrics, with a distinctive chorus of 'boom-de-ya-da, boom-de-ya-da'.

   a. AMAX
   b. ADTECH
   c. ACNielsen
   d. I Love the World

35. _____! was a large-scale United States anti-narcotics campaign by Partnership for a Drug-Free America. Launched in 1987, the campaign used a televised public service announcement.

The PSA features a father confronting his son in his bedroom after finding a box containing an unspecified controlled substance and drug paraphernalia.

   a. ACNielsen
   b. AMAX
   c. ADTECH
   d. I learned it by watching you

36. 'The _____' is an advertisement campaign launched by the National Coffee Association in the 1980s, urging Americans to drink more coffee. The television ads featured celebrities such as David Bowie, actress Cicely Tyson, actress Jane Curtin, author Kurt Vonnegut, then-Cincinnati Bengals quarterback Ken Anderson, and rock group ELO. The campaign's tagline was 'Join the _____!'

The campaign was referenced in the 'Weird Al' Yankovic song Dare to be Stupid.

   a. 180SearchAssistant
   c. Power III

   b. 6-3-5 Brainwriting
   d. Coffee Achievers

37. '_____' was an advertising campaign, part of the U.S. 'War on Drugs', prevalent during the 1980s and early 1990s, to discourage children from engaging in recreational drug use by offering various ways of saying no. Eventually, this also expanded the realm of '_____' to violence, premarital sex, and any other vices that young people might try. The slogan was created and championed by First Lady Nancy Reagan during her husband's presidency.
   a. Life. Be in it.
   c. You Got the Right One, Baby

   b. Got Milk?
   d. Just Say No

38. '_____' was a phrase used to market the Canadian prairies to prospective immigrants. The notion of the _____ is still a common perception of the Canadian west. The phrase was used to advertise the Canadian west abroad, and in Eastern Canada, during the heyday of western settlement from 1896 until the start of the First World War.
   a. Power III
   c. 6-3-5 Brainwriting

   b. 180SearchAssistant
   d. Last best West

39. _____ is an activist campaign promoting immigration reform, propagated through billboards, protests, clothing, advertisements, educational pamphlets, and grass roots support, underwritten by American Apparel. Originating locally in downtown Los Angeles, the company took the campaign national in early 2008.

_____ is billed as an education and media advertising campaign.

   a. Who Makes Movies?
   c. Good things come to those who wait

   b. For Your Consideration
   d. Legalize LA

40. _____ is an Australian government program and advertising campaign encouraging people to be more active and participate in recreational sports or other physical activities.
   a. Just Say No
   c. Life. Be in it.

   b. Slip-Slop-Slap
   d. Give a little nibble

41. '_____' is a former slogan used by the U.S. Army National Guard. It indicated the amount of time an individual would need to spend actively in the Guard to be a Guardsman with benefits. It was dropped during the Iraq War after it became clear that Guardsmen were now serving considerably more time in service.
   a. One weekend a month, two weeks a year
   c. ACNielsen

   b. AMAX
   d. ADTECH

42. _____ or Paid-to-click is a business model that became popular in the late 1990s, prior to the dot-com crash. Essentially, a company places advertising on members' screens and pays them from advertising earnings.

A pay-to-surf company would provide a small program, commonly called a 'viewbar', to be installed on a member's computer.

a. Multi-level marketing
b. Freebie marketing
c. Pay to surf
d. Cross-selling

43. '_____' is an often-quoted phrase that originated in a series of television advertisements by the Australian Tourism Commission starring Paul Hogan from 1984 through to 1990. The actual quote spoken by Hogan is 'I'll slip an extra _____ for you', and the actual slogan of the ad was 'Come and say G'day'. It has since been used, along with some variations, to make reference to Australia in popular culture.

a. Shrimp on the barbie
b. 6-3-5 Brainwriting
c. Power III
d. 180SearchAssistant

44. _____ is the name of a health campaign in Australia exhorting people to 'slip on a shirt, slop on sunscreen, and slap on a hat' when they go out into the sun, in order to protect themselves against an increased risk of skin cancer. It is probably Australia's most recognizable health message.

The campaign started in 1981; its mascot is a seagull called Sid.

a. Slip-Slop-Slap
b. You Got the Right One, Baby
c. Life. Be in it.
d. For Your Consideration

45. '_____' is a student outreach campaign sponsored by the American Institute of Certified Public Accountants (AICPA) to engage high school and college students in pursuing careers in business and accounting, so that they ultimately become certified public accountants (CPAs.) Through a combination of online and print activities, the campaign provides students with business and accounting-related career resources, information and guidance.

a. Start Here. Go Places.
b. 6-3-5 Brainwriting
c. Power III
d. 180SearchAssistant

46. _____ was a brand of cigarettes produced by W.D. ' H.O. Wills (part of Imperial Tobacco), launched in 1959 but withdrawn in the early 1960s. The launch was accompanied by a huge television advertising campaign, You're never alone with a _____.

a. Strand
b. Comparison-Shopping agent
c. GE matrix
d. Better Living Through Chemistry

47. '_____' is an advertising slogan created for Apple Computer in 1997 by the Los Angeles office of advertising agency TBWAChiatDay. It was used in a famous television commercial, several print advertisements, and several television advertisements for Apple products. Apple's use of the slogan was discontinued with the start of the Apple Switch ad campaign in 2002.

a. Think Different
b. Life. Be in it.
c. Who Makes Movies?
d. Give a little nibble

48. _____ was a large-scale US anti-narcotics campaign by Partnership for a Drug-Free America (PDFA) launched in 1987, that used two televised public service announcements (PSAs) and a related poster campaign.

Chapter 10. Test Preparation Part 10

The first PSA, from 1987, showed a man who held up an egg and said, 'This is your brain,' before picking up a frying pan and adding, 'This is drugs.' He then cracks open the egg, fries the contents, and says, '_____.' Finally he looks up at the camera and asks, 'Any questions?' A shorter version of this, simply showing a close-up of an egg dropping into a frying pan, was used a few years later.

The second PSA, from 1998, featured actress Rachael Leigh Cook, who, as before, holds up an egg and says, 'this is your brain', before lifting up a frying pan with the words, 'this is heroin', after which she places the egg on a kitchen counter - 'this is what happens to your brain after snorting heroin' - and slams the pan down on it.

- a. This Is Your Brain on Drugs
- b. Give a little nibble
- c. Life. Be in it.
- d. Buy Kiwi Made

49. '_____!' is an enduring slogan which appeared in magazine, newspaper, and television advertisements for Tareyton cigarettes from 1963 until 1981. It was the American Tobacco Company's most visible ad campaign in the 1960s and 1970s.

The slogan was created by James Jordan of the BBDO advertising agency.

- a. Us Tareyton smokers would rather fight than switch
- b. ACNielsen
- c. ADTECH
- d. AMAX

50. _____? was a commercial campaign for Anheuser-Busch Budweiser beer from 1999 to 2002. The first spot aired during Monday Night Football, December 20 1999. The ad campaign was run worldwide and became a pop culture phenomenon.
- a. Power III
- b. 180SearchAssistant
- c. 6-3-5 Brainwriting
- d. Whassup?

51. _____? was an advertising campaign run jointly by several international associations looking to crack down on copyright infringement of motion pictures, most notably the MPAA, as part of the larger 'Respect Copyrights' campaign. The campaign was endorsed by several motion picture workers' guilds, including the Directors Guild of America, the International Alliance of Theatrical Stage Employees, Moving Picture Technicians, Artists and Allied Crafts, the Motion Picture Editors Guild, the Screen Actors Guild and the Writers Guild of America.

Five short films were created, each profiling the work done by primarily blue-collar workers in the production of a feature film.

- a. Buy Kiwi Made
- b. You Got the Right One, Baby
- c. Just Say No
- d. Who Makes Movies?

52. '_____' is an enduring slogan that appeared in newspaper, magazine, radio, and television advertisements for Winston cigarettes from the brand's introduction in 1954 until 1972. It is one of the best-known American tobacco advertising campaigns. In 1999, Advertising Age ranked the jingle eighth-best out of all the television jingles that aired in the United States in the 20th century.

a. Albert Einstein
b. African Americans
c. Winston tastes good like a cigarette should
d. AStore

53. The phrase '_____' is a commonly-used phrase within New Zealand. It is used to describe items that though famous within New Zealand are unknown in the rest of the world, whereas similar items and people in larger countries would have a far higher media profile and would therefore be famous worldwide. The slogan as it appeared on Lemon ' Paeroa bottles during the early 2000s.

The term is simultaneously both parochially proud and self-deprecating.

a. 6-3-5 Brainwriting
b. 180SearchAssistant
c. Power III
d. World famous in New Zealand

54. '_____' run everywhere (WORE), is a slogan created by Sun Microsystems to illustrate the cross-platform benefits of the Java language. Ideally, this means Java can be developed on any device, compiled into a standard bytecode and be expected to run on any device equipped with a Java virtual machine (JVM.) The installation of a JVM or Java interpreter on chips, devices or software packages has become an industry standard practice.

a. 6-3-5 Brainwriting
b. Write once, run anywhere
c. Power III
d. 180SearchAssistant

55. '_____, Uh Huh' was a popular slogan for Pepsico's Diet Pepsi brand in the United States and Canada from 1990 to 1993. A series of television ads featured singer Ray Charles, surrounded by models, singing a song about Diet Pepsi, entitled 'You Got the Right One Baby, Uh Huh'. The tag-phrase of the song included the words 'Uh Huh!', which (as part of the ad campaign) were featured on Diet Pepsi packaging.

a. Go to work on an egg
b. For Your Consideration
c. Buy Kiwi Made
d. You Got the Right One, Baby

56. _____ is the misleading marketing practice of including a minuscule amount of an active ingredient in a cosmetic, cosmeceutical, dietary supplement, food product insufficient to cause any measurable benefit. The advertising materials may claim that the ingredient is helpful and that the ingredient is contained in the product, both of which are true (with the exception of some extreme cases where the ingredient is so diluted that most units of the product don't even contain a single molecule of the active ingredient.) However, no claim is made that the product contains enough of the active ingredient to have an effect -- this is just assumed by the purchaser.

a. Incomplete comparison
b. Inconsistent comparison
c. Employee pricing
d. Angel dusting

57. In retail sales, a _____ is a form of fraud in which the party putting forth the fraud lures in customers by advertising a product or service at an unprofitably low price, then reveals to potential customers that the advertised good is not available but that a substitute is.

The goal of the bait-and-switch is to convince some buyers to purchase the substitute good as a means of avoiding disappointment over not getting the bait, or as a way to recover sunk costs expended to try to obtain the bait. It suggests that the seller will not show the original product or product advertised but instead will demonstrate a more expensive product.

a. Bait and switch
b. Transpromotional
c. Roll-in
d. Promotional products

58. _____ , Above the line (ATL), and Through the Line (TTL), in organisational business and marketing communications, are advertising techniques.

Promotion can be loosely classified as 'above the line' or '_____'.

Promotional activities carried out through mass media, such as television, radio and newspaper, are classed as above the line promotion.

a. Below the line
b. Customization
c. Rural market
d. Range

59. _____ is a type of branding in which a celebrity uses his or her status in society to promote a product, service or charity. _____ can take several different forms, from a celebrity simply appearing in advertisements for a product, service or charity, to a celebrity attending PR events, creating his or her own line of products or services, and/or using his or her name as a brand. The most popular forms of celebrity brand lines are for clothing and perfume.

a. Master-McNeil
b. Fu Yan Jie
c. Celebrity branding
d. Gee, Your Hair Smells Terrific

1. _____ was a 1909 publicity stunt in Salt Lake City by the (long defunct) Salt Lake Herald-Republican newspaper, involving a pretty girl in a new automobile, in this case an American Traveler. A $500 reward (roughly $25,000 in 2008 dollars) was offered for the 'capture' of Miss _____. No record is available of the outcome of the contest.
   a. Customization
   b. Pearson's chi-square
   c. Dolly Dimples
   d. Market specialization

2. _____ is a selling strategy launched in 2005 by the auto industry in order to attract customers by using the discounted prices that auto industry employees pay for new cars rather than the sticker price MSRP. The program was first offered that year by General Motors, and later followed by Ford, Chrysler, and some local dealerships. While 2005 was the biggest year for the promotion, it has since been used several times, like during the automotive industry crisis of 2008 to stimulate sales.
   a. In-store demonstration
   b. Inconsistent comparison
   c. Incomplete comparison
   d. Employee pricing

3. _____ is one of the four Ps of the marketing mix. The other three aspects are product, promotion, and place. It is also a key variable in microeconomic price allocation theory.
   a. Pricing
   b. Price
   c. Competitor indexing
   d. Relationship based pricing

4. _____s or previews are film advertisements for feature films that will be exhibited in the future at a cinema, on whose screen they are shown. The term '_____' comes from their having originally been shown at the end of a film programme. That practice did not last long, because patrons tended to leave the theater after the films ended, but the name has stuck.
   a. Clustering
   b. Trailer
   c. Rural market
   d. Distribution

5. _____ is the concept of either giving away a sellable item for nothing or charging an extremely low price in order to generate a continual market for another, generally disposable, item. The concept was pioneered by King C. Gillette, inventor of the disposable safety razor and founder of Gillette Safety Razor Company It is a similar concept to loss leader marketing.
   a. Freebie marketing
   b. Pay to surf
   c. Cross-selling
   d. Service provider

6. _____ is defined by the American _____ Association as the activity, set of institutions, and processes for creating, communicating, delivering, and exchanging offerings that have value for customers, clients, partners, and society at large. The term developed from the original meaning which referred literally to going to market, as in shopping, or going to a market to sell goods or services.

_____ practice tends to be seen as a creative industry, which includes advertising, distribution and selling.

   a. Marketing myopia
   b. Customer acquisition management
   c. Product naming
   d. Marketing

7. In advertising, a _____ is an advertisement or campaign that uses a more direct, forceful, and overt sales message. This approach works in opposition to a soft sell.

Theorists have examined the value of repetition for _____ versus soft sell messages to determine their relative efficacy.

a. Rack card
b. Hard sell
c. Comparative advertising
d. GL-70

8. An _____ is a misleading argument popular in advertising. For example, an advertiser might say 'product X is better'. This is an incomplete assertion, so can't be refuted.
a. Inconsistent comparison
b. Employee pricing
c. In-store demonstration
d. Incomplete comparison

9. An _____ is a misleading argument popular in advertising. For example, an advertisement might say 'product X is less expensive than product A, has better quality than product B, and has more features than product C'. This is designed to give the impression that product X is better than products A, B, and C in all respects, but doesn't actually make that claim.
a. In-store demonstration
b. Incomplete comparison
c. Employee pricing
d. Inconsistent comparison

10. A _____ or leader is a product sold at a low price (at cost or below cost) to stimulate other, profitable sales. It is a kind of sales promotion, in other words marketing concentrating on a pricing strategy. The price can even be so low that the product is sold at a loss.
a. Resale price maintenance
b. Penetration pricing
c. Price shading
d. Loss leader

11. A _____ is a short segment of media either an audio clip or a video clip. _____s may be promotional in nature, as with movie clips. For example, to promote upcoming movies, many actors are accompanied by movie clips on their circuits. Additionally, _____s may be raw materials of other productions, such as audio clips used for sound effects.
a. Power III
b. 180SearchAssistant
c. 6-3-5 Brainwriting
d. Media clip

12. _____ or promotional products refers to articles of merchandise that are used in marketing and communication programs. These items are usually imprinted with a company's name, logo or slogan, and given away at trade shows, conferences, and as part of guerrilla marketing campaigns.

Almost anything can be branded with a company's name or logo and used for promotion.

a. Testimonial
b. Promotional products
c. Roll-in
d. Promotional items

13. A _____ is an advertisement or promotion that precedes core video or audio content presented in the same packaging as the core content. _____s are being used increasingly as a method for getting advertising revenue from embeddable online content such as news and entertainment.
a. Roll-in
b. Promotional items
c. Testimonial
d. Promotional products

14. In advertising, a _____ is an advertisement or campaign that uses a more subtle, casual, or friendly sales message. This approach works in opposition to a hard sell.

Theorists have examined the value of repetition for _____ versus hard sell messages to determine their relative efficacy.

   a. Refusal to deal   b. Discontinuation
   c. Jobbing house   d. Soft sell

15. A _____ is a signal or message embedded in another medium, designed to pass below the normal limits of the human mind's perception. These messages are unrecognizable by the conscious mind, but in certain situations can affect the subconscious mind and can negatively or positively influence subsequent later thoughts, behaviors, actions, attitudes, belief systems and value systems. The term subliminal means 'beneath a limen' (sensory threshold.)

   a. 6-3-5 Brainwriting   b. Power III
   c. 180SearchAssistant   d. Subliminal message

16. _____ refers to the practice of making spoofs or parodies of corporate and political advertisements in order to make a statement. This can take the form of a new image or an alteration to an existing image. A subvertisement can also be referred to as a meme hack and can be a part of social hacking or culture jamming.

   a. 6-3-5 Brainwriting   b. 180SearchAssistant
   c. Power III   d. Subvertising

17. A _____ is a low, adjustable introductory rate advertised for a loan or credit card in order to attract potential customers to obtain the service. The _____s are normally too good to be true for the long term, and are far below the common realistic rate for the service. In a competitive market, many companies will compete with each other for the lower _____.

   a. Reseller   b. Whole product
   c. Discontinuation   d. Teaser rate

18. In promotion and of advertising, a _____ or endorsement consists of a written or spoken statement, sometimes from a person figure, sometimes from a private citizen, extolling the virtue of some product. The term '_____' most commonly applies to the sales-pitches attributed to ordinary citizens, whereas 'endorsement' usually applies to pitches by celebrities. See also Testify, Testimony, for historical context and etymology.

   a. Transpromotional   b. Promotional products
   c. Roll-in   d. Testimonial

19. _____ is a technique used in propaganda and advertising. Also known as association, this is a technique of projecting positive or negative qualities (praise or blame) of a person, entity, object, or value (an individual, group, organization, nation, patriotism, etc.) to another in order to make the second more acceptable or to discredit it.

   a. Transfer   b. Micro ads
   c. Supplier   d. Sexism,

20. Transpromo describes a type of document or corporate communication strategy that delivers transactional information and promotional marketing messages. By adding relevant messages to transaction documents, companies can strengthen relationships and increase revenue.

_____ documents combine CRM Customer relationship management and data mining technology with Variable data printing and location intelligence.

Chapter 11. Test Preparation Part 11

a. Promotional items
c. Roll-in
b. Testimonial
d. Transpromotional

21. In business, a _____ is an advertising offer made by a company that is designed to draw potential customers by offering them cash or something of value for acceptance, but following acceptance, the buyer is forced to spend a much larger amount of money, either by being signed into a lengthy contract, from which exit is difficult, or by having money automatically drawn in some other method. The harmful consequences faced by the customer may include spending far above market rate, large amount of debt, or identity theft.

The term, which originated in New England during the 2000s, and has spread to some other parts of the United States, is also sometimes misused in reference to an item offered seemingly at a bargain price.

a. Testimonial
c. Promotional items
b. Below the line
d. Trojan horse

22. _____ refers to the increase of advertising. The virtues of advertising are debated, but _____ especially refers to advertising which is invasive and coercive, like ads in schools, doctor's offices and hospitals, restrooms, elevators, on ATM's, on garbage cans, and on restaurant menus.

a. ADTECH
c. AMAX
b. ACNielsen
d. Ad-creep

23. _____ is a form of communication that typically attempts to persuade potential customers to purchase or to consume more of a particular brand of product or service. 'While now central to the contemporary global economy and the reproduction of global production networks, it is only quite recently that _____ has been more than a marginal influence on patterns of sales and production. The formation of modern _____ was intimately bound up with the emergence of new forms of monopoly capitalism around the end of the 19th and beginning of the 20th century as one element in corporate strategies to create, organize and where possible control markets, especially for mass produced consumer goods.

a. ADTECH
c. ACNielsen
b. AMAX
d. Advertising

24. _____ is a term coined by Simon Broadbent to describe the prolonged or lagged effect of advertising on consumer purchase behavior. It is also known as 'advertising carry-over'. Adstock is an important component of marketing-mix models.

a. ACNielsen
c. AMAX
b. ADTECH
d. Advertising Adstock

25. _____ is a term used to describe the phenomenon of a marketplace being full or even overcrowded with products. It also refers to the extreme amount of advertising the average American sees in their daily lives. _____ is a major problem for marketers and advertisers.

a. Procter ' Gamble
c. Consumption Map
b. Push
d. Clutter

26. In graphic design and advertising, a _____ usually shortened to comp, is the page layout of a proposed design as initially presented by the designer to a client, showing the relative positions of text and illustrations before the specific content of those elements has been decided on, as a rough draft of the final layout in which to build around.

The illustration element may incorporate stock photography, clip art, or other found material that gives an idea of what should be visually communicated, before entering any negotiations concerning the rights to use a specific image for the purpose. Picture agencies may encourage such use free of charge, in the hope that the comp image will end up being used in the final product.

   a. Geo
   b. Comprehensive,
   c. Clutter
   d. Motion Picture Association of America's film-rating system

27. In economics, business, retail, and accounting, a _____ is the value of money that has been used up to produce something, and hence is not available for use anymore. In economics, a _____ is an alternative that is given up as a result of a decision. In business, the _____ may be one of acquisition, in which case the amount of money expended to acquire it is counted as _____.
   a. Transaction cost
   b. Cost
   c. Variable cost
   d. Fixed costs

28. _____ is an advertising and marketing term, describing the cost of acquiring a customer, typically calculated by dividing the total cost of an advertising campaign by the number of conversions. The definition of 'conversion' varies depending upon the situation; it is sometimes considered to be a lead, a sale, or a purchase. .
   a. Rate card
   b. Hard sell
   c. Rack card
   d. Cost per conversion

29. _____ measures the extent to which a consumer has a meaningful brand experience when exposed to commercial advertising, sponsorship, television contact, or other experience.

In March 2006 the Advertising Research Foundation defined _____ as 'turning on a prospect to a brand idea enhanced by the surrounding context'. The ARF has also defined the function whereby _____ impacts a brand:

_____ is complex because a variety of exposure and relationship factors affect _____, making simplified rankings misleading.

   a. Inseparability
   b. Engagement
   c. Automated surveys
   d. Individual branding

30. _____, small print, or 'mouseprint' is less noticeable print smaller than the more obvious larger print it accompanies that advertises or otherwise describes or partially describes a commercial product or service . The larger print that is used in conjunction with _____ is generally ingenuously used by the merchant to, in effect, deceive the consumer into believing the offer is more advantageous than it really is, via a legal technicality which requires full disclosure of all (even unfavorable) terms or conditions, but does not specify the manner (size, typeface, coloring, etc.) of disclosure.
   a. Fine print
   b. False advertising
   c. Power III
   d. Misleading advertising

Chapter 11. Test Preparation Part 11

31. The term _____ refers to the placement of advertisements on the side of trucks, vans, and other forms of transportation that form part of a commercial fleet. This is more than the addition of a company logo, name and number to the vehicles belonging to that company. The crucial difference is that _____, like any other form of advertising, is commercially available.
   a. Fleet media
   b. Power III
   c. 180SearchAssistant
   d. Mind share

32. _____ is an advertising term referring to a high concentration of advertising for a short period of time in a media schedule. If an advertiser's product is more likely to be used at one specific time than at another, the advertiser may choose to _____ the advertising for that time period. For example, a candy manufacturer may opt for _____ advertising during the two weeks prior to Halloween.
   a. Cost per conversion
   b. Rack card
   c. Rate card
   d. Heavy-up

33. _____ is one of the main objectives of advertising and promotion. When people think of examples of a product type or category, they usually think of a limited number of brand names. For example, a prospective buyer of a college education will have several thousand colleges to choose from.
   a. Mind share
   b. Power III
   c. 180SearchAssistant
   d. Nielsen Ratings

34. _____ are audience measurement systems developed by the AC Nielsen Company, (now Nielsen Media Research) to determine the audience size and composition of television programming. Founder Arthur Nielsen was a market analysis specialist whose career had begun in the '20s with brand advertising analysis and expanded into radio market analysis during the '30s, culminating in _____ of radio programming, meant to provide detailed and accurate statistics as to markets of radio shows. In 1950, Nielsen moved to television, developing an offshoot ratings system using the methods he and his company had developed for radio.
   a. Nielsen Ratings
   b. Power III
   c. Mind share
   d. 180SearchAssistant

35. _____ (PI) - also known variously as cost per lead (CPL), pay per lead (PPL) or cost per action (CPer-inquiry advertising) - is a form of direct response marketing in which the advertiser receives free ad time and space while paying only for results. In return, the advertiser gives up control of where and when the ads will run.

Agencies that offer PI have relationships with media outlets - radio, television, print, Internet, movie screens and billboards - and access to their unsold inventory of ad time and space.

   a. Per-inquiry advertising
   b. Lifestyle center
   c. Little value placed on potential benefits
   d. Micro ads

36. _____ or advertising-supported software is any software package which automatically plays, displays, or downloads advertisements to a computer after the software is installed on it or while the application is being used. Some types of _____ are also spyware and can be classified as privacy-invasive software.

Advertising functions are integrated into or bundled with the software, which is often designed to note what Internet sites the user visits and to present advertising pertinent to the types of goods or services featured there.

a. ACNielsen   b. ADTECH
c. Isearch   d. Adware

37. _____ is an adware program that displays pop-ups based on a user's browsing habits.

It has been claimed the product presents ads under some circumstances and that it contacts its maker's site without user permission, leading to it being classified as spyware by some third parties.

The _____ now more often comes under the name Zango.

a. New.net   b. DollarRevenue
c. 180SearchAssistant   d. SpyBouncer

38. _____ is an Adware program developed by Exact Advertising. _____ software monitors Internet usage and displays advertisements based on the websites a user views. The software may also display ads for Exact Advertising programs such as FunGameDownloads and PhotoGizmo.
a. 6-3-5 Brainwriting   b. 180SearchAssistant
c. Power III   d. Bargain Buddy

39. _____ is a BitTorrent client written in C++ for Microsoft Windows. _____ Pro is a recent 'commercial' release of _____. It appears to come bundled with UseNeXT's Usenet service.
a. BitLord   b. Power III
c. 6-3-5 Brainwriting   d. 180SearchAssistant

40. _____, sometimes spelled Bonzi Buddy, _____ was an on-screen 'intelligent software agent' from BONZI Software, released in 1999 and discontinued in 2005. The official website stated it would help a person explore the Internet through various functions along with their own sidekick. It first surfaced as a green talking parrot, before taking the form of an animated purple gorilla that resided on a user's desktop and communicated through the employment of Microsoft Agent technology.
a. DollarRevenue   b. ClipGenie
c. BonziBUDDY   d. The Best Offers

41. _____ was a media marketing software company based in Redwood City, California. It was established in 1998 by Denis Coleman. Its name was often used interchangeably with its Gain advertising network, which it claimed serviced over 40 million users.
a. Power III   b. 180SearchAssistant
c. 6-3-5 Brainwriting   d. Claria Corporation

42. _____ is an adware program that 'brings rich media content to you, directly to your hard drive. Now you can get all the best movies, games and programs downloaded directly to your computer ... while you sleep! And the best part is ...
a. DollarRevenue   b. Comet Cursor
c. ClipGenie   d. BonziBUDDY

43. _____ was a software program manufactured by Comet Systems. It allowed users of the Microsoft Windows Operating System to change the appearance of their mouse's cursor and to allow websites to use customized cursors for visitors. The product was introduced as an enhancement to website design and to enable advertisers to use customized cursors for their campaigns.

   a. Comet Cursor   b. DollarRevenue
   c. Virtual Bouncer   d. SpyBouncer

44. _____ is a broad label that refers to any individuals or households that use goods and services generated within the economy. The concept of a _____ is used in different contexts, so that the usage and significance of the term may vary.

A _____ is a person who uses any product or service.

   a. 6-3-5 Brainwriting   b. Power III
   c. 180SearchAssistant   d. Consumer

45. The _____ is a spyware/adware program for Microsoft Windows that delivers advertisements to a personal computer's desktop. The program has been criticized by users for privacy issues and hijackings of computers. However, the program is considered very low-risk.

   a. Power III   b. Cydoor
   c. MyWay Searchbar   d. Consumer alert system

46. _____ Desktop Media is an Israeli adware company. _____ originally placed ads only in software programs such as Kazaa, but has now expanded into running ads on websites as an advertising network.

Because of _____'s highly controversial practices of running ads in software programs, _____ software is often considered spyware -- and many Anti-Spyware and Antivirus applications will flag the software as such.

   a. Power III   b. MyWay Searchbar
   c. Cydoor   d. ContraVirus

47. _____ is an adware program made by the company of the same name. It displays advertisements on the infected PC and installs the UCMore Toolbar to track internet searches. It usually comes bundled with another program.

   a. DollarRevenue   b. SpyBouncer
   c. Virtual Bouncer   d. WeatherBug

48. The Gator _____ was one of the earlier and better known forms of spyware and/or adware.

The program was described as your helpful online companion, that remembers your online logins and passwords. Unfortunately, the _____ program installs GAIN, which is known to show pop-up ads and hijack Internet search results.

   a. Isearch   b. ADTECH
   c. E-wallet   d. ACNielsen

49. _____ is a Browser Helper Object. By downloading and installing this software, all typing errors in the address bar will cause the browser to be redirected to the _____'s search page, instead of your normal one. It also shows advertisements and popups on the PC.

   a. ACNielsen   b. AMAX
   c. InstaFinder   d. ADTECH

50. _____ is a resilient and common adware program that is often installed on a user's computer from pop-ups or unprotected downloads. Even most firewalls and other computer protection programs are ineffective to stop this program from being downloaded and successfully removed. This program often re-directs pop-ups to your browser, downloads other adware and spy ware programs onto your computer without your consent, captures private details such your local IP address and visited websites, re-installs itself after incomplete deletion, establishes its own .exe program, and disables your firewalls, internet options, homepage, and other vital functions that threaten its own existence.

   a. ADTECH   b. Isearch
   c. E-wallet   d. ACNielsen

51. _____ Media Desktop (once capitalized as '_____', but now usually written '_____') is a peer-to-peer file sharing application using the FastTrack protocol and owned by Sharman Networks.

_____ is commonly used to exchange MP3 music files over the Internet. However it can also be used to exchange other file types, such as videos, applications, and documents.

   a. Kazaa   b. Power III
   c. 6-3-5 Brainwriting   d. 180SearchAssistant

52. _____ 2008, 2009, 2010, and 360; System Antivirus; Vista Antivirus; AntiSpywareMaster; and XP AntiSpyware 2009, is a scareware rogue anti-virus which claims to remove bogus virus infections found on a computer running Microsoft Windows if a user purchases the full version of the software.

_____ is known to infect users using the Microsoft Windows operating system, and is browser independent. One infection method involves the Zlob Trojan.

   a. MS Antivirus   b. 180SearchAssistant
   c. 6-3-5 Brainwriting   d. Power III

53. _____ is a freeware add-on for Windows Live Messenger created by Cyril Paciullo. The software provides additional functionality to Microsoft's Windows Live Messenger by adding its own controls to the main interface. These controls affect Messenger's behaviour and appearance, often through additional dialog boxes.

   a. African Americans   b. AStore
   c. Albert Einstein   d. Messenger Plus! Live

54. _____, MyWay Search Assistant, MyWebSearch or MyWeb Searchbar, is a spyware and search toolbar program that allows the user to query Google, Ask Jeeves, Yahoo!, and LookSmart search engines. HP and Dell pre-install this software on some of their commercially sold PCs. It is also bundled with some versions of Kazaa.

   a. Cydoor   b. MyWay Searchbar
   c. Power III   d. ContraVirus

55. _____ is an alternate DNS root system, and publishes NewDotNet, an application that makes use of these domains. The top-level domains _____ provides include: .agent, .arts, .auction, .chat, .church, .club, .family, .free, .game, .golf, .inc, .kids, .law, .llc, .llp, .love, .ltd, .med, .mp3, .school, .scifi, .shop, .soc, .sport, .tech, .travel, .video, and .xxx. Of these, .travel and possibly soon .kids and/or .xxx are in conflict with official TLDs later authorized by ICANN to be implemented by other registries.
 a. New.net   b. DollarRevenue
 c. ClipGenie   d. The Best Offers

56. _____ is a commercial anti-spyware application developed by SRC Technologies for the Microsoft Windows operating system.

_____ has been listed by Spyware Warrior as a 'rogue anti-spyware' program for its use of aggressive advertising and deliberate false positives. Particularly noted is the use of typosquatting sites such as goggle.com to promote the software, using advertisements which misleadingly suggest that the viewer's computer is infected when it is not.

 a. ClipGenie   b. Virtual Bouncer
 c. WeatherBug   d. SpyBouncer

57. The most important feature of a contract is that one party makes an _____ for an arrangement that another accepts. This can be called a 'concurrence of wills' or 'ad idem' (meeting of the minds) of two or more parties. The concept is somewhat contested.
 a. ADTECH   b. ACNielsen
 c. AMAX   d. Offer

58. _____ is a trojan horse that is mis-represented as an audio and video codec for Windows-based PCs. It exists in various variants with names such as Media Codec, Ecodec, Imediacodec, IntCodec, Pcodec, SVideocodec, Video iCodec, QualityCodec, Vcodec, Zip Codec, zCodec, ZCODEC and began to be widely used in spring 2005.

When visiting certain web sites, in particular pornographic sites, and attempting to view a video file on the site, the user will be directed to download this software, purportedly in order to allow viewing of the video.

 a. Power III   b. 180SearchAssistant
 c. 6-3-5 Brainwriting   d. Trojan.Emcodec.E

59. _____ is a closed source Microsoft Windows-based peer-to-peer client which connects to the Gnutella, Gnutella2, FastTrack, eDonkey, Overnet and BitTorrent network protocols.

It is notable for the claims against it that it has stolen code from the open source Gnucleus, giFT, and avilib projects, which was discovered by disassembling the program, and the response was rapid release of another version with the offending code still remaining, however it was obscured by compressing the executable.

_____ then claimed that it was developing and would release an open source Linux version, however this has still not happened.

a. 180SearchAssistant
b. 6-3-5 Brainwriting
c. Power III
d. TrustyFiles

60. _____ is a Mac OS X, and iPhone OS client for the social networking site Twitter, created by The Iconfactory. It lets users view in real time 'tweets' or micro-blog posts on the Twitter website as well as publish their own. The program's main window uses a translucent black theme similar to certain palettes used in Aperture, iPhoto and other Apple Inc.
a. 180SearchAssistant
b. Power III
c. 6-3-5 Brainwriting
d. Twitterrific

61. _____ is an adware program targeting the Microsoft Windows operating system. It masquerades as anti-spyware software and attempts to contact a server in order to receive instructions.
a. The Best Offers
b. ClipGenie
c. BonziBUDDY
d. Virtual Bouncer

62. _____ is a computer program from AWS Convergence Technologies, Inc. that displays live weather data. The program is available for download from _____'s website, websites of the approximately 85 TV partners, and was formerly distributed through the AOL Instant Messenger installation utility.
a. DollarRevenue
b. New.net
c. WeatherBug
d. ClipGenie

63. _____, formerly known as 121Media, is a digital technology company based in London, New York, and Moscow. The company drew attention when it announced it was in talks with several United Kingdom ISPs to deliver targeted advertising based on user browsing habits by using deep packet inspection. It is one of several companies developing behavioral targeting advertising systems, seeking deals with ISPs to enable them to analyse customers' websurfing habits in order to deliver targeted advertising to them.
a. Sustainable Forestry Initiative
b. Phorm
c. GlobalSpec
d. Mapinfo

64. _____, developed by the company WhenU, is a piece of advertising software generally considered to be adware or spyware. The program delivers advertisements, compares shopping results and other offers to users' computers, and tracks their browsing habits. WhenU is typically installed with other applications, ostensibly to support the free existence of those applications.
a. Just-In-Case
b. Range
c. WhenU Save/SaveNow
d. Lobbying and Disclosure Act of 1995

65. _____ is an archiving program for Windows with its own 'ACE' compressed archive format and built-in support for other common archive formats types such as ZIP, RAR and MS-CAB. There is a text-based version for DOS called Commandline ACE. They also offer a freeware (but not free software) command-line decompression (including listing and testing) program called Unace for Mac OS X and Linux.
a. 6-3-5 Brainwriting
b. 180SearchAssistant
c. WinAce
d. Power III

66. _____ or Thunder Gigaget is a popular Chinese download manager and file sharing client that supports BitTorrent, eDonkey, Kad, and FTP. It is mainly used in the Mainland China and the software is only available in Chinese, although recently an English translation has been released. The client is developed by Thunder Networking Technologies, a Shenzhen startup formerly known as Sandai Technologies (ä¸‰ä»£ç§'æŠ€).

a. Xunlei
c. 6-3-5 Brainwriting
b. 180SearchAssistant
d. Power III

67. The _____ is a trojan horse which masquerades as a needed video codec in the form of ActiveX. It was first detected in late 2005, but only started gaining attention in mid-2006. Once installed, it displays popup ads with appearance similar to real Microsoft Windows warning popups, informing the user that their computer is infected with spyware.
    a. Power III
    b. 180SearchAssistant
    c. Zlob trojan
    d. 6-3-5 Brainwriting

68. The _____ is the independent self-regulatory organisation (SRO) of the advertising industry in the United Kingdom. The _____ is a non-statutory organisation and so cannot interpret or enforce legislation. However, its code of advertising practice broadly reflects legislation in many instances.
    a. Advertising Standards Authority
    b. ADTECH
    c. ACNielsen
    d. AMAX

69. The _____ is the self-regulatory body of the Australian print media. It was established in 1976 with two aims:

- to help preserve the traditional freedom of the press within Australia and;
- to ensure that the free press acts responsibly and ethically.

To carry out its latter function, it serves as a forum to which the public may take a complaint concerning the press. In its attempts to preserve the freedom of the press, it keeps a watching brief on developments which might impinge on such freedoms.

The Council is funded by the newspaper and magazine industries, and its authority rests on the willingness of publishers and editors to respect the Council's views, to adhere voluntarily to ethical standards and to admit mistakes publicly.

a. AMAX
c. ACNielsen
b. Australian Press Council
d. ADTECH

70. The _____ is a New Zealand Crown Entity created by the Broadcasting Act 1989 to develop and uphold standards of broadcasting for radio, free-to-air and pay television.

The main functions of the _____ are:

- Develop and maintain codified broadcasting standards
- Operate a complaints procedure.

The _____ is made up of a board appointed for a fixed term by the Governor General on the advice of the Minister of Broadcasting meaning that practically the Minister of Broadcasting (and Cabinet) appoint the board. The chair is always a barrister. One member is appointed after consultation with broadcasters and one after consultation with public interest groups.

a. 6-3-5 Brainwriting
b. Power III
c. Broadcasting Standards Authority
d. 180SearchAssistant

71. The _____ is an independent, non-governmental organization created by the Canadian Association of Broadcasters to administer standards established by its members, Canada's private broadcasters.

The Council's membership includes more than 630 private sector radio and television stations, specialty services and networks from across Canada, programming in English, French and third languages. As such, the Council allows the private broadcasting industry to be self-regulating and it acts as an intermediary in the regulatory process, which is governed by the Canadian Radio-television and Telecommunications Commission .

a. 180SearchAssistant
b. Power III
c. 6-3-5 Brainwriting
d. Canadian Broadcast Standards Council

72. The _____ is an independent agency of the United States government, created, directed, and empowered by Congressional statute , and with the majority of its commissioners appointed by the current President.

a. Federal Communications Commission
b. 6-3-5 Brainwriting
c. Power III
d. 180SearchAssistant

73. The _____ is a Non Governmental Organisation which exists to uphold standards in the New Zealand print media and promote freedom of speech in New Zealand. Founded in 1975, it is enabled to hear complaints against newspapers and other publications, particularly regarding allegations of bias and inaccuracy. It can order an offending publication to publish a summary of the Council's ruling, and will generally specify the prominence of the summary (for example, where in the newspaper.)

a. New Zealand Press Council
b. 6-3-5 Brainwriting
c. Power III
d. 180SearchAssistant

74. The Office of Communications (Welsh: Y Swyddfa Gyfathrebiadau) or, as it is more often known, _____, is the independent regulator and competition authority for the communication industries in the United Kingdom. _____ was initially established in the enabling device, the Office of Communications Act 2002, but received its full authority from the Communications Act 2003. On 29 December 2003, _____ inherited the duties that had previously been the responsibility of five regulatory bodies:

- the Broadcasting Standards Commission,
- the Independent Television Commission,
- the Office of Telecommunications (Oftel),
- the Radio Authority, and
- the Radiocommunications Agency.

The first chairman of _____ was David Currie, Dean of Cass Business School at City University and a life peer under the title Lord Currie of Marylebone. The first chief executive was Stephen Carter, formerly a senior executive of JWT UK and NTL.

a. AMAX
b. ACNielsen
c. Ofcom
d. ADTECH

75. _____ is an organizational lifecycle function within a company dealing with the planning or marketing of a product or products at all stages of the product lifecycle.

_____ and product marketing (outbound focused) are different yet complementary efforts with the objective of maximizing sales revenues, market share, and profit margins. The role of _____ spans many activities from strategic to tactical and varies based on the organizational structure of the company.

a. Requirement prioritization
c. Service product management
b. Product information management
d. Product management

76. _____ deals with the first of the '4P''s of marketing, which are Product, Pricing, Place, and Promotion. _____, as opposed to product management, deals with more outbound marketing tasks. For example, product management deals with the nuts and bolts of product development within a firm, whereas _____ deals with marketing the product to prospects, customers, and others.

a. Corporate transparency
c. Reverse hierarchy
b. Crisis management
d. Product Marketing

77. _____, is a division of the BSI Group which works with organizations to assess the implementation and administration of their management systems and business processes.

In order to ensure they have derived the most benefit from their management system an organization often decides to publicly prove that it meets the requirements by inviting a certification body like _____ to assess and evaluate their implementation of the management system.

_____ is an accredited registrar certify organizations to international management systems standards, such as ISO 9001 Quality Management, ISO 14001 Environmental Management, ISO/IEC 27001 Information Security Management, SA8000 Social Accountability.

a. 180SearchAssistant
c. BSI Management Systems
b. 6-3-5 Brainwriting
d. Power III

78. _____ was developed by Richard Zultner for his clients in the software industry in the 1990s. The premise was that the House of Quality and other large matrices demanded too much time and resources when speed of development was a critical customer need. The _____ is an efficient subset of Comprehensive QFD as developed by Dr. Yoji Akao, that can be later upgraded with no wasted effort.

a. Category management
c. Market share
b. Cyberdoc
d. Blitz QFD

79. A _____ is a collection of symbols, experiences and associations connected with a product, a service, a person or any other artifact or entity.

_____s have become increasingly important components of culture and the economy, now being described as 'cultural accessories and personal philosophies'.

Some people distinguish the psychological aspect of a _____ from the experiential aspect.

a. Brand
b. Store brand
c. Brand equity
d. Brandable software

80. _____ is a branding strategy used in a business alliance. _____ are divided into three types: A typical Yum! Brands co-branded restaurant that offer products from two or more of the company's brands (in this case, Taco Bell and KFC)

Cobrands are the usage of two or more brands on one certain product. For example, Dell computers carries three brands on their packages and cases: Dell, Microsoft Windows, and Intel.

a. Rack card
b. Comparative advertising
c. Rate card
d. Brand alliances

81. _____ refers to the marketing effects or outcomes that accrue to a product with its brand name compared with those that would accrue if the same product did not have the brand name . And, at the root of these marketing effects is consumers' knowledge. In other words, consumers' knowledge about a brand makes manufacturers/advertisers respond differently or adopt appropriately adapt measures for the marketing of the brand .
a. Product extension
b. Brand equity
c. Brand image
d. Brand aversion

82. _____ or brand stretching is a marketing strategy in which a firm marketing a product with a well-developed image uses the same brand name in a different product category. Organizations use this strategy to increase and leverage brand equity (definition: the net worth and long-term sustainability just from the renowned name.) An example of a _____ is Jello-gelatin creating Jello pudding pops.
a. Web 2.0
b. Brand awareness
c. Brand extension
d. Brand orientation

83. _____ is the application of marketing techniques to a specific product, product line, or brand. It seeks to increase the product's perceived value to the customer and thereby increase brand franchise and brand equity. Marketers see a brand as an implied promise that the level of quality people have come to expect from a brand will continue with future purchases of the same product.
a. Naming rights
b. Brand management
c. Store brand
d. Trademark distinctiveness

84. In marketing and strategy, _____ refers to a reduction in the sales volume, sales revenue, or market share of one product as a result of the introduction of a new product by the same producer.

For example, if Coca Cola were to introduce a similar product (say, Diet Coke or Cherry Coke), this new product could take some of the sales away from the original Coke. _____ is a key consideration in product portfolio analysis.

a. Business-to-consumer
b. Co-marketing
c. Marketing
d. Cannibalization

85. In business, a _____ is a product or a business unit that generates unusually high profit margins: so high that it is responsible for a large amount of a company's operating profit. This profit far exceeds the amount necessary to maintain the _____ business, and the excess is used by the business for other purposes.

A firm is said to be acting as a _____ when its earnings per share (EPS) is equal to its dividends per share (DPS), or in other words, when a firm pays out 100% of its free cash flow (FCF) to its shareholders as dividends at the end of each accounting term.

a. Goal setting
c. Crisis management
b. Corporate transparency
d. Cash cow

86. A _____ is a relatively new executive level position at a corporation, company, organization typically reporting directly to the CEO or board of directors. The _____ is responsible for a brand's image, experience, and promise, and propagating it throughout all aspects of the company. The brand officer oversees marketing, advertising, design, public relations and customer service departments.

a. Power III
c. Financial analyst
b. Chief executive officer
d. Chief brand officer

87. '_____' is a class of statistical techniques that can be applied to data that exhibit 'natural' groupings. _____ sorts through the raw data and groups them into clusters. A cluster is a group of relatively homogeneous cases or observations.

a. Power III
c. Structure mining
b. 180SearchAssistant
d. Cluster analysis

88. _____ is the process of using quantitative methods and qualitative methods to evaluate consumer response to a product idea prior to the introduction of a product to the market. It can also be used to generate communication designed to alter consumer attitudes toward existing products. These methods involve the evaluation by consumers of product concepts having certain rational benefits, such as 'a detergent that removes stains but is gentle on fabrics,' or non-rational benefits, such as 'a shampoo that lets you be yourself.' Such methods are commonly referred to as _____ and have been performed using field surveys, personal interviews and focus groups, in combination with various quantitative methods, to generate and evaluate product concepts.

a. Market analysis
c. Logit analysis
b. Cross tabulation
d. Concept testing

89. _____ is a statistical technique used in market research to determine how people value different features that make up an individual product or service.

The objective of _____ is to determine what combination of a limited number of attributes is most influential on respondent choice or decision making. A controlled set of potential products or services is shown to respondents and by analyzing how they make preferences between these products, the implicit valuation of the individual elements making up the product or service can be determined.

a. Likert scale
c. Semantic differential
b. Power III
d. Conjoint analysis

90. The _____ in statistical process control is a tool used to determine whether a manufacturing or business process is in a state of statistical control or not.

If the chart indicates that the process is currently under control then it can be used with confidence to predict the future performance of the process. If the chart indicates that the process being monitored is not in control, the pattern it reveals can help determine the source of variation to be eliminated to bring the process back into control.

a. Probability sampling
b. Survey research
c. Control chart
d. Statistics

91. _____, are also called Company colours, which are one of the most instantly recognizable elements of a corporate visual identity and promote a strong non-verbal message on the company's behalf.

- Red for Coca-Cola
- Blue for Pepsi

- Corporate logo
- Corporate identity
- Corporate image

a. Visual merchandising
b. Brand equity
c. Brand orientation
d. Corporate colours

92. In marketing, a _____ is the 'persona' of a corporation which is designed to accord with and facilitate the attainment of business objectives. It is usually visibly manifested by way of branding and the use of trademarks.

_____ comes into being when there is a common ownership of an organisational philosophy that is manifest in a distinct corporate culture -- the corporate personality.

a. Brand recognition
b. Corporate identity
c. Brand orientation
d. Brand ambassador

93. A _____ displays the joint distribution of two or more variables. They are usually presented as a contingency table in a matrix format. Whereas a frequency distribution provides the distribution of one variable, a contingency table describes the distribution of two or more variables simultaneously.

a. Logit analysis
b. Marketing research
c. Cross tabulation
d. Marketing research process

94. _____: Marketing and Selling High-Tech Products to Mainstream Customers (1991, revised 1999), is a marketing book by Geoffrey A. Moore that focuses on the specifics of marketing high tech products. Moore's exploration and expansion of the diffusions of innovations model has had a significant and lasting impact on high tech entrepreneurship. In 2006, Tom Byers, Faculty Director of Stanford Technology Ventures Program, described it as 'still the bible for entrepreneurial marketing 15 years later'.

a. Magalog
c. Power III
b. Consumer Reports
d. Crossing the Chasm

95. _____ is defined as: 'The loss or impending loss of manufacturers of items or suppliers of items or raw materials.' _____ and obsolescence are terms that are often used interchangeably. However, obsolescence refers to a lack of availability due to statutory and process changes, as well as new designs; whereas _____ is a lack of sources or materials.

Although it is not strictly limited to electronic systems much of the effort regarding _____ deals with electronic components that have a relatively short lifetime.

a. 6-3-5 Brainwriting
c. DMSMS
b. 180SearchAssistant
d. Power III

96. _____ is the process by which a new idea or new product is accepted by the market. The rate of _____ is the speed that the new idea spreads from one consumer to the next. Adoption is similar to _____ except that it deals with the psychological processes an individual goes through, rather than an aggregate market process.

a. Kano model
c. Market development
b. Perceptual maps
d. Diffusion

97. _____ is a theory of how, why, and at what rate new ideas and technology spread through cultures. Everett Rogers introduced it in his 1962 book, _____s, writing that 'Diffusion is the process by which an innovation is communicated through certain channels over time among the members of a social system.' The adoption curve becomes an s-curve when cumulative adoption is used.

Rogers theorized that innovations would spread through a community in an S curve, as the early adopters select the innovation (which may be a technology) first, followed by the majority, until a technology or innovation has reached its saturation point in a community.

According to Rogers, diffusion research centers on the conditions which increase or decrease the likelihood that a new idea, product, or practice will be adopted by members of a given culture.

a. 6-3-5 Brainwriting
c. Diffusion of innovation
b. 180SearchAssistant
d. Power III

98. _____ is to quit a procedure, and has different meanings for a treatment of an individual and a whole brand of a drug product:

- _____ of a treatment is to stop taking a drug. There are several reasons for _____, e.g.:
    - The ailment or reason it was taken has disappeared.
    - The adverse effects overweight the desired effects.
    - Other, better, alternatives are available.

- _____ for drug products is when a product's manufacture and/or support are stopped by the company that makes the product. This is usually due to low sales, but it does not mean the product never sold well. Many high selling products eventually see a drop in sales and eventual _____, usually after being superseded by a superior product.

- Out of print

a. Discontinuation
c. Reseller
b. Value-based pricing
d. Whole product

99. A _____ or disruptive innovation is a technological innovation that improves a product or service in ways that the market does not expect, typically by being lower priced or designed for a different set of consumers.

Disruptive innovations can be broadly classified into low-end and new-market disruptive innovations. A new-market disruptive innovation is often aimed at non-consumption (i.e., consumers who would not have used the products already on the market), whereas a lower-end disruptive innovation is aimed at mainstream customers for whom price is more important than quality.

a. Google Advertising Professional
c. Disruptive technology
b. Law of disruption
d. Commercial operations management

100. An _____ is a proposed category of trademark that would restrict the use of trademarked words and phrases in online advertising.

The State of Utah proposed this in response to trademark owners' claims that online advertisers have abused trademarked terms. Some online advertisers, particularly search engines, allow trademarked keywords to generate advertisements for a trademark holder's competitors.

a. ACNielsen
c. ADTECH
b. Umbrella brand
d. Electronic registration mark

101. _____ Management is the succession of strategies used by management as a product goes through its _____. The conditions in which a product is sold changes over time and must be managed as it moves through its succession of stages.

The _____ goes through many phases, involves many professional disciplines, and requires many skills, tools and processes.

a. Supplier diversity
c. Chain stores
b. Customer satisfaction
d. Product Life Cycle

Chapter 12. Test Preparation Part 12

1. _____ is a statistical method used to describe variability among observed variables in terms of fewer unobserved variables called factors. The observed variables are modeled as linear combinations of the factors, plus 'error' terms. The information gained about the interdependencies can be used later to reduce the set of variables in a dataset.
   a. Factor analysis
   b. Likert scale
   c. Power III
   d. Semantic differential

2. _____ is a type of global workflow in which tasks are passed around daily between work sites that are many time-zones apart. Such a workflow is set up in order to reduce project duration and increase responsiveness. Thus, the work is 'following the sun' and never stops.
   a. 180SearchAssistant
   b. Power III
   c. Maid in Manhattan
   d. Follow the sun

3. _____

The Four-Phase Model is a model for managers and management consultants developed by Prof.dr.ing. Teun W. Hardjono to analyze the present organisation and to determine what the organisational control points and interventions must be in relation to their strategy. It also points out what the most likely strategy for an organisation is from the point of view of the present organisation.

   a. Positioning
   b. Procter ' Gamble
   c. Maturity of Organizations and Business Excellence - The Four-Phase Model
   d. Product line extension

4. The _____ is an alternative technique used in brand marketing and product management to help a company decide what product(s) to add to its product portfolio, and which market opportunities are worthy of continued investment. Also known as the 'Directional Policy Matrix,' the GE multi-factor model was first developed by General Electric in the 1970s.

Conceptually, the _____ is similar to the Boston Box as it is plotted on a two-dimensional grid.

   a. Perceptual maps
   b. Parity Product
   c. Reinforcement
   d. GE matrix

5. A _____ is a trademark or brand name that has become the colloquial or generic description for a general class of product or service, rather than the specific meaning intended by the trademark's holder. Using a _____ to refer to the general form of what that trademark represents is a form of metonymy.
   a. Genericized trademark
   b. Trade Symbols
   c. Retail design
   d. Lovemarks

6. A _____ or trade mark, identified by the symbols â„¢ (not yet registered) and Â® (registered) business organization or other legal entity to identify that the products and/or services to consumers with which the _____ appears originate from a unique source of origin, and to distinguish its products or services from those of other entities. A _____ is a type of intellectual property, and typically a name, word, phrase, logo, symbol, design, image, or a combination of these elements. There is also a range of non-conventional _____s comprising marks which do not fall into these standard categories.
   a. 180SearchAssistant
   b. Trademark
   c. Risk management
   d. Power III

7. _____ is a quantitative method used in market research. This method involves generating and presenting a number of design alternatives to persons who are participating in the design, selection, or market research exercise.

The participants (referred to as 'selectors') transmit data indicative of their preferences among or between the presented design alternatives, and that data is used to derive a new generation of design alternatives or proposals.

a. ACNielsen
b. Intent scale translation
c. Exploratory research
d. IDDEA

8. _____ is an applied art whereby the aesthetics and usability of mass-produced products may be improved for marketability and production. The role of an _____er is to create and execute design solutions towards problems of form, usability, user ergonomics, engineering, marketing, brand development and sales.

The term '_____' is often attributed to the designer Joseph Claude Sinel in 1919 (although he himself denied it in later interviews) but the discipline predates that by at least a decade.

a. African Americans
b. Albert Einstein
c. AStore
d. Industrial design

9. _____ is a mathematical technique used by marketers to convert stated purchase intentions into purchase probabilities, that is, into an estimate of actual buying behaviour. It takes survey data on consumers purchase intentions and converts it into actual purchase probabilities.

A survey might ask a question using a five-point scale such as :

Which is most true about product X?

___ I definitely would use product X
___ I probably would use product X
___ I might use product X
___ I probably would not use product X
___ I definitely would not use product X

A marketing researcher will first assign numerical values to these intention categories.

a. IDDEA
b. Exploratory research
c. ACNielsen
d. Intent scale translation

10. The _____ is a theory of product development and customer satisfaction developed in the 80's by Professor Noriaki Kano which classifies customer preferences into five categories:

- Attractive
- One-Dimensional
- Must-Be
- Indifferent
- Reverse

These categories have been translated into English using various different names , but all refer to the original articles written by Kano.

The _____ offers some insight into the product attributes which are perceived to be important to customers. The purpose of the tool is to support product specification and discussion through better development team understanding. Kano's model focuses on differentiating product features, as opposed to focusing initially on customer needs.

   a. Customer value proposition   b. Marketing strategy
   c. Kano model   d. Macromarketing

11. The _____ refers to the way in which innovative technologies disrupt the social order or status quo. It first appeared in the book Unleashing the Killer App. According to the authors, societal change is incremental (linear) while technological change is exponential.

   a. Law of disruption   b. Market segment
   c. Customer franchise   d. Market environment

12. _____ is a statistical technique used by marketers to assess the scope of customer acceptance of a product, particularly a new product. It attempts to determine the intensity or magnitude of customers' purchase intentions and translates that into a measure of actual buying behaviour. _____ assumes that an unmet need in the marketplace has already been detected, and that the product has been designed to meet that need.

   a. Marketing research process   b. Logit analysis
   c. Focus group   d. Market analysis

13. _____ is defined by the American _____ Association as the activity, set of institutions, and processes for creating, communicating, delivering, and exchanging offerings that have value for customers, clients, partners, and society at large. The term developed from the original meaning which referred literally to going to market, as in shopping, or going to a market to sell goods or services.

_____ practice tends to be seen as a creative industry, which includes advertising, distribution and selling.

   a. Customer acquisition management   b. Marketing myopia
   c. Product naming   d. Marketing

14. _____ or labeling is the requirement of consumer products to state their ingredients or components.

Moral purchasing and problems like allergies are two things which are enabled by labelling. It is mandated in most developed nations, and increasingly in developing nations, especially for food products, e.g. 'Grade A' meats.

a. SA8000
b. Power III
c. Product stewardship
d. Mandatory labelling

15. A _____ is a technology that has been in use for long enough (for years or more likely decades or longer) that most of its initial faults and inherent problems have been removed or reduced by further development. In some contexts, it may also refer to technology which has not seen widespread use, but whose scientific background is well understood.

One of the key indicators of a _____ is the ease of use for both non-experts and professionals.

a. Requirement prioritization
b. Service life
c. Promise Index
d. Mature technology

16. _____ is a statistical method invented by Jordan Louviere in 1987 while on the faculty at the University of Alberta. The first working papers and publications occurred in the early 1990s. With _____, survey respondents are shown a set of the possible items and are asked to indicate the best and worst items (or most and least important, or most and least appealing , etc.).

a. Situational theory of publics
b. Gruppi di Acquisto Solidale
c. MaxDiff
d. Consumer confidence

17. _____ is a set of related statistical techniques often used in information visualization for exploring similarities or dissimilarities in data. MDS is a special case of ordination. An MDS algorithm starts with a matrix of item-item similarities, then assigns a location to each item in N-dimensional space, where N is specified a priori.

a. Multidimensional scaling
b. Convenience
c. Cocooning
d. Situational theory of publics

18. _____ is a graphics technique used by asset marketers that attempts to visually display the perceptions of customers or potential customers. Typically the position of a product, product line, brand, or company is displayed relative to their competition.

Perceptual maps can have any number of dimensions but the most common is two dimensions.

a. Market environment
b. Kano model
c. Customer franchise
d. Perceptual mapping

19. _____ is a statistical technique used by marketers to determine consumers' preferred core benefits. It usually supplements product positioning techniques like multi dimensional scaling or factor analysis and is used to create ideal vectors on perceptual maps.

Starting with raw data from surveys, researchers apply positioning techniques to determine important dimensions and plot the position of competing products on these dimensions. Next they regress the survey data against the dimensions.

a. Marketing research process b. Focus group
c. Cross tabulation d. Preference regression

20. _____ is a mathematical technique used by marketers to convert stated preferences into purchase probabilities, that is, into an estimate of actual buying behaviour. It takes survey data on consumers' preferences and converts it into actual purchase probabilities.

A survey might ask a question using a ranking scale such as :

Please rate the following products from 1 (most preferred) to 5 (least preferred.)

    __ product A
    __ product B
    __ product C
    __ product D
    __ product E

A marketing researcher will re-specify the numerical values during codification.

a. Market analysis b. Marketing research
c. Logit analysis d. Preference-rank translation

21. _____ is when a large distribution channel member (usually a retailer), buys from a manufacturer in bulk and puts its own name on the product. This strategy is only practical when the retailer does very high levels of volume. The advantages to the retailer are:

- more freedom and flexibility in pricing
- more control over product attributes and quality
- higher margins (or lower selling price)
- eliminates much of the manufacturer's promotional costs

Chapter 12. Test Preparation Part 12

The advantages to the manufacturer are:

- reduced promotional costs
- stability of sales volume (at least while the contract is operative)

- Kumar, Nirmalya; Steenkamp, Jan-Benedict E.M., Private Label Strategy - How to Meet the Store Brand Challenge. Harvard Business Press 2007

- private label
- brand management
- brand
- product management
- marketing

a. Customization
c. Promotion
b. Private branding
d. Rural market

22. A _____ is a collection of symbols, experiences and associations connected with a product, a service, a person or any other artifact or entity.

_____s have become increasingly important components of culture and the economy, now being described as 'cultural accessories and personal philosophies'.

Some people distinguish the psychological aspect of a _____ from the experiential aspect.

a. Brandable software
c. Brand equity
b. Brand
d. Store brand

23. _____ refer to a collection of facts usually collected as the result of experience, observation or experiment or a set of premises. This may consist of numbers, words particularly as measurements or observations of a set of variables. _____ are often viewed as a lowest level of abstraction from which information and knowledge are derived.

a. Pearson product-moment correlation coefficient
c. Data
b. Mean
d. Sample size

24. Product families/lines are quite common in our daily lives, but before a product family can be successfully established, an extensive process has to be followed. This process is known as _____, product line engineering, and software product lines.

Product family/line engineering can be defined as a method that creates an underlying architecture of an organizations product platform.

a. Product lifecycle
b. Promise Index
c. Product information management
d. Product Family Engineering

25. In project management, a _____ is an exhaustive, hierarchical tree structure of components that make up an item, arranged in whole-part relationship.

A _____ can help clarify what is to be delivered by the project and can help build a work breakdown structure.

The PRINCE2 project management method mandates the use of product based planning, part of which is developing a _____.

a. Project planning
b. 180SearchAssistant
c. Power III
d. Product breakdown structure

26. _____ is a marketing strategy that involves offering several products for sale as one combined product. This strategy is very common in the software business (for example: bundle a word processor, a spreadsheet, and a database into a single office suite), in the cable television industry (for example, basic cable in the United States generally offers many channels at one price), and in the fast food industry in which multiple items are combined into a complete meal. A bundle of products is sometimes referred to as a package deal or a compilation or an anthology.

a. Psychographic
b. Primary research
c. Product bundling
d. Technology acceptance model

27. _____ refers to the support of product management in the management of product information in a structured and consistent way in the form of catalogues. This in order to create a cost-effective means to help customers and channel partners understand what the functionalities and usability of certain products or services are. This includes comparison of product features, advising related products and alternative products and services.

a. Product lifecycle
b. Product management
c. Product catalogue management
d. Rapid prototyping

28. In marketing, _____ is the process of distinguishing the differences of a product or offering from others, to make it more attractive to a particular target market. This involves differentiating it from competitors' products as well as one's own product offerings.

Differentiation is a source of competitive advantage.

a. Packshot
b. Marketing myopia
c. Corporate image
d. Product differentiation

29. _____ refers to processes and technologies focused on centrally managing information about products, with a focus on the data required to market and sell the products through one or more distribution channels. A central set of product data can be used to feed consistent, accurate and up-to-date information to multiple output media such as web sites, print catalogs, ERP systems, and electronic data feeds to trading partners. _____ systems generally need to support multiple geographic locations, multi-lingual data, and maintenance and modification of product information within a centralized catalog to provide consistently accurate information to multiple channels in a cost-effective manner.

Chapter 12. Test Preparation Part 12
181

a. Product catalogue management
b. Service product management
c. Promise Index
d. Product information management

30. _____ is the collection and management of information from one or more sources and the distribution of that information to one or more audiences. This sometimes involves those who have a stake in, or a right to that information. Management means the organization of and control over the structure, processing and delivery of information.

a. AMAX
b. ACNielsen
c. Information management
d. ADTECH

31. _____ Management is the succession of strategies used by management as a product goes through its _____. The conditions in which a product is sold changes over time and must be managed as it moves through its succession of stages.

The _____ goes through many phases, involves many professional disciplines, and requires many skills, tools and processes.

a. Product life cycle
b. Supplier diversity
c. Chain stores
d. Customer satisfaction

32. _____ is the succession of strategies used by management as a product goes through its product life cycle. The conditions in which a product is sold changes over time and must be managed as it moves through its succession of stages.

The product life cycle goes through many phases, involves many professional disciplines, and requires many skills, tools and processes.

a. Cross-docking
b. Product life cycle
c. Small business
d. Product life cycle management

33. _____ or product life cycle is the course of a product's sales and profits over time. The five stages of each _____ are product development, introduction, growth, maturity and decline.

Product Life Cycle (Product lifecycleC) deals with the life of a product in the market with respect to business or commercial costs and sales measures.

a. Product lifecycle
b. Promise Index
c. Product Family Engineering
d. Product management

34. _____ is the process of managing the entire lifecycle of a product from its conception, through design and manufacture, to service and disposal. _____ integrates people, data, processes and business systems and provides a product information backbone for companies and their extended enterprise.

_____ is one of the four cornerstones of a corporation's information technology structure.

a. 6-3-5 Brainwriting
c. 180SearchAssistant
b. Power III
d. Product lifecycle management

35. _____ deals with the first of the '4P''s of marketing, which are Product, Pricing, Place, and Promotion. _____, as opposed to product management, deals with more outbound marketing tasks. For example, product management deals with the nuts and bolts of product development within a firm, whereas _____ deals with marketing the product to prospects, customers, and others.

a. Reverse hierarchy
c. Crisis management
b. Corporate transparency
d. Product marketing

36. The _____ is a brand evaluation and performance tool that tracks how well brands are keeping their promises and predicts their future revenue growth. The study is carried out on the annual basis by Promise, a London based brand consultancy, supported by the London School of Economics (LSE.)

Promise Gap is the difference between the image consumers have of a particular brand and the actual experience.

a. Service product management
c. Service life
b. Promise Index
d. Rapid prototyping

37. In engineering and manufacturing, _____ is involved in developing systems to ensure products or services are designed and produced to meet or exceed customer requirements or SLA's. Genetic algorithms are search techniques, used in computing to find exact or approximate solutions to optimization and search problems.

Alternative _____ procedures can be applied on a process to test statistically the null hypothesis, that the process is in control, against the alternative, that the process is out of control.

a. 6-3-5 Brainwriting
c. 180SearchAssistant
b. Quality control
d. Power III

38. _____ is the automatic construction of physical objects using solid freeform fabrication. The first techniques for _____ became available in the late 1980s and were used to produce models and prototype parts. Today, they are used for a much wider range of applications and are even used to manufacture production quality parts in relatively small numbers.

a. Service life
c. Product lifecycle
b. Rapid prototyping
d. Product management

39. _____ is used in Software product management for determining which candidate requirements of a software product should be included in a certain release. Requirements are also prioritized to minimize risk during development so that the most important or high risk requirements are implemented first. Several methods for assessing a prioritization of software requirements exist.

a. Service life
c. Product management
b. Product Family Engineering
d. Requirement prioritization

40. _____ is a concept pioneered by the Total Quality Management movement, which attempts to 'invert' the classical pyramid of Hierarchical organisation.

It promotes the idea that the most important employees are those who deal daily with the organisations' customers, ie those who would normally be at the 'bottom' of the hierarchy. It is then the role of supervisors and managers (normally 'higher' in the hierarchy) to support these employees and to remove the obstacles that hinder them in satisfying their customers' needs.

a. Performance measurement
b. Cash cow
c. Reverse hierarchy
d. Digital strategy

41. _____ is an advertisement in which a particular product specifically mentions a competitor by name for the express purpose of showing why the competitor is inferior to the product naming it.

This should not be confused with parody advertisements, where a fictional product is being advertised for the purpose of poking fun at the particular advertisement, nor should it be confused with the use of a coined brand name for the purpose of comparing the product without actually naming an actual competitor. ('Wikipedia tastes better and is less filling than the Encyclopedia Galactica.')

In the 1980s, during what has been referred to as the cola wars, soft-drink manufacturer Pepsi ran a series of advertisements where people, caught on hidden camera, in a blind taste test, chose Pepsi over rival Coca-Cola.

a. Heavy-up
b. GL-70
c. Cost per conversion
d. Comparative advertising

42. A product's _____ is its expected lifetime, or the acceptable period of use in service. It is the time that any manufactured item can be expected to be 'serviceable' or supported by its originating manufacturer.

Expected _____ consists of business policy, using tools and calculations from maintainability and reliability analysis.

a. Requirement prioritization
b. Software product management
c. Product management
d. Service life

43. _____ deals with managing a service product across it's complete life cycle. This organizational function is equally common between Business-to-business as well as Business-to-consumer businesses. A service product, unlike a hardware or software product, is intangible and manifests itself as pure professional services or as a combination of services with necessary software and/or hardware.

a. Product Family Engineering
b. Promise Index
c. Service life
d. Service product management

44. _____ is an organizational lifecycle function within a company dealing with the planning or marketing of a product or products at all stages of the product lifecycle.

_____ and product marketing (outbound focused) are different yet complementary efforts with the objective of maximizing sales revenues, market share, and profit margins. The role of _____ spans many activities from strategic to tactical and varies based on the organizational structure of the company.

a. Product management
c. Service product management
b. Requirement prioritization
d. Product information management

45. _____ is the process of managing software that is built and implemented as a product, taking into account lifecycle considerations and generally with a wide audience. This is in contrast to software that is delivered in an ad-hoc manner, typically to a limited clientele, e.g. service.

A software product is typically a single application or suite of applications built by a software company to be used by *many* customers, businesses or consumers.

a. Requirement prioritization
c. Product lifecycle
b. Software product management
d. Rapid prototyping

46. In economics, business, retail, and accounting, a _____ is the value of money that has been used up to produce something, and hence is not available for use anymore. In economics, a _____ is an alternative that is given up as a result of a decision. In business, the _____ may be one of acquisition, in which case the amount of money expended to acquire it is counted as _____.

a. Variable cost
c. Transaction cost
b. Fixed costs
d. Cost

47. The _____ is an information systems theory that models how users come to accept and use a technology. The model suggests that when users are presented with a new technology, a number of factors influence their decision about how and when they will use it, notably:

- Perceived usefulness (PU) - This was defined by Fred Davis as 'the degree to which a person believes that using a particular system would enhance his or her job performance'.
- Perceived ease-of-use (PEOU) - Davis defined this as 'the degree to which a person believes that using a particular system would be free from effort' (Davis, 1989.)

_____ is one of the most influential extensions of Ajzen and Fishbein's theory of reasoned action (TRA) in the literature. It was developed by Fred Davis and Richard Bagozzi (Bagozzi et al., 1992; Davis et al., 1989.) _____ replaces many of TRA's attitude measures with the two technology acceptance measures-- ease of use, and usefulness.

a. Technology acceptance model
c. Market development
b. Lifetime value
d. Market segment

48. Most new technologies follow a similar _____ describing the technological maturity of a product. This is not similar to a product life cycle, but applies to an entire technology, or a generation of a technology.

Technology adoption is the most common phenomenon driving the evolution of industries along the industry lifecycle.

a. Surcharge
c. BeyondROI
b. Technology maturity lifecycle
d. Cash carriers

Chapter 12. Test Preparation Part 12

49. In commerce, _____ is the length of time it takes from a product being conceived until its being available for sale. _____ is important in industries where products are outmoded quickly. A common assumption is that _____ matters most for first-of-a-kind products, but actually the leader often has the luxury of time, while the clock is clearly running for the followers.

   a. Product support
   b. Product life cycle management
   c. Time to market
   d. Customer centricity

50. In sociology, a _____ or angle of repose is the event of a previously rare phenomenon becoming rapidly and dramatically more common. The phrase was coined in its sociological use by Morton Grodzins, by analogy with the fact in physics that adding a small amount of weight to a balanced object can cause it to suddenly and completely topple.

Grodzins studied integrating American neighborhoods in the early 1960s.

   a. Tipping point
   b. Completely randomized designs
   c. Manufacturers' representatives
   d. Publicity

51. _____ is an expression as opposed to total cost of ownership (TCO.)

The TBO tries to summarize positive effects on acquisition of new computer components. These effects might be increases in high-value work, improvements in accuracy and efficiency, improvements in decision-making or improvements in customer service.

   a. Consumer-to-business
   b. Niche market
   c. Soft currency
   d. Total benefits of ownership

52. _____ is the state or fact of exclusive rights and control over property, which may be an object, land/real estate, or some other kind of property (like government-granted monopolies collectively referred to as intellectual property.) It is embodied in an _____ right also referred to as title.

_____ is the key building block in the development of the capitalist socio-economic system.

   a. AMAX
   b. ADTECH
   c. Ownership
   d. ACNielsen

53. A _____ is the name which a business trades under for commercial purposes, although its registered, legal name, used for contracts and other formal situations, may be another. Pharmaceuticals also have _____s, often dissimilar to their chemical names

Trading names are sometimes registered as trademarks or are regarded as brands.

   a. Local purchasing
   b. Soft currency
   c. Trade name
   d. Niche market

54. _____ is an important concept in the law governing trademarks and service marks. A trademark may be eligible for registration, or registrable, if amongst other things it performs the essential trademark function, and has distinctive character. Registrability can be understood as a continuum, with 'inherently distinctive' marks at one end, 'generic' and 'descriptive' marks with no distinctive character at the other end, and 'suggestive' and 'arbitrary' marks lying between these two points.
   a. Web 2.0
   b. Brand ambassador
   c. Trademark distinctiveness
   d. Lovemarks

55. Trademark _____ is an important concept in the law governing trademarks and service marks. A trademark may be eligible for registration, or registrable, if amongst other things it performs the essential trademark function, and has distinctive character. Registrability can be understood as a continuum, with 'inherently distinctive' marks at one end, 'generic' and 'descriptive' marks with no distinctive character at the other end, and 'suggestive' and 'arbitrary' marks lying between these two points.
   a. Corporate colours
   b. Distinctiveness
   c. Brand ambassador
   d. Brand implementation

56. _____ is the process of marketing, engineering design, manufacturing, testing and production where each stage of the development process is carried out separately, and the next stage cannot start until the previous stage is finished. Therefore the information flow is only in one direction, and it is not until the end of the chain that errors, changes and corrections can be relayed to the start of the sequence, causing estimated costs to be under predicted. This can cause many problems; such as time consumption due to many modifications being made as each stage does not take into account the next.
   a. Power III
   b. Traditional engineering
   c. 6-3-5 Brainwriting
   d. 180SearchAssistant

57. _____ is a technology acceptance model formulated by Venkatesh and others in 'User acceptance of information technology: Toward a unified view'. The UTAUT aims to explain user intentions to use an information system and subsequent usage behavior. The theory holds that four key constructs (performance expectancy, effort expectancy, social influence, and facilitating conditions) are direct determinants of usage intention and behaviour.
   a. Unified Theory of Acceptance and Use of Technology
   b. E-readiness
   c. ADTECH
   d. ACNielsen

58. The _____ is branding terminology for a unique alphabet which directly and subliminally communicates a company's values and personality through compelling imagery and design style. This alphabet, properly designed, results in an emotional connection between the brand and the consumer. The _____ is a key ingredient necessary to make an authentic and convincing brand strategy that can be applied uniquely and creatively in all forms of brand communications to both employees and customers.
   a. 180SearchAssistant
   b. Power III
   c. Visual brand language
   d. Microbrand

59. _____ is a term used in business to describe the process of capturing a customer's requirements. Specifically, the _____ is a market research technique that produces a detailed set of customer wants and needs, organized into a hierarchical structure, and then prioritized in terms of relative importance and satisfaction with current alternatives. _____ studies typically consist of both qualitative and quantitative research steps.

a. Crisis management
b. Corporate transparency
c. Voice of the customer
d. Digital strategy

60. A _____ is a brand under which goods or services are marketed in parallel but separately by a vendor in order to compete for customers based on price without compromising the prestige of the core brand or to reach out to a certain demographic with a unique approach tailored to their community. Two examples of _____s include Solo Mobile, a youth and value oriented brand under which wireless services are offered by Bell Mobility in Canada and the defunct Delta Air Lines Song brand which was intended to fight JetBlue for leisure travelers in the New York market by emulating the JetBlue experience and fares.

a. 180SearchAssistant
b. Visual brand language
c. Fighter Brand
d. Power III

61. A _____ is a small-scale brand recognized only in a certain geographic location or by consumers in a specific micromarket or niche market. The majority of _____s are owned by a microbusiness, but this trend is beginning to change due to the expansion of the internet and advancement of micromarketing tools. The process of identifying and microsegmenting customers into more refined targets is becoming an efficient and rewarding operation for larger companies and corporations.

a. 180SearchAssistant
b. Visual brand language
c. Power III
d. Microbrand

62. _____, a registered trademark of _____ Inc., is a mass loaded construction membrane material which increases the sound attenuation properties of conventional wall and floor/ceiling designs. _____ material is also used as a component in noise abatement systems. It was introduced in 1999 and is manufactured in the United States.

a. Acoustiblok
b. ADTECH
c. AMAX
d. ACNielsen

63. A _____ is a set of exclusive rights granted by a State to an inventor or his assignee for a limited period of time in exchange for a disclosure of an invention.

The procedure for granting _____s, the requirements placed on the _____ee and the extent of the exclusive rights vary widely between countries according to national laws and international agreements. Typically, however, a _____ application must include one or more claims defining the invention which must be new, inventive, and useful or industrially applicable.

a. Reasonable person standard
b. Product liability
c. Foreign Corrupt Practices Act
d. Patent

64. An _____ is a person who creates or discovers a new method, form, device or other useful means. The word _____ comes form the latin verb invenire, invent-, to find. The system of patents was established to encourage _____s by granting limited-term, limited monopoly on inventions determined to be sufficiently novel, non-obvious, and useful.

a. Inventor
b. ACNielsen
c. ADTECH
d. AMAX

65. An _____ is the manufacturing of a good or service within a category. Although _____ is a broad term for any kind of economic production, in economics and urban planning _____ is a synonym for the secondary sector, which is a type of economic activity involved in the manufacturing of raw materials into goods and products.

There are four key industrial economic sectors: the primary sector, largely raw material extraction industries such as mining and farming; the secondary sector, involving refining, construction, and manufacturing; the tertiary sector, which deals with services (such as law and medicine) and distribution of manufactured goods; and the quaternary sector, a relatively new type of knowledge _____ focusing on technological research, design and development such as computer programming, and biochemistry.

   a. Industry   b. AMAX
   c. ACNielsen   d. ADTECH

66. The verb _____ or grant _____ means to give permission. The noun _____ refers to that permission as well as to the document memorializing that permission. _____ may be granted by a party to another party as an element of an agreement between those parties.
   a. License   b. 180SearchAssistant
   c. Power III   d. 6-3-5 Brainwriting

67. _____ is the practice of using a company's name as a product brand name. It is an attempt to leverage corporate brand equity to create product brand recognition. It is a type of family branding or umbrella brand.
   a. Rebranding   b. Nation branding
   c. Corporate branding   d. Foreign branding

68. _____ is an indirect branding effect in which the communication of company employees serves to characterise their company's employer brand. The term also refers to the effects that company employees have on the image of their employer and the employer brand by publicly voicing their opinion on their place of work.
   a. Organizational culture   b. ACNielsen
   c. Employee branding   d. ADTECH

69. _____ is the concept of branding religious organizations, leaders in the hope of penetrating a media-driven, consumer-oriented culture more effectively. Primary goals include sharing a message of faith, raising money for charity, preaching salvation, building an inner-city outreach, and giving an audience hope. It refers to new rules for branding and communicating a message in the 21st century digital generation.
   a. Foreign branding   b. Faith branding
   c. Rebranding   d. Nation branding

70. _____ is an advertising and marketing term describing the implied cachet or superiority of products and services with foreign or foreign-sounding names.

In English-speaking countries, many cosmetics and fashion brands use French or Italian-styled names to imply a connection to the style-conscious, while northern European and Japanese names imply high quality and efficiency.

- The cold potato and leek soup vichyssoise was invented at the Ritz-Carlton Hotel in New York in the 1910s and was given a French name to make it sound more palatable.

- The name of the French wine-growing district of Chablis is used on bottles of generic-quality American white wine.

- Dolmio sauce has an Italian-sounding name but is not even sold in Italy.

- In the UK, the English company Moben Kitchens trademarked 'Möben' in 1977 because of the perceived higher quality of German and Scandinavian kitchens .

- The electrical retailer Dixons adopted the Japanese-sounding brand Matsui for consumer electronics.

- Ginsu knives have the faux Japanese-sounding name 'Ginsu' .

- In Germany it is common for television advertisements to be mainly in German, but to end with an English-language motto or slogan; recently, however, there has been a notable shift back towards German due to widespread complaints from language purists and studies showing that many target audiences with moderate English proficiency misunderstood the intended message. The most prominent example in this respect is Sat.1 Television, which abandoned its poorly understood corporate slogan 'Powered by Emotion' in favor of 'Sat.1 zeigt's allen', a phrase that is much more catchy to German ears and translates into 'Sat.1 shows it to everybody' or, idiomatically, 'Sat.1 shows everybody how it's done properly' or 'Sat.1 shows everybody how (or why) it is superior'.

a. Foreign branding
c. Nation branding
b. Rebranding
d. Faith branding

71. _____ is the marketing strategy of giving each product in a product portfolio its own unique brand name. This is contrasted with family branding in which the products in a product line are given the same brand name. The advantage of _____ is that each product has a self image and identity that's unique.
    a. Intangibility
    c. Online focus group
    b. Individual branding
    d. Engagement

72. _____ is a field of theory and practice which aims to measure, build and manage the reputation of countries (closely related to place branding.) It applies some approaches from commercial brand management practice to countries, in an effort to build, change, or protect their international reputations. It is based on the observation that the 'brand images' of countries are just as important to their success in the global marketplace as those of products and services.
    a. Faith branding
    c. Rebranding
    b. Nation branding
    d. Foreign branding

73. _____ is the process whereby people and their careers are marked as brands. It has been noted that while previous self-help management techniques were about self-improvement, the _____ concept suggests instead that success comes from self-packaging
   a. Personal branding
   b. Power III
   c. 6-3-5 Brainwriting
   d. 180SearchAssistant

74. _____ is the process by which a product or service developed with one brand, company or product line affiliation is marketed or distributed with a different identity. This may involve radical changes to the brand's logo, brand name, image, marketing strategy, and advertising themes. These changes are typically aimed at the repositioning of the brand/company, usually in an attempt to distance itself from certain negative connotations of the previous branding, or to move the brand upmarket.
   a. Faith branding
   b. Foreign branding
   c. Nation branding
   d. Rebranding

75. The _____ is a 501(c)(3) non-profit organization that promotes conservative Christian values as well as other public policy goals such as deregulation of the oil industry and lobbying against the Employee Free Choice Act. It was founded in 1977 by Rev. Donald Wildmon as the National Federation for Decency and is headquartered in Tupelo, Mississippi.
   a. ACNielsen
   b. AMAX
   c. American Family Association
   d. ADTECH

76. _____ is an ongoing protest and reaction to the commercialization of the North American Christmas season. It started unofficially in 1968, when Ellie Clark and her family decided to publicly disregard the commercial aspects of the Christmas holiday. Contemporarily a movement was created to extend Adbusters' Buy Nothing Day into the entire Christmas season.
   a. Power III
   b. 6-3-5 Brainwriting
   c. 180SearchAssistant
   d. Buy Nothing Christmas

77. _____ is an international day of protest against consumerism observed by social activists. Typically celebrated the Friday after American Thanksgiving in North America and the following day internationally, in 2008 the dates were November 28 and 29 respectively. It was founded by Vancouver artist Ted Dave and subsequently promoted by Adbusters magazine, based in Canada.
   a. 180SearchAssistant
   b. Power III
   c. 6-3-5 Brainwriting
   d. Buy Nothing Day

78. _____ is a movement which seeks to avoid all products of cruelty.

The _____ movement has developed from veganism into a philosophy of life which aims to avoid all the products of cruelty to humans or animals.

Products avoided include those which contain part of a dead animal, those which contain materials obtained from an animal by means of cruelty (such as keeping the animal in a confined space or separating mother from child etc.).

a. 180SearchAssistant
b. 6-3-5 Brainwriting
c. Power III
d. Cruelty-free

79. _____ is the equation of personal happiness with consumption and the purchase of material possessions.

The term is often associated with criticisms of consumption starting with Thorstein Veblen.

Veblen's subject of examination, the newly emergent middle class arising at the turn of the twentieth century, comes to full fruition by the end of the twentieth century through the process of globalization.

In economics, _____ refers to economic policies placing emphasis on consumption.

a. Consumerism
b. Power III
c. 6-3-5 Brainwriting
d. 180SearchAssistant

80. _____, originally named Patriotic Americans Boycotting Anti-American Hollywood (or PABAAH) was a U.S. nationalist-conservative organization that called for the boycott of Hollywood films made by film makers who have made statements deemed by the group to be 'unpatriotic,' 'anti-American' or treasonous. Though it mainly targeted film makers, it targeted other pop-culture figures, including musicians.

PABAAH was formed by Jon Alvarez in reaction to the 'Not in Our Name' Internet petition against the 2003 invasion of Iraq, which included many celebrity signatures.

a. Power III
b. 180SearchAssistant
c. 6-3-5 Brainwriting
d. FireHollywood

81. _____ is a list for goods and materials held available in stock by a business. It is also used for a list of the contents of a household and for a list for testamentary purposes of the possessions of someone who has died. In accounting _____ is considered an asset.

a. Ending Inventory
b. ADTECH
c. ACNielsen
d. Inventory

82. In mathematics, an _____, or central tendency of a data set refers to a measure of the 'middle' or 'expected' value of the data set. There are many different descriptive statistics that can be chosen as a measurement of the central tendency of the data items.

An _____ is a single value that is meant to typify a list of values.

a. AMAX
b. ADTECH
c. ACNielsen
d. Average

83. Under the _____, it is assumed that the cost of inventory is based on the average cost of the goods available for sale during the period. Average cost is computed by dividing the total cost of goods available for sale by the total units available for sale. This gives a weighted-average unit cost that is applied to the units in the ending inventory.

a. Average-cost method
b. Inventory
c. ACNielsen
d. ADTECH

84. In marketing, _____ refers to the total cost of holding inventory. This includes warehousing costs such as rent, utilities and salaries, financial costs such as opportunity cost, and inventory costs related to perishibility, shrinkage and insurance.

When there are no transaction costs for shipment, _____s are minimized when no excess inventory is held at all, as in a Just In Time production system.

a. Reverse auction
b. Vendor Managed Inventory
c. Merchandise management system
d. Carrying cost

85. _____ is the maximum amount of goods that a company can possibly sell during this fiscal year. It have the formula:

Beginning Inventory (at the start of this year)+ Purchases (within this year)+ Production (within this year)= _____

Notice that purchases and production might not be the same throughout the year, since purchase cost and production cost might vary during the year. But at the end, the total cost of purchases and production are added to beginning inventory cost to give _____.

a. Stock obsolescence
b. Cost of Goods Available for Sale
c. Phantom inventory
d. Finished good

Chapter 13. Test Preparation Part 13

1. In economics, business, retail, and accounting, a _____ is the value of money that has been used up to produce something, and hence is not available for use anymore. In economics, a _____ is an alternative that is given up as a result of a decision. In business, the _____ may be one of acquisition, in which case the amount of money expended to acquire it is counted as _____.
   a. Cost
   b. Variable cost
   c. Transaction cost
   d. Fixed costs

2. In financial accounting, _____ or cost of sales includes the direct costs attributable to the production of the goods sold by a company. This amount includes the materials cost used in creating the goods along with the direct labor costs used to produce the good. It excludes indirect expenses such as distribution costs and sales force costs.
   a. Stock demands
   b. FIFO and LIFO accounting
   c. Stock obsolescence
   d. Cost of goods sold

3. _____ refers to the process by which tissues of dead organisms break down into simpler forms of matter. Such a breakdown of dead organisms is essential for new growth and development of living organisms because it recycles the finite chemical constituents and frees up the limited physical space in the biome. Bodies of living organisms begin to decompose shortly after death.
   a. Decomposition
   b. Power III
   c. 6-3-5 Brainwriting
   d. 180SearchAssistant

4. _____ is the amount of inventory a company have in stock at the end of this fiscal year. It is closely related with _____ Cost, which is the amount of money spent to get these goods in stock. It should be calculated at the Lower of Cost or Market.
   a. Ending Inventory
   b. ACNielsen
   c. Inventory
   d. ADTECH

5. _____ is a list for goods and materials held available in stock by a business. It is also used for a list of the contents of a household and for a list for testamentary purposes of the possessions of someone who has died. In accounting _____ is considered an asset.
   a. Ending Inventory
   b. ADTECH
   c. ACNielsen
   d. Inventory

6. _____ methods are means of managing inventory and financial matters involving the money a company ties up within inventory of produced goods, raw materials, parts, components, or feed stocks. FIFO stands for first-in, first-out, meaning that the oldest inventory items are recorded as sold first. LIFO stands for last-in, first-out, meaning that the most recently purchased items are recorded as sold first.
   a. Stock demands
   b. GMROII
   c. Stock forecast
   d. FIFO and LIFO accounting

7. _____ is an acronym which stands for last in, first out. In computer science and queueing theory this refers to the way items stored in some types of data structures are processed. By definition, in a _____ structured linear list, elements can be added or taken off from only one end, called the 'top'.
   a. Retailers' cooperative
   b. Publicity
   c. LIFO
   d. Flyer

8. _____s are goods that have completed the manufacturing process but have not yet been sold or distributed to the end user.

Manufacturing has three classes of inventory:

1. Raw material
2. Work in process
3. _____s

A good purchased as a 'raw material' goes into the manufacture of a product. A good only partially completed during the manufacturing process is called 'work in process'. When the good is completed as to manufacturing but not yet sold or distributed to the end-user is called a '_____'.

a. Stock forecast
c. Stock obsolescence
b. Perpetual inventory
d. Finished good

9. Gross Margin Return on Inventory Investment (_____) is a ratio in microeconomics that describes a seller's income on every dollar spent on inventory. It is one way to determine how valuable the seller's inventory is, and describes the relationship between total sales, total profit from total sales, and the amount of resources invested in the inventory sold. A seller will aim for a high _____.

a. Periodic inventory
c. Stock mix
b. GMROII
d. Stock obsolescence

10. The _____ is an equation that equals the cost of goods sold divided by the average inventory. Average inventory equals beginning inventory plus ending inventory divided by 2.

The formula for _____:

$$\text{Inventory Turnover} = \frac{\text{Cost of Goods Sold}}{\text{Average Inventory}}$$

The formula for average inventory:

$$\text{Average Inventory} = \frac{\text{Beginning inventory} + \text{Ending inventory}}{2}$$

A low turnover rate may point to overstocking, obsolescence, or deficiencies in the product line or marketing effort.

a. ACNielsen
c. ADTECH
b. Inventory turnover
d. AMAX

11. _____ is one of the Accounting Liquidity ratios, a financial ratio. This ratio measures the number of times, on average, the inventory is sold during the period. Its purpose is to measure the liquidity of the inventory.

a. ACNielsen
c. ADTECH
b. Inventory turnover ratio
d. Internality

12. Traditional manufacturing is sometimes referred to as _____ manufacturing by Manufacturing engineers In JIC, manufacturers need to maintain large inventories of supplies, parts, warehousing resources, and extra workers to meet production contingencies. These contingencies, more common in less industrialized countries, can be poor transportation, poor quality control, other suppliers production problems, and environmental.

   a. Positioning
   b. Manufacturers' representatives
   c. Statistical surveys
   d. Just-In-Case

13. _____ is an inventory strategy implemented to improve the return on investment of a business by reducing in-process inventory and its associated carrying costs. In order to achieve JIT the process must have signals of what is going on elsewhere within the process. This means that the process is often driven by a series of signals, which can be Kanban , that tell production processes when to make the next part.

   a. Clutter
   b. Promotion
   c. Just-in-time
   d. Personalization

14. _____ is an approach to valuing and reporting inventory. Normally ending inventory is stated at historical cost (what was paid to obtain it) but there are times when the original cost of the ending inventory is greater than the cost of replacement thus the inventory has lost value. If the inventory has decreased in value below historical cost then its carrying value is reduced and reported on the balance sheet.

   a. Power III
   b. 6-3-5 Brainwriting
   c. 180SearchAssistant
   d. Lower of Cost or Market

15. _____ is a method of evaluating an asset's worth when held in inventory, in the field of accounting. _____ is part of the Generally Accepted Accounting Principles that apply to valuing inventory, so as to not overstate or understate the value of inventory goods. _____ is generally equal to the selling price of the inventory goods less the selling costs (completion and disposal.)

   a. Pick and pack
   b. Promotional mix
   c. Net realisable value
   d. Power III

16. A personal and cultural _____ is a relative ethic _____, an assumption upon which implementation can be extrapolated. A _____ system is a set of consistent _____s and measures that is soo not true. A principle _____ is a foundation upon which other _____s and measures of integrity are based.

   a. Package-on-Package
   b. Supreme Court of the United States
   c. Value
   d. Perceptual maps

17. _____ are old parts for obsolete equipment that have never been sold at retail.

The term refers to merchandise being offered for sale which was manufactured long ago but that has never been used. Such merchandise may not be produced anymore, and the _____ may represent the only market source of a particular item at the present time.

   a. 6-3-5 Brainwriting
   b. 180SearchAssistant
   c. New old stock
   d. Power III

18. _____ is in the most general sense the complete process from point of sales inquiry to delivery of a product to the customer. Sometimes _____ is used to describe the more narrow act of distribution or the logistics function, however, in the broader sense it refers to the way firms respond to customer orders.

The first research towards defining _____ strategies was published by Mather and his discussion of the P:D ratio, whereby P is defined as the production lead-time, i.e. how long it takes to manufacture a product, and D is the demand lead-time, i.e. how long customers are willing to wait for the order to be completed.

   a. ADTECH
   b. AMAX
   c. ACNielsen
   d. Order fulfillment

19. _____ is a system of inventory in which updates are made on a periodic basis. This differs from perpetual inventory systems, where updates are made continuously.
   a. Cost of goods sold
   b. Periodic inventory
   c. Stock demands
   d. FIFO and LIFO accounting

20. In business and accounting/accountancy, _____ or continuous inventory describes systems of inventory where information on inventory quantity and availability is updated on a continuous basis as a function of doing business. Generally this is accomplished by connecting the inventory system with order entry and in retail the point of sale system. In this case, book inventory would be exactly the same as, or almost the same, as the real inventory.
   a. Net realisable value
   b. Stock forecast
   c. Stock mix
   d. Perpetual inventory

21. _____ is a common expression for goods that an inventory accounting system considers to be on-hand at a storage location, but are not actually available. This could be due to the items being moved without recording the change in the inventory accounting system, breakage, theft, data entry errors or deliberate fraud. The resulting discrepancy between the online inventory balance and physical availability can delay automated reordering and lead to out-of-stock incidents.
   a. Cost of goods sold
   b. Phantom inventory
   c. Reorder point
   d. Finished good

22. The _____ is the level of inventory when a fresh order should be made with suppliers to bring the inventory up by the Economic order quantity (EOQ.)

The _____ for replenishment of stock occurs when the level of inventory drops down to zero. In view of instantaneous replenishment of stock the level of inventory jumps to the original level from zero level.

   a. Stock forecast
   b. Reorder point
   c. Net realisable value
   d. Stock obsolescence

23. _____ is a term used by inventory specialists to describe a level of stock that is maintained below the cycle stock to buffer against stockouts. _____ exists to counter uncertainties in supply and demand. _____ is defined as extra units of inventory carried as protection against possible stockouts.
   a. Cross-docking
   b. Product support
   c. Safety stock
   d. Price-weighted

24. _____ is a method of finding out ending inventory cost. It requires a very detailed physical count, so that the company knows exactly how many of each goods brought on specfic dates remained at year end inventory. When this information is found, the amount of goods are multiplied by their purchase cost at their purchase date, to get a number for the ending inventory cost.

a. Phantom inventory
c. Stock mix
b. Reorder point
d. Specific Identification

25. _____ - the demand a customer has for a certain product or products. The demand is influenced by price, availability and position of the product in relation to the consumer. .
   a. Stock mix
   c. Finished good
   b. Stock demands
   d. Perpetual inventory

26. In economics, _____ is the desire to own something and the ability to pay for it. The term _____ signifies the ability or the willingness to buy a particular commodity at a given point of time .

   a. Discretionary spending
   c. Demand
   b. Market dominance
   d. Market system

27. _____ - by evaluating current and past stock demands and stock levels accurate stock forecasting can be made to customer needs. Stock forecasting is integral to managing profitability in any organisation that deals with inventory. .
   a. Reorder point
   c. Stock mix
   b. Stock forecast
   d. Phantom inventory

28. _____ - is the combination of products a company sells or manufactures. The _____ is determined by the demand for certain products and the profitability of those products.
   a. Finished good
   c. Stock forecast
   b. Stock mix
   d. Stock obsolescence

29. _____ consists of the sale of goods or merchandise from a fixed location, such as a department store or kiosk in small or individual lots for direct consumption by the purchaser. _____ may include subordinated services, such as delivery. Purchasers may be individuals or businesses.
   a. Warehouse store
   c. Thrifting
   b. Charity shop
   d. Retailing

30. In retail an _____, draw tenant, anchor tenant is one of the larger stores in a shopping mall, usually a department store or a major retail chain.

When the planned shopping mall format was developed by Victor Gruen in the mid-1950s, signing larger department stores was necessary for the financial stability of the projects, and to draw retail traffic that would result in visits to the smaller stores in the mall as well. Anchors generally have their rents heavily discounted, and may even receive cash inducements from the mall to remain open.

   a. Outlet store
   c. Online ticket brokering
   b. Endcap
   d. Anchor store

31. _____ is a term for the Friday after Thanksgiving in the United States, which is the beginning of the traditional Holiday shopping season. Because Thanksgiving falls on the fourth Thursday in November in the United States, _____ occurs between the 23rd and the 29th of November.

_____ is not an official holiday, but many employees have the day off (with the exception of those employed in retail), which increases the number of potential shoppers.

a. Dunkin' Donuts
b. Black Friday
c. Gold Key Matching Service
d. Statistical surveys

32. _____ is the examining of goods or services from retailers with the intent to purchase at that time. _____ is an activity of selection and/or purchase. In some contexts it is considered a leisure activity as well as an economic one.
a. Hawkers
b. Khodebshchik
c. Discount store
d. Shopping

33. A _____, from the French word for 'shop,' is a small shopping outlet, especially one that specializes in elite and fashionable items such as clothing and jewelry.

The term entered into everyday English use in the late 1960s when, for a brief period, London, UK was the centre of the fashion trade. Carnaby Street and the Kings Road were the focus of much media attention as home to the most fashionable _____s of the era.

a. Warehouse store
b. Catalog merchant
c. Boutique
d. People counter

34. _____ refers to a company which possesses a building for operations. The phrase can be a misnomer since not all buildings are physically constructed from bricks and mortar.

In the jargon of eCommerce, _____ businesses are companies which have a physical presence (for example, a building made of bricks and mortar) -- which offer face-to-face consumer experiences.

a. History of pawnbroking
b. Brick and mortar
c. Warehouse club
d. Strip mall

35. In the jargon of eCommerce, _____es are companies which have a physical presence (for example, a building made of bricks and mortar) - which offer face-to-face consumer experiences. This term is usually used to contrast with a transitory business or an internet-only presence An example would be the brick and mortar movie rental shop Blockbuster Video--the competition from the new online rental services offered by Netflix.
a. Khodebshchik
b. Layaway
c. Brick and mortar
d. Brick and mortar business

36. _____ are a way of selling consumables by weight. The product is stored in bins in a section of the retail floor. A customer can measure out an amount of product into a plastic bag, to be later weighed at the point of sale.
a. Bulk bins
b. Confectionery store
c. Charity shop
d. Khodebshchik

Chapter 13. Test Preparation Part 13

37. A _____ or vehicle local distribution is a business that sells new cars and/or used cars at the retail level, based on a dealership contract with an automaker or its sales subsidiary. It employs automobile salespeople to do the selling. It may also provide maintenance services for cars, thus employing automobile mechanics, stock and sell spare automobile parts, and process warranty claims.
   a. Car dealership
   b. 180SearchAssistant
   c. Power III
   d. 6-3-5 Brainwriting

38. _____ is a form of shelving that uses a gravity-feed rear load design. Each unit consists of one or more inclined runways. Merchandise is loaded in the rear of each runway.
   a. 180SearchAssistant
   b. 6-3-5 Brainwriting
   c. Carton flow
   d. Power III

39. _____ were used in shops and department stores to carry customers' payments from the sales assistant to the cashier and to carry the change and receipt back again.

The earliest type was a wooden ball which ran along sloping rails. One set of rails sloped down from sales desk to cash office and another set sloped in the opposite direction.

   a. Relationship Management Application
   b. Hospitality point of sales systems
   c. Black Friday
   d. Cash carriers

40. _____ is a term for a form of retailing. The typical merchant sold a wide variety of household and personal products, with many emphasizing jewelry. Unlike a self-serve retail store, most of the items are not displayed; customers selected the products from printed catalogs in the store and filled out an order form.
   a. Discount store
   b. Closeout store
   c. Khodebshchik
   d. Catalog merchant

41. _____s function as professionals who deal with trade, dealing in commodities that they do not produce themselves, in order to produce profit.

_____s can be of two types:

   1. A wholesale _____ operates in the chain between producer and retail _____. Some wholesale _____s only organize the movement of goods rather than move the goods themselves.
   2. A retail _____ or retailer, sells commodities to consumers (including businesses.) A shop owner is a retail _____.

A _____ class characterizes many pre-modern societies. Its status can range from high (even achieving titles like that of _____ prince or nabob) to low, such as in Chinese culture, due to the soiling capabilities of profiting from 'mere' trade, rather than from the labor of others reflected in agricultural produce, craftsmanship, and tribute.

In the United States, '_____' is defined (under the Uniform Commercial Code) as any person while engaged in a business or profession or a seller who deals regularly in the type of goods sold.

a. Merchant
b. Retail loss prevention
c. RFM
d. Trade credit

42. _____ are retail outlets, usually corporate owned businesses, that share brands and central management, often with standardized business methods and practices, and these may include stores, restaurants, and some service-oriented businesses.

The displacement of independent businesses by chains has generated controversy in many countries, and has sparked increased collaboration among independent businesses and communities to prevent chain proliferation. Such efforts occur within national trade groups such as the American Booksellers Association, as well as community-based coalitions such as Independent Business Alliances.

a. Supplier diversity
b. Chain stores
c. Customer base
d. Product life cycle management

43. A _____, thrift shop, thrift store, hospice shop (U.S., Canada), resale shop (when not meaning consignment shop (U.S.)), or op shop (Australia/N.Z.) is a retail establishment operated by a charitable organization for the purpose of fundraising.

_____s are a type of social enterprise.

a. Specialty stores
b. Layaway
c. Quality competition in retailing
d. Charity shop

44. _____ is the commercial phenomenon of merchants and retailers exploiting the commercialized status of Christmas by moving up the start of the holiday shopping season. The term was first used in the mid 1980s.

It is associated with a desire of merchants to take advantage of particularly heavy Christmas-related shopping well before Black Friday in the US and before Halloween in Canada, Ireland and the UK.

a. Christmas season
b. Power III
c. 180SearchAssistant
d. Christmas creep

45. A _____ or clearance is the final sale of an item or items to zero inventory. It may be a given model of item that is not selling well, or in the case of the final closure of a retailer because of a relocation, a fire (fire sale), or especially because of a bankruptcy. In the latter case, it is usually known as a going-out-of-business sale, and is part of a liquidation.
a. Warehouse store
b. Bulk bins
c. Khodebshchik
d. Closeout

46. A _____ is a retailer specializing in buying closeout items wholesale from other retailers and selling them at a discount. Big Lots is probably the most well-known _____ chain in the U.S., but other stores such as TJ Maxx, Ross Dress For Less, Marshall's, and Value City are also common, specializing more in clothing and housewares.

Some clearance merchandise is non-returnable at some stores, as the intent is of course to get rid of the items.

a. People counter
b. Same-store sales
c. Charity shop
d. Closeout store

47. A _____ sells confectionery and is usually targeted to children or tourists in the modern retail world. Most confectioners are usually filled with an assortment of sweets far larger than a grocer or convenience store can accommodate, the selection is often nostalgic for many and sometimes overwhelming on the senses. Very often unchanged in layout since their inception, either because the stores are rare survivals in a competitive world or tourism aimed recreations, such stores have a warming and nostalgic feel with vast collections of sweets in jars, with sights and smells to trigger childhood memories.
   a. Thrifting
   b. Scrapstore
   c. Khodebshchik
   d. Confectionery store

48. _____ is the act of consigning, which is placing a person or thing in the hand of another, but retaining ownership until the goods are sold or person is transferred. This may be done for shipping, transfer of prisoners, or for sale in a store (i.e. a _____ shop.)

Features of _____ are as follows: 1)The Relation between the two parties is that of consignor and consignee and not that of buyer and seller 2)The consignor is entitled to receive all the expenses in connection with _____ 3)The consignee is not responsible for damage of goods during transport or any other procedure.

   a. History of pawnbroking
   b. Consignment
   c. Garage sale
   d. Self service

49. _____ is anything that is intended to save time, energy or frustration. A _____ store at a petrol station, for example, sells items that have nothing to do with gasoline/petrol, but it saves the consumer from having to go to a grocery store. '_____' is a very relative term and its meaning tends to change over time.
   a. Convenience
   b. MaxDiff
   c. Marketing buzz
   d. Demographic profile

50. A _____ is a small store or shop that sells candy, ice-cream, soft drinks, lottery tickets, newspapers and magazines, along with a small selection of food and grocery supplies. Stores that are part of gas stations may also sell motor oil, windshield washer fluid, radiator fluid, and maps. Often toiletries and other hygiene products are stocked, and some of these stores also offer money orders and wire transfer services or liquor products.
   a. 180SearchAssistant
   b. Power III
   c. 6-3-5 Brainwriting
   d. Convenience store

51. A _____ is a retail establishment which specializes in selling a wide range of products without a single predominant merchandise line. _____s usually sell products including apparel, furniture, appliances, electronics, and additionally select other lines of products such as paint, hardware, toiletries, cosmetics, photographic equipment, jewelry, toys, and sporting goods. Certain _____s are further classified as discount _____s.
   a. 180SearchAssistant
   b. Power III
   c. 6-3-5 Brainwriting
   d. Department store

52. A _____ is a type of department store, which sell products at prices lower than those asked by traditional retail outlets. Most discount department stores offer wide assortments of goods; others specialize in such merchandise as jewelry, electronic equipment, or electrical appliances. _____s are not dollar stores, which sell goods at a dollar or less.
   a. Sales per unit area
   b. Strip mall
   c. Gruen transfer
   d. Discount store

53. _____ are products such as textiles, ready-to-wear clothing, and sundries. In U.S. retailing, a _____ store carries consumer goods that are distinct from those carried by hardware stores and grocery stores, though '_____' as a term for textiles has been dated back to 1742 in England or even a century earlier. _____ can be carried by stores specializing just in those products (a type of specialty store), or may be carried by a general store or a department store or more recently, a big box store.
   a. 180SearchAssistant
   b. Sample sales
   c. Power III
   d. Dry goods

54. _____s (or stores) are retail outlets that do not apply local or national taxes and duties. Duty-free shopping is a bit of misnomer though because shoppers may still have to pay duties in their home country on items purchased from a _____. They are often found in the international zone of international airports, sea ports or onboard passenger ships.
   a. Duty-free shop
   b. 6-3-5 Brainwriting
   c. Power III
   d. 180SearchAssistant

55. _____ also known by the acronym _____, is a system used by retailers for displaying product pricing on shelves. Typically, electronic display modules are attached to the front edge of retail shelving. These modules use Liquid Crystal Display (LCD) or similar technology to show the current product price to the customer.
   a. Outlet store
   b. Online ticket brokering
   c. Electronic Shelf Label
   d. Endcap

56. _____ is a technological method for preventing shoplifting from retail stores or pilferage of books from libraries. Special tags are fixed to merchandise or books. These tags are removed or deactivated by the clerks when the item is properly bought or checked out.
   a. ACNielsen
   b. ADTECH
   c. AMAX
   d. Electronic article surveillance

57. _____ is a display for a product placed at the end of an aisle. It is perceived to give a brand a competitive advantage. It is often available for lease to a manufacturer in a retail environment.
   a. Online ticket brokering
   b. Electronic Shelf Label
   c. Endcap
   d. Outlet store

58. _____ is an Italian word, formed by analogy with biblioteca ('book repository, library'), which literally means 'wine repository' (from Oeno/Eno- 'wine', and teca θήκη, 'receptacle, case, box'), but is used to describe a special type of local or regional wine shop that originated in Italy. The concept of an _____ has also spread to some other countries. A genuine _____ is primarily directed at giving visitors or tourists the possibility to taste these wines at a reasonable fee and possibly to buy them.
   a. ACNielsen
   b. AMAX
   c. Enoteca
   d. ADTECH

59. A _____ or swap meet is a type of bazaar where inexpensive or secondhand goods are sold or bartered. It may be indoors, such as in a warehouse or school gymnasium; or it may be outdoors, such as in a field or under a tent. The _____ vendors may range from a family that is renting a table for the first time to sell a few unwanted household items to a commercial operation including a large variety of used merchandise, scouts who rove the region buying items for sale from garage sales and other _____s, and several staff watching the stalls.

a. Flea market
b. 6-3-5 Brainwriting
c. 180SearchAssistant
d. Power III

60. A _____ rummage sale, tag sale, attic sale, moving sale is an informal, irregularly scheduled event for the sale of used goods by private individuals, in which 'block sales' are allowed, so that sellers are not required to obtain business licenses or collect sales tax. Some professional companies offer their expert services where they actually come into your house and price everything at fair market value, advertise the sale, and do all the selling for you. One reputable company that offers this service is Sell My Stuff Toronto Yard sale in Spring 2005 in California Yard sale in Summer 2005 in California

Typically the goods in a _____ are unwanted items from the household with the home owners conducting the sale.

a. Self service
b. Self checkout
c. Scrapstore
d. Garage sale

61. _____ or general merchandise is a term used in retail and wholesale business in reference to merchandise not limited to some particular category. General merchandise stores (general stores) address this sector of retail.

According to the North American Industry Classification System 2002, the following types of general merchandise are excluded from the line carried by general stores:

- general line of building and home improvement materials (44411, Home Centres)
- general line of grocery items (44511, Supermarkets and Other Grocery (except Convenience) Stores)
- general line of used goods (45331, Used Merchandise Stores)

- Convenience store

a. Specialist store
b. Brick and mortar
c. Warehouse club
d. General line of merchandise

62. Merchandising refers to the methods, practices and operations conducted to promote and sustain certain categories of commercial activity. The term is understood to have different specific meanings depending on the context. _____ is a sale goods at a store

In marketing, one of the definitions of merchandising is the practice in which the brand or image from one product or service is used to sell another.

a. Merchandise
b. New Media Strategies
c. Merchandising
d. Sales promotion

63. In retail terms, _____ are items of merchandise which must be placed back on the store shelves. They usually accumulate during the store's open hours, and comprise a combination of returned items, items customers have decided not to purchase, and items store employees may have found left lying on the wrong shelf. _____ can often accumulate over several days because businesses, especially larger department stores, tend to have other priorities at the time and not enough employment to put the _____ away.

a. Go-backs
b. Brick and mortar
c. Sales per unit area
d. Garage sale

64. In shopping mall design, the _____ refers to the moment when consumers respond to 'scripted disorientation' cues in the environment. It is named for Austrian architect Victor Gruen (who disavowed such manipulative techniques.) Recently, the _____ has been popularised by Douglas Rushkoff.

a. Stock rotation
b. Thrifting
c. Layaway
d. Gruen transfer

65. _____ is a technique used in propaganda and advertising. Also known as association, this is a technique of projecting positive or negative qualities (praise or blame) of a person, entity, object, or value (an individual, group, organization, nation, patriotism, etc.) to another in order to make the second more acceptable or to discredit it.

a. Micro ads
b. Sexism,
c. Supplier
d. Transfer

66. _____ is the name given to road-side vendors selling merchandise.

Can refer to a vendor selling items in-seat to fans at a sports venue. Such items generally include popcorn, cotton candy, peanuts, beverages, and ice cream.

a. Product line extension
b. Hawkers
c. Statistical surveys
d. Black Friday

67. The _____ began in the earliest ages of the world. Lending money on portable security is one of the oldest professions.

The Mosaic Law struck at the root of pawnbroking as a profitable business, since it forbade the taking of interest from a poor borrower, while no Jew was to pay another for timely accommodation.

a. Bulk bins
b. Power centre
c. History of pawnbroking
d. Same-store sales

68. A _____ sells recreational modelling and craft supplies and specialty magazines for model airplanes (both military craft and airliners), train models, ship models, house and building models. Some hobby shops may also sell dolls, and collectible coins and stamps. A subtype of _____ is a game store, which sells board games and role playing games.

a. Power III
b. Hobby store
c. 6-3-5 Brainwriting
d. 180SearchAssistant

69. _____ commonly refers to the electronic retailing / _____ channels industry, which includes such billion dollar companies as Home shoppingN, QVC, eBay, ShopNBC, Buy.com, and Amazon.com. _____ allows consumers to shop for goods while in the privacy of their own home, as opposed to traditional shopping, which requires you to visit brick and mortar stores and shopping malls.

The _____ / electronic retailing industry was created in 1977 when small market radio talk show host Bob Circosta was asked to sell avocado-green-colored can openers live on the air by station owner Bud Paxson when an advertiser traded 112 units of product instead of paying his advertising bill.

a. Power III
b. 6-3-5 Brainwriting
c. 180SearchAssistant
d. Home shopping

70. _____ is a blanket term used for pre-recorded media that is either sold or hired for home entertainment. The term originates from the VHS/Betamax era but has carried over into the current DVD/Blu-ray Disc age. The first company to duplicate and distribute _____ was Magnetic Video, established in 1968.
a. Home video
b. 180SearchAssistant
c. Power III
d. 6-3-5 Brainwriting

71. _____ are computerized systems incorporating registers, computers and peripheral equipment, usually on a computer network which exist in the food service industry. Like other Point of sale systems, these systems keep track of sales, labor and payroll and can generate records used in accounting and book keeping. They may be accessed remotely by restaurant corporate offices, troubleshooters and other authorized parties.
a. Flighting
b. Shrinkage
c. Comparison-Shopping agent
d. Hospitality point of sales systems

72. _____ or point of service (_____ or PoS) can mean a retail shop, a checkout counter in a shop, or the location where a transaction occurs. By synecdoche _____ often refers to a _____ terminal or more generally to the hardware and software used for checkouts - the equivalent of an electronic cash register. _____ systems are used in supermarkets, restaurants, hotels, stadiums, and casinos, as well as almost any type of retail establishment.
a. Nielsen Media Research
b. Kahala-Cold Stone
c. Point of sale
d. Goodyear Tire ' Rubber Company

73. In commerce, a _____ is a superstore which combines a supermarket and a department store. The result is a very large retail facility which carries an enormous range of products under one roof, including full lines of groceries and general merchandise. In theory, _____s allow customers to satisfy all their routine weekly shopping needs in one trip.
a. 180SearchAssistant
b. 6-3-5 Brainwriting
c. Power III
d. Hypermarket

74. Today, the term _____ refers to a retailer (or wholesaler) of iron goods. This has often been expanded to include consumer goods made of aluminium, brass, or other metals, as well as plastics. In modern usage, it is thus synonymous with a hardware shop.

a. ACNielsen
b. ADTECH
c. Ironmonger
d. AMAX

75. A _____ is a retail store that sells secondhand goods cheaply. A low-quality antique shop may be bordering on a _____.

- Bric-a-brac
- Flea market
- Charity shop

a. Junk shop
b. Strip mall
c. Warehouse store
d. Power centre

76. _____ was a person carrying advertisement hoarding or house-to-house salesman, or trading peddle in 16th-19th centuries in Russia.
a. Power centre
b. Khodebshchik
c. Planogram
d. General line of merchandise

77. _____, also referred to as lay-by in Australia, New Zealand, South Africa and Great Britain, is a way to purchase an item without paying the entire cost at once. However, rather than taking the item home and then repaying the debt on a regular schedule, as in most installment plans or hire purchases, the _____ customer does not receive the item until it is completely paid for. There is sometimes a fee associated with a _____ purchase, since the seller must 'lay' the item 'away' in storage until the payments are completed.
a. Sales per unit area
b. Strip mall
c. Warehouse club
d. Layaway

78. _____ was originally coined by Austrian psychologist Alfred Adler in 1929. The current broader sense of the word dates from 1961.

In sociology, a _____ is the way a person lives.

a. 6-3-5 Brainwriting
b. Lifestyle
c. Power III
d. 180SearchAssistant

79. A _____ is a shopping center or mixed-used commercial development that combines the traditional retail functions of a shopping mall but with leisure amenities oriented towards upscale consumers. _____s, which were first labeled as such by Memphis developers Poag and McEwen in the late 1980s and emerged as a retailing trend in the late 1990s, are sometimes labeled 'boutique malls'. They are often located in affluent suburban areas.
a. Flighting
b. Category Development Index
c. Private branding
d. Lifestyle center

80. A _____ is a form of exterior cardboard packaging for musical compact discs in widespread use in North America in the 1980s and early 1990s.

Chapter 13. Test Preparation Part 13

When compact discs first began to appear in the retail stores, the _____ packaging served a transitional purpose, allowing shops to file new compact discs in the same bins originally used for vinyl records. _____es were 12' tall, and capable of containing two separate discs when necessary.

a. 180SearchAssistant
b. Power III
c. 6-3-5 Brainwriting
d. Longbox

81. A _____ is a large online seller of second-hand and rare books with more than 100,000 listings. _____s offer their books for sale at large online book marketplaces like Amazon, Abebooks and Alibris. Some _____s may not own all the books they are selling.

a. Demand chain management
b. Wholesale
c. Supply chain network
d. Megalister

82. A _____ in the home entertainment business refers to the practice of suspending the sales of DVD movies or DVD boxed sets after a certain period of time. The Walt Disney Company practices _____ more than any other production company, often with releases of classic animated movies in the Disney catalog.

Disney is not the only studio that puts movies on _____.

a. Hospitality point of sales systems
b. Procter ' Gamble
c. Hawkers
d. Moratorium

83. A _____ is a company that sells directly to the public via more than one distribution channel. Most _____s sell through mail order catalogs and 'brick ' mortar' retail stores. Some _____s, sell online as well.

a. Khodebshchik
b. Discount store
c. Gruen transfer
d. Multichannel retailer

84. _____ is the resale of tickets through a web-based ticket brokering service. Prices on ticket brokering websites are determined by demand, availability, and the ticket reseller. Tickets sold through an _____ service may or may not be authorized by the official seller.

a. Outlet store
b. Online ticket brokering
c. Endcap
d. Electronic Shelf Label

85. An _____ or factory outlet or 'Best Saving Outlet' is a retail store in which manufacturers sell their stock directly to the public through their own branded stores. The stores can be brick and mortar or online. Traditionally, a factory outlet was a store, attached to a factory or warehouse.

a. Endcap
b. Electronic Shelf Label
c. Outlet store
d. Online ticket brokering

86. A _____ is an individual or business that offers monetary loans in exchange for an item of value that is given to the pawn broker. The word pawn is derived from the Latin pignus, for pledge, and the items having been pawned to the broker are themselves called pledges or pawns, or simply the collateral.

If an item is pawned for a loan, within a certain contractual period of time the pawner may purchase it back for the amount of the loan plus some agreed-upon amount for interest.

a. Pawnbroker
c. 6-3-5 Brainwriting
b. Power III
d. 180SearchAssistant

87. A _____ is a device used to measure the number and direction of people traversing a certain passage or entrance per unit time. The resolution of the measurement is entirely dependent on the sophistication of the technology employed. The device is often used at the entrance of a building so that the total number of visitors can be recorded.
   a. Closeout store
   c. Khodebshchik
   b. Wardrobing
   d. People counter

88. A _____ is a diagram of fixtures and products that illustrates how and where retail products should be displayed, usually on a store shelf in order to increase customer purchases. They may also be referred to as plano-grams, plan-o-grams, schematics (archaic) or POGs.

A _____ is often received before a product reaches a store, and is useful when a retailer wants multiple store displays to have the same look and feel.

   a. Layaway
   c. Khodebshchik
   b. Power centre
   d. Planogram

89. A _____ is an unenclosed shopping centre with 250,000 square feet (23,000 m^2) to 750,000 square feet (70,000 m^2) of gross leasable area that usually contains three or more big box retailers and various smaller retailers (usually located in strip malls) with a common parking area shared among the retailers. It is likely to have more money spent on features and architecture than a traditional big box shopping centre.

_____s function similar to a traditional shopping mall, but more closely resemble open-air malls and lifestyle centres, rather than the modern enclosed shopping malls of today.

   a. Power centre
   c. Warehouse store
   b. Discount store
   d. Khodebshchik

90. _____

In many retail industries, the most successful firms are the ones that offer the widest selection. For example, Wal-Mart rose to the top of the Fortune 500 by offering consumers a vast array of products at very competitive prices. The emphasis on product variety is particularly strong in the supermarket industry, where the introduction of computerized logistical and inventory management systems in the 1980s allowed firms to stock an ever expanding array of products.

   a. Quality competition in retailing
   c. Retailing
   b. Stock rotation
   d. Scrapstore

91. _____ is a rivalry between individuals, groups, nations for territory, a niche, or allocation of resources. It arises whenever two or more parties strive for a goal which cannot be shared. _____ occurs naturally between living organisms which co-exist in the same environment.

a. Non-price competition
b. Price competition
c. Price fixing
d. Competition

92. _____ is a creative and commercial discipline that combines and utilizes many different design concepts together in the conceptualizing and construction of retail space. _____ is primarily a specialized practice of architecture and interior design, however it also incorporates elements of interior decoration, graphic design, ergonomics, and advertising.

_____ is a very specialized discipline due to the heavy demands placed on retail space.

a. Web 2.0
b. Channel conflict
c. Distinctiveness
d. Retail design

93. _____ is a business that makes money by doing short term loans secured by collateral it loans for. The costs are usually very high, with interest rates of 28%-40%, as well as a fee to put inventory on the floorplan.

Floor planning is commonly used in new and used car dealerships.

a. Clustering
b. Personalization
c. Reinforcement
d. Retail floor planning

94. _____ is a form of private investigation into larceny or theft. The focus of such investigations generally includes shoplifting, package pilferage, embezzlement, credit fraud, and check fraud. 'Loss prevention' or 'LP' is used to describe a number of methods used to reduce the amount of all losses and shrinkage often related to retail trade.

a. Trade credit
b. Merchant
c. RFM
d. Retail loss prevention

95. A _____ is defined by the International Co-operative Alliance's Statement on the Co-operative Identity as an autonomous association of persons united voluntarily to meet their common economic, social, and cultural needs and aspirations through a jointly-owned and democratically-controlled enterprise. It is a business organization owned and operated by a group of individuals for their mutual benefit. A _____ may also be defined as a business owned and controlled equally by the people who use its services or who work at it.

a. Power III
b. 6-3-5 Brainwriting
c. 180SearchAssistant
d. Cooperative

96. In retail, _____ is a standard and usually the primary measurement of store success. The unit of area is usually square metres in the metric system or square feet in U.S. customary units. Square feet are also widely used in retailing in the United Kingdom, but there are signs of a trend towards use of square metres.

a. Sales per unit area
b. Discount store
c. Catalog merchant
d. Scrapstore

97. _____ is a business term which refers to the revenue generated by a retail chain's existing outlets over a certain period of time (often a fiscal quarter or a particular shopping season), compared to an identical period in the past, usually in the previous year. By comparing sales data from existing outlets (that is, by excluding new outlets), the comparison is like-to-like, and avoids comparing data that are fundamentally incomparable.

_____ are also known as comparable store sales or like-store sales.

a. Quality competition in retailing
b. Same-store sales
c. Planogram
d. Garage sale

98. A _____ is a particular type of not for profit organization centered upon the principle of re-use. The basic operational principle of all _____s is the same, although their business models may differ significantly.

_____s operate by taking re-usable, safe, clean waste products ('Scrap') and re-distributing it.

a. Strip mall
b. Smartstores
c. Scrapstore
d. General line of merchandise

99. _____ machines are automated alternatives to the traditional cashier-staffed checkout at retailers. They have been implemented most often in stores like those which sell groceries, and other large scale stores.

_____ machines were first prototyped by companies such as NCR Corporation in 1997.

a. Self service
b. Strip mall
c. Smartstores
d. Self checkout

100. _____ is the practice of serving oneself, usually when purchasing items. Common examples include many gas stations, where the customer pumps their own gas rather than have an attendant do it (self-service gas pumping is illegal in New Jersey ' Oregon); Automatic Teller Machines (ATMs) in the banking world have also revolutionised how people withdraw and deposit funds; most American stores, where the customer uses a shopping cart in the store, placing the items they want to buy into the cart and then proceeding to the checkout counter/aisles; or at buffet-style restaurants, where the customer serves their own plate of food from a large, central selection.

_____ is used on the phone, web and email to facilitate customer service interactions using automation.

a. Warehouse store
b. Gruen transfer
c. Self service
d. Wardrobing

101. _____ is an advertisement in which a particular product specifically mentions a competitor by name for the express purpose of showing why the competitor is inferior to the product naming it.

This should not be confused with parody advertisements, where a fictional product is being advertised for the purpose of poking fun at the particular advertisement, nor should it be confused with the use of a coined brand name for the purpose of comparing the product without actually naming an actual competitor. ('Wikipedia tastes better and is less filling than the Encyclopedia Galactica.')

In the 1980s, during what has been referred to as the cola wars, soft-drink manufacturer Pepsi ran a series of advertisements where people, caught on hidden camera, in a blind taste test, chose Pepsi over rival Coca-Cola.

a. Heavy-up
b. GL-70
c. Cost per conversion
d. Comparative advertising

102. A _____, erotic shop is a shop that sells products such as sex toys, pornography, erotic lingerie, erotic books, and safer sex products such as condoms and dental dams. The euphemisms 'Adult Video Store' and 'Adult Book Store' are commonly used to refer to _____s that sell or rent pornographic videos, books, and magazines. However, many adult films are not rated when released to video or DVD.

a. 180SearchAssistant
b. 6-3-5 Brainwriting
c. Sex shop
d. Power III

Chapter 14. Test Preparation Part 14

1. _____ is the trade of fitting out retail and service shops and stores with equipment and merchandise. The trade applies to all kinds of outlets from a small corner shop to hypermarkets. A shop fitter executes planning, design of shop layout, and most importantly physically stocks the shop with equipment and goods.
   a. Teaser rate
   b. Micromarketing
   c. Value-based pricing
   d. Shop fitting

2. _____ is the examining of goods or services from retailers with the intent to purchase at that time. _____ is an activity of selection and/or purchase. In some contexts it is considered a leisure activity as well as an economic one.
   a. Shopping
   b. Khodebshchik
   c. Hawkers
   d. Discount store

3. _____ is the generic term for next generation retail technologies that use RFID that sell using a full complement of smart technologies including smart shelves, smart carts, smart cards, etc.

   Retailers are fast adopting technologies that enhance the productivity of store space and inventory. Some solutions include kiosks and self-checkout terminals, with RFID keeping track of all incoming and outgoing products.
   a. Charity shop
   b. Closeout
   c. Stock rotation
   d. Smartstores

4. _____ is a method of e-commerce and of traditional shopping in which consumers shop in a social networking environment similar to MySpace. Using the wisdom of crowds, users communicate and aggregate information about products, prices, and deals. Many sites allow users to create custom shopping lists and share them with friends..
   a. Spamvertising
   b. Social shopping
   c. Business-to-government
   d. Locator software

5. A _____ is a shop that caters to one specific retail market. Examples of _____s include camera stores, pharmacies, stationers and bookstores.

   _____s compete with other types of stores such as department stores, general stores, supermarkets and variety stores.
   a. Layaway
   b. Strip mall
   c. Specialist store
   d. Smartstores

6. _____ are small stores which specialize in a specific range of merchandise and related items. Most stores have an extensive width and depth of stock in the item that they specify in and provide high levels of service and expertise. The pricing policy is generally in the medium to high range, depending on factors like the type and exclusivity of merchandise and ownership, that is, whether they are owner operated or a chain operation which has the advantage of bulk purchasing and centralized warehousing system.
   a. Brick and mortar business
   b. Wardrobing
   c. Catalog merchant
   d. Specialty stores

7. _____ is the practice, used in retail and especially in food stores such as supermarkets, of moving products with an earlier sell-by date to the front of a shelf (or in the cooler if the item is on repack so they get worked out before the new product), so they get picked up and sold first, and of moving products with a later sell-by date to the back.

Chapter 14. Test Preparation Part 14

Most, if not all, packaged perishable food products, will have either a sell by date on them or a display until date; in practice, these are exactly the same thing. After this date, it is either illegal for the store to sell them (this is the case in the United Kingdom) or the quality will have deteriorated to the point at which nobody will buy them.

- a. Discount store
- b. Brick and mortar business
- c. Closeout
- d. Stock rotation

8. In business, a _____ is the date a particular product is to be released for sale to the general public.

Typically, retailers receive shipments of stock prior to its _____ release, so that the product can be placed on display shelves for store opening that day. Shipments come marked very clearly with a 'do not sell before release date' label designating a _____ mandated by the distributor.

- a. Time to market
- b. Chain stores
- c. Customer base
- d. Street date

9. A _____ is an open area shopping center where the stores are arranged in a row, with a sidewalk in front. _____s are typically developed as a unit and have large parking lots in front. They face major traffic arterials and tend to be self-contained with few pedestrian connections to surrounding neighborhoods.

- a. Strip mall
- b. Thrifting
- c. Confectionery store
- d. Scrapstore

10. _____ refers to the act of shopping at a thrift store, flea market, garage sale usually with the intent of finding interesting items at a cheap price.

A larger philosophy permeates the act of _____ which celebrates the recycling of formerly-owned items, finding new use and new love for vintage material goods which had been thrown out, and the thrill of imagining what the former life of the item was like.

A 'zine called 'Thrift Score', published in the 1990s by Ms.

- a. Garage sale
- b. Same-store sales
- c. General line of merchandise
- d. Thrifting

11. A _____ is an establishment that has been created with the aim of attracting tourists and their money. _____s will typically provide services, entertainment, souvenirs and other products for tourists to purchase, and these will often be at inflated prices (compared to the local economy.)

While the term may have negative connotations for some, such establishments may be viewed by tourists as fun and interesting diversions.

- a. 6-3-5 Brainwriting
- b. 180SearchAssistant
- c. Power III
- d. Tourist trap

Chapter 14. Test Preparation Part 14

12. _____ is the practice of purchasing an item, using it, and then returning it to the store for a refund. It is most often done with expensive clothing - hence the name - but the practice is also common with tools, electronics, and even computers.

Perhaps one of the most notorious examples of _____ comes from the film My Date With Drew, which was filmed entirely on a wardrobed video camera.

   a. Thrifting
   b. Quality competition in retailing
   c. Warehouse store
   d. Wardrobing

13. A _____ is a commercial building for storage of goods. _____s are used by manufacturers, importers, exporters, wholesalers, transport businesses, customs, etc. They are usually large plain buildings in industrial areas of cities and towns.

   a. 6-3-5 Brainwriting
   b. 180SearchAssistant
   c. Power III
   d. Warehouse

14. A _____ is a retail store, usually selling a wide variety of merchandise, in which customers pay annual membership fees in order to shop. The clubs are able to keep prices low due to the no-frills format of the stores. In addition, customers are required to buy large, wholesale quantities of the store's products, which makes these clubs attractive to both bargain hunters and small business owners.

   a. Warehouse club
   b. Consignment
   c. Self service
   d. Power centre

15. A _____, as opposed to a warehouse club, is a retail location with a limited variety of merchandise sold in bulk at a discount to customers. Unlike a warehouse club, _____s do not require their patrons to obtain a membership nor do they require the payment of any fees.

This type of store is also referred to as a 'Big Box' or 'Price-Impact' store because of the spartan, warehouse style of the interior and the low prices.

   a. Khodebshchik
   b. Closeout store
   c. History of pawnbroking
   d. Warehouse store

16. An _____ is a fast food restaurant where simple foods and drink are served by coin-operated and bill-operated vending machines. Originally, the machines took only nickels but modern _____ vending machines accept bills. In the original format, a cashier would sit in a change booth in the center of the restaurant, behind a wide marble counter with five to eight rounded depressions in it.

   a. AMAX
   b. Automat
   c. ADTECH
   d. ACNielsen

17. _____ is the sale of unsorted confections, nuts, gumballs, toys and novelties (in capsules) selected at random and dispensed generally through non-electrically operated vending machines. _____ is a separate segment of the vending industry from full line vending - i.e., the snack and soda vending industries - and involves different products and strategies. _____ represents less than 1% of the total vending industry.

a. Gashapon
b. Full line vending
c. Maas International
d. Bulk vending

18. A _____ is a machine for charging devices such as mobile phones, PDAs, iPods, PSPs, and other small, mobile electronics. They can be situated in locations between the home and the office, with securable lockers, so devices can be safely charged at the owner's convenience. Other vending machines that are also capable of performing this function are operated by Photo-Me International.
a. 6-3-5 Brainwriting
b. 180SearchAssistant
c. Power III
d. Chargebox

19. A _____ is a type of arcade game known as a merchandiser. They are commonly found in video arcades, supermarkets, restaurants, movie theaters, and bowling alleys.

A claw consists of many parts but the basic components are a PCB, power supply, currency detector, credit/timer display, joystick, wiring harness, bridge assembly, xport and claw.

a. Power III
b. 180SearchAssistant
c. 6-3-5 Brainwriting
d. Claw vending machine

20. _____ is the name of a brewer in a espresso machine, coffee machine or vending machine which is able to brew a cup of coffee as well as an espresso. It is a mechanism in which with ground coffee and hot water (on pressure in case of espresso), a cup of coffee or espresso can be made, and from which, after the drink has been prepared the coffee residue is removed. Cutaway diagram of a _____ mechanism

Firstly ground coffee is dosed into the cylinder chamber.

a. Coex
b. Power III
c. 6-3-5 Brainwriting
d. 180SearchAssistant

21. The _____ is an organization supporting the elimination of pennies and dollar bills from U.S. currency. It is funded by vending machine companies, video arcade owners, and the soft drink industry, who all have an interest in eliminating maintenance costs associated with dollar bill validators. The National Bulk Vendors Association supports the Coalition.
a. Full line vending
b. Coin Coalition
c. Maas International
d. Gashapon

22. _____, Inc. (NASDAQ: CSTR) converts loose change into currency, donations or gift cards via self-service or interactive kiosks. The company was founded in 1991 and David W. Cole serves as CEO.
a. China Compulsory Certificate
b. Partnership for a Drug-Free America
c. RuTube
d. Coinstar

23. A _____ is a device that determines if a piece of currency is counterfeit. These devices are used in vending machines that accept payment and dispense a product to a customer. They are also used in change machines and in slot machines.

a. Power III
c. 6-3-5 Brainwriting
b. Currency detector
d. 180SearchAssistant

24. _____ is a brand of bubble gum and chewing gum often found in gum machines. It is produced by _____ ' Machine Co. The history of the company goes back to 1913, when Ford Mason leased 102 machines and placed them in stores and shops in New York.
   a. 180SearchAssistant
   c. 6-3-5 Brainwriting
   b. Ford Gum
   d. Power III

25. A _____ business uses vending machines to sell cans or bottles of soft drink and individual packages of snacks. Soda sold is usually 12 fl. oz.
   a. Full line vending
   c. Maas International
   b. Coin Coalition
   d. Gashapon

26. _____ or gachapon , also referred to as 'capsule toy', is a Japanese onomatopoeia, made up of two sounds: 'gacha' for the turning of a crank on a toy vending machine, and 'pon' for the sound of the toy capsule dropping into the receptacle. It is used to describe both the machines themselves, and any toy obtained from them.

_____ machines are similar to the coin-operated toy vending machines seen outside of grocery stores and other retailers in other countries.

   a. Gashapon
   c. Full line vending
   b. Maas International
   d. Coin Coalition

27. The _____ was formed in the early 1920's to produce Mutoscope machines and the motion picture reels that the machines played, and continued to manufacture arcade machines, including the claw machine, until 1949.

The mutoscope was a peep show-style movie viewer that was first manufactured by the American Mutoscope and Biograph company, and is notable for being one of the first means by which motion pictures were exhibited. The company gradually changed its focus to motion picture production and projection, and by the early 1920s, had stopped production of both mutoscopes and the movie reels that were played by the machines.

   a. AMAX
   c. ADTECH
   b. ACNielsen
   d. International Mutoscope Reel Company

28. _____ is the largest vending machine manufacturer/operator in the world. Its Global head office is in Eindhoven, The Netherlands.

_____ has 24% of the European vending market with over 160,000 vending machines in operation.

   a. Full line vending
   c. Gashapon
   b. Coin Coalition
   d. Maas International

29. _____ refers to the methods, practices and operations conducted to promote and sustain certain categories of commercial activity. The term is understood to have different specific meanings depending on the context. Merchandise is a sale goods at a store

In marketing, one of the definitions of _____ is the practice in which the brand or image from one product or service is used to sell another.

a. Marketing communication
b. New Media Strategies
c. Merchandising
d. Word of mouth

30. The _____ is the American national trade association of the food and refreshment vending, coffee service and foodservice management industries. Public relations is an important part of its mandate.
a. National Automatic Merchandising Association
b. 6-3-5 Brainwriting
c. 180SearchAssistant
d. Power III

31. _____ is a bulk vending machine company in Morris, Illinois. It was founded in 1909 by Emerson A. Bolen as Northwestern Novelty Company. The 60, Northwestern's bulk vender, began being marketed in 1960.
a. Power III
b. 180SearchAssistant
c. 6-3-5 Brainwriting
d. Northwestern Corporation

32. _____, founded in 1948, is a vending machine company located in Vernon, California. Along with Northwestern Corporation, it is regarded by most people in the vending community as a producer of high-quality equipment.

Oak manufactures bulk venders, including the ever-popular Oak Acorn (their oldest machine), the Oak Vista 300, the Oak Vista 450, the Oak Vista Cabinet Machine, and the Big Oak, which can be a bulk vender, but is usually a Capsule Machine.

a. ACNielsen
b. ADTECH
c. Oak Manufacturing
d. AMAX

33. _____ is the term given to food that can be prepared and served very quickly. While any meal with low preparation time can be considered to be _____, typically the term refers to food sold in a restaurant or store with low quality preparation and served to the customer in a packaged form for take-out/take-away. The term '_____' was recognized in a dictionary by Merriam-Webster in 1951.
a. Fast food
b. 180SearchAssistant
c. Power III
d. 6-3-5 Brainwriting

1. _____ is a chain of fried chicken fast food restaurants, owned since 1993 by the Atlanta-based AFC Enterprises (originally America's Favorite Chicken Company.) According to a company press release dated June 29, 2007, Popeyes is the second-largest 'quick-service chicken restaurant group, measured by number of units', with more than 1,800 restaurants in more than 40 states, the District of Columbia, Puerto Rico and 20 countries worldwide including Turkey, Hong Kong, Iraq, Jordan, Kuwait, United Arab Emirates, Japan, Malaysia, South Africa, South Korea, Singapore, Philippines, Canada, Jamaica, Mexico and Panama. About thirty locations are company-owned, the rest franchised.

  a. Popeyes Chicken ' Biscuits
  b. Superbrands
  c. Phorm
  d. Multinational corporation

2. A _____ is a collection of symbols, experiences and associations connected with a product, a service, a person or any other artifact or entity.

_____s have become increasingly important components of culture and the economy, now being described as 'cultural accessories and personal philosophies'.

Some people distinguish the psychological aspect of a _____ from the experiential aspect.

  a. Store brand
  b. Brand equity
  c. Brandable software
  d. Brand

3. _____ has been in continuous operation since 1978 and is a satellite-delivered Radio network featuring the Adult Standards radio format. Created by record executive and jingle writer Al Ham, _____ has approximately 50 affiliates, mostly AM stations.

The format is hosted by well-known celebrity DJs including TV game show host and singer/entertainer Peter Marshall; as well as singer/entertainer Pat Boone.

  a. Music of Your Life
  b. 180SearchAssistant
  c. Radio format
  d. Power III

4. _____ was a children's television series which ran in the United States from 1953 to 1994 as well as at various times in Australia, Canada, Japan, Puerto Rico and the United Kingdom. The program was targeted at preschoolers .

_____ was a rare case of a series being franchised and syndicated, so local affiliates (Los Angeles and New York City were prime examples) could produce their own versions of _____ instead of airing the national telecast.

  a. Power III
  b. 6-3-5 Brainwriting
  c. 180SearchAssistant
  d. Romper Room

5. _____ was a cable television network operated by Cablevision. While the network did not survive, its basic gameplan (a sports cable network with national programming, but that let each local market get the rights to show their own local teams in their market) survives on in the form of Fox Sports Net, and more recently Comcast SportsNet. SportsChannel New York was the first of these networks and was launched in 1976.

  a. Power III
  b. SportsChannel America
  c. 180SearchAssistant
  d. 6-3-5 Brainwriting

6. _____ was a syndicated game show, in which viewers via telephone control the video game featured in the program, in hopes of winning prizes. _____ was a franchised game show format, hosted locally by hosts at stations that purchased the rights to the program. _____ was syndicated from the late-1970s to the mid-1980s.
   a. Power III
   b. 180SearchAssistant
   c. 6-3-5 Brainwriting
   d. TV POWWW

7. _____ is the practice of using video games to advertise a product, organization or viewpoint. The term 'advergames' was coined in January 2000 by Anthony Giallourakis, and later mentioned by Wired's 'Jargon Watch' column in 2001. It has been applied to various free online games commissioned by major companies.
   a. ADTECH
   b. ACNielsen
   c. AMAX
   d. Advergaming

8. _____ is a form of entertainment designed to educate as well as to amuse. _____ typically seeks to instruct or socialize its audience by embedding lessons in some familiar form of entertainment: television programs, computer and video games, films, music, websites, multimedia software, etc. Examples might be guided nature tours that entertain while educating participants on animal life and habitats, or a video game that teaches children conflict resolution skills.
   a. AMAX
   b. ADTECH
   c. ACNielsen
   d. Edutainment

9. _____ is a form of communication that typically attempts to persuade potential customers to purchase or to consume more of a particular brand of product or service. 'While now central to the contemporary global economy and the reproduction of global production networks, it is only quite recently that _____ has been more than a marginal influence on patterns of sales and production. The formation of modern _____ was intimately bound up with the emergence of new forms of monopoly capitalism around the end of the 19th and beginning of the 20th century as one element in corporate strategies to create, organize and where possible control markets, especially for mass produced consumer goods.
   a. ACNielsen
   b. Advertising
   c. ADTECH
   d. AMAX

10. _____ is a portmanteau of 'Military' and 'entertainment'. It is defined as either entertainment featuring and celebrating the military, or controlled by the military.

The U.S. military in particular excels in the authorship of _____, although the Russian military also has plans to produce their own TV channel.

   a. Militainment
   b. 6-3-5 Brainwriting
   c. 180SearchAssistant
   d. Power III

11. _____ is a digital marketing company, providing publishers, agencies and ad networks the ability to manage, serve and evaluate online advertising campaigns, including display, video and mobile formats. Founded in 1998 and headquartered in Frankfurt, Germany, _____ is the ad serving platform of AOL's digital advertising business. Globally, _____ works with customers in more than 25 countries.
   a. Athena Wissenschaftsmarketing
   b. Advertising Standards Canada
   c. UL 94
   d. ADTECH

12. _____ is an internet based private company that provides online pay-per-click advertising campaigns for advertisers and ad agency clients to generate consumer leads and sales. Revenue is primarily earned from online advertising by delivering contextual and search ad listings based on pre-determined targets and criteria, to third-party ad networks and marketing affiliates.

   a. Oodle   b. Archos

   c. Isense   d. Abcsearch

13. _____s are rapidly growing and accepted online advertising technology platforms for buying, selling and trading online ad impressions and is a field beyond ad networks cited by the Interactive Advertising Bureau (IAB)) advertising trade publications Advertising Age, iMediaConnectionClickZ, and others that provide ways to purchase advertising on many advertising networks or thousands of websites or the pages of websites at the same time to effectively reach the largest or most targeted audience very efficiently in an increasingly fragmented online media world.

They give buyers (online advertisers and ad agency media planners and buyers) places to advertise where audiences are engaged with content today and at the same time give sellers (publisher websites online advertising sellers) a place to compete for advertiser revenue they otherwise would have a difficult time acquiring on their own and a place for these same publisher online advertising sellers to be able to sell various parts of their website(s) ad impression inventory.

_____s offer ways for advertisers to reach more audience efficiently as well as an effective method for managing campaigns to see which ads on which networks perform better or to contextually see how advertising is best performing.

   a. Advertising network   b. Automated Bid Managers

   c. Ad rotation   d. Ad exchange

14. _____ or ad blocking is a service which removes or alters advertising content in a Web page. This content can be represented in a variety of ways including pictures, animations, text, or pop-up windows. More advanced filters allow fine-grained control of advertisements through features like blacklists, whitelists, and regular expression filters.

   a. Ad serving   b. Organic search

   c. Ad filtering   d. Online identity management

15. _____ International N.V. is a public company based in Nuremberg,Germany. The company has 16 offices in 10 countries across Europe ' USA.

_____ operates as an online advertising company with services in display advertising, e-mail marketing, affiliate marketing, ad serving and search engine marketing.

   a. Ameritest   b. Ad pepper media

   c. Aberdeen Group   d. Adbot

16. _____ is the practice of showing multiple advertisements in a single location on a web page. Sometimes the ads are rotated with each new page load, sometimes they are rotated in the context of a single page load, and sometimes both simultaneously. Because the ads are placed in the same location, they are typically the same size.

a. Audience Screening
c. E-mail marketing
b. Internet currency
d. Ad rotation

17. _____ describes the technology and service that places advertisements on web sites. _____ technology companies provide software to web sites and advertisers to serve ads, count them, choose the ads that will make the website or advertiser most money, and monitor progress of different advertising campaigns.

An ad server is a computer server, specifically a web server, that stores advertisements used in online marketing and delivers them to website visitors.

a. Organic search
c. Online identity management
b. Ad serving
d. Online reputation management

18. _____ is a content-filtering extension for the Mozilla Firefox- and Mozilla Application Suite-based web browsers. _____ allows users to prevent page elements, such as advertisements, from being downloaded and displayed.

A forked version called _____ Plus has risen to replace the old _____.

a. Adblock
c. AMAX
b. ACNielsen
d. ADTECH

19. _____, Inc. was a privately held Internet advertising company in Chicago owned and operated by James R. Frith, Jr. The company was a pioneer in the delivery of display advertising on the Internet and had a brief but interesting run from April 1997 to December 1997, at which time it ceased operations due to a legal tangle with the U.S. Securities and Exchange Commission.

a. Adbot
c. Emerging technologies
b. American Family Publishers
d. Amoco Corporation

Chapter 16. Test Preparation Part 16

1. _____ is a form of communication that typically attempts to persuade potential customers to purchase or to consume more of a particular brand of product or service. 'While now central to the contemporary global economy and the reproduction of global production networks, it is only quite recently that _____ has been more than a marginal influence on patterns of sales and production. The formation of modern _____ was intimately bound up with the emergence of new forms of monopoly capitalism around the end of the 19th and beginning of the 20th century as one element in corporate strategies to create, organize and where possible control markets, especially for mass produced consumer goods.

   a. ACNielsen
   b. ADTECH
   c. Advertising
   d. AMAX

2. An _____ or ad network is a company that connects web sites that want to host advertisements with advertisers who want to run advertisements. Increasingly Ad networks are companies that pay software developers as well as web sites money for allowing their ads to be shown when people use their software or visit their sites.

   Online advertising inventory comes in many different forms.

   a. Ad rotation
   b. Automated Bid Managers
   c. Interactive advertising
   d. Advertising network

3. _____ or advertising-supported software is any software package which automatically plays, displays, or downloads advertisements to a computer after the software is installed on it or while the application is being used. Some types of _____ are also spyware and can be classified as privacy-invasive software.

   Advertising functions are integrated into or bundled with the software, which is often designed to note what Internet sites the user visits and to present advertising pertinent to the types of goods or services featured there.

   a. ACNielsen
   b. Adware
   c. Isearch
   d. ADTECH

4. _____ is an Internet-based marketing practice in which a business rewards one or more affiliates for each visitor or customer brought about by the affiliate's marketing efforts.

   _____ is also the name of the industry where a number of different types of companies and individuals are performing this form of Internet marketing, including affiliate networks, affiliate management companies, and in-house affiliate managers, specialized third party vendors, and various types of affiliates/publishers who promote the products and services of their partners.

   _____ overlaps with other Internet marketing methods to some degree, because affiliates often use regular advertising methods.

   a. Affiliate marketing
   b. ADTECH
   c. ACNielsen
   d. AMAX

5. _____ is defined by the American _____ Association as the activity, set of institutions, and processes for creating, communicating, delivering, and exchanging offerings that have value for customers, clients, partners, and society at large. The term developed from the original meaning which referred literally to going to market, as in shopping, or going to a market to sell goods or services.

Chapter 16. Test Preparation Part 16

_____ practice tends to be seen as a creative industry, which includes advertising, distribution and selling.

a. Product naming
c. Marketing
b. Marketing myopia
d. Customer acquisition management

6. _____ is an indie online music store and social network service created in 2006 by Brown University seniors Elliott Breece, Elias Roman, and Joshua Boltuch, in Providence, Rhode Island. They have since graduated and moved the company to Long Island City in Queens, New York.

Their vision for _____ is to become 'the most fun way to discover and buy music online', keep music social, and support the artists.

a. Ed Bradley
c. Ellen Goodman
b. Anne M. Mulcahy
d. Amie Street

7. The _____, a United States federal law enacted in 1999, is part of A bill to amend the provisions of title 17, United States Code, and the Communications Act of 1934, relating to copyright licensing and carriage of broadcast signals by satellite . It makes people who register domain names that are either trademarks or individual's names with the sole intent of selling the rights of the domain name to the trademark holder or individual for a profit liable to civil action. It was sponsored by Senator Trent Lott on November 17, 1999, and enacted on November 29 of the same year.

a. ADTECH
c. AMAX
b. ACNielsen
d. Anticybersquatting Consumer Protection Act

8. _____ is a broad label that refers to any individuals or households that use goods and services generated within the economy. The concept of a _____ is used in different contexts, so that the usage and significance of the term may vary.

A _____ is a person who uses any product or service.

a. 6-3-5 Brainwriting
c. Consumer
b. Power III
d. 180SearchAssistant

9. _____ is a form of government regulation which protects the interests of consumers. For example, a government may require businesses to disclose detailed information about products--particularly in areas where safety or public health is an issue, such as food. _____ is linked to the idea of consumer rights (that consumers have various rights as consumers), and to the formation of consumer organizations which help consumers make better choices in the marketplace.

a. Trademark dilution
c. Consumer Protection
b. Federal Bureau of Investigation
d. Sound trademark

10. _____ is a type of advertising in which businesses write short articles related to their respective industry. These articles are made available for distribution and publication in the marketplace

a. ACNielsen
c. In-text advertising
b. Article marketing
d. ADTECH

11. _____ is a product of AtomPark Software. The first version was published in 2001. It is a group mail sending software for Microsoft Windows.

    a. ACNielsen
    b. ADTECH
    c. AMAX
    d. Atomic Mail Sender

12. Media planning is a science and one that has seen growth and increased discipline over the last few years through the introduction of new technology. These technologies have morphed from audience segmentation to audience profiling, but the most recent wave of technology to affect media planning is based on _____, which can be defined as the opportunity to purchase an actual audience online rather than impressions.

_____ incorporates a number of different technologies including behavioral targeting and the more advanced Conversion optimization platforms.

    a. Audience Screening
    b. Ad rotation
    c. OpenX
    d. Enterprise Search Marketing

13. _____ are an advertising tool used to manage budgets on pay per click (PPC) campaigns. ADM's allow users to prioritize keywords listings and bids. Many _____ have time stamp controls as well a position monitors.

    a. Interactive advertising
    b. Automated Bid Managers
    c. Internet currency
    d. Ad rotation

14. In environmental modeling and especially in hydrology, a _____ model means a model that is acceptably consistent with observed natural processes, i.e. that simulates well, for example, observed river discharge. It is a key concept of the socalled Generalized Likelihood Uncertainty Estimation (GLUE) methodology to quantify how uncertain environmental predictions are.

    a. Behavioral
    b. 180SearchAssistant
    c. 6-3-5 Brainwriting
    d. Power III

15. _____ or behavioural targeting is a technique used by online publishers and advertisers to increase the effectiveness of their campaigns.

_____ uses information collected on an individual's web-browsing behavior, such as the pages they have visited or the searches they have made, to select which advertisements to display to that individual. Practitioners believe this helps them deliver their online advertisements to the users who are most likely to be influenced by them.

    a. Search engine image protection
    b. Hit inflation attack
    c. Contextual advertising
    d. Behavioral targeting

16. _____ is a digital marketing agency. The company was founded in 2002 by Richard J. Pollack in Hallandale, Florida. Satellite locations have been established throughout the United States.

    a. Strict liability
    b. Supplier
    c. Lifestyle city
    d. BeyondROI

17. A _____ is a type of website, usually maintained by an individual with regular entries of commentary, descriptions of events, or other material such as graphics or video. Entries are commonly displayed in reverse-chronological order. '_____' can also be used as a verb, meaning to maintain or add content to a _____.

a. 180SearchAssistant
b. Blog
c. 6-3-5 Brainwriting
d. Power III

18. _____ is the term used to describe internet marketing via web blogs. These blogs differ from corporate websites because they feature daily or weekly posts, often around a single topic. Typically, corporations use blogs to create a dialog with customers and explain features of their products and services.

a. VoloMedia
b. Latitude Group
c. Tribal DDB London
d. Blog marketing

19. A _____ is a relatively new executive level position at a corporation, company, organization typically reporting directly to the CEO or board of directors. The _____ is responsible for a brand's image, experience, and promise, and propagating it throughout all aspects of the company. The brand officer oversees marketing, advertising, design, public relations and customer service departments.

a. Chief executive officer
b. Power III
c. Financial analyst
d. Chief brand officer

20. The _____ is an independent marketing agency specializing in all areas of the marketing and promotions in the entertainment industry, including but not limited to Commercial/non-Commercial Radio Promotion, Publicity, Street/Lifestyle Marketing, Online Marketing, Viral Video Dissemination. Founded in 1999 by Ted Chung, _____ has grown to be one of the west coast largest independent integrated marketing companies, and recently went international opening offices in New York and Mumbai, India. They have coordinated campaigns for the likes of Snoop Dogg, Warner Bros.

a. Customization
b. Clutter
c. Comprehensive,
d. Cashmere Agency

21. _____ is a type of Internet crime that occurs in pay per click online advertising when a person, automated script, or computer program imitates a legitimate user of a web browser clicking on an ad for the purpose of generating a charge per click without having actual interest in the target of the ad's link. _____ is the subject of some controversy and increasing litigation due to the advertising networks being a key beneficiary of the fraud.

Use of a computer to commit this type of Internet fraud is a felony in many jurisdictions, for example, as covered by Penal code 502 in California, USA, and the Computer Misuse Act 1990 in the United Kingdom.

a. Videoplaza
b. Paid inclusion
c. Click fraud
d. Value Per Action

22. _____ is a way of measuring the success of an online advertising campaign. A CTR is obtained by dividing the number of users who clicked on an ad on a web page by the number of times the ad was delivered (impressions.) For example, if a banner ad was delivered 100 times (impressions delivered) and one person clicked on it (clicks recorded), then the resulting CTR would be 1 percent.

a. JICIMS
b. Web analytics
c. Display advertising
d. Click-through rate

23. _____ refers to advertising on Consumer Generated Media. Generally used to refer to sponsored content on blogs, wikis, forums, etc. These sponsored content also known as sponsored posts or paid posts or sponsored reviews, contain links that point to the home page or specific product pages of the website of the sponsor.

   a. Pay for placement
   b. Consumer Generated Advertising
   c. VoloMedia
   d. Peer39

24. _____ is a form of targeted advertising for advertisements appearing on websites or other media, such as content displayed in mobile browsers. The advertisements themselves are selected and served by automated systems based on the content displayed to the user.

A _____ system scans the text of a website for keywords and returns advertisements to the webpage based on what the user is viewing.

   a. Click fraud
   b. Multivariate testing
   c. Click-through rate
   d. Contextual advertising

25. _____, is a Rogue Spyware application that poses as a legitimate anti- spyware program. The application uses a false scanner to force computer users to pay for removal of non-existent spyware items. It may also be known as ExpertAntivirus

_____ may be downloaded as a Trojan Horse, with other software.

   a. Cydoor
   b. MyWay Searchbar
   c. Power III
   d. ContraVirus

26. In internet marketing, _____ is the science and art of creating an experience for a website visitor with the goal of converting the visitor into a customer.

_____ was born out of the need of lead generation and ecommerce internet marketers to improve their website's results. As competition grew on the web during the early 2000's, Internet marketers had to become more measurable with their marketing tactics.

   a. Revenue sharing
   b. Mobile Web Analytics
   c. Pay for placement
   d. Conversion optimization

27. In economics, business, retail, and accounting, a _____ is the value of money that has been used up to produce something, and hence is not available for use anymore. In economics, a _____ is an alternative that is given up as a result of a decision. In business, the _____ may be one of acquisition, in which case the amount of money expended to acquire it is counted as _____.

   a. Variable cost
   b. Transaction cost
   c. Fixed costs
   d. Cost

28. _____ is an online advertising pricing model, where the advertiser pays for an explicit sign-up from an interested consumer interested in the advertiser offer.

In a CPM (Cost-per-Thousand) pricing model, advertisers are forced to pay for wasted impressions. CPC (Cost-per-Click) pricing models, commonly found on search engines, compel advertisers to pay for clicks from people that might never sign up on the advertiser landing page.

a. Direct navigation
b. Web analytics
c. Blog marketing
d. Cost per Lead

29. _____ is an online advertising pricing model, where the advertiser pays for each specified action (a purchase, a form submission, and so on) linked to the advertisement.

Direct response advertisers consider _____ the optimal way to buy online advertising, as an advertiser only pays for the ad when the desired action has occurred. An action can be a product being purchased, a form being filled, etc.

a. Display advertising
b. Value Per Action
c. Cost per action
d. Cost per Lead

30. _____ is one of the first and now-defunct online casinos, which gained it notoriety for one of the largest organised international sponsorship (and gambling) frauds, through its ad serving program. Formed in 1997 and located in Nassau, Bahamas, the company was represented by the Canadian firm Internet Entertainment Enterprises, Inc. (based in Montreal, Canada) which also handled the casino's marketing and banner advertising program.

a. CyberThrill
b. 6-3-5 Brainwriting
c. Power III
d. 180SearchAssistant

31. _____, according to the United States federal law known as the Anticybersquatting Consumer Protection Act, is registering, trafficking in, or using a domain name with bad faith intent to profit from the goodwill of a trademark belonging to someone else. The cybersquatter then offers to sell the domain to the person or company who owns a trademark contained within the name at an inflated price.

The term is derived from 'squatting,' which is the act of occupying an abandoned or unoccupied space or building that the squatter does not own, rent or otherwise have permission to use.

a. Wildcard DNS record
b. Cybersquatting
c. Fast flux
d. Domain name warehousing

32. _____, on the World Wide Web, is making a hyperlink that points to a specific page or image on another website, instead of that website's main or home page. Such links are called deep links.

This link: http://en.wikipedia.org/wiki/Deep_linking is an example of a deep link.

a. 6-3-5 Brainwriting
b. 180SearchAssistant
c. Power III
d. Deep linking

33. In the fields of strategic management, marketing strategy, and operational strategy, _____ is the process of specifying an organization's vision, initiatives and processes in order to deploy their online assets (as of 2007, these include: web sites, mini-sites, mobile sites, digital audio and video content, rich Internet applications, community groups, banner ads, search engine marketing, affiliate programs, etc.) in a manner which maximizes the business benefits they provide to the organization.

There are numerous approaches to conducting _____, but at their core, all go through four steps:1.

   a. Goal setting   b. Digital strategy
   c. Business plan   d. Voice of the customer

34. A _____ is a plan of action designed to achieve a particular goal.

_____ is different from tactics. In military terms, tactics is concerned with the conduct of an engagement while _____ is concerned with how different engagements are linked.

   a. Power III   b. 180SearchAssistant
   c. Strategy   d. 6-3-5 Brainwriting

35. _____ describes the method individuals use to navigate the World Wide Web in order to arrive at specific websites. _____ is a 10 year old term which is generally understood to include type-in traffic.

_____ traffic was first discovered circa 1996.

   a. Pay for placement   b. Contextual advertising
   c. Display advertising   d. Direct navigation

36. A _____ is a technique used by spammers in an attempt to find valid/existent e-mail addresses at a domain by using brute force. The attack is usually carried out by way of a standard dictionary attack, where valid e-mail addresses are found by brute force guessing valid e-mail addresses at a domain using different permutations of common usernames. These attacks are more effective for finding e-mail addresses of companies since they are likely to have a standard format for official e-mail aliases (i.e. jdoe@example.domain, johnd@example.domain, or johndoe@example.domain.)

   a. Phishing   b. Joe job
   c. Telemarketing   d. Directory Harvest Attack

37. _____ is a type of advertising that typically contains text (i.e., copy), logos, photographs or other images, location maps, and similar items. In periodicals, _____ can appear on the same page as, or on the page adjacent to, general editorial content. In contrast, classified advertising generally appears in a distinct section, was traditionally text-only, and was available in a limited selection of typefaces.

   a. Multivariate testing   b. Latitude Group
   c. Display advertising   d. Peer39

38. A _____ is a list containing the expired domain names that will be deleted from the domain name registry in the near future. are typically used by domainers to locate expiring domain names with value.

Chapter 16. Test Preparation Part 16   229

There is no defined date range for data contained with a drop list, as they can contain anywhere between 1 day's worth of expiring domain names, to 30 or more days worth.

a. Domain name drop list
b. Domain tasting
c. Reverse domain hijacking
d. Wildcard DNS record

39. _____ is the practice whereby a domain name registrar uses insider information to register domains for the purpose of re-selling them or earning revenue via ads placed on the domain's landing page. By registering the domains, the registrar locks out other potential registrars from selling the domain to a customer. The registrar typically takes advantage of the 5-day 'domain tasting' trial period, where the domain can be locked without payment.

a. Domain name front running
b. Domain name speculation
c. Top-level domain
d. Typosquatting

40. _____ refers to buying domains with the intent of selling them later for a higher price. The speculative element can be linked to news and current events, though the period during which such domains can be sold or flipped is limited. The main target of _____ is generic words which can be valuable for type-in traffic and for the dominant position they would have in any field due to their descriptive nature.

a. Reverse domain hijacking
b. Domain name warehousing
c. Domain name drop list
d. Domain name speculation

41. _____ is the common practice of registrars obtaining control of domain names with the intent to hold or 'warehouse' names for their use and/or profit. Also see domain name front running and domain tasting, related business practices employed by registrants.

Typically this practice occurs after a domain name has expired and the previous owner (registrant) has not exercised his/her right to renew that name within the allotted time frame (approximately 45 days following expiration.)

a. Wildcard DNS record
b. Typosquatting
c. Domaining
d. Domain name warehousing

42. _____ is the practice of an individual registering a domain name whose registration has lapsed in the immediate moments after expiry. This practice has largely been rendered moot through ICANN's addition of the Redemption Grace Period (RGP), which allows registrants 30 days to reclaim their domain name. By law there are no perpetual rights to domain names after payment of registration fees lapses, aside from trademark rights granted by common law or statute.

a. Domain tasting
b. Wildcard DNS record
c. Top-level domain
d. Domain sniping

43. _____ is the practice of a domain name registrant using the five-day 'grace period' (the Add Grace Period or AGP) at the beginning of the registration of an ICANN-regulated second-level domain to test the marketability of the domain. During this period, when a registration must be fully refunded by the domain name registry, a cost-benefit analysis is conducted by the registrant on the viability of deriving income from advertisements being placed on the domain's website.

Domains that are deemed 'successes' and retained in registrant's portfolio often represent domains that were previously used and have since expired, misspellings of other popular sites, or generic terms that may receive type-in traffic.

a. Top-level domain
b. Typosquatting
c. Domain tasting
d. Domain name warehousing

44. _____ is the business of buying, selling, developing and monetizing Internet domain names not for primary use as a website, but with the goal of profit generation with the intent of resale, like real estate. The noun form is domainer. A domainer is a person who engages in _____.

a. Typosquatting
b. Domain name drop list
c. Wildcard DNS record
d. Domaining

45. _____ is a form of direct marketing which uses electronic mail as a means of communicating commercial or fundraising messages to an audience. In its broadest sense, every e-mail sent to a potential or current customer could be considered _____. However, the term is usually used to refer to:

- sending e-mails with the purpose of enhancing the relationship of a merchant with its current or previous customers and to encourage customer loyalty and repeat business,
- sending e-mails with the purpose of acquiring new customers or convincing current customers to purchase something immediately,
- adding advertisements to e-mails sent by other companies to their customers, and
- sending e-mails over the Internet, as e-mail did and does exist outside the Internet (e.g., network e-mail and FIDO.)

Researchers estimate that United States firms alone spent US$400 million on _____ in 2006.

Chapter 16. Test Preparation Part 16

_____ is popular with companies for several reasons:

- A mailing list provides the ability to distribute information to a wide range of specific, potential customers at a relatively low cost.
- Compared to other media investments such as direct mail or printed newsletters, e-mail is less expensive.
- An exact return on investment can be tracked ('track to basket') and has proven to be high when done properly. _____ is often reported as second only to search marketing as the most effective online marketing tactic.
- The delivery time for an e-mail message is short (i.e., seconds or minutes) as compared to a mailed advertisement (i.e., one or more days.)
- An advertiser is able to 'push' the message to its audience, as opposed to website-based advertising, which relies on a customer to visit that website.
- It is possible to impress the target audience using various unique fonts and formats. This will help in making the email messages more appealing and sweet.
- E-mail messages are easy to track. An advertiser can track users via autoresponders, web bugs, bounce messages, unsubscribe requests, read receipts, click-throughs, etc. These mechanisms can be used to measure open rates, positive or negative responses, and to correlate sales with marketing.
- Advertisers can generate repeat business affordably and automatically.
- Advertisers can reach substantial numbers of e-mail subscribers who have opted in (i.e., consented) to receive e-mail communications on subjects of interest to them.
- Over half of Internet users check or send e-mail on a typical day.
- Specific types of interaction with messages can trigger (1) other messages to be delivered automatically, or (2) other events, such as updating the profile of the recipient to indicate a specific interest category.
- _____ is paper-free (i.e., 'green'.)

Many companies use _____ to communicate with existing customers, but many other companies send unsolicited bulk e-mail, also known as spam.

Internet system administrators have always considered themselves responsible for dealing with 'abuse of the net', but not 'abuse on the net'.

a. Enterprise Search Marketing
c. E-mail marketing
b. Audience Screening
d. Online shopping rewards

46. _____ is a commonly used measurement in advertising. Radio, television, newspaper, magazine, Out-of-home advertising and online advertising can be purchased on the basis of what it costs to show the ad to one thousand viewers . It is used in marketing as a benchmark to calculate the relative cost of an advertising campaign or an ad message in a given medium.

a. Frequency capping
c. Link exchange
b. Cost per time
d. Cost per mille

47. _____ is a subset of Search Engine Marketing that relates specifically to the implementation, management and measurement of SEM programs at scale-across a variety of business units, geographies, budgets, local languages, search engines and target audiences. As with Search Engine Marketing, there are three main methods: Search Engine Optimization, paid search engine advertising or pay per click advertising and paid inclusion.

There are several differences between SEM and Enterprise Search Engine Marketing, one being the requirement for enterprise-class SEM tools and SEM software solutions to enable organic optimization, search campaign management and ROI analysis at scale.

- a. Enterprise Search Marketing
- b. Online shopping rewards
- c. Audience Screening
- d. Automated Bid Managers

48. A _____ is an electronic communication form that appears to originate from a credible, non-biased source, but which in fact is created by a company or organization for the purpose of marketing a product, service, or political viewpoint. The purpose of a _____ is to inspire viral marketing or create an internet meme that generates traffic and interest in a product, much the same as astroturfing (a 'fake grassroots' campaign.)

_____s are corrupted forms of public relations, which as a discipline demands transparency and honesty, according to the Public Relations Society of America's code of ethics and the Word of Mouth Marketing Association's code of ethics.

- a. Power III
- b. 6-3-5 Brainwriting
- c. 180SearchAssistant
- d. Fake blog

49. _____ is a DNS technique used by botnets to hide phishing and malware delivery sites behind an ever-changing network of compromised hosts acting as proxies. It can also refer to the combination of peer-to-peer networking, distributed command and control, web-based load balancing and proxy redirection used to make malware networks more resistant to discovery and counter-measures. The Storm Worm is one of the recent malware variants to make use of this technique.

- a. Domain name speculation
- b. Typosquatting
- c. Fast flux
- d. Domain tasting

50. _____ is a third-party set of filters for the popular Adblock extensions for the Mozilla Firefox web browser. The filterset contains pre-made and regularly updated filters that remove ads from many common ad providers, such as DoubleClick. The filters are based primarily on regular expressions.

- a. 180SearchAssistant
- b. Power III
- c. 6-3-5 Brainwriting
- d. Filterset.G

51. _____ is a content-filtering extension for the Mozilla Firefox- and Mozilla Application Suite-based web browsers. _____ allows users to prevent page elements, such as HTML object tag Browser plug-ins and advertisements, from being displayed.

The extension uses XBL and CSS to prevent elements of Silverlight, Java applets, Macromedia Authorware, Adobe Director and Adobe Flash from being displayed.

a. Flashblock
c. Power III
b. 6-3-5 Brainwriting
d. 180SearchAssistant

52. _____ is a term in advertising that means restricting (capping) the amount of times (frequency) a specific visitor to a website is shown a particular advertisement. This restriction is applied to all websites that serve ads from the same advertising network.

_____ is a feature within ad serving that allows to limit the maximum number of impressions/views a visitor can see a specific ad within a period of time.

a. Link exchange
c. Cost per time
b. Cost per mille
d. Frequency capping

53. _____, Inc. provides services to Internet Service Providers. _____ technology enables an Internet Service Provider (ISP) to insert its own messages to be presented to users as they use their web browsers, such as customer service notices or online advertising.
a. Front Porch
c. Capital Cities/ABC
b. Direct investment
d. Popeyes Chicken ' Biscuits

54. In marketing, _____ is a discipline within marketing analysis which uses geolocation in the process of planning and implementation of marketing activities. It can be used in any aspect of the marketing mix - the Product, Price, Promotion, or Place Market segments can also correlate with location, and this can be useful in targeted marketing.
a. Geo
c. Quantitative
b. Parity Product
d. Containerization

55. _____ in geomarketing and internet marketing is the method of determining the geolocation (the physical location) of a website visitor and delivering different content to that visitor based on his or her location, such as country, region/state, city, metro code/zip code, organization, Internet Protocol (IP) address, ISP or other criteria.

In _____ with geolocation software, the geolocation is based on geographical and other personal information that is provided by the visitor or others.

A typical example for different content by choice in _____ is the FedEx website at FedEx

a. Puffery
c. Driven media
b. Recruitment tool
d. Geo targeting

56. _____ is a video sharing website where users can upload, view and share video clips.

_____ was launched the 1st of July 2008. The website use Adobe Flash technology to display videos.

a. Point of sale
c. CoolBrands
b. Nielsen Media Research
d. HD share

57. _____ is a kind of fraudulent skill used by some advertisement publishers' to earn unjustified revenue on the traffic they drive to the advertisers' Web sites. It is more sophisticated and hard to detect than simple Inflation Attack

This process involves the collaboration of two counterparts, a dishonest publisher, P, and a dishonest Web Site S. Webpages on S have a script that redirects the customer to publisher P's website, and this process is hidden from the customer. So, when User U retrieves a page on S site, which would simulate a click or request to pages on P site.

a. Microsoft adCenter
b. Blog marketing
c. Hit inflation attack
d. Pay per click

58. In economics, _____ is a rise in the general level of prices of goods and services in an economy over a period of time. The term '_____' once referred to increases in the money supply (monetary _____); however, economic debates about the relationship between money supply and price levels have led to its primary use today in describing price _____. Inflation can also be described as a decline in the real value of money--a loss of purchasing power in the medium of exchange which is also the monetary unit of account.

a. Industrial organization
b. ADTECH
c. Inflation
d. ACNielsen

59. _____ uses online or offline interactive media to communicate with consumers and to promote products, brands, services, and public service announcements, corporate or political groups.

In the inaugural issue of the Journal of _____ , editors Li and Leckenby (2000) defined _____ as the 'paid and unpaid presentation and promotion of products, services and ideas by an identified sponsor through mediated means involving mutual action between consumers and producers.' This is most commonly performed through the Internet as a medium.

It is these mutual actions or interactions that enhance what _____ is trying to achieve.

a. Interactive advertising
b. Internet currency
c. Enterprise Search Marketing
d. Audience Screening

60. _____ was a form of electronic money for the Internet. Most sites offering the currency have either been shut down or acquired.

The idea of _____ could possibly date back to 1995, when the first major website that used Internet trade was opened, eBay.

a. E-mail marketing
b. OpenX
c. Ad rotation
d. Internet currency

61. An _____ is an entrepreneur that engages in business on the Internet and helps to shape the future of business on the Internet by being an innovator. One who is able to recognize opportunity and administer resources to take advantage of the opportunities. A pioneer of new technologies and someone who is responsible for the ideas and processes to develop and implement large projects that will inevitably shape the future of the Internet market place.

a. ADTECH
b. AMAX
c. ACNielsen
d. Internet entrepreneur

62. An _____ is a person who has possession of an enterprise and assumes significant accountability for the inherent risks and the outcome. It is an ambitious leader who combines land, labour, and capital to create and market new goods or services. The term is a loanword from French and was first defined by the Irish economist Richard Cantillon.
   a. ADTECH
   b. ACNielsen
   c. AMAX
   d. Entrepreneur

63. _____, also referred to as i-marketing, web marketing, online marketing is the marketing of products or services over the Internet.

The Internet has brought many unique benefits to marketing, one of which being lower costs for the distribution of information and media to a global audience. The interactive nature of _____, both in terms of providing instant response and eliciting responses, is a unique quality of the medium.

   a. Internet marketing
   b. ADTECH
   c. ACNielsen
   d. AMAX

64. _____. is an online semantic advertising company based in London, with research and development facilities in Copenhagen ' Holyhead. The company has offices in New York, Munich, Paris, Stockholm, Madrid, Milan, Hamburg, Dusseldorf, Amsterdam

_____ applies the principles of semantics to online advertising with solutions for publisher sites, including user-generated content, social networks, blogs and online forums.

   a. Aberdeen Group
   b. Ameritest
   c. Isense
   d. Arcis Communications

65. _____ is the world's largest digital agency network. It is part of Aegis Media and therefore a wholly owned subsidiary of Aegis Group plc.Aegis launched its first digital business in 1995 in the UK. By 2000 it was operating in the top 10 markets of the world.
   a. Isobar
   b. Asia Insight
   c. ADTECH
   d. IQ Beats

66. _____ is the practice of promoting products and services using digital distribution channels to reach consumers in a timely, relevant, personal and cost-effective manner.

Whilst _____ does include many of the techniques and practices contained within the category of Internet Marketing, it extends beyond this by including other channels with which to reach people that do not require the use of The Internet. As a result of this non-reliance on the Internet, the field of _____ includes a whole host of elements such as mobile phones, sms/mms, display / banner ads and digital outdoor.

   a. Diversity marketing
   b. Global marketing
   c. Relationship marketing
   d. Digital marketing

67. _____ - Joint Industry Committee for Internet Measurement Systems

Initially a 2003 working party comprising representatives of the IAB (Internet Advertising Bureau), AOP (Association of Online Publishers), IPA (Institute of Practitioners in Advertising) and ISBA (Incorporated Society of British Advertisers) it became a joint industry committee, _____ being inporported as a company in 2007. Its main goal is to develop a single user-centric currency that can be used to trade online media. Online advertising tends to be traded either on CPM, CPC or CPA metrics currently, but in an effort to gain more support from advertisers (especially FMCGs) _____ was created to find a currency that would resemble an existing currency used on another medium (such as TVRs on television.)

   a. JICIMS
   c. Quality Score
   b. Multivariate testing
   d. Blog marketing

68. Online, a _____ is a spam attack using spoofed sender data and aimed at tarnishing the reputation of the apparent sender and/or induce the recipients to take action against him For a related phenomenon that is not targeted directly at a particular victim, see backscatter of email spam.

The name '_____' originated from such a spam attack on Joe Doll, webmaster of Joe's Cyberpost.

   a. Phishing
   c. Joe job
   b. Directory Harvest Attack
   d. Telemarketing

69. In online marketing a _____, sometimes known as a lead capture page, is the page that appears when a potential customer clicks on an advertisement or a search-engine result link. The page will usually display content that is a logical extension of the advertisement or link, and that is optimized to feature specific keywords or phrases for indexing by search engines.

In pay per click (PPC) campaigns, the _____ will also be customized to measure the effectiveness of different advertisements.

   a. Hit inflation attack
   c. Conversion optimization
   b. VoloMedia
   d. Landing page

70. The _____ is a UK search engine marketing agency that specialises in pay-per-click advertising and search engine optimisation. It was founded in 2001 by Dylan Thwaites and is headquartered in London with offices in Cheshire, with more than 100 employees.

Latitude's stated aim is to help companies achieve the best possible position on search engines' results pages and obtain high click through rates and ROI from online marketing.

   a. Conversion optimization
   c. Latitude Group
   b. SiteScreen
   d. Cost per action

71. A _____ is a confederation of websites that operates similarly to a web ring. Webmasters register their web sites with a central organization, that runs the exchange, and in turn receive from the exchange HTML code which they insert into their web pages. In contrast to a web ring, where the HTML code simply comprises simple circular ring navigation hyperlinks, in a _____ the HTML code causes the display of banner advertisements, for the sites of other members of the exchange, on the member web sites, and webmasters have to create such banner advertisements for their own web sites.
   a. Link exchange
   b. Cost per mille
   c. Frequency capping
   d. Cost per time

72. A _____ is a banner ad which is created dynamically (or whose content is created dynamically) at the time of display, instead of being pre-programmed with fixed content. _____s function the same way as traditional web banners: promoting a brand, product, service, or an event, except that the banner content is variable and may even update in real time. _____s are built using technologies such as Adobe Flash, Java, or Microsoft Silverlight, and usually employ animation together with text, images, graphics, sounds and video to catch the viewer's attention.
   a. Consumer-to-consumer
   b. Social shopping
   c. Spam Lit
   d. Live banner

73. _____ is an electronic commerce software module on a website that allows a visitor to find nearby stores and business locations. In its most common form, a visitor inputs a ZIP code and the locator returns all locations in a database within a specified radius. It is often used in conjunction with mapping/driving direction software on brick and click corporate websites to help customers locate a physical business location.
   a. Consumer-to-consumer
   b. Locator software
   c. Spamvertising
   d. Disintermediation

74. _____ is a provider of social media marketing and digital publicity with offices in Los Angeles and New York. Founded in 1998 by Dave Neupert, the agency started as a word-of-mouth marketing agency in Silver Lake and built its success largely by promoting products that fans were eager to embrace, such as bands and television shows with cult followings.

_____ is a founding member of the Word Of Mouth Marketing Association, establishing an official trade association to set ethical standards, standardized terms, and best practices for other marketing agencies to follow.

   a. M80
   b. Consumption Map
   c. Motion Picture Association of America's film-rating system
   d. Spearman's rank correlation coefficient

75. _____ are relatively new to internet marketing. Google's Ad-Words is a prime example of what _____ are. What makes them attractive is the ease at which you can set up an ad and have it posted.
   a. Promotion
   b. BeyondROI
   c. Self branding
   d. Micro ads

76. _____, is the division of the Microsoft Network (MSN) responsible for MSN's advertising services. _____ provides pay per click advertisements.

Microsoft was the last of the 'Big Three' search engines (Microsoft, Google and Yahoo!) to develop its own system for delivering pay per click (PPC) ads.

a. Click fraud
b. Microsoft adCenter
c. Consumer Generated Advertising
d. Paid inclusion

77. _____ studies the behaviour of mobile website visitors, in a similar way to traditional web analytics (or desktop web analytics.) In a commercial context, _____ refers to the use of data collected as visitors access a web site from a mobile phone. It helps to determine which aspects of the website work best for mobile traffic and which mobile marketing campaigns work best for the business; this includes mobile advertising, mobile search marketing, text campaigns and desktop promotion of mobile sites and services.

a. Direct navigation
b. Mobile Web Analytics
c. Microsoft adCenter
d. Search engine image protection

78. _____ is the measurement, collection, analysis and reporting of internet data for purposes of understanding and optimizing web site usage.

There are two categories of _____; off-site and on-site _____.

Off-site _____ refers to web measurement and analysis irrespective of whether you own or maintain a website.

a. Videoplaza
b. Latitude Group
c. VoloMedia
d. Web Analytics

79. In statistics, _____ or multi-variable testing is a technique for testing hypotheses on complex multi-variable systems, especially used in testing market perceptions.

In internet marketing, _____ is a process by which more than one component of a website may be tested in a live environment. It can be thought of in simple terms as numerous split tests or A/B tests performed on one page at the same time.

a. Search engine image protection
b. Search engine marketing
c. Paid inclusion
d. Multivariate testing

80. _____ is a social networking website with an interactive, user-submitted network of friends, personal profiles, blogs, groups, photos, music, and videos for teenagers and adults internationally. Its headquarters are in Beverly Hills, California, USA, where it shares an office building with its immediate owner, Fox Interactive Media; which is owned by News Corporation, which has its headquarters in New York City. In June 2006, _____ was the most popular social networking site in the United States.

a. MySpace
b. Fountain Fresh International
c. Chief marketing officer
d. National Asset Recovery Services

81. _____, a free online animation community that supports content sharing and social networking, was the first online animation community for viewing community animation content in high-definition. After four months of private beta, the site launched publicly in March 2007 during the South by Southwest festival in Austin, Texas, and began distributing member-created animation videos to Internet audiences worldwide. Three weeks after its launch, _____ had received more than 1.5 million unique visitors.

a. Superbrands Council
b. Capital Cities/ABC
c. JPMorgan Chase ' Co.
d. MyToons

82. _____, previously known as Vendare, First Look, and qsrch.net, is a pay-per-click advertising company that specializes in monetizing parked domain names and registrars' wildcard DNS records. _____ is a subsidiary of New.net and an affiliate of the ICANN-accredited registrar Basic Fusion.

In 2007, _____, along with its affiliate registrar Basic Fusion, was sued by Verizon for the registration and domain tasting of 1,392 domain names incorporating Verizon's trademarks (Verizon California, Inc. v. _____, Inc., 2008 WL 2651163 (C.D. Cal.

a. Paid inclusion
b. Web analytics
c. Value Per Action
d. Navigation Catalyst Systems

83. _____ is an American online advertising company based in Redwood City, California, with offices in New York and London and is funded by the investment companies Sierra Ventures and Menlo Ventures. It is one of several companies developing behavioral targeting advertising systems, seeking deals with ISPs to enable them to analyse customer's websurfing habits in order to provide them with more relevant, micro-targeted advertising. Others include Phorm, Perftech, Quarad and Front Porch.

a. Pinstorm
b. Direct investment
c. Mapinfo
d. NebuAd

84. _____ is a relatively new concept utilized by businesses in developing an online community, which allows satisfied customers to congregate and extol the virtues of a particular brand. In most cases, the online community includes mechanisms such as blogs, podcasts, message boards, and product reviews, all of which contribute to a transparent forum to post praises, criticisms, questions, and suggestions.

One of the primary arguments to promote _____ is the premise that traditional advertising is losing its influence on consumers.

a. 180SearchAssistant
b. Viral marketing
c. New Media Marketing
d. Power III

85. _____ is an online intelligence and word-of-mouth marketing company based in Arlington, Virginia.

_____ was founded by pollster Pete Snyder in 1999. As one of the first online media firms of the Web 2.0 era, _____ is a pioneer in online intelligence, word-of-mouth marketing, and digital public relations campaigns.

a. Sales promotion
b. Marketing communication
c. Merchandise
d. New Media Strategies

86. _____ also known as online image management or online personal branding is a set of methods for generating a distinguished Web presence of a person on the Internet. That presence could be reflected in any kind of content that refers to the person, including news, participation in blogs and forums, personal web sites , social media presence, pictures, video, etc.

_____ also refers to identity exposure and identity disclosure, and has particularly developed in the management on online identity in social network services or online dating services .

a. Organic search
b. Ad serving
c. Online reputation management
d. Online identity management

87. _____ is the practice of consistent research and analysis of one's personal or professional, business or industry reputation as represented by the content across all types of online media. It is also sometimes referred to as Online Reputation Monitoring, maintaining the same acronym.

_____ is a relatively new industry but has been brought to the forefront of professionals' consciousness due to the overwhelming and many times unpredictable nature of both professional journalistic content and amateur user-generated content (or UGC), the latter of which there is far more, and not the least because of the wide number websites that offer such an opportunity to visitors, typically with very low barriers to entry--often just by creating a screenname, registering one's birthday and a geographical location, and providing a valid email address to complete the account-creation process.

a. Organic search
b. Online identity management
c. Ad serving
d. Online reputation management

88. _____ portals are a relatively new type of loyalty program.

The advent of online shopping has resulted in the rapid development of a large number of rewards programs that offer incentives for shopping. These programmes may be points-based (redeemable for products or vouchers), cashback, airline frequent flyer-miles-based, hotel points, donations to charity, or even carbon offsets.

a. Advertising network
b. Enterprise Search Marketing
c. Automated Bid Managers
d. Online shopping rewards

89. _____ is the examining of goods or services from retailers with the intent to purchase at that time. _____ is an activity of selection and/or purchase. In some contexts it is considered a leisure activity as well as an economic one.

a. Hawkers
b. Khodebshchik
c. Discount store
d. Shopping

90. _____ is an open-source advertising server (written in PHP and using a MySQL or PostgreSQL database) that is licensed under the GNU General Public License. It features an integrated banner management interface and tracking system for gathering statistics. The product enables web site administrators to rotate banners from both in-house advertisement campaigns as well as from paid or third-party sources, such as Google's AdSense.

a. Interactive advertising
b. Automated Bid Managers
c. OpenX
d. Audience Screening

91. _____ results refers to those listings in search engine results pages that appear by dint of their relevance to the search terms, as opposed to their being adverts.

The Google, Yahoo, MSN and Live! search engines combine advertising and search results on their search results pages. In each case, the adverts are designed to look like the search results, except for minor visual distinctions such as their background colour and/or placement on the page.

a. Online reputation management
b. Ad serving
c. Online identity management
d. Organic search

92. _____ is a search engine marketing product where the search engine company charges fees related to inclusion of websites in their search index. _____ products are provided by most search engine companies, the most notable exception being Google.
a. Microsoft adCenter
b. Paid inclusion
c. Hit inflation attack
d. VoloMedia

93. _____ or Paid-to-click is a business model that became popular in the late 1990s, prior to the dot-com crash. Essentially, a company places advertising on members' screens and pays them from advertising earnings.

A pay-to-surf company would provide a small program, commonly called a 'viewbar', to be installed on a member's computer.

a. Pay to surf
b. Freebie marketing
c. Cross-selling
d. Multi-level marketing

94. _____ is an Internet advertising model in which advertisements appear along with relevant search results from a Web search engine. Under this model, advertisers bid for the right to present an advertisement with specific search terms (i.e., keywords) in an open auction. When one of these keywords is entered into the search engine, the results of the auction on that keyword are presented, with higher ranking bids appearing at the top of the page.
a. Blog marketing
b. Videoplaza
c. Display advertising
d. Pay for placement

95. _____ is an Internet advertising model used on search engines, advertising networks, and content sites, such as blogs, in which advertisers pay their host only when their ad is clicked. With search engines, advertisers typically bid on keyword phrases relevant to their target market. Content sites commonly charge a fixed price per click rather than use a bidding system.
a. Videoplaza
b. Hit inflation attack
c. Pay per click
d. Navigation Catalyst Systems

96. _____ is an online advertising method that plays an audio advertisement on websites. The term '_____' comes from advertisers paying for each audio ad played. Also, the web page playing the audio ad is normally paid for each ad they serve.
a. Pay per play
b. Web data extractor
c. 180SearchAssistant
d. Power III

97. _____ is a website which helps content creators such as bloggers find advertisers willing to sponsor specific content. The advertisers create opportunities ('opps') that describe the content they are looking for (e.g. feedback, reviews, buzz, creative, video.) The bloggers (sometimes referred to as 'Posties') then choose opportunities in their area of interest.

a. VoloMedia
b. PayPerPost
c. M80
d. Forrester Research

98. _____, Inc. is an online semantic advertising company based in New York City, with research and development facilities in Israel.

_____ applies the principles of natural language processing (NLP) and machine learning to online advertising solutions for publisher sites, including user-generated content, social networks, blogs and online forums.

a. Mobile Web Analytics
b. Consumer Generated Advertising
c. Microsoft adCenter
d. Peer39

99. With _____, the advertiser pays only for measurable results.

With other forms of advertising they pay regardless of results. _____ is becoming more common with the spread of electronic media, notably the Internet, where it is possible to directly measure user actions that result from the advertisement.

a. Door-to-door
b. Fast moving consumer goods
c. Performance-based advertising
d. Business structure

100. _____ is an ad-blocking utility for the Apple Safari web browser.

_____ began in January 2003 as one user's utility to filter content in Safari and has since become a popular utility for other users of Apple's web browser.

As of May 2008 _____'s most recent version is 2.8.4, which works with Safari 3.2.1.

a. 180SearchAssistant
b. 6-3-5 Brainwriting
c. PithHelmet
d. Power III

101. _____ is a form of display advertising on the web, in which the cost of each advertisement is calculated dependent on the number of pixels it occupies.

_____ gained popularity in the last quarter of 2005 when British student Alex Tew created a website named The Million Dollar Homepage, and solicited advertisers to buy ad space measured in pixels on the homepage. The price was set at $1 USD per pixel, and there were 1 million pixels of space available.

a. Pay per ship
b. Copy testing
c. Driven media
d. Pixel advertising

102. _____ is a variable used by Google, Yahoo! (called Quality Index), and MSN that can influence both the rank and cost per click (CPC) of ads.

To determine the order in which ads are listed, each ad has the following formula run against it: bid * _____. Ads are then listed in descending order based on the result of that equation.

a. Cost per action
b. Peer39
c. Conversion optimization
d. Quality Score

Chapter 17. Test Preparation Part 17

1. In business, _____ refers to the sharing of profits and losses among different groups. One form shares between the general partner(s) and limited partners in a limited partnership. Another form shares with a company's employees, and another between companies in a business alliance.

   a. Pay per click
   b. Revenue sharing
   c. Cost per Lead
   d. Videoplaza

2. The term _____ refers to the practice of acquiring domain names from owners by accusing them of violating trademarks with the domain name, and demanding that the domain be transferred.

   The name refers to the practice of domain hijacking, in which a domain name consisting of a trademark or another well-known name is registered solely with the intent of selling it to the trademark owner later on.

   A widely regarded case of _____ occurred in 2000, when the Deutsche Welle attempted to acquire the domain dw.com from software company Diamond Ware.

   a. Top-level domain
   b. Reverse domain hijacking
   c. Domain name front running
   d. Type-in traffic

3. _____ was a pioneer in the movement to commercialize the World Wide Web.

   A media buyer with the San Francisco ad agency Hal Riney ' Partners, Boyce was recruited by HotWired's chief executive officer, Andrew Anker, to be HotWired's director of business development when the company was founded in the fall of 1994. Boyce was responsible for organizing the first, widespread effort to sell banner ads.

   a. Rick Boyce
   b. Nouveau riche
   c. Paschal Eze
   d. Peter Ferdinand Drucker

4. _____ is a Russian online video sharing and transmitting service. As of 2008, it is visited by 400,000 people daily and plays over 40 million videos every month. According to TNS Gallup Media, over 4 million unique users visit it every month.

   a. Nielsen Media Research
   b. RuTube
   c. Forrester Research
   d. Phorm

5. _____ combines the expertise of Search Engine Marketing and PR, and is designed to protect a company or brand against incorrect negative publicity via the Internet.

   By using _____ strategies to push potentially damaging information out of the top search engine rankings, marketers hope to protect their brand image and make a good impression on Internet users who may be researching a future purchase.

   _____ draws on a combination of SEM and public relations strategies to supplant unflattering online content with brand-friendly content.

   a. Mobile Web Analytics
   b. Pay for placement
   c. Web analytics
   d. Search engine image protection

Chapter 17. Test Preparation Part 17

6. _____ is a form of Internet marketing that seeks to promote websites by increasing their visibility in search engine result pages (SERPs.) According to the _____ Professional Organization, _____ methods include: search engine optimization (or SEO), paid placement, contextual advertising, and paid inclusion. Other sources, including the New York Times, define _____ as the practice of buying paid search listings.
   a. Search engine marketing
   b. Pay for placement
   c. Display advertising
   d. Blog marketing

7. _____ is defined by the American _____ Association as the activity, set of institutions, and processes for creating, communicating, delivering, and exchanging offerings that have value for customers, clients, partners, and society at large. The term developed from the original meaning which referred literally to going to market, as in shopping, or going to a market to sell goods or services.

   _____ practice tends to be seen as a creative industry, which includes advertising, distribution and selling.

   a. Customer acquisition management
   b. Product naming
   c. Marketing
   d. Marketing myopia

8. _____ is the process of improving the volume and quality of traffic to a web site from search engines via 'natural' ('organic' or 'algorithmic') search results. Typically, the earlier a site appears in the search results list, the more visitors it will receive from the search engine. _____ may target different kinds of search, including image search, local search, and industry-specific vertical search engines.
   a. Power III
   b. Search engine optimization
   c. 6-3-5 Brainwriting
   d. 180SearchAssistant

9. _____ is a music website set up by Johan Vosmeijer (ex Sony/BMG), Pim Betist (ex Shell), and Dagmar Heijmans (ex Sony/BMG) in August 2006 to allow music ensemblebands to raise the money to record a professional album. Their offices are located in Amsterdam, Netherlands, but it's a German company that started in Bocholt, Germany.

On December 18, 2007 a partnership with the British site from Amazon.com was announced.

   a. Power III
   b. 6-3-5 Brainwriting
   c. 180SearchAssistant
   d. Sellaband

10. _____ applies semantic technologies to online advertising solutions. The function of _____ technology is to semantically analyze every web page in order to properly understand and classify the meaning of a web page and accordingly ensure that the web page contains the most appropriate advertising. _____ increases the chance that the viewer will click-thru because only advertising relevant to what they are viewing, and therefore their interests, should be displayed.
    a. Power III
    b. 6-3-5 Brainwriting
    c. 180SearchAssistant
    d. Semantic advertising

11. _____ is a form of communication that typically attempts to persuade potential customers to purchase or to consume more of a particular brand of product or service. 'While now central to the contemporary global economy and the reproduction of global production networks, it is only quite recently that _____ has been more than a marginal influence on patterns of sales and production. The formation of modern _____ was intimately bound up with the emergence of new forms of monopoly capitalism around the end of the 19th and beginning of the 20th century as one element in corporate strategies to create, organize and where possible control markets, especially for mass produced consumer goods.
   a. ADTECH
   b. ACNielsen
   c. AMAX
   d. Advertising

12. A _____ is a relatively new executive level position at a corporation, company, organization typically reporting directly to the CEO or board of directors. The _____ is responsible for a brand's image, experience, and promise, and propagating it throughout all aspects of the company. The brand officer oversees marketing, advertising, design, public relations and customer service departments.
   a. Chief brand officer
   b. Financial analyst
   c. Chief executive officer
   d. Power III

13. _____. is an online semantic advertising solution, developed by iSense, a company based in London, with research and development facilities in Copenhagen ' Holyhead. The company has offices in New York, Munich, Paris, Stockholm, Madrid, Milan, Hamburg, Dusseldorf, Amsterdam

_____ applies the principles of semantics to online advertising with solutions to block the placement of advertisements alongside Internet content that could be seen as being controversial.

   a. Revenue sharing
   b. SiteScreen
   c. Blog marketing
   d. Pay per click

14. _____ is a set of methods for generating publicity through social media, online communities and community websites. Methods include adding RSS feeds, social news buttons, blogging, and incorporating third-party community functionalities like images and videos.
   a. Quality Score
   b. Social media optimization
   c. Videoplaza
   d. Pay per click

15. _____ is defined as snippets of nonsensical verse and prose embedded in spam e-mail messages. Some of the snippets are made up, others are passages from public domain works, and others are conglomerations of several creative public domain works, which are often be copied from the internet. _____ is included in spam emails selling or purporting to sell a products such as software, male enhancement pills, and computers.
   a. Social shopping
   b. Permission marketing
   c. Spam Lit
   d. Business-to-government

16. _____ is computer software that is installed surreptitiously on a personal computer to intercept or take partial control over the user's interaction with the computer, without the user's informed consent.

While the term _____ suggests software that secretly monitors the user's behavior, the functions of _____ extend well beyond simple monitoring. _____ programs can collect various types of personal information, such as Internet surfing habits, sites that have been visited, but can also interfere with user control of the computer in other ways, such as installing additional software, and redirecting Web browser activity.

Chapter 17. Test Preparation Part 17

a. 180SearchAssistant
c. 6-3-5 Brainwriting
b. Spyware
d. Power III

17. _____ LLC is a New York City independent game development company, formed in 1997 by Peter Mack and several associates to create video games for clients looking to market products and services on the Internet, which in turn would fund internal development of proprietary titles. The company was originally located on the Lower East Side, but moved its offices to Chinatown in 2003. Templar continues to be managed by Peter Mack (President ' Creative Director)and Gordon Klimes (Animation Director.)

a. Templar Studios
c. 6-3-5 Brainwriting
b. 180SearchAssistant
d. Power III

18. _____, also referred to as i-marketing, web marketing, online marketing is the marketing of products or services over the Internet.

The Internet has brought many unique benefits to marketing, one of which being lower costs for the distribution of information and media to a global audience. The interactive nature of _____, both in terms of providing instant response and eliciting responses, is a unique quality of the medium.

a. ACNielsen
c. AMAX
b. ADTECH
d. Internet Marketing

19. Founded in 1995, BMP InterAction was the primary operating arm of interactive R'D and client service provision until being rebranded as Tribal DDB in August 2000, following DDB Worldwide's merging of the interactive services arm of BMP DDB with DDB Digital. The UK branch became _____.

A full-service, interactive agency, _____ work with their clients to create brand demand through digital marketing campaigns.

a. Pay for placement
c. Cost per Lead
b. Tribal DDB London
d. Quality Score

20. _____ is one of the largest video sharing websites in China, where users can upload, view and share video clips. _____ went live on April 15, 2005 and by September 2007, served over 55 million videos each day.

_____ states they are one of the world's largest bandwidth users, moving more than 1 Petabyte per day to 7 million users.

a. Goodyear Tire ' Rubber Company
c. Tudou
b. Kahala-Cold Stone
d. GlobalSpec

21. _____ is a term describing visitors landing at a web site by entering a keyword or phrase (with no spaces or a hyphen in place of a space) in the web browser's address bar (and adding .com or in a mobile browser address bar and adding .mobi or any other gTLD (generic top-level domain) or ccTLD extension (country code top-level domain); rather than following a hyperlink from another web page, using a browser bookmark, or a search-box search. _____ is a form of direct navigation.

Example: If you are interested in widgets, then instead of performing a search-engine search for the term 'widgets' you might type 'widgets.com' or 'widgets.mobi in your mobile browser address bar to see if such a web site exists, and, if so, what content is there.

a. Type-in traffic
b. Domain name speculation
c. Domain tasting
d. Domain name warehousing

22. _____ is a form of cybersquatting which relies on mistakes such as typographical errors made by Internet users when inputting a website address into a web browser. Should a user accidentally enter an incorrect website address, they may be led to an alternative website owned by a cybersquatter.

Generally, the victim site of _____ will be a frequently visited website.

a. Domaining
b. Domain name front running
c. Fast flux
d. Typosquatting

23. A personal and cultural _____ is a relative ethic _____, an assumption upon which implementation can be extrapolated. A _____ system is a set of consistent _____s and measures that is soo not true. A principle _____ is a foundation upon which other _____s and measures of integrity are based.

a. Supreme Court of the United States
b. Package-on-Package
c. Perceptual maps
d. Value

24. _____ refers to an online marketing business model similar to the Cost Per Action (CPA) model. While Cost Per Action provides a low risk arrangement in which the seller only pays an advertising fee when a consumer takes action (such as purchasing their product) _____ extends that model to add revenue sharing with the consumer.

Using the _____ model, sellers don't incur advertising/marketing costs until a sale takes place, and can increase the likelihood of a sale by increasing the adverstising dollars.

a. Consumer Generated Advertising
b. Click-through rate
c. Value Per Action
d. Search engine image protection

25. _____ is an instructional video website, which aims to provide a how-to guide for many differing subjects such as 'How to eat sushi' to 'How to tie a tie' using windsor knots, a half windsor knot, or a four-in-hand knot. It launched as a beta online in 2006 and about a month later went gold.

The website provides both professionally made videos produced internally, as well as videos produced by and uploaded by amateurs.

a. Sustainable Forestry Initiative
b. GlobalSpec
c. VideoJug
d. Multinational corporation

26. _____ AB is a video adserving company based in Sweden.

_____ AB was founded during the fall of 2007 by Sorosh Tavakoli, Dante Buhay and Alfred Ruth in Stockholm, Sweden. The company is backed by the Swedish VC firm Creandum and private investors Rolf Skoglund, Joakim Jardenberg, Andy Chen, Henrik Torstensson and Magnus Hultman.

- a. Quality Score
- b. Latitude Group
- c. Videoplaza
- d. Conversion optimization

27. _____ is a Sunnyvale, California based advertising network that has developed technology to enable advertisements to be dynamically inserted into downloadable audio and video, such as podcasts. Large media publishers such as Public Radio International, MSNBC and FOX News utilize their technologies in order to provide free downloadable programming. The company is funded by venture capital firms Mayfield Fund, Sutter Hill Ventures and Worldview Technology Partners.
- a. Cost per Lead
- b. Search engine marketing
- c. Display advertising
- d. VoloMedia

28. _____ is an online music creation community and user-generated record label founded in 2007 by hip-hop star and award-winning actor Christopher 'Ludacris' Bridges headquartered in New York City. It is a privately held joint venture between Ludacris' Disturbing tha Peace label and MegaMobile TV (a company founded by veteran TV creator Matthew Apfel.) Officially launched in April 2008, the service is a social network as well as a content browsing/filtering structure similar to YouTube.
- a. 6-3-5 Brainwriting
- b. 180SearchAssistant
- c. Power III
- d. WeMix.com

29. _____ is the measurement, collection, analysis and reporting of internet data for purposes of understanding and optimizing web site usage.

There are two categories of _____; off-site and on-site _____.

Off-site _____ refers to web measurement and analysis irrespective of whether you own or maintain a website.

- a. Latitude Group
- b. Web analytics
- c. VoloMedia
- d. Videoplaza

30. _____, button graphics, badges or stickers are pictures in some World Wide Web pages which are typically used to advertise programs that were used to create or host the site (for example, MediaWiki sites often have a 'Powered by Mediawiki' button on the bottom right corner of the page), programs that are recommended to view the site, or that the site passes W3C HTML validation. The buttons are linked to the advertised sites. These were first popularized by Netscape and Microsoft during the browser wars.
- a. Strand
- b. Supplier
- c. Consumocracy
- d. Web buttons

31. _____ is a shareware _____ utility for Microsoft Windows.

The software allows to extract URL, Meta Tag, Body Text, Email, Phone and Fax directly from web sites and save them in various formats for future use. Program has numerous special filters to restrict session, for example: URL filter, date modified, file size, etc.

   a. Geo
   b. Web data extractor
   c. Range
   d. Push

32. _____ refer to a collection of facts usually collected as the result of experience, observation or experiment or a set of premises. This may consist of numbers, words particularly as measurements or observations of a set of variables. _____ are often viewed as a lowest level of abstraction from which information and knowledge are derived.
   a. Mean
   b. Sample size
   c. Pearson product-moment correlation coefficient
   d. Data

33. A _____ is a record in a DNS zone that will match requests for non-existent domain names. A _____ is specified by using a '*' as the left most label (part) of a domain name, e.g. `*.example.com`. The exact rules for when a wild card will match are specified in RFC 1034, but the rules are neither intuitive nor clearly specified.
   a. Wildcard DNS record
   b. Top-level domain
   c. Domain sniping
   d. Domain name speculation

34. _____, founded in 1930 as the Merchant's Advertising Service, began as a publisher of independent telephone directories. Based in Uniondale (Long Island), New York, the company mission has always been to provide a vehicle to connect consumers with local businesses. Today that is done online and in print.
   a. 180SearchAssistant
   b. Power III
   c. Yellowbook
   d. 6-3-5 Brainwriting

35. _____ is a form of targeted advertising for advertisements appearing on websites or other media, such as content displayed in mobile browsers. The advertisements themselves are selected and served by automated systems based on the content displayed to the user.

A _____ system scans the text of a website for keywords and returns advertisements to the webpage based on what the user is viewing.

   a. Click fraud
   b. Click-through rate
   c. Multivariate testing
   d. Contextual advertising

36. In economics, business, retail, and accounting, a _____ is the value of money that has been used up to produce something, and hence is not available for use anymore. In economics, a _____ is an alternative that is given up as a result of a decision. In business, the _____ may be one of acquisition, in which case the amount of money expended to acquire it is counted as _____.
   a. Fixed costs
   b. Transaction cost
   c. Variable cost
   d. Cost

37. _____ is an online advertising pricing model, where the advertiser pays for each specified action (a purchase, a form submission, and so on) linked to the advertisement.

Chapter 17. Test Preparation Part 17

Direct response advertisers consider _____ the optimal way to buy online advertising, as an advertiser only pays for the ad when the desired action has occurred. An action can be a product being purchased, a form being filled, etc.

a. Cost per Lead
c. Value Per Action

b. Display advertising
d. Cost per action

38. _____ is the amount of money an advertiser pays search engines and other Internet publishers for a single click on its advertisement that brings one visitor to its website.

- Ad serving
- Click-through rate (CTR)
- Compensation methods
- Cost per action (CPA)
- Cost per impression (CPI)
- Cost per mille (CPM), Also Cost per thousand
- Google AdSense
- Interactive advertising
- Internet marketing
- Online advertising
- Pay Per Click (PPC)
- Search engine marketing (SEM)
- Search engine optimization (SEO)

a. Cost per conversion
c. Comparative advertising

b. Flighting
d. Cost per click

39. _____ is an online advertising pricing structure introduced into the market in 2008.

Differing from cost per impression or click through rate models, a _____ model means advertising impressions are free and advertisers pay only when a user engages with their ad unit. Engagement is defined as a user interacting with an ad in any number of ways, including playing a game, taking a poll, rolling over an ad unit for a specified amount of time or taking a product tour.

a. Hover ads
c. Search advertising

b. Cost per engagement
d. Keyword advertising

40. _____ measures the extent to which a consumer has a meaningful brand experience when exposed to commercial advertising, sponsorship, television contact, or other experience.

In March 2006 the Advertising Research Foundation defined _____ as 'turning on a prospect to a brand idea enhanced by the surrounding context'. The ARF has also defined the function whereby _____ impacts a brand:

_____ is complex because a variety of exposure and relationship factors affect _____, making simplified rankings misleading.

- a. Inseparability
- b. Automated surveys
- c. Individual branding
- d. Engagement

41. _____ refers to a form of Internet advertising, where the buyer pays for an advertisement to be placed on a website for a set amount of time. It differs from cost per impression, in which a buyer pays for the ad to be displayed a set number of times. Cost for time permits the ad to displayed unlimited times over the term of the contract.

- a. Link exchange
- b. Frequency capping
- c. Cost per mille
- d. Cost per time

42. _____ is a type of advertising that typically contains text (i.e., copy), logos, photographs or other images, location maps, and similar items. In periodicals, _____ can appear on the same page as, or on the page adjacent to, general editorial content. In contrast, classified advertising generally appears in a distinct section, was traditionally text-only, and was available in a limited selection of typefaces.

- a. Latitude Group
- b. Peer39
- c. Multivariate testing
- d. Display advertising

43. _____ is associated with the concept of Contextual Advertising but differs in its ability to match advertising to content in a much more specific manner For example, there is no chance that an Auto Mechanic could advertise next to an article about the Detroit Pistons.

- a. ACNielsen
- b. ADTECH
- c. AMAX
- d. Editorial Related Advertising

44. _____ are a special type of pop-up ads created using Dynamic HTML, JavaScript and similar web browser technologies. Because they do not scroll with the web page, they appear to 'hover' over the page, usually obscuring the content.

Being among the most effective forms of web advertising, pop-up ads acquired a certain share of online advertising solutions and technologies.

- a. Keyword advertising
- b. Semantic targeting
- c. Search advertising
- d. Hover ads

45. On the World Wide Web, _____s are web pages that are displayed before an expected content page, often to display advertisements or confirm the user's age.

Some people take issue with this form of online advertising. Less controversial uses of _____ pages include introducing another page or site before directing the user to proceed; or alerting the user that the next page requires a login, or has some other requirement which the user should know about before proceeding.

- a. ADTECH
- b. AMAX
- c. ACNielsen
- d. Interstitial

46. _____ refers to any advertising that is linked to specific words or phrases. Common forms of _____ are known by many other terms including pay per click (PPC) and cost per action (CPA.) There are multiple variations each starting with 'pay per' or 'cost per' such as pay per action (PPA), pay per cost (PPC), cost per mille (CPM.)
- a. Hover ads
- b. Semantic targeting
- c. Search advertising
- d. Keyword advertising

47. _____ is a form of promotion that uses the Internet and World Wide Web for the expressed purpose of delivering marketing messages to attract customers. Examples of _____ include contextual ads on search engine results pages, banner ads, Rich Media Ads, Social network advertising, online classified advertising, advertising networks and e-mail marketing, including e-mail spam.

Online video directories for brands are a good example of interactive advertising.

- a. ADTECH
- b. AMAX
- c. ACNielsen
- d. Online advertising

48. _____ is a search engine marketing product where the search engine company charges fees related to inclusion of websites in their search index. _____ products are provided by most search engine companies, the most notable exception being Google.
- a. VoloMedia
- b. Hit inflation attack
- c. Microsoft adCenter
- d. Paid inclusion

49. _____ is an online advertisement pricing system where the publisher or website owner is paid on the basis of the number of sales that are directly generated by an advertisement. It is a variant of the CPA (Cost Per Action) model where the advertiser pays the publisher/website only and in proportion to the number of actions committed by the readers or visitors to the website.

In many cases it's not practical to track all the sales generated by an advertisement, however it is more easily tracked for full online transactions, such as for selling songs directly on the internet.

- a. Price war
- b. Break even analysis
- c. Price points
- d. Pay Per Sale

50. _____ is a term used in Internet marketing to define a popular pricing model whereby a marketing agency will receive a bounty from an advertiser for each new lead or new customer obtained for the advertiser through the agency's online marketing efforts. The agency creates advertising campaigns and promotions to convert the maximum number of new leads or customers and gets paid for its work only when a new lead or a new customer is passed on to the advertiser.

PPP advertising became popular with the advent of the world wide web that allows real time measurement of an advertising campaign's ROI (return on investment.)

- a. 6-3-5 Brainwriting
- b. 180SearchAssistant
- c. Power III
- d. Pay for performance advertising

51. _____ is an Internet advertising model in which advertisements appear along with relevant search results from a Web search engine. Under this model, advertisers bid for the right to present an advertisement with specific search terms (i.e., keywords) in an open auction. When one of these keywords is entered into the search engine, the results of the auction on that keyword are presented, with higher ranking bids appearing at the top of the page.

   a. Blog marketing
   c. Display advertising
   b. Videoplaza
   d. Pay for placement

52. _____ is an Internet advertising model used on search engines, advertising networks, and content sites, such as blogs, in which advertisers pay their host only when their ad is clicked. With search engines, advertisers typically bid on keyword phrases relevant to their target market. Content sites commonly charge a fixed price per click rather than use a bidding system.

   a. Hit inflation attack
   c. Navigation Catalyst Systems
   b. Pay per click
   d. Videoplaza

53. _____ are a form of online advertising on the World Wide Web intended to attract web traffic or capture email addresses. It works when certain web sites open a new web browser window to display advertisements. The pop-up window containing an advertisement is usually generated by JavaScript, but can be generated by other means as well.

   a. Power III
   c. Customer intelligence
   b. Pop-up ads
   d. Project Portfolio Management

54. In Internet Marketing, _____ is a method of placing online advertisements on Web pages that show results from search engine queries. Through the same search-engine advertising services, ads can also be placed on Web pages with other published content.

Search advertisements are targeted to match key search terms (called keywords) entered on search engines.

   a. Keyword advertising
   c. Semantic targeting
   b. Hover ads
   d. Search advertising

55. _____ is a technique enabling the delivery of targeted advertising, a form of contextual advertising, for advertisements appearing on websites and is used by online publishers and advertisers to increase the effectiveness of their campaigns. The selection of advertisements are served by automated systems based on the content displayed to the user.

_____ has originated from the developments arising from Semantic Web.

   a. Search advertising
   c. Hover ads
   b. Keyword advertising
   d. Semantic targeting

56. _____ is the practice of sending E-mail spam, advertising a website. In this case, it is a portmanteau of the words 'spam' and 'advertising'.

It also refers to vandalizing wikis, blogs and online forums with hyperlinks in order to get a higher search engine ranking for the vandal's website.

a. Live banner	b. Disintermediation
c. Locator software	d. Spamvertising

57. In packaging, a _____ or BIB is a type of container for the storage and transportation of liquids. It consists of a strong bladder (or plastic bag), usually made of metallised film or other plastics, seated inside a corrugated fiberboard box. The bag is filled by the manufacturer with the desired liquid and sealed.

a. Foam take-out container	b. 180SearchAssistant
c. Power III	d. Bag-In-Box

58. _____ is a term for several types of pre-formed plastic packaging used for small consumer goods.

The two primary components of a _____ are the cavity or pocket made from a 'formable' web, either plastic or aluminium - and the lidding, made from paper, carton, plastic or aluminium. The 'formed' cavity or pocket contains the product and the 'lidding' seals the product in the package..

a. Flavor scalping	b. Blister pack
c. Quilt packaging	d. Child-resistant packaging

59. _____ are production lines that fill a product, generally a beverage, into bottles on a large scale.

The first step in bottling wine is depalletising, where the empty wine bottles are removed from the original pallet packaging delivered from the manufacturer, so that individual bottles may be handled. The bottles may then be rinsed with filtered water or air, and may have carbon dioxide injected into them in attempt to reduce the level of oxygen within the bottle.

a. Manufacturers' representatives	b. Pearson's chi-square
c. Bottling lines	d. GE matrix

60. A _____ is an apparatus used to seal a container, such as a bottle, tube or barrel. Unlike a lid which encloses a container from the outside without displacing the inner volume, a _____ is partially inserted inside the container to act as a seal. The lids for safety overpacks for 55 gallon drums sometimes may have a _____ built in for access of the contents of the container.

a. 180SearchAssistant	b. Power III
c. 6-3-5 Brainwriting	d. Bung

61. _____ is the measurement of the amount of carbon dioxide gas that passes through a substance over a given period. It is mostly carried out on non-porous materials, where the mode of transport is diffusion, but there are a growing number of applications where the transmission rate also depends on flow through apertures of some description.

- Moisture vapor transmission rate
- Permeation
- Oxygen transmission rate

- Brody, A. L., and Marsh, K, S., 'Encyclopedia of Packaging Technology', John Wiley ' Sons, 1997, ISBN 0-471-06397-5
- Massey,L K, 'Permeability Properties of Plastics and Elastomers', 2003, Andrew Publishing, ISBN 978-1-884207-97-6

a. Carbon dioxide transmission rate
b. Retail Ready Packaging
c. Foam take-out container
d. Flavor scalping

62. _____ or C-R packaging is special packaging used to reduce the risk of children ingesting dangerous items. It is often required by regulation for prescription drugs, over-the-counter medications, pesticides, and household chemicals.

No package is childproof.

a. Discbox Slider
b. Child-resistant packaging
c. Spray foam
d. Living hinge

63. A _____ is a temperature-controlled supply chain. An unbroken _____ is an uninterrupted series of storage and distribution activities which maintain a given temperature range. It is used to extend and to help ensure the shelf life of products such as chemicals, foods and drugs.

a. Power III
b. Cold chain
c. Shelf life
d. 180SearchAssistant

64. _____, usually abbreviated as _____ is the name given to an ISO shipping container pre-fabricated into a living quarters. Such containers can be transported by container ships, railroad cars, planes, and trucks that are capable of transporting intermodal freight transport cargo.

Container Housing units are related to the site and land occupied during a certain amount of time by the need of water supply and evacuation, electricity, telecommunications, etc.

a. Slip sheet
b. Demand chain management
c. Drop shipping
d. Containerized housing unit

65. A _____ is a design of cartons for bottled wine that holds two rows of five bottles, developed by the Helm Wines winery, Canberra, Australia, to replace traditional dozen-bottle cartons. The quoted motivation is that demographics reports show that females buy more than 50 percent of wine in Australia. According to the OH'S regulations, a female should not lift more than 15 kilograms (33 lbs), which is only the minimum gross weight of a standard 12-bottle carton, which can weigh up to 20 kg for some types of bottles.

Chapter 17. Test Preparation Part 17

a. Discbox Slider
c. Carbon dioxide transmission rate
b. Snap case
d. Decimal Dozen

66. _____ is a patented style of compact disc or DVD packaging, and is a registered trademark of AGI Media, a MeadWestvaco, Inc. resource, which acquired the original trademark holder, IMPAC Group, Inc., in 2000. MeadWestvaco licenses the name and designs to manufacturers around the world.
   a. 180SearchAssistant
   c. Digipak
   b. Power III
   d. 6-3-5 Brainwriting

67. The _____ is a 100% carton board optical disc packaging concept developed by the international paper and board company Stora Enso. The case is comparable with plastic jewel or amaray cases when it comes to size but it holds more of the features of the LP style cases in terms of light weight and printability. The DBS case opens up from the side by moving the slider part from the sleeve.
   a. Decimal Dozen
   c. Squround
   b. Snap case
   d. Discbox Slider

68. _____ is one of the four elements of marketing mix. An organization or set of organizations (go-betweens) involved in the process of making a product or service available for use or consumption by a consumer or business user.

The other three parts of the marketing mix are product, pricing, and promotion.

   a. Japan Advertising Photographers' Association
   c. Comparison-Shopping agent
   b. Better Living Through Chemistry
   d. Distribution

69. A _____ is a sealed plastic bag that is designed to stand upright. _____s are commonly used for powders or ready to drink beverages. They can be aseptically filled or filled on normal packaging lines.
   a. Snap case
   c. Filament tape
   b. Doypack
   d. Spray foam

70. _____ is an Authentication service provided by one remote server to other distributed servers, on the Internet or Intranet.Similar to Credit Cards verification services that are provided by third parties to eCommerce Web Sites, _____ service is providing Identity verification services primarily to Web sites but also to Intranet servers.There are a number of _____ implementations in the markets today. Some use Radius based eAuthetication and other are using a more elaborate proprietary API.
   a. ADTECH
   c. AMAX
   b. ACNielsen
   d. EAuthentication

71. _____ is a major discipline within the field of electronic engineering, and includes a wide variety of technologies. It refers to enclosures and protective features built into the product itself, and not to shipping containers. It applies both to end products and to components.
   a. ADTECH
   c. AMAX
   b. ACNielsen
   d. Electronic packaging

72. The _____ is a US law that applies to labels on many consumer products. It requires the label to state:

- The identity of the product;
- The name and place of business of the manufacturer, packer, or distributor; and
- The net quantity of contents.

The contents statement must include both metric and U.S. customary units.

Passed under Lyndon B. Johnson in 1966, the law first took effect on July 1, 1967. The metric labeling requirement was added in 1992 and took effect on February 14, 1994.

a. 180SearchAssistant
c. Power III
b. 6-3-5 Brainwriting
d. Fair Packaging and Labeling Act

73. _____ or strapping tape is a pressure sensitive tape used for several packaging functions such as closing corrugated fiberboard boxes, reinforcing packages, bundling items, pallet unitizing, etc. It consists of a pressure sensitive adhesive coated onto a backing material which is usually a polypropylene or polyester film and fiberglass filaments embedded to add high tensile strength.

Most often, the tape is 12 mm (aprox 1/2 inch) to 24 mm (aprox 1 inch) wide but is also used in other widths.

a. K-Cup
c. Skin pack
b. Tamper-evident
d. Filament tape

74. _____ is a term used in the packaging industry to describe the loss of quality of a packaged item due to either its volatile flavors being absorbed by the packaging or the item absorbing undesirable flavors from its packaging. A classic example is the absorption of various plastic flavors when soft drinks are stored in plastic bottles for an extended period.

- cork tainting

a. Squround
c. Flavor scalping
b. Hermetic seal
d. Living hinge

75. An _____ is a container used for transport and storage of fluids and bulk materials. The construction of the _____ container and the materials used are chosen depending on the application, i.e. there are various types available in the market.

- Foldable (collapsable) _____ Container
- Plastic composite _____ Container
- Steel _____ Container
- Stainless steel _____ Container

There are many advantages of the _____ concept:

- They are generally cubic in form and therefore can transport more material in the same area than cylindrically shaped containers and far more than might be shipped in the same space if packaged in consumer quantities.
- They rely on plastic liners that can be filled and discharged with a variety of systems.
- The manufacturer/processor of a product can bulk package a product in one country and ship to many other countries at a reasonably low cost where it is subsequently packaged in final consumer form in accordance with the regulations of that country and in a form and language suitable for that country.

_____s range in size but are generally between 700 mm and 2000 mm in height or 46 inches to 52 inches. The length and width of an _____ is usually dependent on the country's pallet dimension standard.

a. AMAX
b. Intermediate bulk container
c. ACNielsen
d. ADTECH

76. _____ is a form of printing process which utilizes a flexible relief plate. It is basically an updated version of letterpress that can be used for printing on almost any type of substrate including plastic, metallic films, cellophane, and paper. That's why it's widely used for printing on the non-porous substrates required for various types of food packaging (it is also well suited for printing large areas of solid color.)

a. 180SearchAssistant
b. Security printing
c. Power III
d. Flexography

77. A _____ is a disposable container for take-out food used internationally by restaurants. Such containers are most commonly used to serve takeout food, and are also available by request in some restaurants for diners who wish to take the remainder of their meal home.

_____s are made from XPS foam, or another type of polystyrene foam, and produced by injecting the foam into a mold.

a. Foam take-out container
b. Punnet
c. Power III
d. 180SearchAssistant

78. _____ refers to 'controlling human or societal behaviour by rules or restrictions.' _____ can take many forms: legal restrictions promulgated by a government authority, self-_____, social _____, co-_____ and market _____. One can consider _____ as actions of conduct imposing sanctions (such as a fine.) This action of administrative law, or implementing regulatory law, may be contrasted with statutory or case law.

a. Non-conventional trademark
b. Rule of four
c. CAN-SPAM
d. Regulation

79. _____ is a scientific discipline describing handling, preparation, and storage of food in ways that prevent foodborne illness. This includes a number of routines that should be followed to avoid potentially severe health hazards. Food can transmit disease from person to person as well as serve as a growth medium for bacteria that can cause food poisoning.

a. Power III
c. Food safety
b. 180SearchAssistant
d. Shelf life

80. _____ is divided into two types of glass: sheet glass made by the float glass process and glass container production.

Modern glass container factories are broadly divided into three parts: the batch house, the hot end and the cold end. The batch house is concerned with raw materials.

a. Glass production
c. Power III
b. 180SearchAssistant
d. 6-3-5 Brainwriting

81. _____ are claims by manufacturers of food products that their food will reduce the risk of developing a disease or condition. For example, it is claimed by the manufacturers of oat cereals that oat bran can reduce cholesterol, which will lower the chances of developing serious heart conditions.

In the United States, these claims, usually referred to as 'qualified health claims', are regulated by the Food and Drug Administration in the public interest.

a. 6-3-5 Brainwriting
c. Power III
b. Health claims on food labels
d. 180SearchAssistant

82. A _____ is a machine used to seal products, packaging, and other thermoplastic materials using heat.

- Continuous _____s- (also known as Band type _____s) utilize heated moving belts.

- Impulse _____s- use a stationary element which is heated with each sealing cycle .An impulse sealer is a system often found on a 'bottom weld' machine. This type of machine uses two sealing elements, an upper and lower which fuse the material from both sides at the same time. The purpose of 'Impulse sealing' is to improve the bonding of the two layers of film.

a. Power III
c. 180SearchAssistant
b. 6-3-5 Brainwriting
d. Heat sealer

83. A _____ is a seal which, for practical purposes, is considered airtight. The term is often used to describe electronic parts that are designed and intended to secure against the entry of microorganisms and other foreign bodies in order to maintain the proper functioning and reliability of their contents.

The word hermetic comes from the syncretism of the Greek god Hermes and the Egyptian Thoth; this figure was also a mythological alchemist known as Hermes Trismegistus.

a. Video game packaging
c. Decimal Dozen
b. Tamper-evident
d. Hermetic seal

84. A _____ is a thin flask for holding a distilled beverage; its size and shape are suited to a trouser pocket.

_____s are often made of stainless steel with a leather cover for decoration. Some come with small cups to make sharing easier, although generally liquid is drank directly from the flask.

a. 6-3-5 Brainwriting
c. 180SearchAssistant
b. Power III
d. Hip flask

Chapter 18. Test Preparation Part 18

1. A _____ is a type of hydration system built as a backpack or waistpack containing a reservoir or 'bladder' commonly made of rubber or flexible plastic. The reservoir contains a capped mouth for filling with liquid and a hose that allows the wearer to drink hands-free. Most hoses end with a 'bite valve' that opens when the user bites down on it; the valve may be protected by a dust cover.

   a. Power III
   b. 6-3-5 Brainwriting
   c. Hydration pack
   d. 180SearchAssistant

2. _____ are containers primarily used in retail to hold fruit and vegetables. They are attractive due to their ability to be stacked in many different configurations, much like Lego, either when flattened or completely upright, and due to their reusable nature. They can also be folded up for storage purposes.

   a. AMAX
   b. ACNielsen
   c. Ifco trays
   d. ADTECH

3. _____, otherwise known as cap sealing, is a non-contact method of heating a metallic disk to hermetically seal the top of plastic and glass containers. This sealing process takes place after the container has been filled and capped. A Hand Held induction sealer Automatic Waterless Induction Sealer An induction sealer with a conveyor

   The closure is supplied to the bottler with foil liner already inserted.

   a. Induction sealing
   b. AMAX
   c. ACNielsen
   d. ADTECH

4. _____s are a type of packaging used to ship temperature sensitive products such as foods, pharmaceuticals, and chemicals. They are used as part of a cold chain to help maintain product freshness and efficacy.

   An _____ might be constructed of:

   1. a vacuum flask, similar to a 'thermos' bottle
   2. fabricated thermal blankets or liners
   3. molded expanded polystyrene foam (EPS, styrofoam, etc), similar to a cooler
   4. other molded foams such as polyurethane, polyethylene, etc
   5. sheets of foamed plastics
   6. reflective materials: (metallised film, etc)
   7. bubble wrap or other gas filled panels
   8. other packaging materials and structures

   Some are designed for single use while others are returnable for reuse. Some empty containers are sent to the shipper disassembled or 'knocked down', assembled and used, then knocked down again for easier return shipment.

   a. ACNielsen
   b. AMAX
   c. ADTECH
   d. Insulated shipping container

5. _____ is the final stage of semiconductor device fabrication per se, followed by IC testing.

Chapter 18. Test Preparation Part 18   263

In the integrated circuit industry it is called simply packaging and sometimes semiconductor device assembly, or simply assembly. Also, sometimes it is called encapsulation or seal, by the name of its last step, which might lead to confusion, because the term packaging generally comprises the steps or the technology of mounting and interconnecting of devices

   a. ACNielsen
   c. AMAX
   b. ADTECH
   d. Integrated circuit packaging

6. An _____ is a container used for transport and storage of fluids and bulk materials. The construction of the _____ container and the materials used are chosen depending on the application, i.e. there are various types available in the market.

   - Foldable (collapsable) _____ Container
   - Plastic composite _____ Container
   - Steel _____ Container
   - Stainless steel _____ Container

There are many advantages of the _____ concept:

   - They are generally cubic in form and therefore can transport more material in the same area than cylindrically shaped containers and far more than might be shipped in the same space if packaged in consumer quantities.
   - They rely on plastic liners that can be filled and discharged with a variety of systems.
   - The manufacturer/processor of a product can bulk package a product in one country and ship to many other countries at a reasonably low cost where it is subsequently packaged in final consumer form in accordance with the regulations of that country and in a form and language suitable for that country.

_____s range in size but are generally between 700 mm and 2000 mm in height or 46 inches to 52 inches. The length and width of an _____ is usually dependent on the country's pallet dimension standard.

   a. ACNielsen
   c. AMAX
   b. ADTECH
   d. Intermediate bulk container

7. _____ portion packs are used with Keurig single cup brewing systems to brew a cup of coffee, tea, or hot chocolate. Each _____ is a plastic container with a coffee filter inside. Ground coffee beans are packed in the _____ and sealed air-tight with a combination plastic and foil lid.
   a. Discbox Slider
   c. Pilferage
   b. Child-resistant packaging
   d. K-Cup

8. A _____ or poly-box is a type of DVD (and sometimes CD) packaging. One well known manufacturer is Amaray, which is why this type of case is sometimes called an amaray case. Amaray case has become a genericized trademark for DVD case among the people in the disc duplication and replication industry.

a. 180SearchAssistant
c. Power III
b. 6-3-5 Brainwriting
d. Keep case

9. A _____ is a thin flexible hinge (flexure bearing) made from plastic (rather than cloth, leather allowing them to bend along the line of the hinge. It is typically manufactured in an injection molding operation that creates all three parts at one time as a single part, and if correctly designed and constructed, it can remain functional over the life of the part. Polyethylene and polypropylene are considered to be the best resins for _____s, due to their excellent fatigue resistance.
  a. Child-resistant packaging
  c. Living hinge
  b. Spray foam
  d. Pilferage

10. A _____ is a form of exterior cardboard packaging for musical compact discs in widespread use in North America in the 1980s and early 1990s.

When compact discs first began to appear in the retail stores, the _____ packaging served a transitional purpose, allowing shops to file new compact discs in the same bins originally used for vinyl records. _____es were 12' tall, and capable of containing two separate discs when necessary.

  a. 180SearchAssistant
  c. Power III
  b. 6-3-5 Brainwriting
  d. Longbox

11. _____ or labeling is the requirement of consumer products to state their ingredients or components.

Moral purchasing and problems like allergies are two things which are enabled by labelling. It is mandated in most developed nations, and increasingly in developing nations, especially for food products, e.g. 'Grade A' meats.

  a. Power III
  c. Mandatory labelling
  b. Product stewardship
  d. SA8000

12. _____ , also water vapor transmission rate (WVTR), is a measure of the passage of water vapor through a substance.

There are many industries where this property is critical. Moisture sensitive foods and pharmeceuticals are put in packaging with controlled _____ to achieve the required quality, safety, and shelf life.

  a. 180SearchAssistant
  c. Power III
  b. Moisture vapor transmission rate
  d. 6-3-5 Brainwriting

13. An _____ is traditionally a strip of paper looped around the left side or folded over the top of Japanese LP albums. _____s are also found folded over the left side of music CDs, video games, DVDs and even on the covers of books when they are sold new. The Japanese word 'Obi' refers to the traditional sash or belt worn with a kimono.
  a. ACNielsen
  c. Oxygen transmission rate
  b. Obi strip
  d. Unit dose

Chapter 18. Test Preparation Part 18 265

14. _____ is a standardized container in large dimensions for storing for example vegetables, granules of plastics or other dry products. It is made of thick cardboard with an optional inner polyethylene bag and normally measures from 80 x 120 cm to 120 x 120 cm and varies in height from 50 cm up to 200 cm. It's capacity is normally around 1000 kg but the larger units can store even 1700 kg.
   a. Oxygen transmission rate
   b. Octabin
   c. Unit dose
   d. ACNielsen

15. _____ is the measurement of the amount of oxygen gas that passes through a substance over a given period. It is mostly carried out on non-porous materials, where the mode of transport is diffusion, but there are a growing number of applications where the transmission rate also depends on flow through apertures of some description.

It relates to the permeation of oxygen through packaging to sensitive foods and pharmaceuticals.

   a. Unit dose
   b. ACNielsen
   c. Octabin
   d. Oxygen transmission rate

16. _____ is an integrated circuit packaging technique to allow vertically combining discrete logic and memory ball grid array (BGA) packages. Two or more packages are installed on top of one another, i.e. stacked, with a standard interface to route signals between them. This allows higher density, for example in the mobile telephone / PDA market.
   a. Good things come to those who wait
   b. Bottling lines
   c. Package-on-Package
   d. Flighting

17. _____ is the theft of part of the contents of a package. It may also include theft of the contents but leaving the package, perhaps resealed with bogus contents. Small packages can be pilfered from a larger package such as a shipping container.
   a. Skin pack
   b. Child-resistant packaging
   c. Squround
   d. Pilferage

18. _____ refers to 'controlling human or societal behaviour by rules or restrictions.' _____ can take many forms: legal restrictions promulgated by a government authority, self-_____, social _____, co-_____ and market _____. One can consider _____ as actions of conduct imposing sanctions (such as a fine.) This action of administrative law, or implementing regulatory law, may be contrasted with statutory or case law.
   a. Rule of four
   b. Non-conventional trademark
   c. CAN-SPAM
   d. Regulation

19. In computing, a _____ is a style of case for computers. They tend to be very thin, normally one or two rack units (1U or 2U) in height, making them wide and flat. The result is a case that looks like boxes used to deliver pizza.
   a. 180SearchAssistant
   b. Power III
   c. 6-3-5 Brainwriting
   d. Pizza box

20. A _____ is a basket for displaying and collecting fruits or flowers. Farmers' markets sometimes sell fruits and berries in plastic _____s. Decorative _____s are often made of felt and seen in flower and craft arrangements.
   a. 180SearchAssistant
   b. Punnet
   c. Foam take-out container
   d. Power III

21. _____ is an electronic packaging technology under research that allows microchips made of dissimilar materials to be attached like squares in a quilt. Chips are connected in a way that minimizes both thermal stress and interchip delay times. The reflection coefficient s11 has been measured at less than -25dB at 40GHz in high resistivity silicon.

  a. K-Cup
  b. Foam take-out container
  c. Discbox Slider
  d. Quilt packaging

22. _____ refers to the containers and packaging for retail goods which are ready to be displayed instantly or with little set up for retail consumption by consumers.

_____ is a retail industry term used by both retail stores and retail goods producers. An example of _____ is the cardboard boxes that hold several packs of gum which are placed near cash registers at supermarkets and retail stores.

  a. Foam take-out container
  b. Retail Ready Packaging
  c. Quilt packaging
  d. Snap case

23. A _____ is a small disposable bag, often used to contain single-use quantities of consumer goods, such as ketchup or shampoo.

A _____ can also be a fabric bag containing pot pourri.

Sale of products, such as shampoo and detergents, in _____s is very popular in India and other Eastern countries.

  a. 180SearchAssistant
  b. Sachet
  c. 6-3-5 Brainwriting
  d. Power III

24. _____ is the field of the printing industry that deals with the printing of items such as banknotes, passports, tamper-evident labels, stock certificates, postage stamps and identity cards. The main goal of _____ is to prevent forgery, tampering, or counterfeiting.

A number of technical methods are used in the _____ industry.

  a. Security printing
  b. Hot stamping
  c. 180SearchAssistant
  d. Power III

25. The _____ is an eighteen digit number used to identify logistics units. The _____ is encoded in a barcode, generally GS1-128, and used in electronic commerce transactions.

The _____ comprises an extension digit, a GS1 company prefix, a serial reference, and a check digit.

  a. 6-3-5 Brainwriting
  b. Serial Shipping Container Code
  c. 180SearchAssistant
  d. Power III

Chapter 18. Test Preparation Part 18

26. _____ is that length of time that food, drink, medicine and other perishable items are given before they are considered unsuitable for sale or consumption. In some regions, a best before, use by or freshness date is required on packaged perishable foods.

_____ is the recommendation of time that products can be stored, during which the defined quality of a specified proportion of the goods remains acceptable under expected (or specified) conditions of distribution, storage and display.

a. Shelf life
c. Power III
b. Food safety
d. 180SearchAssistant

27. A _____, packing list, packing slip docket, delivery list is a shipping document that accompanies delivery packages, usually inside an attached shipping pouch or inside the package itself. It commonly includes an itemized detail of the package contents and may or may not include customer pricing. It serves to inform all parties, including transport agencies, government authorities, and customers, about the contents of the package.

a. Power III
c. Shipping list
b. 6-3-5 Brainwriting
d. 180SearchAssistant

28. _____ are bottles designed and manufactured in Switzerland from aluminium or in China from stainless steel. The aluminum bottles are made by an extruding press which forms an aluminum puck into a cylinder in a single movement after which it is pressed into one of several possible bottle sizes. A separate threading ring is inserted and secured.

a. Good things come to those who wait
c. LIFO
b. Manufacturers' representatives
d. Sigg bottles

29. _____ is a type of carded packaging where a product (or products) is placed on a piece of paperboard, and a thin sheet of transparent plastic is placed over the product and paperboard.

The printed paperboard usually has a heat-seal coating. The plastic film (LDPE, PVC, ionomer, etc.)

a. Living hinge
c. Child-resistant packaging
b. Decimal Dozen
d. Skin pack

30. _____s are thin pallet-sized sheets made of plastic or fiberboard, used in commercial shipping.

The _____ is used as a unit load support device in vehicle delivery and transportation of products. When _____s are supported by a pallet board, roller conveyor surface, flat load carrying surface, or a cart or lift truck, the structural strength of the _____ supports the product loads weight.

a. Demand chain management
c. Slip sheet
b. Megalister
d. Supply network

31. A _____ is a type of optical disc packaging. It consists of a cardboard flap (where the cover art is printed) which is held closed by a narrow plastic strip which has a 'snap' closure. The strip is part of a single piece of plastic which forms the disc tray, and protective edges at the top and bottom.

Chapter 18. Test Preparation Part 18

a. Flavor scalping
b. K-Cup
c. Skin pack
d. Snap case

32. _____ is a very specialised packing material, often required for use in shipping valuable fragile items. Engineered packaging principles are designed to protect sculptures, vases, large fossils, lamp bases, busts, computers, furniture, chandeliers and other objects of unusual shape. By virtue of the liquid foam expanding by up to 280 times the volume of its liquid state, it efficiently protects almost any size, form and weight.
   a. Skin pack
   b. Spray foam
   c. Video game packaging
   d. Squround

33. _____ is a portmanteau for 'square round' (cartons), referring to a compromise between a square and a round carton. It is also sometimes known as the scround.

The term applies almost exclusively to ice cream packaging design, where the switch to a _____ from paperboard bricks, cylindrical half-gallons and other containers is motivated by consumer preference.

   a. Squround
   b. Snap case
   c. Pilferage
   d. Spray foam

34. _____ is the development and use of packaging which results in improved sustainability. It involves increased use of life cycle inventory and life cycle assessment to help guide the use of packaging which reduces the environmental impact and ecological footprint. The goals are to improve the long term viability and quality of life for humans and the longevity of natural ecosystems.
   a. Simple living
   b. Sustainable development
   c. Power III
   d. Sustainable packaging

35. _____ is resistance to tampering by either the normal users of a product, package, or system or others with physical access to it. There are many reasons for employing _____.

_____ ranges from simple features like screws with special heads to more complex devices that render themselves inoperable or encrypt all data transmissions between individual chips.

   a. 180SearchAssistant
   b. Power III
   c. 6-3-5 Brainwriting
   d. Tamper resistance

36. _____ describes a device or process that makes unauthorized access to the protected object easily detected. Seals, markings or other techniques may be tamper indicating.

Tampering involves the deliberate altering or adulteration of a product, package, or system.

   a. Doypack
   b. Pilferage
   c. Discbox Slider
   d. Tamper-evident

37. _____ is a manufacturing process where plastic sheet is heated to a pliable forming temperature, formed to a specific part shape in a mold, and trimmed to create a usable product. The sheet, or 'film' when referring to thinner gauges and certain material types, is heated in an oven to a high-enough temperature that it can be stretched into or onto a mold and cooled to a finished shape.

In its simplest form, a small tabletop or lab size machine can be used to heat small cut sections of plastic sheet and stretch it over a mold using vacuum.

   a. 180SearchAssistant
   b. 6-3-5 Brainwriting
   c. Power III
   d. Thermoforming

38. _____ is an industrial technique whereby high-frequency ultrasonic acoustic vibrations are locally applied to workpieces being held together under pressure to create a solid-state weld. It is commonly used for plastics, and especially for joining dissimilar materials. In _____, there are no connective bolts, nails, soldering materials, or adhesives necessary to bind the materials together.

   a. Ultrasonic welding
   b. ADTECH
   c. AMAX
   d. ACNielsen

39. A _____ is the amount of a medication administered to a patient in a single dose.

Unit-dose packaging is the packaging of a single dose in a nonreusable container. It is increasingly used in hospitals, nursing homes, etc.

   a. Oxygen transmission rate
   b. Octabin
   c. ACNielsen
   d. Unit dose

40. A _____ combines packages or items into a single 'unit' of a few thousand kilograms that can be moved easily with simple equipment. A _____ packs tightly into warehouse racks, containers, trucks, and railcars, yet can be easily broken apart at a distribution point, usually a distribution center, wholesaleer, retail store, etc. Forklift truck handling stretch wrapped _____.

Most consumer and industrial products move through the supply chain in unitized or _____ form for at least part of their distribution cycle.

   a. ACNielsen
   b. AMAX
   c. ADTECH
   d. Unit load

41. _____ is a method of storing food and presenting it for sale. Appropriate types of food are stored in an airless environment, usually in an air-tight pack or bottle to prevent the growth of microorganisms. The vacuum environment removes atmospheric oxygen, protecting the food from spoiling by limiting the growth of aerobic bacteria or fungi, and preventing the evaporation of volatile components.

   a. Power III
   b. Vacuum packing
   c. 6-3-5 Brainwriting
   d. 180SearchAssistant

42. The term box art can refer to the artwork on the front of computer or _____. Box art is usually flashy and bombastic, in the vein of movie posters, and serves a similar purpose. Historically, art featured on the box has been in excess of what the computer or console was technically capable of displaying.
   a. Retail Ready Packaging
   b. K-Cup
   c. Decimal Dozen
   d. Video game packaging

43. _____ is a group creativity technique used in marketing, advertising, design, writing and product development originally developed by Professor Bernd Rohrbach in 1968.

Based on the concept of Brainstorming, the aim of _____ is to generate 108 new ideas in half an hour. In a similar way to brainstorming, it is not the quality of ideas that matters but the quantity.

   a. 6-3-5 Brainwriting
   b. Power III
   c. BATBYGOBSTOPL
   d. 180SearchAssistant

44. _____ is a group creativity technique designed to generate a large number of ideas for the solution of a problem. The method was first popularized in the late 1930s by Alex Faickney Osborn in a book called Applied Imagination. Osborn proposed that groups could double their creative output with _____.
   a. Albert Einstein
   b. AStore
   c. Brainstorming
   d. African Americans

45. _____ is a recursive process where two or more people or organizations work together toward an intersection of common goals -- for example, an intellectual endeavor that is creative in nature--by sharing knowledge, learning and building consensus. _____ does not require leadership and can sometimes bring better results through decentralization and egalitarianism. In particular, teams that work collaboratively can obtain greater resources, recognition and reward when facing competition for finite resources. _____ is also present in opposing goals exhibiting the notion of adversarial _____, though this notion is atypical of the annotation that people have given towards their understanding of _____.
   a. 180SearchAssistant
   b. 6-3-5 Brainwriting
   c. Power III
   d. Collaboration

46. _____ is a business strategy, work process and collection of software applications that facilitates different organizations to work together on the development of a product. It is also known as collaborative Product Definition Management (cPDM.)

Introduction

Exactly what technology comes under this title does vary depending on who you ask; however, it usually consists of the PLM areas of: Product Data Management (PDM); Product visualization; team collaboration and conferencing tools; and supplier sourcing software.

   a. Power III
   b. 180SearchAssistant
   c. 6-3-5 Brainwriting
   d. Collaborative Product Development

47. In business and engineering, new _____ is the term used to describe the complete process of bringing a new product or service to market. There are two parallel paths involved in the Nproduct development process: one involves the idea generation, product design, and detail engineering; the other involves market research and marketing analysis. Companies typically see new _____ as the first stage in generating and commercializing new products within the overall strategic process of product life cycle management used to maintain or grow their market share.
   a. Product Development
   b. New product screening
   c. New product development
   d. Specification tree

48. _____ is a process by which products are designed with ease of assembly in mind. If a product contains fewer parts it will take less time to assemble, thereby reducing assembly costs. In addition, if the parts are provided with features which make it easier to grasp, move, orient and insert them, this will also reduce assembly time and assembly costs.
   a. Specification tree
   b. New product development
   c. Specification
   d. Design for Assembly

49. _____ is the redesign of a product, not for resale, but by a consumer (end user.) Historically, concept and craft were often more significant components of products as they were intended to last indefinitely (with proper maintenance and repair.) Modern products have 'life expectancies' due to rapid innovation rate, disposability, automation, and shorter-term finance paradigms which can decrease product service life-terms.
   a. ADTECH
   b. AMAX
   c. End user retro-engineering
   d. ACNielsen

50. _____ is the ability to make changes in the product being developed or in how it is developed, even relatively late in development, without being too disruptive. Consequently, the later one can make changes, the more flexible the process is, and the less disruptive the change is, the greater the flexibility.

Flexibility is important because the development of a new product naturally involves change from what came before it.

   a. 180SearchAssistant
   b. Power III
   c. Project planning
   d. Flexible product development

51. _____ is a systematic method and procedure for company-supportive product modularisation. It consists of five major steps. It starts with Quality Function Deployment (QFD) analysis to establish customer requirements and to identify important design requirements with a special emphasis on modularity.
   a. Power III
   b. 180SearchAssistant
   c. Modular Function Deployment
   d. 6-3-5 Brainwriting

52. In business and engineering, _____ is the term used to describe the complete process of bringing a new product or service to market. There are two parallel paths involved in the _____ process: one involves the idea generation, product design, and detail engineering; the other involves market research and marketing analysis. Companies typically see _____ as the first stage in generating and commercializing new products within the overall strategic process of product life cycle management used to maintain or grow their market share.
   a. Specification
   b. Product optimization
   c. Product development
   d. New product development

53. _____ is the process of filtering or screening new product developments before they enter the stage gate process and start to consume significant resources. The Stage-Gate process was created by Dr. Robert Cooper and is a method described by Cooper and Kleinshmidt of a systematic moving of a new product through various stages from the screening process to product launch.

The screening stage is one that permits new product opportunities to be rejected early in the stage gate process.

   a. Specification
   b. Specification tree
   c. Product development
   d. New product screening

54. _____ is the process of a product becoming obsolete and/or non-functional after a certain period or amount of use in a way that is planned or designed by the manufacturer. _____ has potential benefits for a producer because the product fails and the consumer is under pressure to purchase again, whether from the same manufacturer (a replacement part or a newer model), or from a competitor which might also rely on _____. The purpose of _____ is to hide the real cost per use from the consumer, and charge a higher price than they would otherwise be willing to pay (or would be unwilling to spend all at once.)

   a. 180SearchAssistant
   b. 6-3-5 Brainwriting
   c. Planned obsolescence
   d. Power III

55. _____ can be defined as the idea generation, concept development, testing and manufacturing or implementation of a physical object or service. _____ers conceptualize and evaluate ideas, making them tangible through products in a more systematic approach. The role of a _____er encompasses many characteristics of the marketing manager, product manager, industrial designer and design engineer.

   a. AStore
   b. African Americans
   c. Albert Einstein
   d. Product design

56. A _____ is a statement of what a not-yet-designed product is intended to do. Its aim is to ensure that the subsequent design and development of a product meets the needs of the user.

The _____ acts as an initial boundary in the development of products.

   a. Power III
   b. 180SearchAssistant
   c. 6-3-5 Brainwriting
   d. Product design specification

57. A _____ is an explicit set of requirements to be satisfied by a material, product, or service.

In engineering, manufacturing, and business, it is vital for suppliers, purchasers, and users of materials, products, or services to understand and agree upon all requirements. A _____ is a type of a standard which is often referenced by a contract or procurement document.

   a. Product optimization
   b. Product development
   c. New product development
   d. Specification

58. _____ is the practice of making changes or adjustments to a product to make it more desirable.

A product has a number of attributes. For example, a soda bottle can have different packaging variations, flavors, nutritional values.

a. Product optimization
c. Specification tree
b. Product development
d. New product development

59. A _____ is an established norm or requirement. It is usually a formal document that establishes uniform engineering or technical criteria, methods, processes and practices.

A _____ can also be a controlled artifact or similar formal means used for calibration.

a. Power III
c. 6-3-5 Brainwriting
b. Technical standard
d. 180SearchAssistant

60. A _____ shows all specifications of a technical system under development in a hierarchical order.

For a spacecraft system it has the following levels:

- System (requirements) specification - generated by customer
    - System (design to) specification - generated by system responsible prime contractor
        - Subsystem specifications - generated by system responsible prime contractor
            - Assembly¹ specifications - generated by subsystem responsible contractors
                - Unit specifications - generated by subsystem (or assembly) responsible contractors.

¹ An assembly level is defined as intermediate level when the subsystem contractor prefers to contract a group of units with complex interfaces to another contractor (for instance the operating system and subsystem application software can be an assembly of the data management subsystem.)

a. New product screening
c. Specification
b. Product development
d. Specification tree

61. _____ is a United States certification program developed by the Electronic Industries Association (EIA) and the National Association of Broadcasters (NAB) in 1993. This quality control program addressed both consumer receiver developments and air chains of broadcast AM transmission stations. Tuners and receivers offering _____ Stereo were designed to capture the widest audio frequency response and stereo separation of AM stereo broadcasts, where available.
a. ACNielsen
c. ADTECH
b. AMAX
d. AMOCO

62. _____, also known in its home market as the British Standards Institution (or BSI) is a multinational business services provider whose principal activity is the production of standards and the supply of standards-related services.

_____ was founded as the Engineering Standards Committee in London in 1901. It subsequently extended its standardization work and became the British Engineering Standards Association in 1918, adopting the name British Standards Institution in 1931 after receiving its Royal Charter in 1929.

a. BSI Group
b. Population Reference Bureau
c. World Trade Organization
d. Merchandise Mart

63. _____, is a division of the BSI Group which works with organizations to assess the implementation and administration of their management systems and business processes.

In order to ensure they have derived the most benefit from their management system an organization often decides to publicly prove that it meets the requirements by inviting a certification body like _____ to assess and evaluate their implementation of the management system.

_____ is an accredited registrar certify organizations to international management systems standards, such as ISO 9001 Quality Management, ISO 14001 Environmental Management, ISO/IEC 27001 Information Security Management, SA8000 Social Accountability.

a. BSI Management Systems
b. Power III
c. 6-3-5 Brainwriting
d. 180SearchAssistant

64. _____s are produced by British Standardl _____s, a division of British Standardl Group that is incorporated under a Royal Charter and is formally designated as the National Standards Body (NSB) for the UK. Products and services which British Standardl certifies as having met the requirements of specific standards within designated schemes are awarded the Kitemark.

The standards produced are titled _____ XXXX[-P]:YYYY where XXXX is the number of the standard, P is the number of the part of the standard (where the standard is split into multiple parts) and YYYY is the year in which the standard came into effect.

a. BSI Group
b. John F. Kennedy International Airport
c. World Trade Organization
d. British Standard

65. _____ is the world's only independent standard for creating high-quality emission reductions projects in the Clean Development Mechanism (CDM) Joint Implementation (JI) and Voluntary Carbon Market. It was designed to ensure that carbon credits are not only real and verifiable but that they make measurable contributions to sustainable development worldwide.

To be eligible for Gold Standard Certification, a project must:

1. Be an approved Renewable Energy or Energy Efficiency project type
2. Use the United Nations Framework Convention on Climate Change (UNFCCC) additionality tool
3. Make a net-positive contribution to the economic, environmental and social welfare of the local population that hosts it

_____ for CDM (GS CER) was developed in 2003 by World Wide Fund for Nature (WWF), SouthSouthNorth, and Helio International. The Voluntary Gold Standard (GS VER), a methodology for use within the voluntary carbon market, was launched in May 2006.

a. The Gold Standard

b. Madrid system for the international registration of marks

c. Statistical surveys

d. Comprehensive,

66. _____ refers to the confirmation of certain characteristics of an object, person, or organization. This confirmation is often, but not always, provided by some form of external review, education, or assessment. One of the most common types of _____ in modern society is professional _____, where a person is certified as being able to competently complete a job or task, usually by the passing of an examination.

a. 6-3-5 Brainwriting

b. 180SearchAssistant

c. Power III

d. Certification

67. A _____ on a commercial product indicates five things:

- The existence of a legal follow-up or product certification agreement between the manufacturer of a product and an organisation with national accreditation for both testing and certification,
- Legal evidence that the product was successfully tested in accordance with a nationally accredited standard,
- Legal assurance the accredited certification organization has ensured that the item that was successfully tested and is identical to that which is being offered for sale,
- Legal assurance that the successful test has resulted in a certification listing, which is considered public information, which sets out the tolerances and conditions of use for the certified product, to enable compliance with the law through listing and approval use and compliance,
- Legal assurance that the manufacturer is being regularly audited by the certification organisation to ensure the maintenance of the original process standard that was employed in the manufacture of the test specimen that passed the test. If the manufacturer should fail an audit, all product that was certified, including labels of stock on hand, on construction sites, with end-user customers and on distributor store shelves, can be mandated by the cirtification organisation in charge to be immediately removed, and can insist that all stakeholders be informed that the de-listed product certification is no longer eligible for use in field installations.

On the part of the certifier, the label itself is a type of trademark whereby the listee, or manufacturer, uses the mark to indicate eligibility of the products for use in field installations in accordance with the requirements of the code, and/or the origin, material, mode of manufacture of products, mode of performance of services, quality, accuracy of other characteristics of products or services.

_____s differ from collective trade marks. The main difference is that collective trade marks may be used by particular members of the organization which owns them, while _____s are the only evidence of the existence of follow-up agreements between manufacturers and nationally accredited testing and certification organisations. Certification organisations charge for the use of their labels and are thus always aware of exact production numbers.

a. Kitemark
c. Conformance mark
b. Certification mark
d. Recognized Component Mark

Chapter 19. Test Preparation Part 19

1. The _____ mark, commonly known as _____ Mark, is a compulsory safety mark for many products sold on the Chinese market. It became effective on May 1, 2002. It is the result of the integration of China's two old compulsory inspection systems, namely 'CCIB' and 'CCEE' (also known as 'Great Wall' Mark, for electrical commodities in 7 product categories), into a single procedure.
   a. Consumers Union
   b. China Compulsory Certificate
   c. Tudou
   d. Mapinfo

2. The _____ is the first agency in the People's Republic of China to oversee organic food standards. The Center was established in November 1992, under the jurisdiction of the Ministry of Agriculture of the People's Republic of China, and is headquartered in Beijing.

The _____ oversees two Green Food Standards: A and AA (which is more stringent, allowing less use of such chemicals, and is consequently less popular with agricultural producers.)

   a. 180SearchAssistant
   b. 6-3-5 Brainwriting
   c. Power III
   d. China Green Food Development Center

3. The _____ was a set of ethical standards adopted by the National Association of Broadcasters (NAB) for television. The code was established on December 6, 1951. Compliance with the code was indicated by the 'Seal of Good Practice,' displayed during during closing credits on most United States television programs from 1952 through the early 1970s.
   a. 6-3-5 Brainwriting
   b. 180SearchAssistant
   c. Power III
   d. Code of Practices for Television Broadcasters

4. Much equipment and tools have _____s stamped, inscribed, moulded, or printed on them to indicate that the tool or equipment in question meets the standards set by the body indicated by the mark or marks in question.

They are different from maker's marks that indicate the origin of manufacture.

An early example of a _____ might be the use of a hallmark on precious metals to indicate that the marked item will meet a particular assay standard.

   a. Recognized Component Mark
   b. Conformance mark
   c. Radura
   d. Kitemark

5. _____ is a type of double-sided optical disc product developed by a group of record companies including EMI Music, Universal Music Group, Sony/BMG Music Entertainment, Warner Music Group, and 5.1 Entertainment Group and now under the aegis of the Recording Industry Association of America (RIAA.) It features an audio layer similar to a CD (but not following the Red Book CD Specifications) on one side and a standard DVD layer on the other. In this respect it is similar to, but distinct from, the DVD Plus invented in Europe by Dieter Dierks and covered by European patents.
   a. DualDisc
   b. 6-3-5 Brainwriting
   c. Power III
   d. 180SearchAssistant

6. _____ is an international standard for energy efficient consumer products. It was first created as a United States government program in 1992, but Australia, Canada, Japan, New Zealand, Taiwan and the European Union have also adopted the program. Devices carrying the _____ logo, such as computer products and peripherals, kitchen appliances, buildings and other products, save 20%-30% on average.

a. Express warranty
b. Energy Star
c. Imperial Group v. Philip Morris
d. Office for Harmonization in the Internal Market

7. _____ is a certification mark of the Recording Industry Association of America for various technologies that combine audio and computer data for use in both compact disc and CD-ROM players.

The primary data formats for _____ disks are mixed mode, CD-i, hidden track, and multisession

The technology was popular in the late 90s with the increase of computer usage.

a. ACNielsen
b. ADTECH
c. E-readiness
d. Enhanced CD

8. The _____ is a certification mark used in Canada and in the United States. It appears on products as an independent guarantee that disadvantaged producers in the developing world are getting a better deal. The _____ is the North American equivalent of the International Fairtrade Certification Mark used in Europe, Africa, Asia, Australia and New Zealand.

a. 6-3-5 Brainwriting
b. Fair Trade Certified Mark
c. 180SearchAssistant
d. Power III

9. The _____ is a registered trademark which stands for guaranteed toothfriendly quality.

The _____ mark distinguishes products that are not harmful for teeth. All products carrying the _____ symbol have been scientifically tested and found not to be cariogenic or erosive.

a. Radura
b. Kitemark
c. Conformance mark
d. Happy Tooth

10. A _____ is the special certification marking found on the packages of products that have been certified as kosher (meaning 'fit' for consumption.) In Halakha (Jewish law), the dietary laws of kashrut specify food items that may be eaten and others that are prohibited as set out in the commandments of the Torah. Observant Jews generally will only eat permitted foods.

a. Gerl
b. Goodyear Tire ' Rubber Company
c. Compensation methods
d. Hechsher

11. The _____ consists of the letters IP followed by two digits and an optional letter. As defined in international standard IEC 60529, it classifies the degrees of protection provided against the intrusion of solid objects (including body parts like hands and fingers), dust, accidental contact, and water in electrical enclosures. The standard aims to provide users more detailed information than vague marketing terms such as 'waterproof'.

a. AMAX
b. ADTECH
c. ACNielsen
d. IP Code

12. _____ refers to the confirmation of certain characteristics of an object, person, or organization. This confirmation is often, but not always, provided by some form of external review, education, or assessment. One of the most common types of _____ in modern society is professional _____, where a person is certified as being able to competently complete a job or task, usually by the passing of an examination.

a. Power III
b. 6-3-5 Brainwriting
c. 180SearchAssistant
d. Certification

13. A _____ on a commercial product indicates five things:

- The existence of a legal follow-up or product certification agreement between the manufacturer of a product and an organisation with national accreditation for both testing and certification,
- Legal evidence that the product was successfully tested in accordance with a nationally accredited standard,
- Legal assurance the accredited certification organization has ensured that the item that was successfully tested and is identical to that which is being offered for sale,
- Legal assurance that the successful test has resulted in a certification listing, which is considered public information, which sets out the tolerances and conditions of use for the certified product, to enable compliance with the law through listing and approval use and compliance,
- Legal assurance that the manufacturer is being regularly audited by the certification organisation to ensure the maintenance of the original process standard that was employed in the manufacture of the test specimen that passed the test. If the manufacturer should fail an audit, all product that was certified, including labels of stock on hand, on construction sites, with end-user customers and on distributor store shelves, can be mandated by the cirtification organisation in charge to be immediately removed, and can insist that all stakeholders be informed that the de-listed product certification is no longer eligible for use in field installations.

On the part of the certifier, the label itself is a type of trademark whereby the listee, or manufacturer, uses the mark to indicate eligibility of the products for use in field installations in accordance with the requirements of the code, and/or the origin, material, mode of manufacture of products, mode of performance of services, quality, accuracy of other characteristics of products or services.

_____s differ from collective trade marks. The main difference is that collective trade marks may be used by particular members of the organization which owns them, while _____s are the only evidence of the existence of follow-up agreements between manufacturers and nationally accredited testing and certification organisations. Certification organisations charge for the use of their labels and are thus always aware of exact production numbers.

a. Conformance mark
b. Kitemark
c. Recognized Component Mark
d. Certification Mark

14. The _____ is an independent certification mark used in over 50 countries. It appears on products as an independent guarantee that disadvantaged producers in the developing world are getting a better deal.

The _____ is owned and protected by FLO International, on behalf of its 23 member Fairtrade producer networks and labelling initiatives.

a. AMAX
b. ACNielsen
c. ADTECH
d. International Fairtrade Certification Mark

15. The _____ is a voluntary European certification mark demonstrating compliance with the European Standard (EN.) It is owned by CEN the European Committee for Standardization, and CENELEC, the European Committee for Electrotechnical Standardization.

The _____ is the European mark based on the principle 'one standard, one test, accepted everywhere' It is operated by certification bodies which have been empowered by CEN or CENELEC and who are accredited on the basis of EN 45011 (ISO/IEC Guide 65) by a signatory to the multilateral agreement (MLA) of the European Co-operation for Accreditation (EA.)

a. Keymark
b. Power III
c. 6-3-5 Brainwriting
d. 180SearchAssistant

16. The _____ is a UK product and service quality certification mark which is owned by the British Standards Institution (BSI Group) and operated by its Product Services division.

The _____ is most frequently used to identify products where safety is paramount, such as crash helmets, smoke alarms and flood defences. In recent years the _____ has also been applied to a range of services, such as electrical installations; car servicing and accident repair; and window installations.

a. Happy Tooth
b. Radura
c. Recognized Component Mark
d. Kitemark

17. _____ is an incentive program and marketing campaign of the City of New York Mayor's Office of Film, Theatre and Broadcasting. Under the program, television and film productions which complete at least 75% of their shooting and rehearsal work in New York City are eligible for marketing incentives and tax credits, and can display the _____ logo in their closing credits.

a. Power III
b. Made in NY
c. 6-3-5 Brainwriting
d. 180SearchAssistant

18. The _____ is used in the U.S. and its territories to rate a film's thematic and content suitability for certain audiences. It is one of various motion picture rating systems used to help patrons decide what movies are appropriate for children, for adolescents, and for adults.

In the U.S., the MPAA's rating system is the most recognized classification system for determining potentially offensive content, but usually is not used outside the film industry, because the MPAA has trademarked each rating.

a. Hospitality point of sales systems
b. Distribution
c. Promotion
d. Motion Picture Association of America's film-rating system

19. Founded in 1974, _____ is an American nonprofit membership organisation dedicated to supporting and advocating organic food and farming, based in Salem, Oregon. _____ provides independent certification of organic food producers and suppliers. The _____ Certified Organic label (Oregon TilthCO) was established in 1982 and is renowned as one of the most rigorous and stringent in the United States.

a. EarthLink
b. Intuit
c. American Family Publishers
d. Oregon Tilth

Chapter 19. Test Preparation Part 19

20. _____ is a certification process for producers of organic food and other organic agricultural products. In general, any business directly involved in food production can be certified, including seed suppliers, farmers, food processors, retailers and restaurants. Requirements vary from country to country, and generally involve a set of production standards for growing, storage, processing, packaging and shipping that include:

- avoidance of most synthetic chemical inputs (e.g. fertilizer, pesticides, antibiotics, food additives, etc), genetically modified organisms, irradiation, and the use of sewage sludge;
- use of farmland that has been free from chemicals for a number of years (often, three or more);
- keeping detailed written production and sales records (audit trail);
- maintaining strict physical separation of organic products from non-certified products;
- undergoing periodic on-site inspections.

In some countries, certification is overseen by the government, and commercial use of the term organic is legally restricted. Certified organic producers are also subject to the same agricultural, food safety and other government regulations that apply to non-certified producers.

a. ACNielsen
b. ADTECH
c. Organic certification
d. AMAX

21. The _____ is the international symbol indicating a food product has been irradiated. The _____ is usually green and resembles a plant in circle. The top half of the circle is dashed.
a. Happy Tooth
b. Recognized Component Mark
c. Radura
d. Kitemark

22. The _____ is a type of quality mark issued by Underwriters Laboratories. It is borne on components which are intended to be part of a UL listed product, but which cannot bear the full UL logo themselves. The general public does not ordinarily come across it, as it is borne on components which make up finished products.
a. Radura
b. Conformance mark
c. Voluntary Carbon Standard
d. Recognized Component Mark

23. The universal _____ is an internationally-recognized symbol used to designate recyclable materials. It is composed of three chasing arrows that form a Möbius strip or unending loop.

In 1969 and early 1970, worldwide attention to environmental issues reached a crescendo, culminating in the first Earth Day.

a. Recycling symbol
b. 180SearchAssistant
c. Power III
d. 6-3-5 Brainwriting

24. _____ is a global social accountability standard for decent working conditions, developed and overseen by Social Accountability International (SAI.) Detailed guidance for implementing or auditing to _____ are available from its website. SAI offers training in _____ and other workplace standards to managers, workers and auditors.
a. Political consumerism
b. Power III
c. Product stewardship
d. SA8000

Chapter 19. Test Preparation Part 19

25. The _____ is a blue, six-pointed star, outlined with a white border which features the Rod of Asclepius in the center, originally designed and governed by the U.S. National Highway Traffic Safety Administration (NHTSA) (under the United States Department of Transportation, DOT.) Traditionally in the United States the logo was used as a stamp of authentication or certification for ambulances, paramedics or other EMS personnel. Internationally, it represents emergency medical services (EMS) units and personnel.

   a. Power III
   b. 6-3-5 Brainwriting
   c. Star of Life
   d. 180SearchAssistant

26. _____ was the official Soviet mark for the certification of quality established in 1967.

It was used to mark the consumer goods and production and technical goods to ensure their high quality and, in general, to increase the effectiveness of production system in USSR.

It was applied directly on the goods or their packing, as well as in the accompanying documentation, labels or tags.

   a. 6-3-5 Brainwriting
   b. 180SearchAssistant
   c. Power III
   d. State Quality Mark of the USSR

27. The _____ is a program to certify forests to insure they are being managed in a sustainable manner.

_____ was started in 1994 by members of the American Forest and Paper Association. As of January 1, 2007, the _____ program became fully independent, being governed by an independent board of directors that includes nonprofit environmental groups and forest products companies.

   a. Phorm
   b. Hechsher
   c. Superbrands Council
   d. Sustainable Forestry Initiative

28. _____ is a plastics flammability standard released by Underwriters Laboratories of the USA.

The standard classifies plastics according to how they burn in various orientations and thicknesses. From lowest (least flame-retardant) to highest (most flame-retardant), the classifications are:

- HB: slow burning on a horizontal specimen; burning rate < 76 mm/min for thickness < 3 mm.
- V2 burning stops within 30 seconds on a vertical specimen; drips of flaming particles are allowed.
- V1: burning stops within 30 seconds on a vertical specimen; no drips allowed.
- V0: burning stops within 10 seconds on a vertical specimen; no drips allowed.
- 5VB: burning stops within 60 seconds on a vertical specimen; no drips allowed; plaque specimens may develop a hole.
- 5VA: burning stops within 60 seconds on a vertical specimen; no drips allowed; plaque specimens may not develop a hole

Tests are generally conducted on a 5' x 1/2' specimen of the minimum approved thickness. For 5VA and 5VB ratings, tests are performed on both bar and plaque specimens, and the flame ignition source is approximately five times as severe as that used for testing the other materials.

a. Eight Partnership
c. Asia Insight
b. Access Commerce
d. UL 94

29. _____ Inc. is a U.S. privately owned and operated, independent, third party product safety testing and certification organization. Based in Northbrook, Illinois, _____ develops standards and test procedures for products, materials, components, assemblies, tools and equipment, chiefly dealing with product safety.
   a. InfoUSA
   c. Intuit
   b. Underwriters Laboratories
   d. Outdoor Advertising Association of America

30. The _____ is a quality standard for voluntary carbon offset industry. Based on the Kyoto Protocol's Clean Development Mechanism, _____ establishes criteria for validating, measuring, and monitoring carbon offset projects.
   a. Recognized Component Mark
   c. Conformance mark
   b. Voluntary Carbon Standard
   d. Radura

31. A _____ or trade mark, identified by the symbols â„¢ (not yet registered) and Â® (registered) business organization or other legal entity to identify that the products and/or services to consumers with which the _____ appears originate from a unique source of origin, and to distinguish its products or services from those of other entities. A _____ is a type of intellectual property, and typically a name, word, phrase, logo, symbol, design, image, or a combination of these elements. There is also a range of non-conventional _____s comprising marks which do not fall into these standard categories.
   a. Risk management
   c. Power III
   b. Trademark
   d. 180SearchAssistant

32. A _____ or in the alternative spelling trade mark attorney, is a person who is qualified to act in matters involving trademark law and practice and provide legal advice on trade mark and design matters.

In many countries, most notably the United Kingdom, trade mark attorneys are a separate recognised legal profession, along with solicitors and barristers, and are recognised as lawyers under the Legal Services Act 2007. In other jurisdictions, most notably the United States, the profession is less clearly defined, with _____s being a part of the general legal profession, who simply specialise in advising on trade mark law.

   a. Copyright
   c. Patent
   b. Reasonable person standard
   d. Trademark attorney

33. A _____ is a collection of symbols, experiences and associations connected with a product, a service, a person or any other artifact or entity.

_____s have become increasingly important components of culture and the economy, now being described as 'cultural accessories and personal philosophies'.

Some people distinguish the psychological aspect of a _____ from the experiential aspect.

   a. Brand
   c. Brand equity
   b. Store brand
   d. Brandable software

34. _____ is the act of naming a product in a manner which can result in confusion with other better known brands. It can occur with either partial integration of the name of the better known brand, or simply by changing the spelling of the product's name. The effect is similar to that of phishing, whereby the trust of the customer is gained through association with the brand name version of the product.

   a. Brand piracy
   b. Trademark dilution
   c. Rule of four
   d. Colour trademark

35. In the USA, a _____ is a trademark or service mark which is given special statutory protection separate from the usual registration of trade marks and service marks. A _____, in effect, is a type of trademark/servicemark in which the organization is granted the mark 'by charter', i.e. by express grant of the legislature. When an organization is granted a _____, no one else may use the same mark at all for any purpose.

   a. Confusing similarity
   b. Trespass to land
   c. Social Norms Approach
   d. Chartered mark

36. A _____ or collective mark is a trademark owned by an organisation (such as an association), whose members use them to identify themselves with a level of quality or accuracy, geographical origin, or other characteristics set by the organisation.

_____s are exceptions to the underlying principle of trade marks in that most trade marks serve as 'badges of origin' - they indicate the individual source of the goods or services. A _____, however, can be used by a variety of traders, rather than just one individual concern, provided that the trader belongs to the association.

   a. Reasonable person standard
   b. Consumer protection
   c. Geographical indication
   d. Collective trade mark

37. A _____ is a non-conventional trademark where at least one colour is used to perform the trademark function of uniquely identifying the commercial origin of products or services.

In recent times colours have been increasingly used as trade marks in the marketplace. However, it has traditionally been difficult to protect colours as trademarks through registration, as a colour as such was not considered to be a distinctive 'trademark'.

   a. Regulation
   b. Geographical indication
   c. Community Trade Mark
   d. Colour trademark

38. A _____ is any trademark which is pending registration or has been registered in the European Union as a whole (rather than on a national level within the EU.)

The _____ system creates a unified trademark registration system in Europe, whereby one registration provides protection in all member states of the EU. The _____ system is unitary in character.

   a. Right to Financial Privacy Act
   b. Trademark attorney
   c. Covenant not to compete
   d. Community Trade Mark

Chapter 19. Test Preparation Part 19

39. In trademark law, _____ is a test used during the examination process to determine whether a trademark conflicts with another, earlier mark, and also in trademark infringement proceedings to determine whether the use of a mark infringes a registered trade mark.

In many jurisdictions this test has been superseded by the concepts of similarity and likelihood of confusion, due to the harmonizing effects of the Agreement on Trade-Related Aspects of Intellectual Property Rights.

Where mark X is not identical to a registered trademark, the use of mark X may still amount to an infringement if it is 'confusingly similar' to the registered trademark.

- a. Contributory negligence
- b. Consumer protection
- c. Confusing similarity
- d. Federal Bureau of Investigation

40. _____, according to the United States federal law known as the Anticybersquatting Consumer Protection Act, is registering, trafficking in, or using a domain name with bad faith intent to profit from the goodwill of a trademark belonging to someone else. The cybersquatter then offers to sell the domain to the person or company who owns a trademark contained within the name at an inflated price.

The term is derived from 'squatting,' which is the act of occupying an abandoned or unoccupied space or building that the squatter does not own, rent or otherwise have permission to use.

- a. Fast flux
- b. Wildcard DNS record
- c. Cybersquatting
- d. Domain name warehousing

41. _____ is an Italian quality assurance label for food products and especially wines (an appellation.) It is modelled after the French AOC. It was instituted in 1963 and overhauled in 1992 for compliance with the equivalent EU law on Protected Designation of Origin, which came into effect that year.

- a. Specific Performance
- b. Patent
- c. Denominazione di origine controllata
- d. Fair trade law

42. _____ is a trademark law concept permitting the owner of a famous trademark to forbid others from using that mark in a way that would lessen its uniqueness. In most cases, _____ involves an unauthorized use of another's trademark on products that do not compete with, and have little connection with, those of the trademark owner. For example, a famous trademark used by one company to refer to hair care products might be diluted if another company began using a similar mark to refer to breakfast cereals or spark plugs.

- a. Trespass to land
- b. Federal Bureau of Investigation
- c. Trademark attorney
- d. Trademark dilution

43. _____ is an important concept in the law governing trademarks and service marks. A trademark may be eligible for registration, or registrable, if amongst other things it performs the essential trademark function, and has distinctive character. Registrability can be understood as a continuum, with 'inherently distinctive' marks at one end, 'generic' and 'descriptive' marks with no distinctive character at the other end, and 'suggestive' and 'arbitrary' marks lying between these two points.

- a. Trademark distinctiveness
- b. Lovemarks
- c. Web 2.0
- d. Brand ambassador

44. Trademark _____ is an important concept in the law governing trademarks and service marks. A trademark may be eligible for registration, or registrable, if amongst other things it performs the essential trademark function, and has distinctive character. Registrability can be understood as a continuum, with 'inherently distinctive' marks at one end, 'generic' and 'descriptive' marks with no distinctive character at the other end, and 'suggestive' and 'arbitrary' marks lying between these two points.
   a. Brand implementation
   b. Corporate colours
   c. Brand ambassador
   d. Distinctiveness

45. An _____ is a proposed category of trademark that would restrict the use of trademarked words and phrases in online advertising.

The State of Utah proposed this in response to trademark owners' claims that online advertisers have abused trademarked terms. Some online advertisers, particularly search engines, allow trademarked keywords to generate advertisements for a trademark holder's competitors.

   a. Umbrella brand
   b. ADTECH
   c. Electronic registration mark
   d. ACNielsen

46. In trademark law, the _____ prevents manufacturers from protecting specific features of a product by means of trademark law. This separates trademarks from patents -- trademarks serve to protect a firm's reputation and goodwill, whereas patents serve to protect processes, machines, and material inventions.

If a feature gives a producer a competitive advantage which is not related entirely to its function as a brand identifier, then it cannot be trademarked.

   a. Functionality doctrine
   b. Gripe site
   c. Patent
   d. Trespass to land

47. A _____ is a trademark or brand name that has become the colloquial or generic description for a general class of product or service, rather than the specific meaning intended by the trademark's holder. Using a _____ to refer to the general form of what that trademark represents is a form of metonymy.
   a. Lovemarks
   b. Trade Symbols
   c. Retail design
   d. Genericized trademark

48. A _____ is a name or sign used on certain products which corresponds to a specific geographical location or origin (eg. a town, region, or country.) The use of a _____ may act as a certification that the product possesses certain qualities, or enjoys a certain reputation, due to its geographical origin.
   a. Trademark attorney
   b. Specific Performance
   c. Federal Bureau of Investigation
   d. Geographical indication

49. _____ are trade marks which closely simulate ordinary words or phrases used in the course of trade, and which are not intended to be used as genuine trade marks.

In the case of Imperial Group v. Philip Morris 1982 FSR 72, the plaintiff endeavoured to register the trade mark 'MERIT' for cigarette products, but was unable to do so on the grounds that the trade mark was too descriptive.

Chapter 19. Test Preparation Part 19

a. Perceptual maps
c. Lobbying and Disclosure Act of 1995
b. Just-In-Case
d. Ghost marks

50. A _____ is a type of website devoted to the critique and or mockery of a person, place, politician, corporation or institution. They are also known as 'complaint' or 'sucks' sites. The Internet provides a low cost public platform for anyone, even of modest means, to reach a global audience via a 'gripe' website.
    a. Community Trade Mark
    c. Denominazione di origine controllata
    b. Colour trademark
    d. Gripe site

51. A _____ is a non-conventional trademark where a picture sequence is used to perform the trademark function of uniquely identifying the commercial origin of products or services.

In recent times holograms have been increasingly used as trade marks in the marketplace. However, it has traditionally been difficult to protect holograms as trademarks through registration, as a hologram was not considered to be a 'trademark'.

   a. Trade dress
   c. Geographical indication
   b. Sound trademark
   d. Hologram trademark

52. In _____, 1982 FSR 72, the plaintiff endeavoured to register the trade mark 'MERIT' for cigarette products, but was unable to do so on the grounds that the trade mark was too descriptive. Instead, it registered the mark 'NERIT', without any intention of using the mark, but in order to prevent other traders from using the mark 'MERIT' because it would be considered too similar to the registered mark 'NERIT'.
    a. Energy Star
    c. Office action
    b. Imperial Group v. Philip Morris
    d. Express warranty

53. _____ is a violation of the exclusive rights attaching to a trademark without the authorization of the trademark owner or any licensees (provided that such authorization was within the scope of the license.) Infringement may occur when one party, the 'infringer', uses a trademark which is identical or confusingly similar to a trademark owned by another party, in relation to products or services which are identical or similar to the products or services which the registration covers. An owner of a trademark may commence legal proceedings against a party which infringes its registration.
    a. Trademark classification
    c. Passing off
    b. Fair Debt Collection Practices Act
    d. Trademark infringement

54. _____ is a slogan, implying that Juan Valdez, a fictional character created by the Federación Nacional de Cafeteros de Colombia , drinks coffee from Costa Rica. In Costa Rica, the slogan is popular on bumper stickers. The slogan prompted a lawsuit for the first time in 2006, when Federación Nacional de Cafeteros de Colombia sued Café Britt following a t-shirt dispute.
    a. 6-3-5 Brainwriting
    c. Power III
    b. 180SearchAssistant
    d. Juan Valdez drinks Costa Rican coffee

55. The _____ is an organization which administers the 'Linux' trademark on behalf of Linus Torvalds for computer software which includes the Linux kernel, computer hardware utilizing Linux-based software, and for services associated with the implementation and documentation of Linux-based products.

The Linux trademark is owned by Linus Torvalds in the U.S., Germany, the European Community, and Japan. In the U.S., the mark is registered (Serial Number: 74560867) for 'Computer operating system software to facilitate computer use and operation.' The assignment of the trademark to Torvalds occurred after an attorney, one William R. Della Croce, Jr, in 1996 began sending letters to various Linux distributors claiming to own the Linux trademark and demanding royalties.

   a. Linux Mark Institute
   b. Power III
   c. 6-3-5 Brainwriting
   d. 180SearchAssistant

56. The _____ for the international registration of marks, also conveniently known as the _____ or simply Madrid, is the primary international system for facilitating the registration of trademarks in multiple jurisdictions around the world.

The _____ provides a centrally administered system of obtaining a bundle of trademark registrations in separate jurisdictions. Registration through the _____ does not create an 'international' registration, as in the case of the European CTM system, rather it creates a bundle of national rights, able to be administered centrally.

   a. Registered trademark symbol
   b. Madrid system
   c. Collective mark
   d. Trademark dilution

57. A _____ is any new type of trademark which does not belong to a pre-existing, conventional category of trade mark, and which is often difficult to register, but which may nevertheless fulfill the essential trademark function of uniquely identifying the commercial origin of products or services.

The term is broadly inclusive as it encompasses marks which do not fall into the conventional set of marks, and therefore includes marks based on appearance, shape, sound, smell, taste and texture.

   a. Non-conventional trademark
   b. Federal Trade Commission Act
   c. Hologram trademark
   d. Sound trademark

58. The _____, also known as Norwegian Patent Office (Norwegian: Patentstyret) is a government agency responsible for regstriation of patents, trademarks and design in Norway. The agency is subordinate the Ministry of Trade and Industry and located in Oslo. It has about 270 employees within the fields of law, technology, administration, marketing and information.
   a. VideoJug
   b. BSI Group
   c. Japan Advertising Photographers' Association
   d. Norwegian Industrial Property Office

59. An _____ is a document written by an examiner in a patent or trademark examination procedure and mailed to an applicant for a patent or trademark. The expression is used in many jurisdictions.

In United States trademark law, an _____ is a rejection of an application to register a trademark issued by an examiner for the United States Patent and Trademark Office (USPTO.)

a. Express warranty
b. Office action
c. Office for Harmonization in the Internal Market
d. Imperial Group v. Philip Morris

60. An _____ operates inside an organizations or set of organizations which have decoupled internal components. Each component trades its services and interfaces with the others. Often a set of government or government-funded set of organizations will operate an _____.

a. Unified market
b. Ever-normal granary
c. ACNielsen
d. Internal Market

61. The _____ is the trademark and industrial designs registry for the internal market of the European Union. It is based in Alicante, Spain, and its president is Wubbo de Boer.

The task of OHIM is to promote and manage Community Trade Marks and Community Designs within the European Union.

a. Energy Star
b. Imperial Group v. Philip Morris
c. Express warranty
d. Office for Harmonization in the Internal Market

62. The _____, signed in Paris, France, on March 20, 1883, was one of the first intellectual property treaties. As a result of this treaty, intellectual property systems, including patents, of any contracting state are accessible to the nationals of other states party to the Convention.

The 'Convention priority right', also called 'Paris Convention priority right' or 'Union priority right', was also established by this treaty.

a. Paris Convention for the Protection of Industrial Property
b. Power III
c. 6-3-5 Brainwriting
d. 180SearchAssistant

63. _____ is a common law tort which can be used to enforce unregistered trademark rights. The tort of _____ protects the goodwill of a trader from a misrepresentation that causes damage to goodwill.

The law of _____ prevents one person from misrepresenting his or her goods or services as being the goods and services of the claimant, and also prevents one person from holding out his or her goods or services as having some association or connection with the plaintiff when this is not true.

a. Trade dress
b. Right to Financial Privacy Act
c. Fair trade law
d. Passing off

64. In patent, industrial design rights and trademark laws, a _____ or right of priority is a time-limited right, triggered by the first filing of an application for a patent, an industrial design or a trademark respectively. The _____ belongs to the applicant or his successor in title and allows him to file a subsequent application in another country for the same invention, design or trademark and benefit, for this subsequent application, from the date of filing of the first application for the examination of certain requirements. When filing the subsequent application, the applicant must 'claim the priority' of the first application in order to make use of the right of priority.

a. Non-conventional trademark
c. Collective mark
b. Priority right
d. Celler-Kefauver Act

65. Protected Designation of Origin (PDO), Protected Geographical Indication (PGI) and Traditional Speciality Guaranteed (TSG) are geographical indications, or more precisely regimes within the _____ framework defined in European Union law to protect the names of regional foods. The law (enforced within the EU and being gradually expanded internationally via bilateral agreements of the EU with non-EU countries) ensures that only products genuinely originating in that region are allowed in commerce as such. The legislation came into force in 1992.
   a. Protected Geographical Status
   c. 180SearchAssistant
   b. Power III
   d. 6-3-5 Brainwriting

66. The _____, designated by ® (a circled 'R'), is a symbol used to provide notice that the preceding mark is a trademark or service mark that has been registered with a national trademark office. Trademarks not so registered are instead marked with the trademark symbol ™, while unregistered service marks are marked with the service mark symbol ℠. The proper manner to display the symbol is immediately following the mark in superscript style.
   a. Mediation
   c. Registered trademark symbol
   b. Reasonable person standard
   d. Regulatory

67. The term _____ refers to the practice of acquiring domain names from owners by accusing them of violating trademarks with the domain name, and demanding that the domain be transferred.

The name refers to the practice of domain hijacking, in which a domain name consisting of a trademark or another well-known name is registered solely with the intent of selling it to the trademark owner later on.

A widely regarded case of _____ occurred in 2000, when the Deutsche Welle attempted to acquire the domain dw.com from software company Diamond Ware.

   a. Reverse domain hijacking
   c. Domain name front running
   b. Type-in traffic
   d. Top-level domain

68. _____ is an advertisement in which a particular product specifically mentions a competitor by name for the express purpose of showing why the competitor is inferior to the product naming it.

This should not be confused with parody advertisements, where a fictional product is being advertised for the purpose of poking fun at the particular advertisement, nor should it be confused with the use of a coined brand name for the purpose of comparing the product without actually naming an actual competitor. ('Wikipedia tastes better and is less filling than the Encyclopedia Galactica.')

In the 1980s, during what has been referred to as the cola wars, soft-drink manufacturer Pepsi ran a series of advertisements where people, caught on hidden camera, in a blind taste test, chose Pepsi over rival Coca-Cola.

   a. GL-70
   c. Heavy-up
   b. Cost per conversion
   d. Comparative advertising

Chapter 19. Test Preparation Part 19

69. In some countries, notably the United States, a trademark used to identify a service rather than a product is called a _____ or servicemark. When a _____ is federally registered, the standard registration symbol Â® or 'Reg U.S. Pat ' TM Off' may be used (the same symbol is used to mark registered trademarks.) Before it is registered, it is common practice (but has no legal standing) to use the _____ symbol â„ (a superscript '_____'.)
    a. Trademark classification
    b. Screener
    c. Trespass to land
    d. Service mark

70. The _____ was adopted in Singapore on March 27, 2006. It will enter into force on March 16, 2009, following the ratification or accession of ten countries, namely Singapore, Switzerland, Bulgaria, Romania, Denmark, Latvia, Kyrgyzstan, United States of America, Republic of Moldova, and Australia. The treaty establishes common standards for procedural aspects of trademark registration and licensing.
    a. Reasonable person standard
    b. Product liability
    c. Non-conventional trademark
    d. Singapore Treaty on the Law of Trademarks

71. A _____ is a non-conventional trademark where sound is used to perform the trademark function of uniquely identifying the commercial origin of products or services.

    In recent times sounds have been increasingly used as trademarks in the marketplace. However, it has traditionally been difficult to protect sounds as trademarks through registration, as a sound was not considered to be a 'trademark'.

    a. Regulatory
    b. Collective trade mark
    c. Functionality doctrine
    d. Sound trademark

72. The _____ is the law governing trademarks within the United Kingdom and the Isle of Man. It implements an earlier EU Directive which forms the framework for the trade mark laws of all EU member states, and replaced an earlier law, the Trade Marks Act 1938. Although the UK's trade mark regime covers the Isle of Man, it does not extend to the Channel Islands which have their own trade mark registers.
    a. 6-3-5 Brainwriting
    b. Trade Marks Act 1994
    c. Power III
    d. 180SearchAssistant

73. _____ is a legal term of art that generally refers to characteristics of the visual appearance of a product or its packaging (or even the design of a building) that signify the source of the product to consumers. _____ is a form of intellectual property. In the U.S., like trademarks, a product's _____ is legally protected by the Lanham Act, the federal statute which regulates trademarks and _____.
    a. Geographical indication
    b. Gripe site
    c. Wheeler-Lea Act
    d. Trade dress

74. A _____ is a way the trademark examiners and applicants' trademark attorneys arrange documents, such as trademark and service mark applications, according to the description and scope of the types of goods or services to which the marks apply. The same trademark or service may be (or in many cases MUST be) classified in several classes, and some countries permit several classes to be registered in the same document. There are fees ordinarily associated with each classification, whether for initial application or later renewal.
    a. Social Norms Approach
    b. Madrid system
    c. Mediation
    d. Trademark classification

75. _____ is a form of cybersquatting which relies on mistakes such as typographical errors made by Internet users when inputting a website address into a web browser. Should a user accidentally enter an incorrect website address, they may be led to an alternative website owned by a cybersquatter.

Generally, the victim site of _____ will be a frequently visited website.

a. Domain name front running
c. Domaining

b. Fast flux
d. Typosquatting

76. _____ are markets where the potential consumers face a severely limited amount of competitive suppliers; their only choices are to purchase what is available or to make no purchase at all. _____ result in higher prices and less diversity for consumers. The term therefore applies to any market where there is a monopoly or oligopoly.

a. Perfect market
c. Regulated market

b. Market system
d. Captive markets

Chapter 20. Test Preparation Part 20

1. A _____ is an organization holding securities either in certificated or uncertificated (dematerialized) form, to enable book entry transfer of securities. In some cases these organizations also carry out centralized comparison, and transaction processing such as clearing and settlement of securities. The physical securities may be immobilised by the depository, or securities may be dematerialised (so that they exist only as electronic records.)
   a. Forward market
   b. Market price
   c. Central Securities Depository
   d. Power III

2. Competitiveness is a comparative concept of the ability and performance of a firm, sub-sector or country to sell and supply goods and/or services in a given market. Although widely used in economics and business management, the usefulness of the concept, particularly in the context of national competitiveness, is vigorously disputed by economists, such as Paul Krugman.

   The term may also be applied to markets, where it is used to refer to the extent to which the market structure may be regarded as perfectly _____.

   a. Customs union
   b. Free trade zone
   c. Geographical pricing
   d. Competitive

3. Competitive market equilibrium is the traditional concept of economic equilibrium, appropriate for the analysis of commodity markets with flexible prices and many traders, and serving as the benchmark of efficiency in economic analysis. It relies crucially on the assumption of a competitive environment where each trader decides upon a quantity that is so small compared to the total quantity traded in the market that their individual transactions have no influence on the prices.

   A _____ consists of a vector of prices and an allocation such that given the prices, each trader by maximizing his objective function (profit, preferences) subject to his technological possibilities and resource constraints plans to trade into his part of the proposed allocation, and such that the prices make all net trades compatible with one another ('clear the market') by equating aggregate supply and demand for the commodities which are traded.

   a. Marketization
   b. Two-sided markets
   c. Part exchange
   d. Competitive equilibrium

4. In economics, a _____ is a market served by only one firm, but with mandated 'competitive' pricing, so as to second the monopoly held by said firm on said market. Its fundamental feature is low barriers to entry and exit; a perfectly _____ would have no barriers to entry or exit. _____s are characterised by 'hit and run' entry.
   a. Palengke
   b. Market penetration
   c. Contestable market
   d. Product-Market Growth Matrix

5. _____ is a form of radical transparency: The construct removing all barriers to --and facilitating of-- free and easy public access to corporate, political and personal information and the laws, rules, social connivance and processes that facilitate and protect those individuals and corporations who freely join, develop and embellish the process. The goal of radical transparency is:

1. Complete personal and _____.
2. The health, safety, and wellbeing of individuals, neighborhoods, communities, institutions, governments and social support systems that subscribe.
3. The protection of the natural environment.
4. The dynamic development of the social assumptions, laws, and conviviance that construct the radical transparency paradigm.

The idea of radical transparency is diametrically opposite--though not opposed and often synched to the ultimate goals of those of privacy advocates. Central is the idea of free access to 'personal' information. But melded to that element is the idea of private ownership of that publicly accessible information.

a. Business plan
b. Reverse hierarchy
c. Corporate transparency
d. Product marketing

6. A high degree of market _____ can result in disintermediation due to the buyer's increased knowledge of supply pricing.

_____ is important since it is one of the theoretical conditions required for a free market to be efficient.

Price _____ can, however, lead to higher prices, if it makes sellers reluctant to give steep discounts to certain buyers, or if it facilitates collusion.

a. Comparison-Shopping agent
b. Spearman's rank correlation coefficient
c. Transparency
d. Package-on-Package

7. _____s is the social science that studies the production, distribution, and consumption of goods and services. The term _____s comes from the Ancient Greek οáΌ°κονομῖα from οáΌ¶κος (oikos, 'house') + vÏŒμος (nomos, 'custom' or 'law'), hence 'rules of the house(hold)'. Current _____ models developed out of the broader field of political economy in the late 19th century, owing to a desire to use an empirical approach more akin to the physical sciences.

a. Industrial organization
b. ADTECH
c. Economic
d. ACNielsen

8. In economics, _____ is simply a state of the world where economic forces are balanced and in the absence of external influences the (equilibrium) values of economic variables will not change. It is the point at which quantity demanded and quantity supplied are equal. Market equilibrium, for example, refers to a condition where a market price is established through competition such that the amount of goods or services sought by buyers is equal to the amount of goods or services produced by sellers.

a. ACNielsen
b. Economic equilibrium
c. Internal market
d. Unified market

9. The _____ is an economic term that refers to a buffer stock scheme where an agricultural product is stored in a granary at constant supply in an effort to stabilize prices. The _____ is maintained by a large entity, typically a government, who buys and sells grain to offset surpluses and shortages that would otherwise cause prices to fluctuate. In this way, the _____ protects against the potential volatility of agricultural prices that can be caused by a variety of situations such as disease or drought.

   a. ACNielsen
   b. Unified market
   c. Ever-normal granary
   d. Internal market

10. _____ is an online trading community established in late 1996 which allows people to trade video games, books, music, movies, and other items through negotiating with other traders from countries worldwide. Once a trade is completed, a record is created on the site for future reference.

    _____ has forums and a trading/matching system that contains a large number of tools necessary for tracking and recording online trading transactions.

    a. 6-3-5 Brainwriting
    b. GameTZ.com
    c. Power III
    d. 180SearchAssistant

11. The _____ is the distribution of refurbished, used, repaired, recycled, discontinued or new products that are in working condition. They are sold through brokers and resellers, not through the original manufacturer. These goods are suitable for resale to customers as a lower cost alternative to buying new goods from standard distribution channels such as retail stores.

    a. Free trade zone
    b. Grey market
    c. Customs union
    d. Green market

12. A _____ or gray market is the trade of a commodity through distribution channels which, while legal, are unofficial, unauthorized, or unintended by the original manufacturer. In contrast, a black market is the trade of goods and services that are illegal in themselves and/or distributed through illegal channels, such as the selling of stolen goods or illegal items such as heroin or unregistered handguns.

    The two main types of _____ are imported manufactured goods that would be normally unavailable or more expensive in a certain country and unissued securities that are not yet traded in official markets.

    a. Green market
    b. Zone pricing
    c. Countervailing duties
    d. Grey market

13. A _____ is a market which meets a given need of a wide variety of industries, rather than a specific one.

    In technology, _____s consist of customers that share a common need that exists in many or all (vertical) industries. For example, customers that need to purchase computer security services or software exist in such varied industries as finance, healthcare, government, etc.

    a. Market system
    b. Two-sided markets
    c. Horizontal market
    d. Marketization

14. _____ is the realization of an application idea, model, design, specification, standard, algorithm an _____ is a realization of a technical specification or algorithm as a program, software component, or other computer system. Many _____s may exist for a given specification or standard.
   a. ACNielsen
   b. ADTECH
   c. AMAX
   d. Implementation

15. In financial markets, _____ is the difference between the decision price and the final execution price (including commissions, taxes, etc.) for a trade. This is also known as the 'slippage'.
   a. Implementation shortfall
   b. Inflation rate
   c. Income distribution
   d. ACNielsen

16. _____ is a field of economics that studies the strategic behavior of firms, the structure of markets and their interactions. The study of _____ adds to the perfectly competitive model real-world frictions such as limited information, transaction cost, cost of adjusting prices, government actions, and barriers to entry by new firms into a market. It then considers how firms are organized and how they compete.
   a. Inflation
   b. Industrial organization
   c. ADTECH
   d. ACNielsen

17. An _____ operates inside an organizations or set of organizations which have decoupled internal components. Each component trades its services and interfaces with the others. Often a set of government or government-funded set of organizations will operate an _____.
   a. ACNielsen
   b. Ever-normal granary
   c. Unified market
   d. Internal market

18. _____ is a belief that the market, in the economic sense, should be completely eliminated from society. Market abolitionists argue that markets are morally abhorrent, anti-social and ultimately incompatible with human and environmental survival and that if left unchecked the market will annihilate both.

In large countries in the modern world, the only significant alternative to a market economy has been central planning or coordinatorism as was practiced in the early U.S.S.R and in the People's Republic of China before the 1990s.
   a. 180SearchAssistant
   b. Power III
   c. Market abolitionism
   d. 6-3-5 Brainwriting

19. In finance, _____ is the size of an order needed to move the market a given amount. If the market is deep, a large order is needed to change the price. _____ closely relates to the notion of liquidity, the ease to find a trading partner for a given order: a deep market is also a liquid market.
   a. Market depth
   b. Partial equilibrium
   c. Competitive equilibrium
   d. Palengke

20. _____ is a term from economics referring to the use of money exchanged by buyers and sellers with an open and understood system of value and time trade offs to produce the best distribution of goods and services. The use of the _____ does not imply a free market: there can be captive or controlled markets which seek to use supply and demand, or some other form of charging for scarcity, both in social situations and in engineering.

Chapter 20. Test Preparation Part 20

The _____ assumes perfect competition and is regulated by demand and supply.

a. Contestable market
c. Public market
b. Horizontal market
d. Market mechanism

21. _____ is one of the four growth strategies of the Product-Market Growth Matrix defined by Ansoff. _____ occurs when a company enters/penetrates a market with current products. The best way to achieve this is by gaining competitors' customers (part of their market share.)

a. Marketization
c. Pasar pagi
b. Market penetration
d. Horizontal market

22. A _____ is any systematic process enabling many market players to bid and ask: helping bidders and sellers interact and make deals. It is not just the price mechanism but the entire system of regulation, qualification, credentials, reputations and clearing that surrounds that mechanism and makes it operate in a social context.

Because a _____ relies on the assumption that players are constantly involved and unequally enabled, a _____ is distinguished specifically from a voting system where candidates seek the support of voters on a less regular basis.

a. Market system
c. Perfect market
b. Public market
d. Market penetration

23. _____ is the process that enables the state-owned enterprises to act like market-oriented firms. This is achieved through reduction of state subsidies, deregulation, organizational restructuring, decentralization and privatization. These steps, it is argued, will lead to the creation of a functioning market system.

a. Two-sided markets
c. Partial equilibrium
b. Contestable market
d. Marketization

24. A _____ is the space, actual or metaphorical, in which a market operates. The term is also used in a trademark law context to denote the actual consumer environment, ie. the 'real world' in which products and services are provided and consumed.

a. 180SearchAssistant
c. 6-3-5 Brainwriting
b. Power III
d. Marketplace

25. A _____, broadcast market, media region, designated market area (DMA), Television Market Area (FCC term) or simply market is a region where the population can receive the same (or similar) television and radio station offerings, and may also include other types of media including newspapers and Internet content. They can coincide with metropolitan areas, though rural regions with few significant population centers can also be designated as markets. Conversely, very large metropolitan areas can sometimes be subdivided into multiple segments.

a. 180SearchAssistant
c. 6-3-5 Brainwriting
b. Power III
d. Media market

26. A _____ is the subset of the market on which a specific product is focusing on; Therefore the market niche defines the specific product features aimed at satisfy specific market needs, as well as the price range, production quality and the demographics that is intending to impact.

Every single product that is on sale can be defined by its _____. As of special note, the products aimed at a wide demographics audience, with the resulting low price (due to Price elasticity of demand), are said to belong to the Mainstream niche, in practice referred only as Mainstream or of high demand.

   a. Local purchasing   b. Soft currency
   c. Commodity chain   d. Niche market

27. _____ refers to internal and external organizing and correcting factors that provide order to market and other types of societal institutions and organizations - economic, political, social and cultural - so that they may function efficiently and effectively as well as repair their failures.

The expression _____ is increasingly found in the title, abstract and text of articles, chapters and papers in the business, management, organization, strategy, social-issues, political-science and sociology literatures. The ABI/Inform Global source located 1748 such uses of both expressions in October 2008, compared with 31 in 1991 and 247 in 2002.

   a. Power III   b. Total revenue
   c. Nonmarket   d. 180SearchAssistant

28. A _____ is a type of public market common throughout the Philippines.

A _____ is usually composed of several dozen stalls arranged in rows under a shared roof. Management is usually by the local governmental units whose jurisdiction encompasses the physical location of the markets.

   a. Palengke   b. Contestable market
   c. Marketization   d. Perfect market

29. A _____ is a product category or set of categories where the several brands within that category possess functionally equivalent attributes, making one brand a satisfactory substitute for most other brands in that category.
   a. Dunlop   b. Retail floor planning
   c. Parity Product   d. Manufacturers' representatives

30. _____ is a term that originated in the United Kingdom and refers to the swapping or bartering or exchange of goods or services. The exact definition for _____ is 'the exchange of resources or services for mutual advantage' and many believe this concept goes back to the start of mankind, it even operates in the animal and plant kingdoms. Barter or _____ amongst humans pre-dates the use of even the earliest forms of money.
   a. Marketization   b. Part exchange
   c. Partial equilibrium   d. Regulated market

31. A _____ is a type of economic equilibrium, where the clearance on the market of some specific goods is obtained independently from prices and quantities demanded and supplied in other markets. In other words, the prices of all substitutes and complements, as well as income levels of consumers are constant. Here the dynamic process is that prices adjust until supply equals demand.

a. Palengke
b. Partial equilibrium
c. Market penetration
d. Part exchange

32. _____ is a type of market found in Malaysia, quite similar to a wet market. _____ and pasar malam are different - _____ opens in the daytime everyday while Pasar malam opens at night and only on selected days of a week. _____ is where many housewives and old folk appear and the things which are on sale are vegetables, fish, meat, clothing and all kinds of daily products.
   a. Horizontal market
   b. Market depth
   c. Contestable market
   d. Pasar pagi

33. In neoclassical economics and microeconomics, _____ describes a market in which there are many small firms, all producing homogeneous goods. In the short term, such markets are productively inefficient as output will not occur where mc is equal to ac, but allocatively efficient, as output under _____ will always occur where mc is equal to mr, and therefore where mc equals ar. However, in the long term, such markets are both allocatively and productively efficient.
   a. Money
   b. Gross domestic product
   c. Market structure
   d. Perfect competition

34. _____ is a rivalry between individuals, groups, nations for territory, a niche, or allocation of resources. It arises whenever two or more parties strive for a goal which cannot be shared. _____ occurs naturally between living organisms which co-exist in the same environment.
   a. Non-price competition
   b. Price competition
   c. Competition
   d. Price fixing

35. A _____ is heuristic and has the following assumptions :

- Rationality of all market actors (Rationality in meaning of the actor's utility maximization)
- No transaction costs (particularly no information costs and no taxes)
- Price taking behavior - there is a sufficiently large number of participants such that no individual can affect the market
- given rare resources
- freedom of decision to do something or to let it be (no external effects)

Share and foreign exchange markets are commonly seen to be the most similar to the _____. The real estate market is an example of a very imperfect market. a free market economy is also related to this _____ system as the public have free will

Other characteristics of a _____ include:-

- No barriers to entry to (or exit from) the market
- Perfect knowledge
- Normal profits

Normal profits are defined as that level of profit which just induces the participants to stay in the market. In other words companies in a _____ pay no dividends, as super-normal profits would induce other participants into the market and drive profits back to the 'normal' level.

This attribute of _____s has profound political and economic implications, as many people assume that the purpose of the market is to enable participants to make profits.

a. Market depth
b. Partial equilibrium
c. Marketization
d. Perfect market

36. _____ in economics and business is the result of an exchange and from that trade we assign a numerical monetary value to a good, service or asset. If I trade 4 apples for an orange, the _____ of an orange is 4 - apples. Inversely, the _____ of an apple is 1/4 oranges.

a. Pricing
b. Discounts and allowances
c. Price
d. Contribution margin-based pricing

37. A _____ or market-based mechanism is any of a wide variety of ways to match up buyers and sellers.

An example of a _____ uses announced bid and ask prices. Generally speaking, when two parties wish to engage in a trade, the purchaser will announce a price he is willing to pay (the bid price) and seller will announce a price he is willing to accept (the ask price.)

a. Price mechanism
b. Regulated market
c. Product-Market Growth Matrix
d. Pasar pagi

38. The _____ as quoted in news generally refers to the spot price of either WTI/Light Crude as traded on the New York Mercantile Exchange (NYMEX) for delivery at Cushing, Oklahoma into which the International Petroleum Exchange has been incorporated) for delivery at Sullom Voe. The price of a barrel of oil is highly dependent on both its grade, determined by factors such as its specific gravity or API and its sulphur content, and its location. The vast majority of oil is not traded on an exchange but on an over-the-counter basis.

a. 180SearchAssistant
b. Power III
c. 6-3-5 Brainwriting
d. Price of petroleum

39. A _____ index is a stock market index where each constituent makes up a fraction of the index that is proportional to its price. For a stock market index this implies that stocks are included in proportions based on their quoted prices. A stock trading at $100 will thus be making up 10 times more of the total index compared to a stock trading at $10.

a. Safety stock
b. Business stature
c. Chain stores
d. Price-weighted

40. The Ansoff _____ is a marketing tool created by Igor Ansoff and first published in his article 'Strategies for Diversification' in the Harvard Business Review (1957.) The matrix allows marketers to consider ways to grow the business via existing and/or new products, in existing and/or new markets - there are four possible product/market combinations. This matrix helps companies decide what course of action should be taken given current performance.

a. Market system
b. Market penetration
c. Partial equilibrium
d. Product-Market Growth Matrix

41. _____s are markets, in public spaces, where independent merchants can sell their products to the public. Typical products sold at _____s include fresh produce, meats and various other food items and crafted goods. Pike Place Market in Seattle, Washington, looking west on Pike Street from First Avenue Soulard Market located in St. Louis, Missouri

- Granville Island
- Lonsdale Quay
- Westminster Quay

_____s are not a new phenomenon. This city market in Grand Rapids, Michigan, occurred about 1910.

- Downtown Phoenix _____ - Phoenix, Arizona
- Eastern Market - Washington, D.C.
- Findlay Market - Cincinnati, Ohio
- Haymarket Square (Boston) - Boston, Massachusetts
- North Market - Columbus, Ohio
- Pike Place Market - Seattle, Washington
- Portland _____ - Portland, Oregon
- Rochester (New York) _____ - Rochester, New York
- Soulard Market - St. Louis, Missouri
- West Side Market - Cleveland, Ohio
- Lexington Market - Baltimore, Maryland
- Hollins Market - Baltimore, Maryland

- Farmers' market
- Souk
- Street food
- palengke

a. Market penetration
c. Regulated market
b. Public market
d. Perfect market

42. A _____ or controlled market, is the provision of goods or services that is regulated by a government appointed body. The regulation may cover the terms and conditions of supplying the goods and services and in particular the price allowed to be charged. It is common for a _____ to control natural monopolies such as aspects of telecommunications, water, gas and electricity supply.

a. Perfect market
c. Two-sided markets
b. Market system
d. Regulated market

43. A _____ is the economic term for a single market where goods, services, capital and people can move freely without regard to national boundaries. These 'four freedoms' are implemented by, among other things, removal of tariffs on the transfer of goods and services among the member nations, imposition of uniform product standards, revision of laws to permit 'market-wide' financial services, and the restructuring of most government procurement practices, so as not to favour local businesses over other member states' businesses.

Chapter 20. Test Preparation Part 20

a. ACNielsen
b. Ever-normal granary
c. Internal market
d. Unified market

44. The _____ is an internationally reaching standards organization dedicated to reducing the costs of technology through standards. Since 1993, ARTS has been delivering application standards exclusively to the retail industry. ARTS has four standards: The Standard Relational Data Model, UnifiedPOS, ARTS XML and the Standard RFPs.
   a. UnifiedPOS
   b. ADTECH
   c. ACNielsen
   d. Association for Retail Technology Standards

45. An _____ or zapper is a software that falsifies the electronic records of point of sale (POS) systems for the purpose of tax evasion.

Most jurisdictions levy a sales tax or a value added tax on commercial transactions such as sales in stores or food served in a restaurant. These transactions are now most often recorded by a POS system rather than a mechanical cash register.

   a. ACNielsen
   b. UnifiedPOS
   c. ADTECH
   d. Automated sales suppression device

46. The first merchant accreditation contract was signed on May 6, 1994 with Rustan's Corp. but the service was first made available later that year at the Robinsons Galleria Supermarket. Given this was the second payment service enabled by BN (with Bill (payment) on the ATM launched the year before), the brand _____ was coined at around the same time.
   a. Power III
   b. BancNet Payment System
   c. JavaPOS
   d. Personal shopping system

47. _____, is a standard for interfacing point of sale (POS) software, written in Java, with the specialized hardware peripherals typically used to create a point of sale system. The advantages are reduced POS terminal costs, platform independence, and reduced administrative costs. _____ was based on a Windows POS device driver standard known as OPOS.
   a. Power III
   b. Personal shopping system
   c. POS terminal
   d. JavaPOS

48. A _____ is a device that can do transactions with a debit card or a credit card. It also may be used to buy telephone PINs.

A _____ manages the selling process by a salesperson accessible interface.

   a. POS terminal
   b. Power III
   c. JavaPOS
   d. Personal shopping system

49. A _____ is a system designed to help people while they are buying in a supermarket or any kind of self-service retailer. In this system, when the customer arrives at a supermarket, instead of picking a shopping cart, he(she) picks an equipment (PDA or similar) which provides a friendly shopping interface.

Using some known technologies (barcode or RFID), the equipment is capable of showing on the screen all sort of information about any product available on the shelves.

a. POS terminal
b. JavaPOS
c. Power III
d. Personal shopping system

50. _____ is the examining of goods or services from retailers with the intent to purchase at that time. _____ is an activity of selection and/or purchase. In some contexts it is considered a leisure activity as well as an economic one.
   a. Shopping
   b. Khodebshchik
   c. Discount store
   d. Hawkers

51. _____ or UPOS is a retailer-driven initiative to combine two existing device interface standards under one specification to allow retailers freedom of choice in the selection of Point of Service devices.

Developed by a team of joint retailer and industry technical experts following published policies and procedures, _____ provides a consistent and exact framework for programming point of sales devices that is platform independent and vendor neutral.

The _____ standard is managed by Association for Retail Technology Standards (ARTS) through two committees.

   a. ACNielsen
   b. ADTECH
   c. Automated sales suppression device
   d. UnifiedPOS

52. _____, Inc. is a payment and transaction processor located in New Jersey, USA, serving businesses throughout the US. _____ currently handles the merchant accounts for over 100,000 merchant locations and processing in excess of $9 billion annually.
   a. United Bank Card
   b. Arbitron
   c. Arcis Communications
   d. Eddie Bauer

53. The _____ is the dominant distribution and retail network for North American comic books. It consists of one dominant distributor and the majority of comics specialty stores, as well as other retailers of comic books and related merchandise. The name is no longer a fully accurate description of the model by which it operates, but derives from its original implementation: retailers bypassing existing distributors to make 'direct' purchases from publishers.
   a. 180SearchAssistant
   b. Power III
   c. 6-3-5 Brainwriting
   d. Direct market

54. A _____ or swap meet is a type of bazaar where inexpensive or secondhand goods are sold or bartered. It may be indoors, such as in a warehouse or school gymnasium; or it may be outdoors, such as in a field or under a tent. The _____ vendors may range from a family that is renting a table for the first time to sell a few unwanted household items to a commercial operation including a large variety of used merchandise, scouts who rove the region buying items for sale from garage sales and other _____ s, and several staff watching the stalls.
   a. 180SearchAssistant
   b. Power III
   c. 6-3-5 Brainwriting
   d. Flea market

55. _____ or night bazaars are street markets operating at night that are generally dedicated to more leisurely strolling, shopping, and eating than more businesslike day markets.

The most well-known _____ are those in Taiwan or other areas inhabited by ethnic Chinese such as Hong Kong, Macau, Singapore, Malaysia, China, Thailand, and Chinatowns worldwide.

Taiwan hosts numerous _____ in each of its major cities.

   a. Night markets
   b. Wet market
   c. Power III
   d. 180SearchAssistant

56. _____s are defined as those segments of overall market of any economy, which are distinct from the other types of markets like stock market, commodity markets or Labor economics. _____s constitute an important segment of overall economy, for example, in the USA, out of about 3000 counties, around 2000 counties are rural, that is, non-urbanized, with population of 55 million. Typically, a _____ will represent a community in a rural area with a population of 2500 to 30000.

   a. Japan Advertising Photographers' Association
   b. Product line extension
   c. Bottling lines
   d. Rural market

57. A _____ is an outdoor market such as traditionally held in a market square in a market town, and are often held only on particular days of the week. Very similar markets, or bazaars can also be found in large enclosed spaces, instead of on a street.

_____s in Greece are called laikes agores (λαϊṡκὶς αγορὶς) in the plural, or λαϊṡκῖ® αγορῖ¬ (laiki agora) in the singular, meaning 'people's market'.

   a. Power III
   b. 6-3-5 Brainwriting
   c. Street market
   d. 180SearchAssistant

58. The _____ or black market is a market where all commerce is conducted without regard to taxation, law or regulations of trade. The term is also often known as the underdog, shadow economy, black economy, parallel economy or phantom trades.

In modern societies the _____ covers a vast array of activities.

   a. ACNielsen
   b. ADTECH
   c. AMAX
   d. Underground economy

59. A _____ is generally an open food market. Some of the common names include 'Cultural Markets', 'traditional markets', 'Gaai Si', 'Gaai See'.

The floors and surroundings are often routinely sprayed and washed with water--to the extent of flooding it at frequent intervals--which gave it the name '_____'.

   a. Wet market
   b. 180SearchAssistant
   c. Rural market
   d. Power III

Chapter 20. Test Preparation Part 20

60. _____ is one of the four aspects of promotional mix. (The other three parts of the promotional mix are advertising, personal selling, and publicity/public relations.) Media and non-media marketing communication are employed for a pre-determined, limited time to increase consumer demand, stimulate market demand or improve product availability.
   a. Marketing communication
   b. Merchandise
   c. New Media Strategies
   d. Sales promotion

61. _____ involves disseminating information about a product, product line, brand, or company. It is one of the four key aspects of the marketing mix. (The other three elements are product marketing, pricing, and distribution). P>_____ is generally sub-divided into two parts:

   - Above the line _____: Promotion in the media (e.g. TV, radio, newspapers, Internet and Mobile Phones) in which the advertiser pays an advertising agency to place the ad
   - Below the line _____: All other _____. Much of this is intended to be subtle enough for the consumer to be unaware that _____ is taking place. E.g. sponsorship, product placement, endorsements, sales _____, merchandising, direct mail, personal selling, public relations, trade shows

   a. Bottling lines
   b. Cashmere Agency
   c. Promotion
   d. Davie Brown Index

62. '_____' is a common form of sales promotion. While rarely presented to customers in acronym form, this marketing technique is universally known in the marketing industry by the acronym _____ or just BOGO, and it is regarded as one of the most effective forms of special offers for goods.

   Originally, 'buy one get one free' was a sudden end-of-season or stock clearance method used by shops who were left with a large quantity of stock that they were looking to sell quickly.

   a. Demand generation
   b. Blind taste test
   c. Pinstorm
   d. Buy one, get one free

63. A _____ is a retail product display, so named because it is a length of material (either plastic or metal) with clips or hooks at regular intervals, upon which merchandise is hung. The _____ is then hung off a shelf or end-cap and serves as an impulse buy to a customer wandering the aisles of a store. Though the term '_____' is a registered trademark of _____ Corp (the company that invented and produced the first '_____'), many display and POP professionals use the term synonymously with 'merchandising strips' - the proper term for these clever display products.
   a. Wiki wiki dollar
   b. Doorbuster
   c. Power III
   d. Clip strip

64. In marketing a _____ is a ticket or document that can be exchanged for a financial discount or rebate when purchasing a product. Customarily, _____s are issued by manufacturers of consumer packaged goods or by retailers, to be used in retail stores as a part of sales promotions. They are often widely distributed through mail, magazines, newspapers, the Internet, and mobile devices such as cell phones.
   a. Merchandise
   b. Marketing communication
   c. Merchandising
   d. Coupon

65. _____ are reductions to a basic price of goods or services. They can occur anywhere in the distribution channel, modifying either the manufacturer's list price (determined by the manufacturer and often printed on the package), the retail price (set by the retailer and often attached to the product with a sticker), or the list price (which is quoted to a potential buyer, usually in written form.) The market price (also called effective price) is the amount actually paid.

   a. Price shading   b. Discounts and allowances
   c. Price   d. Price points

66. A _____ is a very low-priced item designed to draw people into a sale, such as during Boxing Day or Black Friday. As such, items being sold at a loss to the retailer are common during _____ events.

The term is generally used in conjunction with short and much better sales that occur during the beginning hours of a longer sale, sometimes called an 'early bird' sale.

   a. Wiki wiki dollar   b. Power III
   c. Serverbuster   d. Doorbuster

67. The _____ was a marketing promotion begun in 1992 in which the British division of The Hoover Company promised free airline tickets to customers who purchased more than Â£100 worth of their products. However, what Hoover had not anticipated was that huge numbers of customers started buying Hoover products not because they wanted the actual appliances, but simply because they wanted the tickets.

Initially the offer was for two round-trip tickets to Europe, but later it was expanded to the USA, at which point the consumer response increased enormously, as the normal price of these flights was several times more than the Â£100 purchase required to get free tickets.

   a. Co-branding   b. Hoover free flights promotion
   c. Customerization   d. Product planning

68. The _____ is an organisation in the UK that represents brand owners, agencies and service partners engaged in promotional marketing. Formed in 1933, it was established as the ISP in 1979 and provides professional diplomas and certificates, best-practice guidelines and representation for the sales promotion industry. It is based in Islington, London.

   a. AMAX   b. ACNielsen
   c. Institute of Sales Promotion   d. ADTECH

69. A _____ is a promotional copy of a magazine, usually in a 12-page catalog format. _____s help introduce magazines to new readers. It can also help existing readers see new or upcoming changes, additions, or improvements to the magazine.

   a. Magalog   b. Crossing the Chasm
   c. Consumer Reports   d. Power III

70. _____ is anything that is generally accepted as payment for goods and services and repayment of debts. The main uses of _____ are as a medium of exchange, a unit of account, and a store of value. Some authors explicitly require _____ to be a standard of deferred payment.

   a. Leading indicator   b. Money
   c. Law of supply   d. Microeconomics

71. A _____ is essentially a simple guarantee that, if a buyer is not satisfied with a product or service, a refund will be made.

The _____ was a major tool of early U.S. mail order sales pioneers in the United States such as Richard Sears and Powel Crosley Jr. to win the confidence of consumers.

a. Money back guarantee
c. Service-profit chain
b. Whole product
d. Reseller

72. _____ or point of service (_____ or PoS) can mean a retail shop, a checkout counter in a shop, or the location where a transaction occurs. By synecdoche _____ often refers to a _____ terminal or more generally to the hardware and software used for checkouts - the equivalent of an electronic cash register. _____ systems are used in supermarkets, restaurants, hotels, stadiums, and casinos, as well as almost any type of retail establishment.

a. Kahala-Cold Stone
c. Nielsen Media Research
b. Goodyear Tire ' Rubber Company
d. Point of sale

73. In advertising, a lightbox is an accepted term in the advertising industry for an illuminated _____. Generally, a light box uses fluorescent tubes to illuminate a poster inserted into the light box from either the side or rear, in a similar manner to a photographer's lightbox.

- Sales promotion
- Packaging and labelling

a. 180SearchAssistant
c. 6-3-5 Brainwriting
b. Power III
d. Point of sale display

74. A _____ is a deliberate reduction in the selling price of retail merchandise. It is used to increase the velocity (rate of sale) of an article, typically for clearance at the end of a season, or to sell off obsolete merchandise at the end of its life.

The timing and level of markdowns in a selling season is critical to maximising return on sales.

a. Cost-plus pricing
c. Price maintenance
b. Competitor indexing
d. Price markdown

75. _____ is a lightweight markup language, originally created by John Gruber and Aaron Swartz to help maximum readability and 'publishability' of both its input and output forms. The language takes many cues from existing conventions for marking up plain text in email. _____ converts its marked-up text input to valid, well-formed XHTML and replaces left-pointing angle brackets ('<') and ampersands with their corresponding character entity references.

a. 180SearchAssistant
c. Power III
b. Markdown
d. 6-3-5 Brainwriting

76. _____ or promotional products refers to articles of merchandise that are used in marketing and communication programs. These items are usually imprinted with a company's name, logo or slogan, and given away at trade shows, conferences, and as part of guerrilla marketing campaigns.

Almost anything can be branded with a company's name or logo and used for promotion.

   a. Roll-in
   c. Testimonial
   b. Promotional products
   d. Promotional items

77. A _____ is an amount paid by way of reduction, return, or refund on what has already been paid or contributed. It is a type of sales promotion marketers use primarily as incentives or supplements to product sales. The mail-in _____ is the most common.
   a. Strand
   c. Rebate
   b. Personalization
   d. Lifestyle city

78. _____ is defined by the American _____ Association as the activity, set of institutions, and processes for creating, communicating, delivering, and exchanging offerings that have value for customers, clients, partners, and society at large. The term developed from the original meaning which referred literally to going to market, as in shopping, or going to a market to sell goods or services.

_____ practice tends to be seen as a creative industry, which includes advertising, distribution and selling.

   a. Marketing myopia
   c. Product naming
   b. Marketing
   d. Customer acquisition management

79. The _____ is a local tradition that has taken place since 1947 at Filene's Basement in downtown Boston that has held a one-day sale of wedding gowns, garnering local media attention because of the sight of hundreds of brides-to-be scrambling for bargains.

The store stocks thousands of gowns for that day, and marks them down drastically. Prospective brides, and their hovering mothers, have been known to line up as early as 6 the morning of the sale.

   a. Power III
   c. 6-3-5 Brainwriting
   b. 180SearchAssistant
   d. Running of the Brides

80. _____ are used by retail businesses in order to discard excess merchandise. Sometimes these samples have been used by agencies to sell products that they will distribute to local vendors. _____ are often associated with the fashion industry.
   a. Pay per ship
   c. Consumption Map
   b. Lobbying and Disclosure Act of 1995
   d. Sample sales

81. A _____, similar to a doorbuster, is a very low-priced or free item designed to draw people to a website, such as during Black Friday or Cyber Monday. As such, items being sold at a loss to the retailer are not uncommon during _____ events. The term originates from the frequency of server crashes that result from shoppers exceeding server capacity during these sales.
   a. Wiki wiki dollar
   c. Doorbuster
   b. Serverbuster
   d. Power III

Chapter 20. Test Preparation Part 20

82. _____ are a promotion and distribution technique commonly employed by direct marketers. They describe, graphically and verbally, a limited range of products. _____ are a good promotion/distribution choice for new products.
   a. Target audience
   b. Specialty catalogs
   c. Cross merchandising
   d. Brand parity

83. The _____ is a student loyalty discount program in Canada, offering discounts and deals on items such as fashion, food, shoes, and travel and more.

The program's membership include high school and college students throughout Canada. The program has a reported 525,000 members and 120 participating retail chains.

   a. Power III
   b. 180SearchAssistant
   c. Student Price Card
   d. 6-3-5 Brainwriting

84. _____, until recently called simply merchandising, is the activity of promoting the sale of goods, especially by their presentation in retail outlets.. This includes combining product, environment, and space into a stimulating and engaging display to encourage the sale of a product or service. It has become an important element in retailing that is a team effort involving senior management, architects, merchandising managers, buyers, the _____ director, designers, and staff.
   a. Status brand
   b. Trade Symbols
   c. Brand licensing
   d. Visual merchandising

85. _____ refers to the methods, practices and operations conducted to promote and sustain certain categories of commercial activity. The term is understood to have different specific meanings depending on the context. Merchandise is a sale goods at a store

In marketing, one of the definitions of _____ is the practice in which the brand or image from one product or service is used to sell another.

   a. Word of mouth
   b. New Media Strategies
   c. Merchandising
   d. Marketing communication

86. A _____ was a giveaway promotion in the United States from the Chevron gasoline company during the 1960s. The advertising campaign featured a wiki wiki girl, played by dancer Irene Tsu, dressed in a grass skirt and performing a brisk hula while standing on a gasoline pump.

The Hawaiian use of the word 'wiki' was the local pronunciation of the word 'quickly' spoken to them by missionaries trying to get their flocks to work more to Western timeframes than the more laid back Hawaiian work ethic of getting it done in plenty of time.

   a. Serverbuster
   b. Doorbuster
   c. Wiki wiki dollar
   d. Power III

87. _____ is a private corporation, which operates or licenses Blimpie, Cereality, Cold Stone Creamery, Frullati Cafe ' Bakery, Great Steak ' Potato Company, Johnnie's NY Pizzeria, NRgize Lifestyle Cafe, Ranch1, Rollerz, Samurai Sam's Teriyaki Grill, Surf City Squeeze, TacoTime and Wafflo restaurants worldwide. Based in Scottsdale, Arizona, it is one of North America's largest franchise fast food restaurant companies.

_____ was created in 1998 originally as Surf City Squeeze by Kevin Blackwell and his wife Kathi.

a. Center for a New American Dream
b. Goodyear Tire ' Rubber Company
c. Kahala-Cold Stone
d. Sustainable Forestry Initiative

Chapter 1

1. b	2. d	3. d	4. d	5. d	6. a	7. b	8. b	9. b	10. c
11. d	12. d	13. b	14. a	15. d	16. b	17. c	18. d	19. a	20. b
21. d	22. d	23. d	24. d	25. d	26. d	27. d	28. d	29. b	30. d
31. d	32. d	33. b	34. b	35. d	36. b	37. d	38. d	39. d	40. d
41. d	42. c	43. b	44. d	45. c	46. c	47. a	48. d	49. b	50. d
51. d	52. d	53. d	54. d	55. d	56. d	57. b	58. d	59. a	60. d
61. d	62. d	63. b	64. c	65. c	66. d	67. d	68. b	69. b	70. d
71. b	72. d	73. b	74. a	75. d	76. d	77. d	78. d	79. b	80. d
81. a	82. d	83. d	84. d	85. c	86. a	87. b	88. d	89. a	90. d
91. b	92. d	93. d	94. c	95. d	96. b	97. d	98. d	99. b	

Chapter 2

1. d	2. d	3. d	4. d	5. c	6. a	7. d	8. a	9. b	10. b
11. d	12. d	13. d	14. d	15. b	16. b	17. d	18. c	19. c	20. d
21. a	22. a	23. c	24. d	25. d	26. c	27. b	28. a	29. d	30. d
31. d	32. d	33. b	34. d	35. b	36. b	37. d	38. c	39. d	40. b
41. d	42. d	43. d	44. d	45. d	46. c	47. d	48. d	49. d	50. d
51. d	52. c	53. d	54. a	55. d	56. b	57. c	58. d	59. d	60. c
61. a	62. d	63. b	64. a	65. d	66. d	67. d	68. b	69. c	70. b
71. d	72. d	73. d	74. c	75. b	76. a	77. d	78. b	79. d	80. c
81. c	82. d	83. b	84. a	85. d	86. d	87. d	88. d	89. b	90. d
91. b	92. d	93. b	94. d	95. d	96. b	97. c	98. d	99. d	100. c
101. d	102. d	103. d	104. c	105. b	106. d	107. d	108. d	109. d	110. a
111. b	112. d	113. d	114. b	115. d	116. b				

Chapter 3

1. d	2. d	3. a	4. d	5. c	6. d	7. d	8. b	9. a	10. d
11. d	12. a	13. d	14. d	15. d	16. b	17. d	18. d	19. d	20. d
21. d	22. b	23. b	24. c	25. b	26. a	27. d	28. c	29. d	30. a
31. b	32. d	33. d	34. c	35. a	36. b	37. a	38. c	39. a	40. d
41. d	42. b	43. b	44. d	45. c	46. c	47. d	48. c	49. c	50. a
51. d	52. d	53. c	54. a	55. a	56. b	57. c	58. a	59. d	60. d
61. d	62. a	63. a	64. b	65. d	66. a	67. d	68. c	69. b	70. c
71. d	72. a	73. c	74. a	75. d	76. c	77. d	78. d	79. a	80. a
81. d	82. a	83. d	84. a	85. d	86. d	87. b	88. b	89. b	90. b
91. d	92. c	93. c	94. b	95. d	96. a	97. d	98. a		

ANSWER KEY

Chapter 4

1. d	2. d	3. d	4. d	5. d	6. d	7. c	8. b	9. d	10. d
11. d	12. d	13. c	14. b	15. b	16. d	17. c	18. c	19. d	20. c
21. d	22. d	23. d	24. d	25. b	26. b	27. b	28. d	29. a	30. b
31. b	32. d	33. a	34. d	35. c	36. d	37. d	38. b	39. d	40. d
41. d	42. c	43. b	44. a	45. b	46. d	47. d	48. d	49. b	50. d
51. a	52. a	53. c	54. c	55. c	56. d	57. c	58. c	59. a	60. a
61. c	62. d	63. a	64. d	65. a	66. a	67. b	68. a	69. d	70. d
71. a	72. d	73. d	74. d	75. d	76. c	77. d	78. c	79. d	80. d
81. d	82. b	83. a	84. c	85. a	86. b	87. b	88. b	89. c	90. c

Chapter 5

1. a	2. d	3. b	4. d	5. d	6. a	7. b	8. d	9. d	10. b
11. d	12. c	13. d	14. b	15. a	16. a	17. b	18. d	19. d	20. d
21. c	22. d	23. d	24. d	25. b	26. d	27. b	28. d	29. b	30. d
31. c	32. d	33. c	34. c	35. d	36. d	37. d	38. d	39. c	40. d
41. b	42. d	43. d	44. b	45. c	46. c	47. d	48. c	49. d	50. a
51. a	52. a	53. c	54. a	55. d	56. d				

Chapter 6

1. d	2. c	3. d	4. b	5. a	6. d	7. a	8. d	9. c	10. c
11. a	12. a	13. b	14. d	15. b	16. b	17. d	18. b	19. d	20. d
21. c	22. d	23. c	24. d	25. d	26. d	27. d	28. d	29. c	30. d
31. d	32. a	33. d	34. d	35. c	36. d	37. c	38. c	39. a	40. d
41. b	42. d	43. b	44. d	45. d	46. b	47. d	48. d	49. b	50. d
51. b	52. c	53. d	54. d	55. d	56. b	57. a	58. a	59. a	60. a
61. d	62. a	63. a	64. d	65. b	66. d	67. b	68. d	69. c	70. c
71. d	72. b	73. d	74. d	75. d	76. c	77. d	78. d	79. d	80. c
81. a	82. d	83. d	84. a	85. a	86. b	87. a	88. c	89. d	90. c

Chapter 7

1. d	2. d	3. d	4. b	5. d	6. a	7. c	8. c	9. b	10. b
11. d	12. d	13. b	14. b	15. d	16. a	17. d	18. b	19. d	20. d
21. d	22. a	23. a	24. d	25. b	26. c	27. d	28. a	29. b	30. a
31. d	32. d	33. b	34. b	35. d	36. b	37. d	38. d	39. c	40. d
41. d	42. a	43. d	44. c	45. a	46. c	47. c	48. d	49. a	50. d
51. c	52. b	53. b	54. d	55. c	56. d	57. d	58. b	59. c	60. c
61. d	62. c	63. a							

Chapter 8

1. a	2. b	3. a	4. a	5. d	6. a	7. c	8. c	9. a	10. d
11. c	12. b	13. c	14. c	15. a	16. c	17. b	18. c	19. d	20. a
21. b	22. d	23. d	24. d	25. a	26. d	27. a	28. b	29. a	30. d
31. d	32. a	33. d	34. b	35. b	36. c	37. b	38. a	39. d	40. d
41. c	42. a	43. d	44. d	45. b	46. d	47. d	48. d	49. a	50. a
51. d	52. a	53. a	54. c	55. b					

Chapter 9

1. b	2. d	3. d	4. d	5. c	6. d

Chapter 10

1. b	2. b	3. b	4. d	5. d	6. c	7. d	8. a	9. d	10. a
11. b	12. a	13. d	14. b	15. d	16. d	17. a	18. a	19. b	20. d
21. b	22. c	23. d	24. d	25. d	26. d	27. a	28. d	29. d	30. d
31. d	32. b	33. c	34. d	35. d	36. d	37. d	38. d	39. d	40. c
41. a	42. c	43. a	44. a	45. a	46. a	47. a	48. a	49. a	50. d
51. d	52. c	53. d	54. b	55. d	56. d	57. a	58. a	59. c	

Chapter 11

1. c	2. d	3. a	4. b	5. a	6. d	7. b	8. d	9. d	10. d
11. d	12. d	13. a	14. d	15. d	16. d	17. d	18. d	19. a	20. d
21. d	22. d	23. d	24. d	25. d	26. b	27. b	28. d	29. b	30. a
31. a	32. d	33. a	34. a	35. a	36. d	37. c	38. d	39. a	40. c
41. d	42. c	43. a	44. d	45. d	46. c	47. a	48. c	49. c	50. b
51. a	52. a	53. d	54. b	55. a	56. d	57. d	58. d	59. d	60. d
61. d	62. c	63. b	64. c	65. c	66. a	67. c	68. a	69. b	70. c
71. d	72. a	73. a	74. c	75. d	76. d	77. c	78. d	79. a	80. d
81. b	82. c	83. b	84. d	85. d	86. d	87. d	88. d	89. d	90. c
91. d	92. b	93. c	94. d	95. c	96. d	97. c	98. a	99. c	100. d
101. d									

Chapter 12

1. a	2. d	3. c	4. d	5. a	6. b	7. d	8. d	9. d	10. c
11. a	12. b	13. d	14. d	15. d	16. c	17. a	18. d	19. d	20. d
21. b	22. b	23. c	24. d	25. d	26. c	27. c	28. d	29. d	30. c
31. a	32. d	33. a	34. d	35. d	36. b	37. b	38. b	39. d	40. c
41. d	42. d	43. d	44. a	45. b	46. d	47. a	48. b	49. c	50. a
51. d	52. c	53. c	54. c	55. b	56. b	57. a	58. c	59. c	60. c
61. d	62. a	63. d	64. a	65. a	66. a	67. c	68. c	69. b	70. a
71. b	72. b	73. a	74. d	75. c	76. d	77. d	78. d	79. a	80. d
81. d	82. d	83. a	84. d	85. b					

ANSWER KEY

Chapter 13

1. a	2. d	3. a	4. a	5. d	6. d	7. c	8. d	9. b	10. b
11. b	12. d	13. c	14. d	15. c	16. c	17. c	18. d	19. b	20. d
21. b	22. b	23. c	24. d	25. b	26. c	27. b	28. b	29. d	30. d
31. b	32. d	33. c	34. b	35. d	36. a	37. a	38. c	39. d	40. d
41. a	42. b	43. d	44. d	45. d	46. d	47. d	48. b	49. a	50. d
51. d	52. d	53. d	54. a	55. c	56. d	57. c	58. c	59. a	60. d
61. d	62. a	63. a	64. d	65. d	66. b	67. c	68. b	69. d	70. a
71. d	72. c	73. d	74. c	75. a	76. b	77. d	78. b	79. d	80. d
81. d	82. d	83. d	84. b	85. c	86. a	87. d	88. d	89. a	90. a
91. d	92. d	93. d	94. d	95. d	96. a	97. b	98. c	99. d	100. c
101. d	102. c								

Chapter 14

1. d	2. a	3. d	4. b	5. c	6. d	7. d	8. d	9. a	10. d
11. d	12. d	13. d	14. a	15. d	16. b	17. d	18. d	19. d	20. a
21. b	22. d	23. b	24. b	25. a	26. a	27. d	28. d	29. c	30. a
31. d	32. c	33. a							

Chapter 15

1. a	2. d	3. a	4. d	5. b	6. d	7. d	8. d	9. b	10. a
11. d	12. d	13. d	14. c	15. b	16. d	17. b	18. a	19. a	

Chapter 16

1. c	2. d	3. b	4. a	5. c	6. d	7. d	8. c	9. c	10. b
11. d	12. a	13. b	14. a	15. d	16. d	17. b	18. d	19. d	20. d
21. c	22. d	23. b	24. d	25. d	26. d	27. d	28. d	29. c	30. a
31. b	32. d	33. b	34. c	35. d	36. d	37. c	38. a	39. a	40. d
41. d	42. d	43. c	44. d	45. c	46. d	47. a	48. d	49. c	50. d
51. a	52. d	53. a	54. a	55. d	56. d	57. c	58. c	59. a	60. d
61. d	62. d	63. a	64. c	65. a	66. d	67. a	68. c	69. d	70. c
71. a	72. d	73. b	74. a	75. d	76. b	77. b	78. d	79. d	80. a
81. d	82. d	83. d	84. c	85. d	86. d	87. d	88. d	89. d	90. c
91. d	92. b	93. a	94. d	95. c	96. a	97. b	98. d	99. c	100. c
101. d	102. d								

Chapter 17

1. b	2. b	3. a	4. b	5. d	6. a	7. c	8. b	9. d	10. d
11. d	12. a	13. b	14. b	15. c	16. b	17. a	18. d	19. b	20. c
21. a	22. d	23. d	24. c	25. c	26. c	27. d	28. d	29. b	30. d
31. b	32. d	33. a	34. c	35. d	36. d	37. d	38. d	39. b	40. d
41. d	42. d	43. d	44. d	45. d	46. d	47. d	48. d	49. d	50. d
51. d	52. b	53. b	54. d	55. d	56. d	57. d	58. b	59. c	60. d
61. a	62. b	63. b	64. d	65. d	66. c	67. d	68. d	69. b	70. d
71. d	72. d	73. d	74. c	75. b	76. d	77. a	78. d	79. c	80. a
81. b	82. d	83. d	84. d						

Chapter 18

1. c	2. c	3. a	4. d	5. d	6. d	7. d	8. d	9. c	10. d
11. c	12. b	13. b	14. b	15. d	16. c	17. d	18. d	19. d	20. b
21. d	22. b	23. b	24. a	25. b	26. a	27. c	28. d	29. d	30. c
31. d	32. b	33. a	34. d	35. d	36. d	37. d	38. a	39. d	40. d
41. b	42. d	43. a	44. c	45. d	46. d	47. a	48. d	49. c	50. d
51. c	52. d	53. d	54. c	55. d	56. d	57. d	58. a	59. b	60. d
61. b	62. a	63. a	64. d	65. a	66. d	67. b			

Chapter 19

1. b	2. d	3. d	4. b	5. a	6. b	7. d	8. b	9. d	10. d
11. d	12. d	13. d	14. d	15. a	16. d	17. b	18. d	19. d	20. c
21. c	22. d	23. a	24. d	25. c	26. d	27. d	28. d	29. b	30. b
31. b	32. d	33. a	34. a	35. d	36. d	37. d	38. d	39. c	40. c
41. c	42. d	43. a	44. d	45. c	46. a	47. d	48. d	49. d	50. d
51. d	52. b	53. d	54. d	55. a	56. b	57. a	58. d	59. b	60. d
61. d	62. a	63. d	64. b	65. a	66. c	67. a	68. d	69. d	70. d
71. d	72. b	73. d	74. d	75. d	76. d				

Chapter 20

1. c	2. d	3. d	4. c	5. c	6. c	7. c	8. b	9. c	10. b
11. d	12. d	13. c	14. d	15. a	16. b	17. d	18. c	19. a	20. d
21. b	22. a	23. d	24. d	25. d	26. d	27. c	28. a	29. c	30. b
31. b	32. d	33. d	34. c	35. d	36. c	37. a	38. d	39. d	40. d
41. b	42. d	43. d	44. d	45. d	46. b	47. d	48. a	49. d	50. a
51. d	52. a	53. d	54. d	55. a	56. d	57. c	58. d	59. a	60. d
61. c	62. d	63. d	64. d	65. b	66. d	67. b	68. c	69. a	70. b
71. a	72. d	73. d	74. d	75. b	76. d	77. c	78. b	79. d	80. d
81. b	82. b	83. c	84. d	85. c	86. c	87. c			

Chapter 21